MADE
IN
BIRMINGHAM

MADE IN BIRMINGHAM

The Memoirs of

DENIS HOWELL

Macdonald
Queen Anne Press

With love and gratitude to Brenda, and to the family: Andrew and Ceri; Michael and Liz; Kate, Mick, Oliver and Jack; and especially to David.

A QUEEN ANNE PRESS BOOK

© Denis Howell 1990

First published in Great Britain in 1990 by
Queen Anne Press, a division of
Macdonald & Co (Publishers) Ltd
Orbit House
1 New Fetter Lane
London
EC4A 1AR

A member of Maxwell Macmillan Pergamon Publishing Corporation

Front cover illustrations: *Main photograph:* Birmingham Design and Photographic Team. *Inset:* Birmingham Post and Mail (*left*), Press Association (*right*).

British Library Cataloguing in Publication Data
Howell, Denis, *1923–*
  Made in Birmingham: the memoirs of Denis Howell.
  1. Great Britain, Politics. Howell, Denis, 1923–
  I. Title
  941.085'092'4

  ISBN 0–356–17645–2

Every effort has been made to trace the copyright owners of the photographs used. Any copyright holders not credited are invited to inform the publisher.

Typeset, printed and bound in Great Britain by Butler & Tanner Ltd, Frome

ACKNOWLEDGEMENTS

I have every cause to express my heartfelt appreciation to all those kind friends who have assisted me in so many ways in the preparation of this book. To Anne Symonds who edited every word, made many excellent suggestions and corrected my errors; to Frank Owens and Leon Hickman who read and commented upon all the chapters. To an enthusiastic and able research team led by Patrick Cheney and including James and Andrew Perry, as well as, from time to time, American students working in my office on research projects. These included Dorothy Cheung, Dan Gabrielli, Margaret McNally, Peter Clemens, Bill Selent, Tom Fuccillo. To the staff of the Birmingham and House of Commons Reference Libraries to whom I am indebted for all their endeavours on my behalf. To Alan Hughes, who very kindly read and corrected Chapter 6, MP Referee; to Jimmy Munn and his colleagues for their assistance in respect of matters concerning the Birmingham Olympic bid. To Charles Waterhouse and Peter Lawson of the CCPR for factual information and for their comments. Finally, and most definitely, to my secretaries, Jackie Howell and Margaret Emsden, for their never-failing help in the production of the manuscript and to Julie Mackintosh and to Kate for their assistance in helping to make it all possible.

FOREWORD

'Vanity – all is vanity' (Ecclesiastes Chapter 2, Verses 12–26). This truth can only be appreciated by anyone who has written an autobiography. Aneurin Bevan put the matter differently: 'I prefer to take my fiction straight.' I now know the meaning of both. The temptation to vanity and to adapt the facts is ever-present. I have done my best to avoid both pitfalls, I fear not always successfully. Yet it seems to me that if men and women in public life do not express their own interpretation of events, of timing and of motives the full story will rarely emerge from the pen of others. And I have enjoyed the whole experience, trying always to follow the sage advice of Polonius 'This above all, to thine own self be true ...'. I was urged to record my story by old friends Frank and Olwyn Owens, who thought it specially important that I should write about my early days, which is a comment on some of the social history of Birmingham. Well, in our Centenary year I hope that I have justified their faith. For the rest it is a book which expresses my sense of gratitude to and affection for my home town, and offers my grandchildren and those of other Brummies a sense of the city's contribution to our national life and the part played in it by some of its most devoted sons and daughters. Above all I have tried to express the elation I felt in the creation of the Ministry for Sport and to tell something of its early history, as well as providing an account of the many sporting and political controversies in which I have been involved. I hope these will be of some value to students, administrators and friends of sport and politics.

DENIS HOWELL
March 1990

CONTENTS

PART ONE
FROM QUIET HOMES

PART TWO
MINISTER FOR SPORT

PART I

FROM
QUIET
HOMES

From quiet homes and first beginnings,
Out to the undiscovered ends,
There's nothing worth the wear of winning,
But laughter and the love of friends.

Hilaire Belloc

1

THE BACKYARDS OF BIRMINGHAM

PROLOGUE

The Birmingham into which I was born was a product of the Industrial Revolution, as are its citizens. We are here because the city was built on sand, close to coal, and is geographically central for the movement of iron ore. Our furnaces, and those of the neighbouring 'Black Country', turned the ore into metal for the newly created manufacturing industry. James Brindley dug his 'cuts' and so provided the canal system which still goes to all parts of the country, and which took our goods to the sea ports. The canals all meet in Birmingham, giving us more miles of canals than even Venice possesses.

The Soho foundries on our western boundary were built in 1802–03 to accommodate the genius of Bolton, Watt and Murdoch. These great men had pews in St Paul's Church, Hockley, where I worship still, in Birmingham's one remaining Georgian square. Before them, in 1791, Joseph Priestley, not only a chemist but also a philosopher and a Unitarian minister, developed oxygen and outraged our forefathers with his advanced views on the rights of the people to be involved in their government. On the second anniversary of the French Revolution, Priestley and his colleagues decided to celebrate the event and this led the 'beggarly, brazen-faced Birmingham mob' to burn down his home and the homes of other sympathisers such as Thomas Russell, the financier, William Hutton, the Historian of Birmingham, and John Taylor, a metal manufacturer who produced small domestic items such as buckles, buttons and combs. The mob got totally out of hand as they marched to other areas of the city and were halted only by the intervention of the army when they reached the house of John Taylor at Moseley, very close to my present home.

William Murdoch invented the gas mantle and so produced light from power. He teamed up with James Watt, the inventor of the steam engine and at Soho Foundries, just outside our boundary in Smethwick, they cradled the Industrial Revolution. The third partner in the Soho Foundries enterprise was Matthew Boulton, who founded the Lunar Society. This was a remarkable gathering of outstanding intellects which met regularly to discuss philosophy and science. These local men inspired others throughout the world to establish branches of the society, giving Birmingham's intellectuals an outstanding international reputation. The society was created in the 1770s and met on the night of the full moon. Among the giants who became members, in addition to Boulton and Watt, were Oliver Lodge, Erasmus Darwin, Joseph Priestley and, from neighbouring Staffordshire, Josiah Wedgwood. What an assembly of talent! Other Birmingham men of great distinction included Rowland Hill, who invented the postage stamp, and thus the Post Office, and John Baskerville, the printer who produced a much acclaimed edition of Virgil's poems.

Birmingham's university was first established as a scientific college by Sir Josiah Mason in 1875. He was a Wesleyan who had created a machine for manufacturing the slit steel pin, a remarkably successful invention. He used his wealth to promote good causes, the Science College and almshouses to care for women and orphans having pride of place. His university was taken up by Joseph Chamberlain and Charles Beale, four times Lord Mayor of Birmingham, whose family still serve upon its Court of Governors. Professor Oliver Lodge was the first principal of the college and Sir Edward Elgar the first professor of music. It now has fine facilities spanning all the faculties and is superbly located, thanks to the generosity of the Calthorpe Trust, only three miles from the city centre. The Calthorpe Trust has been an extremely generous benefactor to the city and in addition to other gifts provided the land for the superb Warwickshire Test cricket ground at Edgbaston.

The new industries needed workers, many of them attracted from distant parts, especially from Wales and Scotland. Our immigration is no new phenomenon. In Birmingham we all descend from immigrant stock! The workers needed to be housed, and row upon row of houses were thrown up. Densities were of no concern. In the central areas the houses were back to back, or built as terraces, sometimes with more than 30 on each side, without water supply or individual sanitation. It was into such a house that I was born and lived for some 30 years of my life.

Our lives were dominated by factories. My brother Stan and I, together with our friends, went day in and day out to the Burbury Street 'park' – in fact a tarmacadam recreation ground. There we played our games beneath the towering walls of Joseph Lucas where so many of our neighbours worked. At Witton, close by, and in the shade of Aston Villa Football Club was Kynoch's Works, which made munitions in two world wars and zip fasteners. A little further afield was Dunlop. To us no other tyre was of any consequence. The tyres were moulded for companies that led the world in the manufacture of cars, motorcycles and bicycles. They were all 'made in Birmingham' and saw us through the depressions of the 1930s better than most, though that is not saying a lot. Herbert Austin produced his wonder car, the Austin Seven, and built his factory on our southern boundary. The Norton motorcycle was produced in Aston, or to be accurate, Aston Manor, where we lived. In Small Heath was the Birmingham Small Arms company, never known as anything other than BSA, which produced rifles and motorcycles. In my childhood Norton and BSA took on the world in motorcycle racing and beat them, at the Isle of Man TT Races and everywhere else. The Hercules Cycle Company made and sold bikes to the whole world from their factory in Aston and Raleigh Cycles operated from nearby Smethwick. Another dominating firm there was Guest, Keen and Nettlefold, which Joseph Chamberlain came to Birmingham to help create.

But Birmingham was not just a big industrial city. We were 'a city of a thousand trades'. The jewellery quarter was outstanding in this respect. Every one of its old houses was turned over to jewellery manufacture; not just one firm in one house but one firm in each room of each house. So the homes around the church of St Paul's were transformed into places of manufacture and trade. The people moved out and the jewellers moved in, changing the nature of the church and, immediately after the Second World War, transforming it into the centre of Birmingham's industrial chaplaincy. The first industrial chaplain ever appointed anywhere was the Rev Ralph Stevens. He served there for 40 years and, along with other industrialists and trade unionists, he attracted me back to the church. St Paul's is the home church of the Industrial Revolution.

Birmingham had been a collection of urban villages, created one city by Royal Charter in 1838 when Aston Manor, Kings Norton and Handsworth were finally united. No city has enjoyed a greater reputation for its civic government and its leaders were drawn largely from its industry. They were mainly non-conformists, Quakers and Unitarians. Among these Joseph Chamberlain towered above them all. Supported by the Cadburys and the Barrows and people of similarly progressive outlook, he created the finest municipal services this country has known. Our water service was internationally renowned, so was our gas supply and our electricity. Chamberlain went on to establish the Birmingham Municipal Bank (although this idea owed much to an early socialist pioneer, Eldred Hallas) and he bought the land for Corporation Street, still one of our principal shopping streets, and kept the freehold values for our citizens.

Following Chamberlain came the Cadburys, especially George, who not only founded the company but became a very early Labour councillor, and Dame Elizabeth around whom much of Birmingham's voluntary social service seemed to revolve. Later on came Paul Cadbury, who followed in the family tradition as one of the country's leading town planning authorities, an interest no doubt derived from the Bournville

Village Trust which the family created around them – a factory in a garden city – a delightful environment but no pubs! The family tradition still burns bright, mainly through Sir Adrian, recently president of the CBI.

Harrison Barrow ran a food business and several restaurants but he also became a pioneer Labour councillor. His strong advocacy was for regional government, an idea years ahead of his time. I was to serve on the council with him and his nephews George (Labour) and Richard (Conservative). The Nettlefolds produced their city leaders as did two other families who were household names in the Birmingham into which I was born; the Kenricks, notably Byng, and the Martineaus. Byng Kenrick and Wilfrid Martineau were two of the finest educationalists the city has known. Along with the Barrows, they maintained a wonderful family tradition. George Barrow and Wilfrid Martineau became Lord Mayors of the city and when Denis Martineau also assumed that office in recent years he was the sixth member of his family to do so. As is well known, Joseph Chamberlain's two sons also became national figures: Austen, who was expected to be the family front-runner, never attained the Premiership, the Foreign Office being the pinnacle of his public career. Neville, however, after serving as Lord Mayor, became the country's controversial Prime Minister, but not before he had served as a most successful Minister of Health.

The religious life of Birmingham was dominated by the chapels of the Congregational, Methodist and Baptist faiths and by the meeting houses of the Quakers. Their social consciousness was a direct consequence of their Christian non-conformity. Dr R.W. Dale of Carrs Lane Congregational Church was a figure of enormous importance in the life of the city. He once wrote after a holiday in Lucerne that he 'loved the smoky streets of Birmingham better than Lake Lucerne'. F.L. Wiseman of the Methodist Central Mission was another figure of great inspiration. The Sunday Schools thrived in the back streets where we lived. We owed to them nearly everything we knew in terms of community life. The Church of England was late on the scene. Charles Gore was our first Bishop, a learned and academic figure who brought these gifts in good measure to the new, thriving industrial centre of Britain's manufacturing industry. The church of St Philip's was promoted to the status of the Anglican cathedral and although it is one of the smallest cathedrals in the land it is beautifully positioned in the centre of the city where it commands the presence of the people of Birmingham. Charles Gore had many like-minded successors who developed a warm affection for the city and its people and did not stand aside from the great social issues of the day. Bishop Edward Barnes was foremost among these with his towering intellect and deep social commitment. He probably could not have survived in any other diocese but that of Birmingham. He spoke for us. Bishop Leonard Wilson added the enormous courage gained through his Christian witness in a Japanese prisoner of war camp. Hugh Montefiore, of Jewish stock, shared both the intellect and the courage of his predecessors. Mark Santer bodes well for the future on both counts. The Roman Catholic Church has had its giants too, notably Cardinal John Henry Newman, who founded the Oratory and wrote 'Praise to the Holiest in the Heights': one of the most moving and inspirational of all hymns. We are also fortunate to have a marvellously designed Roman Catholic Cathedral, St Chad's, the architect of which was Augustus Welby Pugin who was also responsible for the internal architecture of the House of Commons.

Our leisure time was dominated by sport and theatre, both legitimate and variety. The Birmingham Repertory Theatre of Barry Jackson was an institution of which the city was proud but it was not well known to us in our back streets. We were never taken there by our schools nor, in those days, did we listen to our orchestra, but middle-class Birmingham thrived on both. Barry Jackson's theatre was one of the great actor training theatres in the country. It produced such stars as Sir Felix Aylmer, Dame Edith Evans, Birmingham-born Margaret Leighton, Albert Finney, Dulcie Gray, Stephen Murray, Eric Porter, Paul Scofield and a host of others. It was here that I went with Ken Ford, my school chum, to see my first play – Bernard Shaw's *Doctor's Dilemma*, and thus was born a lifetime love of the theatre. Another play indelibly stamped in my memory was John Drinkwater's *Abraham Lincoln*, with Felix Aylmer playing the lead. It was breathtaking. Drinkwater, Birmingham born and director of the Rep. from 1913 to 1918, made a great partnership with Sir Barry Jackson and provided us with a fine theatrical foundation. The City of Birmingham Symphony Orchestra bids fair these days to be the finest orchestra in the land, wonderfully directed by Simon Rattle and justifiably gaining an international reputation. It was created in 1920, and its first performance was conducted by Sir Edward Elgar OM and included his great cello concerto. In 1923 Neville Chamberlain made a public plea for a public hall befitting an orchestra of this quality. Symphony Hall, probably the finest concert hall built since the war, will open in 1991, and form part of the new International Convention Centre. In between times the orchestra has been directed by such masters as Adrian Boult (twice) Leslie Heward, George Weldon and has for so long enjoyed as associate conductor Birmingham's own Harold Gray. Theatres to us meant the Royal, the Queens and the Hippodromes of Aston and of Birmingham, where we could see all the finest variety acts of our generation, if we could afford it, which was not very often. One of the finest of the old-time artists my father talked about, as did most other fathers in our district, was Vesta Tilley, a pioneer in the role of the male impersonator. In the Lozells district of Aston we knew only one football team, Aston Villa. We had won the Cup more times than any club in the land. As children that was the source of all our pride and loyalty. My father used to tell me that wherever you went in the world, as soon as it was known that you were from Birmingham, you would be asked about

Aston Villa, Joe Chamberlain and Vesta Tilley, in that order. Not a bad tradition! Because he was a namesake, Harry Howell, a demon bowler of Warwickshire County Cricket Club fame attracted our interest in that sport, but we were not taken to cricket anywhere near as often as we were to Villa Park. Later on we took ourselves to see R.E.S. 'Bob' Wyatt and to watch Bradman and Hammond, but these were occasional delights.

This then, was the Birmingham into which I was born in 1923, on 4 September. Brummies have great pride in their city and they fiercely assert it. Certainly, it was a city of politics and sport and it is these passions which have stuck with me. Throughout my life I have never been sure whether I have been engaged in the sport of politics or the politics of sport.

LOZELLS

The Manor of Aston had two districts: one bore that name and housed the Holte family who lived in Aston Hall. The Holte family were supporters of Charles I, and in the Civil War were besieged by the parliamentary forces. The staircase was struck by a cannon ball, still to be seen. The place from which this attack was mounted is not certain; some say it was from Cannon Hill Park but Rupert Street and Cromwell Street in my constituency have equal claims. Aston is also the home of Aston Villa, one of the original 12 founder clubs of the Football League, established by William MacGregor, who lived in our neighbourhood. The Villa was formed at the Aston Villa Methodist Church, also in my constituency.

The other district of Aston is Lozells. So far as I am aware no other place in the world shares that name with us, so it is a bit special. The earliest reference to Lozells was recorded in 1546 when the Lordship of Aston granted a lease for the district known as either Lorres Hill or Lowshill. In 1653 Sir Thomas Holte made a declaration referring to the extent of the park at these two same locations. The southern boundary of Lozells is about two miles from the city centre and is established by a brook first named Hockley Brook and later Aston Brook. It is still there today but after serious flooding, well within the memory of my parents, it was culverted and now runs entirely underground.

From this brook, hills rise on both sides, to the city centre in one direction and to what is now Lozells Road in the other. Near Lozells Road stands Gower Street where I went to my first school. Research shows that this is the site of a Roman cemetery where soldiers were buried in cells. It seems therefore that the first syllable comes from the parkland and the second from the cells. So was derived the name of Lozells.

What had been the pleasant hills and brooks of Lozells were transformed by row upon row of terraced houses built to house the workforce of industrial Birmingham. It was a closely-knit community: people were dependent upon each other, and knew each other's business; hard working when they could be, always seeking work when denied it. Life was tough but our parents, our neighbours, our churches and our schools all continued to make it worthwhile. We were deprived, but as children we were never allowed to know it.

MY PARENTS

My father, Herbert, was a man of firm principles, great loyalties and warm affections. I like to think that some of these qualities have found their way to me. He was the essence of working-class respectability and denounced those who betrayed his standards with trenchant phrases: 'He ought to be horsewhipped', or 'He ought to have his face blacked'. His greatest contempt was reserved for anyone who did not stand his round or in any way sought to take advantage of his friends. He came from a large family of four sons and two daughters, one of whom died early on. The other, Aunt Rhoda, remained a spinster and kept house for her brothers and family. In spite of the hardships of his life he encouraged us whatever the difficulties, 'always keep your pecker up' being his invariable advice.

What I am pretty sure I have inherited from my father is a sense of righteous indignation. This was important to him in making his judgments on the world and testing their standards against his own. Dad's proudest possessions were his bowler hat and his watch and chain. I can see him now brushing his hat with the sleeve of his coat and setting off to take us lads for a Sunday morning stroll. This was preceded by a tram car ride to Perry Barr where we would stand in wonder as the driver unhooked the pole and wheel from overhead electric cables and ran it round to the front of the tram where it was reunited with the cable to turn the tram round.

From Perry Barr we would walk through the park where we were bought an ice cream, and then it was on to the Boar's Head for a glass of lemonade which was brought outside while Dad had his usual mild and bitter and his Woodbine, five for twopence, presented in a thin paper packet. Then home to Sunday dinner – never lunch – which was the most sacred meal of the week. We sat round the table and discussed the news of the day and matters requiring family talk. I am glad to say that we still follow this tradition in my own family whenever it is possible for us to get together. In our early life nothing was more fascinating for my brother Stan and myself than to sit in on these family occasions. Talk and argument flowed. It was a great entertainment for us but an even better education.

My father's eldest brother, Harry, had done a bit of boxing in his time and was well known throughout Birmingham. He and Dad and some of their friends liked a day at the races. They used to regale us with stories of bookmakers who made off with their takings unable to pay out, and of how the crowd would give chase, shouting to attract the attention of the police. And whenever we set off by train to some distant football match he would insist that if ever we saw anyone playing cards on the train we should leave the carriage. He was excessively concerned that we should never fall for the 'three-card trick', another phrase he would use to describe anyone who had been taken in. He loved to have a bet. He could never afford more than a shilling which he would invest in three fourpenny doubles, all first favourites which he selected after hours of studying the *Daily Herald*. He would take the bet to our local bookmaker, George Davis, who had a man stationed behind a chained door, as street betting was illegal. If Dad was ill I had to deliver it. George Davis never paid him less than half a crown – two shillings and sixpence – and as his winnings rarely reached that sum he made a profit, enough to buy a drink and place another bet the next day. It kept him going for years and taught me that bookmakers have big hearts for good causes. But nothing pleased him more than when the Villa had won.

When the FA Cup was stolen in 1895 from the window of William MacGregor's shop, Shillcocks, which was just around the corner from the family home, Dad and his brothers reckoned they knew 'the villains' and told us the Cup was melted down within half an hour of it having been stolen. It was to Shillcocks that we were taken to buy our first pair of football boots as well as a jar of dubbin to treat them. Some of the happiest moments we enjoyed with our father were hearing him retell with great relish stories of his Villa heroes – Sam Hardy, Tommy Smart, Charlie Wallace, 'Happy' Harry Hampton, Pongo Waring and many others. He saw Villa play in the final at Crystal Palace in 1912 and was at Wembley in 1923, part of the crowd which overflowed on to the pitch and had to be cleared back to the touch-line by a policeman on a white horse.

In those days my father worked at the Parkinson Stove factory where he was the foreman in the fitting shop. He considered himself a craftsman and was a member of a small union, the Heating and Domestic Engineers. I am told that I attended my first trade union meeting at the age of three during the General Strike of 1926 when Father 'kept the door' during the meetings of the Birmingham Committee at the King Edward pub in New Corporation Street (now the home of the Birmingham Press Club). Mother was not well and so I sat on his knee while he scrutinised all comers. His other duties during that traumatic dispute were to deliver the TUC news sheet around the city. Dad was the only staff member at his firm who supported the strike, a cause of sadness but pride to him. His union called out its members at Parkinson's. They had to support the miners, they had to be loyal to the leadership. As the union representative he must lead them out. His employers begged him not to but it was a matter of duty for him. Within two years of the strike he was sacked. Blacklisted, he found no work in Birmingham for more than six years, years of tramping the streets, writing hundreds of letters seeking work, and his pride was deeply hurt. As letters of rejection came he would throw them down on the table, unable to speak, near to despair. Eventually he got a job in his trade at Exeter but he was never able to unite the family and, after five years of trying to keep two homes going, his health finally broke down and he returned to Birmingham. The constant worry of being parted from his family took its toll. He wrote home every week and sent Mom his earnings. Mother made sure that we wrote back every week. When he came home for holidays he would tell us about life in Exeter. It mainly consisted of his work at Willey's, also stovemakers, and walks along the riverside. On Sundays he would go to the YMCA where he was made very welcome. His landlady was a staunch Conservative and a leading light in local political activity. On one of his visits home, Dad could not contain his joy: he had told the lady that Labour would win a local election and to her shock and disbelief he was right. It was a source of great satisfaction. When his health finally gave way stomach ulcers were diagnosed and for a few more years he regularly took some powder prescribed by his doctor and drank a lot of milk. Eventually he returned to work but after two or three years he needed surgery and he did not return to Exeter again.

Mother was a Watkins, christened Bertha Amelia, so we have Welsh blood on both sides of the family. We could not trace back the Watkins pedigree but we were always told that the Howells came to Birmingham from West Wales via Cornwall. It seems that our forefathers went there when the tin trade began, so I presume they had previously been mining in Wales. Bertha was known to everyone, as were her two sisters, Annie and Elizabeth, who both had small draper's shops in the Lozells area. Mom too came from a large family who maintained the working-class tradition of the family get-together, usually as a sing-song around the piano. No crisis or call for help went unanswered by Mother. Births, deaths, sickness and marriages were her stock-in-trade, and she was sent for whenever help was needed. She was a great driving force. Her finest quality was application, and she would never give up.

My mother took great pride in our appearance, knitting all our suits when we were very young. Throughout her life she suffered from pernicious anaemia and rheumatism but her determination was boundless. She took in washing, cleaned offices, and always sought ways to earn a few extra shillings, every penny of which was spent on the family. My brother and I would go and collect the washing in suitcases and return it in spotless condition, washed and ironed. Often, when Mother's rheumatic hands would not allow her to 'wring out' the washing, Stan and I were pressed into service to operate the mangle.

When my sister Margaret was born some seven years after my brother, Mom had a very difficult confinement. She was constantly looked after by our devoted family doctor, Dr Orton, to whom we paid a few pence per week to be included on his list of patients. He not only prescribed the medicines but made them up himself. At ten months Margaret developed meningitis. It was a Sunday morning. Dad took my brother and me and walked two miles to the surgery. By the time we had returned home the doctor had been fetched from church and was at our house. He prescribed three hot baths a day, which my mother dutifully carried out, and constant ice packs. Dr Orton himself visited us three times a day to supervise the treatment. These were the days when you provided your own health service, and there was no finer example than in our household. Stan and I would go off every day to Hodson's, the local undertaker, as it was the only place where we could find ice. At first they charged us for the ice but when they learned what it was for they told us to take as much as we needed with their compliments. We had no water in the house so the bathing was done in front of the fire with water heated in kettles on the gas stove, which was also in the living-room. Margaret survived – it was a triumph of dedicated medical care and family devotion.

Mom and Dad liked to go out together at the weekends. They would visit one or other of their favourite local pubs, mainly for the company. The Barton Arms, still fully operational, was without doubt the finest building in our district. These days it has been cleaned up and is protected as a listed building. The other pub was the Acorn where they held 'free and easies' in the concert room. It was at the Acorn during the war that I first learned the art of chairmanship. We ran concerts for the Red Cross, for Labour Party funds, and for any other good causes that attracted our sympathy. We used to book three acts through the Variety Artists' Federation. I would sit in the chairman's large seat, next to the stage, introduce the 'turns' and make the appeal for funds.

It was through this experience that I learned how to develop a relationship with an audience, how to create enthusiasm for the objectives of the meeting, how to introduce the performers, and how to get the audience to identify with them. Later on I was to chair many a political rally and to put these arts to good use. I did this for 12 years when, as the president of APEX, the trade union to which I have belonged all my life, I presided over its Annual Conference.

Sadly, today the qualities of chairmanship have fallen largely into disuse, certainly as far as political rallies are concerned. We hardly ever hold them these days and when we do, or when chairmen of conferences besport themselves, they all seem to think they are television announcers rather than chairmen of a live occasion in which both audience and platform are essential participants. The chairman's duty is to weave them together, to create an identity of purpose between the floor and the platform, to generate an enthusiasm for the cause. Public life is the poorer for this deficiency. Members of Parliament do not serve their apprenticeship these days; they have not been through the testing grounds of the public meeting, where they might learn the arts of exposition, the disciplines of defending their case in the face of penetrating and hostile opposition, always remaining master of the occasion. More and more of them come to Parliament trained by their parties purely to be television performers, concerned much more with the presentation of their case than with its content, and all too often allowing the television interviewers who question them and the opposing ministers to 'get away with murder'.

Our cheapest and most usual entertainment was to be found at our local cinemas. If we had no money we would wait at the side door until someone came out and would sneak in before the door closed. Very often the manager saw us but he did not seem to mind. We watched mainly cowboy films but later on we would go to the Lozells cinema for Sunday night special performances. This cinema possessed the wonderful attraction of an electric organ. This instrument would rise up from below floor level with the organist playing away. His name was Frank Newman and he was tremendous. He would play all the latest hits and such gems as 'In a Monastery Garden' and 'Sanctuary of the Heart' written by Albert W. Ketelbey, who was born down the road in Alma Street. So we produced our 'cultural' giants as well as our sporting heroes.

On Sundays we would go in a party of friends, led by the Hands family who lived down one of the long terraces. Those who were old enough to be working, such as my friend Harry Hands, would buy chocolates and ice cream during the interval and share them with us without giving it a second thought. Ours was a generous and sharing community and it provided the basis for a lifetime of lasting friendships.

Very few of our homes had books and I cannot recall much of a school library at my primary school. But our teachers encouraged us to join the public library, a wonderful service, certainly in Birmingham. Our library is still in operation in Witton Road, about a half a mile away from Villa Park. The building used to be the Aston Manor Council House and was converted to library use when Aston was absorbed into Birmingham. For us it was a wonderland of treasure. I would go there once a week and take out one book for myself – *Treasure Island*, the Just William books, or something of that sort – and one for my mother. To walk around the shelves enjoying the luxury of such a choice and receiving the advice of the ever-helpful staff, especially in choosing my mother's book, was a great experience, and led me naturally to the Central Reference Library in the city centre, where I was later to spend so much of my time and, as I hope will be seen, repaying some part of the debt I owe to it.

A HOUSE OF OUR OWN

The backyards of Birmingham, more accurately Lozells, were the world of our childhood. When I was about three, and my brother a year younger, we had news of a house that our family could call its own. It was a back-to-back house in Clifford Street, just around the corner from Guildford Street where I had been born at number 117. There we had been lodgers in the two front rooms and we owed our good fortune in obtaining this new home to my aunt Annie, mother's sister, who lived in the front house of the other pair of back-to-back houses which shared our backyard and facilities. Aunt Annie was a widow and she lived there with my cousin Joan. They had the tiniest of living-rooms which was divided by a counter from which she ran a shop which sold ladies' clothes and household linen. The window of the room was converted into a shop window. So it was that when number 2 at the back became empty, my aunt prevailed upon the landlord to let us have it. Access to the two back houses was by means of a covered entry which ran from the street between the two sets of back-to-backs and ended in our backyard. The yard was our castle. It still provides happy memories of hours of child's play and games. But it reminds me also of the drudgery and the hardships associated with the unemployment and the despairing search for work that was the lot of my parents for much of the time we lived there.

The house had three rooms, one on top of the other, and a cellar below. When we had water installed the sink was fitted into the small space at the top of the cellar steps. This was a red letter day. Soon we had an Ascot heater fitted. The gas stove remained in the small living-room where the cooking was undertaken.

The 'facilities' for the four houses were built down the left-hand side of the yard starting some ten feet from our living-room window. First came the 'brewhouse' – the wash house – to which each family was allocated a day to do their washing. For this labour there was a sink with a tap from which we also drew our house water until two or three years later when – Oh, happy day – the landlord provided a supply to the house. The sink had an outlet to the 'suff' as it was known, the drain to other people. There was also a copper boiler in which the water was boiled. All the water had to be put into it by bucket and ladled out down the 'suff' afterwards, a much more difficult task. Underneath the boiler was the fire which we had to get going well before the washing could be attempted. Next to the brewhouse came the two lavatories or the 'La Pom' as it was called by the neighbour who shared one with us.

Then came the 'miskin' or 'midden' which received not only the refuse of the four houses in our yard, but of the six houses in the next yard too. When we moved into this house there were no dustbins. Once a week the dustmen would arrive with their cart and their galvanised tin baths and shovel the ashes and the refuse into the baths, place them on top of their heads, protected only by an old cloth cap, and carry them across the yard and up the entry, to be deposited in their dustcart. It took many journeys to complete this operation and on a windy day there was almost as much refuse to be cleared up after the dustmen had gone than before they came.

The miskin provided a wonderful 'double knack' through which we children escaped, via the next backyard, whenever trouble threatened, which was fairly often. There were two other means of escape provided by walls on two sides of our yard over which we would climb, but alas they were much too low to prevent our footballs and cricket balls from disappearing into our neighbours' yards, a source of constant irritation to them, and trouble for us, especially when we broke a window, as we often did! This backyard staged the finest football and cricket matches ever played in Birmingham. Over the wall in the next yard lived the Weir family – Jack, who became a JP, and his brother Terry, now the official photographer of Aston Villa – and their neighbours, Jim and John Smith. They joined the two Howells and the sides were made up of a player from each family. The clothes line, which stretched from wall to wall, became the cross-bar for our soccer matches and we chalked our wickets on the narrow piece of brickwork between the house next door and the entry when we played cricket. A hit reaching the walls of the yard was worth two runs, or four if it didn't bounce. A shot over the wall was six and out. It was tremendous stuff.

One of the benefits of such a play area was the wall. I spent hours kicking a ball against the wall of the house learning how to trap a returning ball and to shoot with either foot. Likewise, cricket practice took the form of hitting the ball against the wall, and from whichever angle it came back, catching it or hitting it back again. Aided by a good imagination and a desire to emulate my heroes, Frank Broome and Eric Houghton of Aston Villa or the great Eric Hollies of Warwickshire, I entertained myself for hours. Years later, as Minister for Sport, I made a speech about the importance of walls and urged local authorities to start building them again. A few did but the basic skills of football and cricket still go undeveloped in most working-class communities, to the detriment of our national games.

There were no bathrooms in our neighbourhood, of course. So every Friday night or Saturday morning, mother packed us off to the municipal 'slipper baths'. There we would wait our turn in the reception room and when it came the attendant would shout 'next' and in you went. He would clean down the bath from the previous occupants, using a wire brush dipped in some powder, and turn on the hot tap by means of a special key which provided your proper measure of hot water. This took about five minutes. After another 20 minutes he would bang the door with his brush and shout 'time's up'.

When Mother's washing was out to dry we took to the streets where cars were few and far between and the handcarts or horse carts presented no problems. There we played tip-cat with a home-made wooden bat. The tip-cat was a piece of wood about one inch thick and four inches long, cut away at each end so that when you chopped the bat down on the end, the cat would fly into the air. As it came down you hit it with the bat and ran round the course, which was set out like a rounders court. The girls in the locality were always pleased when we played these street games because they could join in. We also played rounders, hopscotch and tracking, where one team would go off marking the pavement with chalk, and the other would try to track them down.

We were always well turned out. Special clothes were knitted or sewn for the Sunday School Anniversary, for Christmas and holidays. Sunday School was at the Lozells Congregational Church in Wheeler Street, still there, but now a Sikh temple. Whenever I visit it these days I like to remind the congregation that I too worshipped there as a lad, and that although we may belong to different religions we worship one God. This should be a unifying thought for both the old and the new communities. Sunday School was an event to be looked forward to, conducted by wonderful people who cared about us all. The highlight of our year was the Sunday School Anniversary for which we rehearsed for weeks until the hymns and anthems were mastered. Then rows of wooden benches were erected in front of the pulpit and some 200 youngsters would march in and take their seats, all dressed in their Sunday best. The church was also the home of the 81st Troop of the scouts and its wolf cub pack. We owed much to its dedicated leaders, Miss Alice Wakelin, the Akela, and to Dennis Bellman, the skipper, who was also a football referee. Some of us went to watch him referee in the local parks, thus generating a new interest which was to lead on to another of my lifetime loves. The cubs and the scouts meant a great deal to us youngsters. Not only the weekly meetings where we pursued all the usual scouting interests, but the marches, the church parades, and the camping. A great thrill was to march in the monthly district church parade when all the neighbouring scout troops would assemble near the Lozells Road with all their flags flying and a massed band at the head. Off we would march at about ten o'clock on a Sunday morning, waking up the entire community as we paraded through the streets for a service at one or other of our churches. Then it was back again to be dismissed and sent home to Sunday dinner. There was always a sense of occasion, an excitement which we needed in our lives and, although we didn't recognise it at the time, an early introduction to the ecumenical character of the true Christian church, for the churches we marched to were of every religious faith.

But the greatest joy was camping. For years the only holidays most of us had were the scout camps. We would go off to Yorks Wood, the Birmingham scout camp, whenever we could on weekend holidays, such as Easter and Whitsun. There we would learn to light camp fires, to cook and wash up, to pitch tents and to make beds, to sing our songs and to take turns at contributing to the evening's entertainment. We would camp in all weathers. I well recall a very snowy Easter when our fathers arrived to insist upon us returning home. We had already anticipated them and had fried and consumed a whole week's supply of bacon and beans, tinned fruit and other goodies. There was no way we were returning home with unused stores. August saw our greatest treat: two lorries would arrive by courtesy of Miss Wakelin's employers and we would load these up with all our camping gear and off we would go, cubs, scouts and leaders, for two weeks at Llangollen or Towyn or some other Welsh beauty spot. It is fashionable these days to question the motives of such men as Baden Powell. I don't know what they were, nor do I care overmuch: I do know that he gave us an excitement, a little self-discipline and an early sense of real comradeship which we would not otherwise have known had we been left to the deprivations and limitations of the back streets of Birmingham. And without the camps we would never have enjoyed any holiday during the lean years of the 1930s.

The Temperance Movement also had a strong presence in our neighbourhood through the Band of Hope and the International Order of Good Templars. For a time I was a member of the latter which met in the primitive Methodist church. They conducted their affairs at well-ordered meetings where minutes were read out, regalia was worn and many good social occasions were enjoyed. I parted company with them when I learned to distinguish between teetotalism, in which they believed, and temperance, in which I believe.

TO SCHOOL

The Gower Street Elementary School for Infants and Juniors was a great influence on all our lives. Almost all of us went there. We were admitted at five years of age to the class of Miss Amen. She was an institution. Miss Amen bestrode the streets carrying the largest handbag ever seen. I never see Oscar Wilde's play without thinking of her – 'A handbag!' She had a loud voice and knew every family in the district. She not only taught the children, she had taught most of their parents, too. She practised the ideal that education was indivisible; what went on in the home was just as much her concern as what went on in the classroom. After a year in her charge she handed us on as fit recipients for the ministrations of the rest of the teaching staff.

The headteacher of both the infant and the junior schools was Miss Williams. She was a most caring headteacher who created a fine bond of friendship and loyalty to the school. Later on I often went back to see her when I had a free afternoon. The first prize I ever won, and the first watch I ever possessed, was awarded to me by Miss Williams for being top boy pupil in the school. The other abiding influence was the deputy head, Mr Trevor. He gave me a life's interest in two subjects, history and cricket. Somehow our family had managed to get one of the first 'wireless sets' owned in our neighbourhood, a KB Pup. In the summer of 1934 Australia came over to play and during the Test match I was called upon by Mr Trevor to run home, turn on the wireless and return to school with the lunch-time score which we then discussed for the first few minutes of the afternoon lesson. At the age of ten I took the 'Grammar School' examination. I passed and in due course went for an interview with the headmaster of George Dixon School. I then discovered that the school played rugby, not soccer, and I spent the journey home convincing my father that I could not possibly go there, such was the extent of my prejudice. A year later I passed the exam again and this time went on to Handsworth Grammar School where soccer was played.

By the time my own three sons had to be entered for their secondary schools we had no hesitation in sending them to George Dixon and we have never felt the slightest cause for regret. In the course of time I came to believe that school is the place where you introduce youngsters to all the sports so that they can then choose for themselves. We had no school gym at Gower Street so our PE was held in either the playground or the school hall. In the final year of the juniors we were introduced to the water and the playing field – days of sheer wonder. On Monday mornings we were walked a mile to the swimming baths and on Wednesday afternoons a double-decker bus arrived to take us to the school playing fields for cricket or football. I can remember no coaching for either but we would have been offended at the very suggestion. To this day, nothing angers me more than to learn that in the interests of economy local authorities first cancel the swimming lessons and then school transport to the playing fields: the true sign of the educational moron.

Handsworth Grammar School was entirely different. We had our own playing fields where we played form and house games on Wednesday afternoons and school matches after school on Saturdays. The school had a fine sporting tradition but when I transferred there in 1935 it was just beginning to feel the effects of a new headmaster, the Rev J.J. Walton, who thought that the sporting tradition was being maintained at the expense of its academic life. The suffering caused by his approach seemed to be universal and it was met with concern by the elderly 'Mr Chips' on the school staff, opposition from the strong Old Boys' Association and disgust from most of my fellow pupils. Years later when I found myself a member of the school governors I was told by the secretary that the headmaster had not worn a dog collar when he came for his interview and he would not have been appointed had he done so!

The greatest problem with Walton was his abhorrence of any sort of collective voice raised by the pupils on occasions such as the joint Grammar Schools Sports held at the Birchfield Harriers ground. We had a first class athlete, H.H. Clarke, and we had a faith in him that was unshakeable – and justified. When we won the championship we carried him back to school through the streets of Handsworth accompanied by banners and crowds of schoolboys. The head had specifically forbidden this in one of his typically lengthy addresses to us in assembly and his wrath knew no bounds. It was this sense of collective loyalty and responsibility that was one of the most important lessons I learned at Handsworth Grammar School. It was a school life I enjoyed and from which I made many life-long friendships. It also introduced me to the art of debating through one of its many societies and that love of argument has certainly been a life-long blessing.

In 1935 I entered the form of one of only two women teachers. She was Miss Janet Keeling and without doubt she was the finest teacher I ever had. She remained in charge of us for some three years, teaching us maths and geography. On one occasion I managed to get every question right in a maths exam but she rebuked me for putting ∴ meaning therefore when I should have put ∵ meaning because, and she deducted four marks. I don't think teachers believe it is right that their pupils should get a 100 per cent mark. Janet Keeling took a great personal interest in us all. She regularly looked us over, even inspecting our knees and our shoes to make sure that we were fit for her form. Where she excelled was in making certain that we had a full team for form matches. If we were one or two players short then she would be approached by Dennis Roberts, our team captain, who went on to play good professional football in the Birmingham League; Ken Ford, my school chum, later to be best man at my wedding and godfather to one of my sons; or by myself, and told of our predicament. Miss Keeling's outrage at such a state of affairs always solved the problem in double quick time and earned our lasting respect. Nothing dimmed my gratitude to her – not even the fact that when I was selected to stand as the Labour candidate for Small Heath at the 1961 by-election Janet Keeling emerged as president of the Small Heath Conservatives, actually proposing the nomination of my opponent. She was yet another teacher I was fortunate to encounter at a difficult period of home circumstances and who left an indelible mark of caring and concern.

PAPERBOY

With Dad out of work and Mother struggling to make ends meet something had to be done to help supplement the family income. Stan and I contrived many initiatives. The biggest trouble I faced was that these efforts conflicted with the homework requirements of my new school, but they had to be undertaken, and doing homework in one family room with competition from the wireless and gramophone was no easy task. Our first piece of entrepreneurial activity concerned a wonderful pork butcher, Freeth's of Wheeler Street, run by two very charming ladies. They were famed for all the best working-class delicacies and when my father wanted faggots and peas or tripe and onions we had to take our jug at lunch-time with a piece of paper indicating the order and put the jug in a queue then we returned at night to collect it. Other delicacies sold there included cowheel and chitterlings as well as home cured bacon cut to your own requirements, pork chops and similar delights. All these sales meant that there were a lot of bones to be disposed of so my brother and I persuaded Dad to make us a cart and twice a week we would collect the bones tied up in a large jute bag and take it to the local factory who weighed the bag and gave us sixpence or a shilling which we shared or spent on something for the house. The smell of the boneyard was terrible but the finance was much appreciated.

Then we discovered Mr Rudd, who sold eggs for a living. He provided us with a large basket and we would travel the neighbourhood knocking on doors persuading people to buy the eggs at a penny each or 13 for a shilling, a most competitive price. At Easter time we sold hot cross buns which Mr Rudd also supplied.

One of our most lucrative activities was to 'let in the New Year' for our neighbours. We would tour the district collecting orders to perform this ritual and then on New Year's Eve we raced around hammering their doors, going into our customers' homes and doing our chants. My own family still expect me to repeat this performance at our own New Year's celebrations. Indeed, they bring their friends to enjoy the show. The necessary equipment is simple: a piece of coal to be carried in one hand and a fire poker in the other. We would hammer the staircase, rake out the fire and sing away:

> New Year in. New Year in.
> We wish you a Merry Christmas
> and a Happy New Year.
> New Year in. New Year in.
> Open the door and let the old year out
> and the New Year in. New Year in.
> The cat ran up the plum tree
> The hen came chuckling by.
> We wish you a Merry Christmas,
> A big fat pig in the sty,
> A cellar full of beer
> To last you all the year.
> Open the door and let the old year out
> And the New Year in.
> New Year in. New Year in. New Year in.

Nowadays we round off the ritual by singing the 'Miner's Dream of Home' but when we were 'working' we had to get on to the next house as quickly as we could. Usually we were given a mince pie and half a crown. At about one o'clock we would pack up but we would be off again at five in the morning for those who had to be up early for work like the local milkman. It was all good fun and earned us a pound or two which was luxury.

All this was helpful but we needed to earn regular money week in and week out. There was only one way – delivering newspapers. At first I did a morning and evening round for a small local shop for two shillings and ninepence. Then I heard of a shop in Handsworth,

Hallgarth's, which was much larger. Hallgarth employed eight news-boys and paid three shillings and ninepence. My brother and I were taken on and for this money, plus the tips which doubled our income, we would deliver two rounds of papers every morning, including Sundays, and one round every evening, of the *Birmingham Mail* and *Evening Despatch*, our two evening newspapers. I always read them before pushing them through the doors and later, when I was a young city councillor defending the rights of newsboys from attack by those who wanted to end the practice, I was able to tell the council that 'I used tò deliver the papers of one of the elderly Conservative councillors sitting in the Chamber and, My Lord Mayor, I knew then from the papers he read that there was no hope for him!'.

Mr Hallgarth was a very small man and combined pomposity and arrogance in equal measure. He obviously enjoyed the managerial power of supervising eight newsboys. A collision course looked inevi-table. Matters came to a head over Good Friday when no newspapers were printed. Hallgarth decided to stop sixpence out of our wages since we did not have to work on that day. Our indignation knew no bounds. The newsboys met outside his shop and I was appointed spokesman. 'You will get no sixpence out of me', he told me. So the boys went home and left him with 16 rounds of newspapers to deliver. At night we met again and refused to carry into the shop the bundles of evening newspapers dumped on the pavement to await us. I again approached Mr Hallgarth, but the experience of being left with so many undelivered newspapers had not improved his temper, nor widened his experience of life. Again we went home. The same thing happened again next morning but by then we were into a new learning experience. First came the strike-breaker. The mother of one of our boys was a widow. She needed the money, little as it was, so he returned to work. Another boy provided some excellent intelligence. On the next corner was another newsagent – Knowles – who paid his boys four shillings and sixpence. Not only had he not stopped his boys any money for Good Friday but he had actually given each of them an Easter present. One of our lads told us he was going to pack it all in anyway, so we were down to six.

Mr Knowles was a much more intelligent man to deal with. I explained the position to him. Yes, he needed four boys, but he would agree to take the six of us, one of our conditions, which meant that we could have a day off from time to time. There was a condition – we had to go to Mr Hallgarth and explain in a straightforward way that we were leaving him and moving to Mr Knowles. I collected the six shoulder bags in which we carried our newspapers and delivered them back to Hallgarth with a suitable explanation. He went purple in the face and I left hurriedly before he exploded. Mr Knowles was a good businessman. At the weekend when he paid us our wages he took me to one side and asked whether the boys would like to recruit some new customers. He would pay us half a crown for every new customer still with us after a month. We were delighted and visited all our old customers explaining the situation and collecting new orders. We were rich beyond compare.

SPORTING DAYS

Throughout these years our sport mostly took the form of games we organised for ourselves in the backyards where we would play home and away on each other's territory, or in the streets if there was no policeman about, or at Burbury Street recreation ground, where we could organise matches with a full side or even more if there were lads looking for a game. This happened often and we would end up with games of 20 players on each side. Usually we would arrange the matches as street challenges. Our street – Clifford Street – and Guildford Street, our neighbours, would challenge other streets in the vicinity or we would take up such a challenge. No matches in the Football League or the County Championship were ever taken more seriously. At weekends or in the holidays we would take ourselves off to Perry Hall or Perry Barr parks, if we could get hold of a case ball or a proper cricket ball. That was sheer delight. As we got older Aston Villa and Warwickshire cricket also dominated our lives.

In 1935 Aston Villa were relegated to the Second Division for the first time in their history. It was a disaster; the whole community felt a sense of outrage. These days when speculators seek to take over leading clubs and Ministers suggest that market forces are the dominant factor, or that ground-sharing might be the answer, they show deplorable ignorance of the social purpose of sport, and especially of the fact that a football team is the natural expression of the loyalty of the community from which it springs. So it was with us. Villa were down and so were the supporters in the streets, the factories and the pubs. And didn't the supporters of Birmingham City and West Bromwich Albion let us know it!

Rescue came in the form of Mr Jimmy Hogan, a superb coach who was taken on as manager after international experience in Austria. He was a perfect gentleman with a fine football brain who put together the finest team of players that I have ever seen in the Villa colours. I can recite their names now without a moment's hesitation: Biddlestone, Callaghan, Cummings, Massie, Allen, Iveson, Broome, Haycock, Shell, Starling and Houghton. George Cummings was a very tough left-back and I never saw Stanley Matthews have a good game against him. Jimmy Allen, the centre-half, was bought from Portsmouth in June 1934 for the record sum of £10,500. He was the first 'stopper' centre-half we had seen at Villa Park playing what came to be known as the third back game. It was not popular to start with but was soon universally accepted. Alex Massie was a wonderful Scottish half-back. Bob Iveson scored the fastest goal I have ever seen: nine and three fifths of a second into the Cup tie against Charlton Athletic in 1938. Freddie Haycock was a workhorse who never stopped running at a fantastic pace while Ronnie Starling was a ball-player supreme. But the heroes were Frank Broome, my idol, who played on the right wing and had tremendous ball control at great speed, and Eric Houghton, still a very dear friend, who had the hardest shot in the game. His penalty kicks were unstoppable. He never messed about but fired the ball at the iron stanchions just inside the goal-posts and he could do this with both feet. I never saw him miss a penalty.

Going to Villa Park in those days was the magic of our lives. I was there in 1938 standing at the very top corner of the Holte End terrace when there was a record crowd of 75,000 spectators. There was no trouble, we were just packed together enjoying our sport, part of a united community. I took a school friend to a match against Manchester City in the sixth round of the FA Cup. The gates were closed well before the match started and my friend, who was twice my size, fainted. We handed him over the heads of the crowd and the next I saw of him he was being revived near the touch-line from where he was allowed to sit and watch the game. I stood at exactly the same spot when a new ground record was created in March 1946 against Derby County with an attendance of 76,588. In 1938 we won back our place in the First Division but then came the war and much promise was dissipated.

Summer times for us meant Warwickshire cricket and occasionally Birchfield Harriers. The County side was skippered by R.E.S. 'Bob' Wyatt, now the oldest living England captain and a man whose friendship I am privileged to share. He had constant difficulties with Mr Ryder, a dictatorial county secretary, but even in those days Bob Wyatt was bringing on two of our latter-day heroes, Eric Hollies and Tom Dollery, who became the first professional to skipper a County side and led us to victory in the 1951 County Championship. In pre-war years Birchfield Harriers automatically calls to mind the names of Jack Lovelock and Sidney Wooderson. Both of them ran there from time to time and provided us with a window on another world, as did Dorothy Round, the girl from Dudley, who became a Midlands heroine when she won the Ladies' Championship at Wimbledon in 1934. She started off a lifetime's interest in yet another sport. We lived on this pride until Birmingham's own Ann Jones recharged it by winning the Championship for us in 1969 when I was Minister for Sport. Ann had previously done splendidly in the World Table Tennis Championships so she conquered two worlds and has, for me, provided another lasting friendship.

POLITICAL AWAKENINGS

In 1937 my father returned home unexpectedly from his work in Exeter. 'There is an election,' he said, 'everyone must vote and on Sunday night I will take you to the election meeting.' The election was necessitated by the death of Sir Austen Chamberlain, our Member for the constituency of West Birmingham. We had not seen much of Sir Austen. During the 1935 election he had paraded up our backyards accompanied by a bevy of agents. I remember the occasion well; he did not look very much at ease. His discomfort was soon complete when our neighbour, Jack Weir, a strong Labour man, spotted this procession and leaped through his door to address it in basic working-class language. No retreat ever proceeded more quickly. Sir Austen made a distinguished contribution to international affairs but the rows and rows of terraced houses whose inhabitants he represented, many of them without water, bathrooms or proper sanitation, did not appear to engage his attention.

So on that Sunday evening in 1937 I was taken to my first election meeting. The Labour candidate was a young academic hopeful from Oxford, hitherto little known, by the name of R.H.S. Crossman. Dick Crossman, who was going to become one of the most controversial of the intellectual politicians in the Labour movement, was a brilliant thinker – too brilliant, since he would often destroy his own arguments in the course of the same speech by a lack of understanding of how working people actually think and feel. No such contradictions appeared on the night I first heard him. He spoke with great fervour and total command and the reception he received created a wonderful atmosphere. His supporting speakers excited me even more. They were Ellen Wilkinson, the auburn-haired heroine of the Jarrow march of the unemployed to London and Philip Noel-Baker, a distinguished Olympic athlete in his own right with whom, some 20 years later, I was to strike up a firm personal friendship. He was one of the Party's leading foreign policy experts. Icknield Street School was packed out for the occasion. Rarely since then have I experienced such a night of magic, such an electric atmosphere, such compelling oratory. For a boy of 13 it was heady stuff. I was hooked on politics from that night and there was never to be any turning back. I delivered leaflets and marched the streets singing 'Vote, vote, vote for Richard Crossman'. The Tory candidate was Walter Higgs, a local industrialist, whose path I was later to cross in quite astonishing circumstances. When the result was announced on 29 April it confirmed that Birmingham, the citadel of the Chamberlains, still supported the cause, but for us it was the first of many 'moral' victories. The result was: Higgs W.F. 12,552; Crossman R.H.S. 9,632; Majority 2,920. Austen Chamberlain's 1935 'Unionist' majority of 7,371 had been more than halved.

This by-election seemed to trigger off a veritable torrent of political activity in our neighbourhood. The National Union of Fascists came to harangue us closely followed by the Communists. The Independent Labour Party put in an appearance, so did the Social Credit Party, or Douglas Credit as we called it, after its Alberta founder. Hardly a week went by without a meeting. Mostly they were lost causes but they provided a good apprenticeship for political life. We soon returned to mainstream politics. In 1939 the Conservative MP for the adjacent constituency of Aston died and another by-election was called. The Labour candidate was Dr Sam Segal (later to become Lord Segal). For some time the streets had been whitewashed with the slogan 'Chamberlain must go', and here in the heartland of Chamberlainism there was no way that the issue of Neville Chamberlain's appeasement and the question of re-armament was to be avoided. This time the star speaker was the leader of the Labour Party himself, Major C.R. Attlee. With some of my friends I went to Lozells Street School and at another packed meeting I heard Clem Attlee attack appeasement, defend Labour's defence policy and call for re-armament in the face of the growing threat posed by Hitler, Mussolini and Franco. At the time of the by-election Chamberlain was totally immersed in his appeasement policies. No other issue seemed of any importance. What impressed me most about Attlee was not so much his speech but his masterly handling of questions. He was cryptic and dismissive in a single sentence.

It was an entirely different meeting from the one I had experienced in West Birmingham but it showed how the great national issues could change and take on a new dimension in a short period of time. This meeting had none of the festival atmosphere that I had found so exhilarating at my first election meeting. We were drifting into war and this seemed to be accepted by everyone present. Two things stuck in my mind from Clem Attlee's speech and remained there for months afterwards: the issue of collective security and the need to support the League of Nations which, until that meeting, I had hardly had cause to think about. The policies of Neville Chamberlain were not going to be overturned at this by-election in his home town, but the result announced on 17 May 1939 showed that the Tory majority was down from 10,355 to 5,901. The citadel was creaking. For me politics took on a new meaning. It was not now totally about unemployment and bad housing, it was also about war and peace and far off countries like Czechoslovakia. Clem Attlee had ensured that at least one member of his audience had registered their importance.

WAR DECLARED

As the international crisis grew, things were changing all around us. Dad came home from Exeter, his health broken by the struggle to keep two houses going and the long enforced absences from his family. He needed stomach surgery at the General Hospital but we were never told what the problem actually was. In those days patients did not receive such confidences from their doctors, much less from their surgeons, but he recovered to rejoin the ranks of the unemployed. He never returned to Exeter. Talk of evacuation was in the air and plans were conveyed to the schools informing them where they should report should the need arise. My brother Stan had left school at the age of 14 and my eight-year-old sister Margaret was marched off to take the train for Hereford amid great sadness. Volunteers who had become air raid wardens visited our houses to demonstrate gas masks, which they persuaded us all first to try on, and then to collect from a central store. The final proof that life was never to be the same again came with the arrival of the council builders who erected a strong brick air raid shelter in our backyard, at one stroke destroying both our football and our cricket pitches. War was inevitable. I told my parents that I wanted to leave school and they agreed. I went to see my headmaster and he did not ask me a single question about this decision, nor in any way seek to persuade me otherwise, so I left. I answered an advertisement in the local newspaper for an office boy at the Hercules Cycle Company and my mother took me for an interview. I was offered seven shillings and sixpence a week and assigned to the managing director's office where my job was to race round the factory every hour and record in special books how many cycles or parts of cycles each department had produced in the hour. Thus did a lowly-paid office boy help the managing director to control his empire. After four weeks I asked his secretary for a rise and this was granted. My wages increased to ten shillings.

On 4 September 1939, I had my sixteenth birthday. War had been declared a day earlier. We heard Neville Chamberlain's announcement on our radios and then all the neighbours came to their doors in the street and discussed what it would mean. Almost without exception they believed that 'it will not be like the last time, it will be over very quickly'. As we talked on that Sunday morning we had our first air raid warning. It was a false alarm but it sent us all post haste to our air raid shelters. We had not yet fitted them out with lights or bunk beds, not really believing that we would need to. We were to learn differently. Like it or not, politics were for real and, as if in an instant, I was transformed from a schoolboy to a man. There was no time for adolescence.

2

INTO BATTLE

WARTIME BRUM

No Brummie was going to have an easy war. We were a city of a million people, and the industrial heartland of the nation. We had the Austin Motor Company, the Imperial Chemical Industry, BSA, Serk Radiators, Dunlop, Metropolitan Cammell and Carriage, Guest Keen and Nettlefold and, right there in our own neighbourhood, Joseph Lucas.

Close by, in the Black Country, we had the great foundry industry upon which all depended. And less than 20 miles to the east stood Coventry, home of the motor industry. We were a natural target for the enemy and for the next six years this fact dominated all our lives, but it was not until 9 August 1940 that the first bomb was to land in our streets, at Erdington, when a single raider dropped two bombs. It was thought to be attempting to hit Fisher and Ludlow which was building aircraft. Before this we had the 'phoney war' when all was quiet in the city. Air raid wardens had been recruited into the ARP (Air Raid Precautions Services) as early as 1937. After demonstrating gas masks and inspecting our air raid shelters, they also supervised the black-out of all our houses. If a chink of light showed they would hammer on the door and their cry of 'Put that light out' was a rebuke to be dealt with at all speed.

The shelters became an urgent priority. Houses with cellars had them reinforced with steel girders. Houses with gardens got an 'Anderson' shelter, named after Sir John Anderson, the Minister designated to take care of the home front. These shelters were made from corrugated steel and were round at the top where they were bolted together. Later on other houses without cellars or gardens were supplied with a 'Morrison' shelter which was in fact a steel table under which the family could take shelter. This refuge was named after Herbert Morrison, the Home Secretary when Labour joined Churchill to form a coalition.

Very soon after war was declared, my mother had news of the

vacancy of a 'through' house – with a front room, living-room and small kitchen – at 119 Guildford Street. It also had an outside toilet next to the kitchen – an absolute luxury to us, as were the three bedrooms and the 20 yards of garden. Neighbours put in a good word with the landlord and so we moved to this home just two doors from the house in which I had been born. I was to live there until 1955 when, at the age of 31, I was elected Member of Parliament and married Brenda. The first job was to build the Anderson shelter. My brother and I dug a large hole at the end of the garden some three feet deep, fitted the shelter into it and then filled as many sacks as we could with soil or sand to give the shelter a protective wall some two feet thick. It served our purpose well when shrapnel showered down upon us.

The Fire Brigade had been augmented by the formation of the Auxiliary Fire Service, more than 12,000 strong when war was declared, which was housed in hastily-erected temporary fire stations. Unattended factories and shops were a considerable hazard, especially at night, and a fire watch service was an obvious need as a means of first defence against fire bombs. So the Fire Guard Service was formed. The city had been divided into some 2,300 sectors, each housing several hundred people. The air raid wardens came around recruiting volunteers for the new service and I soon offered to join. We had some basic training from the Fire Service at the old home of Sir Austen Chamberlain. It was there that we were trained to smother incendiary bombs with sandbags and to use stirrup pumps for elementary fire-fighting. For advanced training we were given instruction in the use of hosepipes operated from temporary fire engines.

At the age of 16 I was appointed the sector officer, and so I assumed my first position of authority. Very soon I was advancing up the ladder: within a year I became the deputy group fire guard officer. The group officer, Ernie Hall, is a friend to this day. We went from house to house recruiting as many volunteers as we could and passing on the techniques we had been taught. We arranged the rota on the basis of one night's full duty in every eight days and a full turn-out when an alarm was sounded. When stirrup pumps, buckets, sandbags and sand became available we organised working parties to fill them and store them at designated assembly points. Then we had to visit all the business premises and ensure that fire watchers were on duty at all times. As we were working six and a half days a week at our normal jobs this activity had to be organised at night or on Sunday afternoons.

When the raids started Ernie and I would divide up the area and each tour one half of the sectors in our group, making sure that all sector posts were manned and that all premises were covered. Quite often they were not and this caused us some problems. Our biggest headache was the Midland Oil Company, which stored large quantities of oil poured into containers by the most primitive of methods and then distributed to various garages around the country. The floor of this factory was caked in oil. By a miracle no bomb ever dropped on it. The company met their fire-watching obligations by engaging a local resident to cover for them, but he liked his drink and was rarely at his post. So my first duty when the alarm sounded was to visit the pub, locate him and return him to his post. As I was 17 at the time and the minimum age for entering a pub was 18, I was breaking the law every time I had to enforce it! When the air raids became intense the strain of working all day and doing fire guard duty all night became very exhausting. For weeks on end I never managed to get into bed. At lunch-time I would run the mile or so from work to home and have a quick meal after which I would collapse into a chair for 20 minutes of deep sleep. So began for me one of the greatest blessings of life, the cat-nap. Since then, whether on train, plane or ship I have been able to put my head down and sleep. After ten minutes or so I can wake totally refreshed and ready to face another day.

In the autumn of 1941 the number of voluntary fire guards dried up as more men were called up for war service and it was decreed that fire guard service was to be compulsory. There were still not enough men available to guarantee total fire guard cover so women were also required to do service. This created another problem. My chief, Ernie Hall, was quite a character but he was partially deaf. More and more he tended to leave things to me as he had difficulty in responding quickly to what was being said to him. When the women had to be recruited and organised we delivered a notice to every house requiring them to attend a Sunday meeting at Lozells Street School where we would register them for rota duty and provide basic instruction in their duties and in the techniques of fire-fighting. We arrived at the school to find the place packed. Several hundred women filled the hall, the corridors and classrooms. Ernie took one look at this gathering and turned to me. 'You will have to talk to them, I wouldn't hear their questions.' So I was launched into a lifetime of public speaking. It was an exhilarating occasion for me, especially the applause.

At this time I was called up for my own medical examination and fully expected to be drafted into the services but it was not to be. I was placed in category C because both my feet have hammer toes, a family inheritance. The medical officer told me that I could never wear army boots and on hearing what I was doing, told me I would probably face more action in Birmingham than most people would care for. I found out later that the Civil Defence Service was also keen for me to remain in Birmingham. The city was ready for Hitler, but there was also the task of learning a trade.

HERCULES

At Hercules I soon got into my stride. My hourly tour of every department in the factory, recording the production levels for the managing director, the general manager and the works manager took me from the stores to tube bending, to sandblasting and plating and so to the wheels assembly and wheel truing frame assembly, packing and despatch. Every hour was a voyage of discovery. I met some wonderful people in all these departments. Each section had its own progress clerk who would give me the hourly production figure and then I would spend time talking to one or other of the workforce. No one ever matured more quickly than I did. We talked about everything: sports, politics, life in all its aspects, but especially the progress of the war. During the factory tea break I would contrive to be passing through the section where the progress clerks met for their ten-minute break. One such occasion remains indelibly in my memory. News had come through of our retreat to Dunkirk, and the talk could not have been more sombre. It was the first time that I had seen a grown man in tears as one of my friends in the group told us all that 'You don't realise what this means. It is defeat, we have lost the war'. Most of the group thought otherwise but we were sad and shaken that morning as we realised that defeat was indeed staring us in the face.

Everyone had to be mobilised to face the possibilities of invasion. The LDV (Local Defence Volunteers), which later became the Home Guard, was formed. The Hercules platoon was established and most of us joined it. We had few weapons and shared what rifles were allocated to us for drill parade. We certainly had no ammunition but we were taken off one Sunday to the ranges at Kingsbury where we could practise with real bullets. The commanding officer told us that in the event of an invasion we would defend the junction of Wake Green Road and Yardley Wood Road in Moseley, a mile away from my present home. We would go there on occasions for an all-night exercise, lying in the gardens of the local houses, without rifles or ammunition, discussing among ourselves from which direction the enemy was likely to appear. Fortunately, the residents showed every sympathy with our vigil and kept us supplied with pots of tea. Later on, when Birmingham was under attack and Hercules were making aircraft wings, our Home Guard duty took the form of fire-watching from a tower specially built on the roof from where we had a tremendous view of the whole of Birmingham and could give early alarm.

After a couple of years as the office boy it was thought right that my career should be advanced. My first move was to the Drawing Office, where I was put on to tracing and sent to Saturday afternoon classes at the Birmingham Technical School. As we were working six and a half days a week this was a welcome break but after some months it dawned upon the management and upon me that technical drawing was not my forté so I moved on to the commercial side. First to the Invoice Department, then to Buying and finally to Accounts. It was a good apprenticeship. By 1942 I had decided that on principle I should belong to a trade union. I called the Clerical and Administrative Workers' Union and they sent along a Mr Walter Smart, later to be-come the Yorkshire area secretary of the union. We had a very large office staff but not one of them, nor anyone in the drawing office, belonged to any trade union. I arranged a meeting at a local school one night and some 30 or so of the staff joined the union. So began my lifetime association with the APEX – the Association of Professional, Executive, Clerical and Computer Staffs.

News of the formation of a branch of the union was received with disbelief by the management. After two years or so they decided that we should part company and, as was the practice, I was directed by the Ministry of Labour to work at the firm of Higgs Motors. Here I remained for the rest of the war but it was to prove a most traumatic experience. However, in those two years I met Arthur Lummis Gibson, the Midlands area secretary of the union. He was later to become an outstanding Lord Mayor of Birmingham but in those early days he introduced me to the educational possibilities of the Labour colleges and to courses in trade unionism.

BIRMINGHAM UNDER ATTACK

Between 9 August 1940, when Birmingham experienced its first air raid, and 31 July 1941, the city sustained 76 air attacks. There was to be one further isolated raid on 23 April 1943. During this 12-month bombardment 2,000 citizens were killed and more than 3,000 seriously injured. Some 12,000 houses were damaged and 4,000 destroyed as were more than 1,000 shops, offices, factories and public buildings. At first there were sporadic raids and these served to test our civil defence and fire guard arrangements. On the night of 25 August we suffered our first major raid on the city centre when our famous Market Hall was destroyed. Exactly two months later a large scale incendiary attack did great damage in the centre of the city when the Marshall and Snelgrove store was totally destroyed by fire. Soon the enemy was to change tactics and make daytime attacks on Birmingham industry, scoring hits on both Dunlop and Austin Aero.

However, the major enemy concentration upon the Midlands was signalled on 14 November when a sustained attack was made upon the city of Coventry. The sirens sounded in Birmingham too and we stood in our streets that night hearing wave after wave of aircraft, continuous distant explosions and looking at an eastern sky lit up like a vast red sea. The men on duty were full of foreboding, would it be our turn next? We were soon to know. Five days later, on 19 November, 350 enemy bombers left their calling cards. The attack lasted from just before seven in the evening until some time after four the following morning. More than 1,350 people were killed or injured; a direct hit upon the BSA works at Small Heath caused 53 deaths. Every section of our civil defence service was stretched to the full but as dawn arrived we were proud in the knowledge that Birmingham had coped. We snatched a couple of hours' sleep and then made our way to work through mountains of rubble.

We had also been bombed the previous night and we knew that the city centre was without water. The mains had been destroyed and many of the buildings burned on uncontrollably. My brother Stan was on fire-watch duty at the old university buildings in Edmund Street. He was one of eight youngsters, all members of the ATC (Air Training Corps) under the leadership of a professor of music! He returned home to give us a graphic account of the carnage. A direct hit set alight a gas main in Victoria Square opposite the Town Hall and the Council House. It burned like a gigantic torch, the flame reaching as high as the tall buildings and providing the raiders with a directional flare they could not have dared to hope for.

At work that day I found my workmates in the factory and the office in a state of shock. Many people had not got through to work. We wondered anxiously about them. All of us were full of doubts. The same questions were on everyone's lips, would the Germans come again that night? How could we cope without water? But there was no sense of defeatism. The mood was defiant but apprehensive. The Luftwaffe did not come for a third night. We were saved. Magnificent work was done to patch things up in the city centre and to repair the mains so that we could face the next onslaught but that night we manned our quiet sector post in disbelief. It was a miracle.

Almost the last really heavy raid on the city came in the following year, 1941, when on 9 April we were attacked for six hours by some 250 bombers who dropped 650 high explosives and 170 incendiary bombs. More than 1,100 of our people died or were seriously injured. There was a follow-up attack of some five hours the next night but again there was no third consecutive night of bombing. Why, we shall never know, but our city centre was again ablaze from end to end. Fires in High Street and New Street were out of control, the Bull Ring was burning, the Prince of Wales theatre in Broad Street was destroyed. During these raids the General Hospital was hit and the emergency hospital set up in the basement of Lewis's store was brought into service. The whole of the basement area was covered with rows of the desperately injured. Blood was everywhere. Doctors were few and far between. The Imperial War Museum publication *After a Raid*, written by C.J. Rice, described the scene. 'Stretcher cases covered the whole basement . . . When I glanced at the wide stairway leading to the basement it was crammed from side to side with blood-soaked cloth-ing . . . the unfortunate people of Birmingham row on row, the air raid victims . . . only the faces of the people lying there were showing. All the faces bore the same reddy brown colour, caused by brick dust from demolished houses. Nearly all were badly injured . . . Here and there a doctor or a nurse but medical attention was minimal. Many of them were children. I found the eyes of one face, that of a boy looking towards me. He asked faintly where he was. I told him and said I would come back later. When I came back he had died. It was Good Friday.'

So it was on the streets. The Fire Brigade and their Auxiliary comrades fought like Trojans but were totally overwhelmed. The rescue services and ambulances were working all out but were often unable to get through the rubble to the next incident. The air raid wardens and the fire guard service, the people, whether trained or not, with shrapnel falling all around them, sought to rescue the trapped, put out the fires and comfort the distressed.

It was during these raids that I believe the first explosive incendiary bombs to be dropped in Britain fell in the area for which we were responsible. They were certainly the first we had met. This occurred in Wheeler Street, Lozells. One of our fire guards approached it as he had been instructed, with a sandbag to smother it, when it exploded, killing him outright. We were all stunned and Ernie and I hastily made our way round each of our sectors instructing everyone not to approach incendiary bombs until they had exploded.

On the same night one of these bombs set fire to the Lozells picture house. Only the manager was on duty – he was killed and our favourite cinema was destroyed for ever. Around the corner another fire bomb destroyed someone's home and our team dealt with this incident without help from the fire service, who could not get through to attend. These three incidents were in a straight line, obviously the result of a stick of bombs.

There were three other major incidents in our neighbourhood resulting from high explosive bombs, and they all caused great distress to us. In one of these a whole family was wiped out when the water main was ruptured by the bomb and flooded the cellar where the family had taken shelter. A second bomb landed at the top of a long terrace with some 20 or more houses on each side. It totally blocked the neck of the terrace and rescue work was frantically attempted from both the terrace side and the street side of the wrecked house. Among the families trapped in the terrace and helping in the rescue were the Hands family, great friends of ours and well-known in the neighbourhood. Harry Hands and I saw a lot of each other through football and had gone to many pre-war political meetings together. On this night he and his brother-in-law, Wally Cusack, a bricklayer, tunnelled through to rescue the three people who were trapped, Wally giving advice as to which bricks to move and Harry bringing the family out to safety. I actually heard the fall of the third bomb and remember it vividly. One or two of us were standing by the entry to our houses when we heard a loud 'swoosh' immediately before the explosion. Instinctively we threw ourselves to the ground. I thought my own time had come as I was hit in the back by an enormous force which temporarily knocked me out. When I recovered I found that this force was in fact the 20-stone body of our next-door neighbour!

One other memory stands out. It was a night when two searchlights captured an enemy bomber in their beams right over our heads. Men stood in the roadway waving their fists and shouting 'bastard, bastard'. It was the release of two years of pent-up emotion. Sadly, the plane climbed into the clouds before the anti-aircraft fire arrived.

No one who lived through this time when enemy aircraft filled our skies, when our city burned as we stood helpless without water, when men tore into the rubble with bare hands to rescue friends and neighbours or fought against incendiary bombs, can be filled with anything but tremendous pride at the endurance and the comradeship of his fellow Brummies. Birmingham worked by day and defended itself by night, although the night shifts often performed both duties. I cannot recall that anyone believed there was anything heroic in this service and sacrifice. It was a community of free people asserting its rights to existence with no thoughts of defeat, nor doubts about duty. One million citizens united to defend their freedom. It was a privilege to be one of them. Whatever the future was to hold or whatever future endeavours one would make in the interests of Birmingham they would be but a tiny contribution towards a mammoth obligation to a great city and a wonderful people.

JOINING UP WITH LABOUR

By 1942 the worst was over on the home front. We began easing ourselves into more normal preoccupations as it became possible to walk the streets at night, to attend meetings, to go about more civilised pursuits. Of course, the war effort continued at full speed in the factories and we never relaxed our watch in civil defence and the fire service although we had time now to organise social events in those areas too. Football had been suspended during the year of the bombings. It was now time to kick a ball about once more. The problem was that this had to be organised on Sunday afternoons, our only free time. The Football Association had set its face against Sunday games. Before the war it hounded out of the sport any person found guilty of such blasphemy. When the boys in the factories heard of these prohibitions they regarded them as a monumental irrelevance.

So, on a Sunday afternoon in the early autumn of 1942 I went with a team formed at the firm where my brother was working to a match arranged against another scratch team at Perry Hall park. To our amazement several hundreds of people out for a stroll waited expectantly on the touch-lines. No one had thought of providing a referee, much less a whistle. The inevitable happened ... I refereed the match dressed in my Sunday best, waving a handkerchief and shouting foul, corner and so on. At half-time a man wandered over to me. 'Are you a registered referee?' he asked. 'No', I replied, fearing some official onslaught. 'Well, you should be,' he said. 'I am a member of the Referees' Association. Will you come to our meeting next Friday and we will sign you up and give you some coaching?' Flattered, I agreed, and so I was launched into a refereeing career which was to take me to every major ground in the country.

The man who talked me into it was Jack Price, a delightful friend, a gentleman in every way, probably too nice to advance to the very top of a refereeing career but a fine referee nonetheless. When in 1956 I was to referee my first Football League match at Southend I was thrilled that Jack drove me there as a mission of friendship and of duty. Jack had a much better claim to fame. He became the first, or one of the first, radio cricket statisticians. He kept copious score books and records and developed early systems of advising Brian Johnston and his friends of the essential facts around which they could weave their stories.

The success of that first Sunday afternoon match convinced the boss of my brother's firm that a league should be started. Since no one else seemed interested he contacted me and we called a meeting at the Chamber of Commerce, which we advertised in the *Birmingham Mail*, for people interested in forming a 'friendly Sunday' league. We were inundated. Among those who turned up was a Mr W.H. 'Billy' Rogers, a wonderful character who had once kept goal for West Bromwich Albion, trod the boards as a variety artist around the world and was never to be seen without a large Havana cigar. He explained that he had been secretary of the pre-war Monday League operated for the benefit of butchers and market traders. He came with the authority of Mr E.A. 'Teddy' Eden, secretary of the Birmingham County Football Association and one of the most enlightened of all football administrators, who responded to the situation by registering us as the Birmingham Monday League Sunday section. Sunday football was officially born and has gone from strength to strength, providing millions of youngsters with a happy, healthy and innocent pastime.

I joined the Referees' Association, attended referees' courses and got myself kitted out with the help of a black jacket retrieved from the wardrobe of one of my fellow office workers.

The *Evening Despatch* was Birmingham's second evening newspaper. One of its most popular features was its correspondence page, 'Public Opinion'. As we moved towards victory its columns contained letters expressing the hopes of the people and debates about the future. I decided to join in and had many letters published. One correspondent suggested that in view of the time it took to reply to the letters the newspaper should encourage the formation of a readers' organisation where we could meet weekly and debate the issues of the day. The Public Opinion Action Association was created and its chairman was Wallace Lawler, later to become Birmingham's lone Liberal MP. I was appointed his deputy. Our debates were tremendously stimulating. The first, well covered by the BBC and the *Daily Mirror*, was on 'What is the meaning of democracy?' Week by week we debated every subject under the sun. Taking part were Conservatives, Communists, Socialists, supporters of Social Credit and Monetary Reform, religious adherents of every persuasion, atheists, humanists and anyone who had anything to say, or just came to listen or to vote on the motion. Rarely did a week go by when I did not enter the fray and take on the world. When I joined the Labour Party my colleagues thought that all this was an irrelevant frivolity but I knew better. It was a foundation course for public life for which I have been eternally grateful. Most important of all, it was an introduction to a hundred different points of view and it taught me how to engage the opposition. These arts are as important as those of simple advocacy.

In the last two years of the war the mood of the whole country seemed to be changing. Winning the war was not going to be enough, though winning it sooner rather than later was an increasing demand. A campaign developed to 'Open the Second Front Now', partly out of a desire to get it all over with and to get on with winning the peace and largely out of a tremendous admiration for the heroic sacrifices of the Russian people. This was the first national campaign in which I found myself caught up. I soon discovered that it was dominated by the Communist Party for the very simple reason that the other political parties rigidly adhered to their electoral pact not to engage in political activity while supporting the coalition Government. The campaign was led by large scale public meetings – I attended several at the Town Hall where the proceedings were relayed to enthusiastic overflow crowds outside. I listened to Dr Hewlett Johnson, the Dean of Canterbury, who made a most moving speech. However, I soon became suspicious of the direction of the campaign. I attended one or two meetings organised by members of the Party and when a difference of opinion broke out as to what had been previously agreed I asked for the minutes to be produced. There were no minutes. There was not going to be any democracy here; this was a campaign to be directed by the leadership and we could take it or leave it. I left it.

The dilemma of how to pursue our political ideals and plans to change society the moment the war was won, and yet still to give full support to the war effort, was thrust upon us in dramatic fashion when the MP for Aston, Major Kellett, was tragically killed. A new political party, the Commonwealth Party, had been formed to give expression to the view that normal political life should be re-established in the form of parliamentary elections so that attention could be focused upon the nature of post-war Britain. It met with much success and had already won the only previous wartime by-election. The Commonwealth Party decided to fight the Aston seat and so a by-election was called. Once more campaigning got underway in the streets where we lived. Meetings were held and literature was delivered, only this time there was an astonishing difference. The Labour Party and the Liberals took no part in the election, advising their supporters to vote for the Conservative candidate! The Communists went one better, they actually put up Jessie Eden, one of their star performers, to speak on the Conservative platform. It was very confusing.

This campaign brought me into contact with Jim Meadows, who was later to become the full-time Labour Party agent for Aston. He encouraged me to join the Labour Party, which I did. This was the beginning of 40 years of wonderful friendship. We found that apart from sport, which used to leave him cold, we had many interests in common, especially music and poetry. Often I went late to his house and his wife Edna would make us a large pot of tea and announce, 'I shall leave you to your reading. I'm going to bed'. Jim and I would read for hours. Sometimes from the Bible, sometimes poetry from which we both found inspiration. We had a special fondness for John Addington Symonds' poem which, later on, Jim would urge me to use as a peroration to my speeches. 'Go on,' he would say, 'make sure you finish up with "These Things Shall Be".' Still, today, I know of no poem which better states my philosophy and idealism than these words:

> These things shall be: a loftier race
>   Than e'er the world has known, shall rise,
> With flame of freedom in their souls
>   And light of knowledge in their eyes.
>
> They shall be gentle, brave and strong
>   To spill no drop of blood, but dare
> All that may plant man's lordship firm
>   On earth and fire, and sea, and air.
>
> They shall be simple in their homes
>   And splendid in their public ways,
> Filling the mansion of the state
>   With music and with hymns of praise.
>
> Nation with nation, land with land,
>   Unarmed shall live as comrades free;
> In every heart and brain shall throb
>   The pulse of one fraternity.
>
> New arts shall bloom of the loftier mould,
>   And mightier music thrill the skies,
> And every life shall be a song
>   When all the earth is paradise.

Rarely do we sing it in church these days, which is sad, because it says so much about practical Christianity. Jim and I would also argue about every subject under the sun, often very violently, for we both passionately and obstinately clung to our own views. Usually our arguments were conducted to a background of classical music, which we loved. But in all the years nothing ever shook our friendship. He led me to understand that idealism had to be harnessed to political reality and so to the Labour Party. Later on I partly repaid my debt by persuading him that his talents extended far beyond the role of political organisation. He overcame his doubts, became a fine member of the city council, and he and Edna occupied the office of Lord Mayor and Lady Mayoress with great distinction.

HIGGS MOTORS

In 1944 I left Hercules Cycles and was directed to take up employment with Higgs Motors. I did not want to go there but I had no option, and I found myself working in their Buying Department. They had no union so I set about creating one. It was quite a feat to have some trade union organisation in the office when none existed in the factory. Walter Higgs was the Conservative MP who had won the 1937 by-election in West Birmingham. I joined the Labour Party in that constituency and soon became its secretary. The stage was set for conflict but it was not of my making. Higgs did not believe in unions, he had a 'Works Council'. I set about getting myself elected to it and circulated an election address which dealt with working conditions in the office. I was elected with an overwhelming majority. I was told that Mr Higgs always took the chair at meetings of the Works Council. He was soon to break that habit – he came only to the first meeting that I attended and thereafter apologised for his absence.

The firm decided that they did not like me. First they tried to talk me into leaving and actually told me that I ought to go and work for a firm that believed in my principles, such as Cadbury's. I told them that as I had been directed to work for them I could not leave even if I wished to do so, and I had no such desire. They changed tack. On three occasions they applied to the Ministry of Labour for permission to discharge me, giving all sorts of spurious reasons. On three occasions their application was sent to me for my observations as was required in those days. On three occasions I wrote: 'Mr Walter Higgs is the Conservative MP for West Birmingham. I am the secretary of the West Birmingham Labour Party. That is the reason for this application!' On three occasions Higgs' application was rejected. I was finding life fascinating! Higgs were not to achieve their objective until after the General Election campaign of 1945, when West Birmingham elected its first Labour MP and so helped to bring about the Labour Government. Almost the first act of that Government was to end the Essential Works Order under which I had been directed to work at Higgs Motors. On the morning this new situation came into being the company secretary was waiting by the time clock. 'Good morning Mr Howell, I don't think there is any need for you to clock in today, do you?' I was the first man in Britain to be sacked, and that as a result of a Labour Government!

Later on, after losing his seat, Higgs went to Australia and made what was to become an infamous speech – 'Britain needs empty bellies to make her work harder, eleven men after ten jobs'. I saw a report of this speech in the lunch-time edition of the *Birmingham Mail*. By the evening edition it had disappeared. Too late. The cutting was transmitted from Labour's Regional Office to Transport House and was soon used to such effect in Parliament that Winston Churchill was forced to intervene and explain that Higgs was an unknown back-bencher of whom he had never heard – even though they had served together in the Commons for some eight years!

ELECTION 1945

No sooner was the war won in Europe than Winston Churchill decided that he would end the Coalition Government and go for a 'khaki' election, expecting to be swept back to power on a flood of emotion as Britain's war leader. It was a monumental miscalculation. As he toured the country the rapturous reception he rightly received as our national saviour served only to mask the other public emotion that was being expressed even more strongly: that it was time for a change. There could be no going back to the Britain of the dole queues, of bad housing, to the old ways. Two or three developments brought this about. First was the work of the ABCA (Army Bureau of Current Affairs). They had been carrying out education work wherever British forces were stationed. They started serious thinking about current affairs and so about politics. This was a completely new experience for most of the men and women in our services, many of whom wrote home and said they would be voting Labour.

The Beveridge Report also had great influence. Sir William Beveridge had been asked to work on a plan for the future of the social services. The clarity of his proposals for establishing a new social order was so convincing that it swept the nation and achieved universal acceptance. Hardly a voice was raised against it. The only doubts were about the competence and commitment of old rulers to carry it out. Then there was the brilliant pamphleteering of Victor Gollancz and his Left Book Club Publications like *Guilty Men*, which told the story of pre-war misrule and disaster and sold by the tens of thousands. Particularly telling was *Your MP*, which gave a record of how Members of Parliament had voted on a number of key issues. This had a profound effect upon my first involvement in a major election campaign in the constituency. We used the information provided to great effect.

Our candidate was Jim Simmons, an outstanding disciple of our cause and a great Birmingham Labour leader. Jim lost a leg at Vimy Ridge in the First World War, and came home to marry Beatrice, who was herself to become an outstanding chairman of Birmingham's Housing Committee. Together they gave ceaseless devotion to the Party, tramping the country from end to end, sustained by the families of miners and other workers who would put Jim up for the night, organise a meeting and then give him the fare to his next port of call. Jim Simmons had already won the Erdington seat in Birmingham during the 1929–31 Parliament and throughout the Second World War he was the Birmingham Party secretary and the editor of our weekly newspaper the *Town Crier*. He was a born propagandist – I learned more from Jim about organisation, platform performance and campaigning, than from any other person in the movement. When the election was announced he appointed Sid Watts, an experienced trade unionist, to be his agent, and asked me to be the deputy agent. No constituency could have had a more exciting election.

The Conservative candidate was Mr Walter Higgs, who had succeeded Sir Austen Chamberlain at that memorable by-election in 1937 and for whom I was still working at this time. I asked for three weeks' leave to organise his opponent's election campaign. The look of disbelief on the faces of my employers remains vividly with me to this day. Their refusal was instant. So was my response – the cause of democracy required my services, and if the boss could have time off to conduct his campaign so could his staff. I would return to work after polling day. To their consternation I left the office, determined to relish the battle ahead. We had a tremendous campaign, based upon all the wiles that our candidate possessed. We would hold meetings in row after row of terraced houses. No microphones or amplification – we just stood in a terrace or on a street corner and shouted.

At my first meeting one Sunday morning I found myself called upon to open up and keep going until Jim arrived from another meeting. No one was about. An old campaigner in charge of meetings told me not to worry, there soon would be. He got a banana box from a greengrocer's shop and off I started. Within minutes came shouts from the opposite corner. 'You ought to be locked up, you're a disgrace to the King and country.' I looked up and was astonished to find it was our local agent. His abuse grew louder. Within ten minutes we had an audience of 60 to 100 people out for their Sunday morning walk. My friend gave me a broad smile, raised his Homburg hat and disappeared into the local pub which had just opened.

Other meetings were equally memorable, especially the one we held outdoors on the final Sunday night in a local shopping area. We calculated the meeting to be nearly 2,000 strong. It was a great experience to be the first speaker and to get the meeting off to an enthusiastic start. The organisational side of the election was a revelation to me. Every polling district was thought about, in every street we appointed a street captain who was expected to get his own team together, to canvass the electors, to deliver literature and to knock up on polling day. In no election since then have I experienced such numbers of volunteers or such enthusiasm.

West Birmingham constituency embraced two wards, St Paul's and All Saints. The fact that the jewellery quarter was at the heart of the constituency gave us the inspiration for our campaign slogan: Vote Simmons – 22 Carat. We painted it in whitewash on every street corner, a practice which, thank goodness, has long gone out of fashion. At an

early campaign meeting we decided we would make old age pensions
the main policy issue of the election, for Walter Higgs had voted against
a motion proposed by Clem Attlee in 1938–39 to raise the pension from
seven shillings and sixpence to ten shillings a week. Sid Watts, the
agent, had a poetic turn of mind. He took me into his confidence and
a short verse of doggerel was produced. We had it printed on over 500
posters which we displayed all over the constituency and on thousands
of leaflets which we delivered to every house:

> OLD AGE PENSIONS WILL BE AT A LOSS
> IF THEY SUPPORT A TORY BOSS,
> BUT A VOTE FOR SIMMONS WILL MAKE SURE
> OF AN OLD AGE THAT IS SECURE.

It was a winner. We could hardly believe our luck next day when the
Tory candidate was pictured in the local press boarding a train for
London in order to consult lawyers and issue a writ against Jim
Simmons and his agent.

We had our own legal opinion close at hand in the person of Julius
Silverman, another firm pillar of Birmingham's Labour movement.
Julius, a barrister, was our candidate for the Erdington seat and he
advised us that we could continue to campaign on the pensions issue
until the moment a writ was served on the candidate or agent. We
needed time to deliver our response to Higgs so Simmons and Watts
were given leave of absence and kept out of sight while I took over the
campaign and organised our reply. First stop was the Birmingham
Reference Library, one of my favourite places, where I soon found the
appropriate *Hansard* carrying the motion of Labour's leader, Clem
Attlee, to put up the pension. Higgs W.F. was recorded as voting
against. I took down the date of this debate and the line recording the
fatal vote, and then made for our printer. He worked non-stop to
produce another 500 posters and thousands of leaflets giving this information and stating that we had made special arrangements for this
volume of *Hansard* to be available at the library for the inspection of
any constituent. A team of bill-posters and workers was quickly organised and they worked through the night to get the message out to every
household. No more was heard from Mr Higgs on this subject, and
Jim Simmons reappeared to conduct his campaign.

Because of the war and the bombings endured by so many schools,
the city council decided that if a school had two halls it would agree to
two political meetings being held simultaneously in that school. This
happened with our eve of poll meeting at Smith Street School, Hockley.
The Tories were allowed the upstairs hall and we were put downstairs.
The pensions controversy ensured a massive turn-out. It was almost
impossible to get into Smith Street, much less the school playground
or either of the school halls. Everyone seemed to be supporting us. All,
that is, except for a number of departmental heads from Higgs Motors
who had turned up to sort me out. Unfortunately for one of them, who

became too aggressive when he tried to tell me where my duty lay, he found himself confronted by a large building worker who decided that I needed protection. The invaders beat a hasty retreat.

Meanwhile, Mr Higgs arrived at the school. The commotion started as he reached Smith Street, gathered in intensity as he walked through the playground, up the stairs and into the hall, where it reached a climax. It was time to send for Jim Simmons, who had been told by me not to leave his earlier meeting until he was sent for. He received a hero's welcome. No sooner did he start speaking than he banged his stick on the platform and then pointed it up to the ceiling, to the meeting being held up above. 'There is no need to refer the pensions issue to the capitalist courts,' he said. 'I propose that a delegation be appointed to go upstairs and challenge my opponent to come down to the playground. We can combine the two meetings and settle the matter here and now.' A small delegation was appointed. They interrupted Higgs and issued the challenge. Mr Higgs delivered the last words of his campaign: 'Tell Mr Simmons that as far as I am concerned he is the scum of the earth.' Jim's riposte was equal to the taunt: 'The scum always rises to the top'!

The election was held on Thursday 5 July 1945 and the counting of votes was delayed for two weeks to allow for the service votes to be delivered. I returned to work – the atmosphere was electric. I applied for further leave to be present at the count as one of the counting agents. 'Can't Mr Simmons be represented by housewives who don't need time off work?' I was asked. 'Yes, certainly, if Mr Higgs is also going to be represented by housewives' was my reply. The counting of votes was a two-stage business. We gathered on the afternoon of 15 July and the votes were checked against the number of papers issued to each box and then put away until the next morning when they would be divided and counted. But we already knew we had won. On the following day the result was announced: J. Simmons (Labour) 12,639; W. Higgs (Conservative) 7,253; Majority 5,386.

Our celebrations went on into the night. We draped the arms of the Chamberlain clock in the jewellery quarter with black-out material and planted the red flag on top. It seemed the only gesture appropriate to mark the end of Chamberlain and to herald the new dawn. As Edward Carpenter had written in his great socialist hymn, which we sang in our Labour church, 'England is risen! And the day is here!'

3

THE BIRMINGHAM TRADITION

JOINING THE COUNCIL

The autumn of 1945 was a milestone for me: I laid the foundation of a lifetime of elected office and in doing so I met Brenda, who was to become my life's partner. Both these events began with a knock on my door shortly after the General Election. It was Steve Willson, who was secretary of the Handsworth Ward Labour Party. The November municipal elections were the first since the war began and all councillors who had been elected unopposed during the war now had to stand for election. In Handsworth that meant that three councillors would be elected and Steve asked me if I would consider becoming one of them. As I was only just 21 I thought that I was too young but he was very persuasive: 'I have had my eye on you at Party meetings and read of your contribution to the Public Opinion Action Association and your letters to the press; you will not win this seat but it will be good experience and we shall give them a run for their money!' As I had no job I decided that I might as well have a go. I enjoyed the fight.

The weather was fine and the new Labour Government was exciting all its supporters, raising the political temperature of the whole country. Our meetings were well-attended and noisy. Our opponents turned up to ask us questions, no doubt thinking that they could expose our inexperience. My father retaliated by going to one of their meetings in the Tory heartland and distributing our pamphlets to the audience during the speeches of their candidates. One day I was campaigning in the Cherry Orchard estate when I saw Ruth Willson, Steve's wife, and Brenda, their youngest daughter, delivering our election addresses. Brenda was wearing her school uniform and obviously enjoying the election work. It was good to know that Steve's family shared his political enthusiasms and we found many opportunities after a night's canvassing to sit around the fire and put the world right. Some eight years later when Steve lay very ill I renewed my association with the family and Brenda, and this led to our marriage two years later.

As Steve had forecast, we did not win Handsworth although we won seats all over Birmingham. We polled three times more votes than ever before in this ward – my tally was 3,295 – but we lost by about 1,400. Two elections in four months was heady stuff. Electioneering was now a permanent part of my life. I was soon adopted to fight my own ward of St Paul's where I had always lived, and which made up half of the West Birmingham constituency where I was the Party secretary. The houses were almost all back-to-back properties like the one we had lived in, or rows of terraced houses without any inside sanitation. We took the message to the people holding meeting after meeting in these terraces and backyards under the gas lamps. During the campaign we came across a newly-formed brass band practising in a church hall, and they agreed to make their first public appearance marching the streets on polling night with me at the head. It caused a sensation. Large crowds joined our procession and marched behind us to the polling station. I polled 1,000 more votes than we had in 1945, and had the great thrill of taking my seat in the very council chamber where Joseph and Neville Chamberlain, and generations of other great Birmingham civic leaders had sat. It was an awe-inspiring experience.

On our side of the council we had as our leader Albert Bradbeer, a Quaker who worked at Cadbury's. He was a man of the highest standards, determined to provide an administration which would implement the policies upon which we had won the election, especially in the fields of housing and civic development. We also had our own civic tradition represented by such fine pioneers as Percy Shurmer, Victor Yates, Julius Silverman and Ted Wheeldon, who all became MPs; Harrison Barrow and his nephew George Corbyn Barrow and some excellent trade union leaders including Walter Lewis (Electricians), Teddy Ager (Engineers), Jim Crump (T&GWU) and Arthur Lummis Gibson (Clerks). The next ten years were to be years of continuous excitement and achievement, a training for national political life that was unequalled. Indeed, when it was suggested to me at a Labour Party summer school that I ought to give it up and go to university, my reluctance was strengthened by Jim Simmons whom I consulted. 'You are being educated in the university of adversity', he told me. While the fact that I never enjoyed a university education has always been a regret to me it has never been an obsession, as it has with some other people. Not only were these years some of the most rewarding of my life, they also provided that greatest of all satisfactions for a politician: increased majorities. In 1950 I put another 1,000 votes on my poll and increased my majority by some 50 per cent. Three years later, in my final local government election, I doubled my majority. It was unremitting hard work but these election results were more than adequate reward.

Throughout this time councillors received no salaries or compensation for loss of earnings and I never drew a penny for expenses of any kind. This resulted in considerable difficulties for many of my colleagues, especially those with families. Where they worked for companies with a sense of public duty they were extremely fortunate. Others suffered real hardship, losing pay and having to provide the costs of their own postage, secretarial and other expenses. In my own ward my colleague Jack Farrell, who had been a great supporter of my candidature, lost his job after taking time off from work to attend council committees. This led to so much worry for him that he became ill and never recovered, leaving a wife and family with precious little financial support. The Labour movement in Birmingham responded to an appeal I put out for help, but this experience convinced me that it was no longer possible to expect councillors to find time week in and week out to provide the government of such a city on a voluntary basis. Even today the payment for civic duty is inadequate and as a result the calibre of men and women coming forward to serve in local government suffers. In my own case I was fortunate to find work in the office of the Standard Gas Fitting Company. It was a small company with about four of us in the office where I was responsible for invoices and for wages. My boss, a strong Conservative who thoroughly disapproved of my politics, nevertheless allowed me to go into the office early or to work late after council meetings. His attitude was that I could carry out my civic duties providing the work of the office did not suffer. But when opportunities arose for advancement they were not for me and I had no complaint. He believed that he was making his contribution to the life of Birmingham by enabling me to carry out my own duties and so he was. When I decided to stand for Parliament some five years after joining the firm our relationship changed and soon came to an end.

By this time I had become the secretary of the Labour Group, in effect the principal organiser of the city council, and more and more of my time was taken up with committees and consultations with officials. I enjoyed it all and it was an invaluable political education but it took all my time. I could not see how I was going to find work in these circumstances. I was rescued from this dilemma by Hubert Humphreys who was one of our aldermen, a lifelong Fabian and friend of Bernard Shaw, the Coles and the Webbs. Hubert had been a talented actor in his youth. He turned to business and with his wife, Gertrude, he founded the Midland Fan Company, a firm manufacturing and erecting extracting and ventilating equipment. They wanted to support my work as secretary of the Labour Group and found me a job in their office where I could 'do anything that was useful' and have all the time off I needed. I was extremely grateful. My useful work consisted of negotiating a special deal with the Birmingham Sheet Metal Workers' Union so that we could employ one apprentice for every skilled man, well above the normal quota, and creating and supervising a sandwich course of training. It was a tribute to the quality of the firm and to its reputation that we were able to reach this agreement. My other contribution was to institute a system of workers' participation in the costing system which was a great success. When we received an enquiry for an order and the design work had been completed we would offer the job to one of the skilled men and ask him to quote for the number of hours it would take to make and install it. We would base our quote on this estimate, and if we secured the order the estimate took on the form of an incentive. If the work was completed inside the time estimated then a bonus was paid to the skilled tradesman and his apprentice.

POLITICAL FRIENDS

St Paul's Ward Labour Party brought me many new colleagues, people who gave their all, week in and week out, without thought of recognition. They belonged to the Labour movement, not just to the Party or the trade union or the co-operative movement. They have supported me in election after election and encouraged me in the lifelong belief that democratic socialism cannot be defined in economic terms alone, important as these are. Democratic socialism has to be expressed in human terms. The paraphernalia of the State or the local authority, and the economic strength of industry and commerce govern all our lives but they are not, as the Marxists would have us believe, an end in themselves. The purpose of democratic socialism is the development and expression of human personality; the exercise of choice in the lives of our people in housing, employment, education, the social services and leisure interests; a choice certainly made possible by economic security and collective provision but a choice that is based upon personal fulfilment tempered by a concern for our fellow citizens. These ideals have to be asserted and fought for, often they have to be defended from within, since democratic socialism is always infiltrated by minorities who use our party as a vehicle for their own purposes. They have a contempt for the values and judgment of working-class people which is why they have to be defeated – it is an electoral necessity as well as an act of faith. The terrible thing is that in doing so we make ourselves politically vulnerable, which is what they want, but which causes the disillusionment of so many of our supporters.

In St Paul's our band of good comrades would meet regularly, certainly every Sunday morning and often in the evenings, and we would debate all these ideals and try to relate them to the issues of the day, to the politics we were practising as well as preaching. How could we speed up the demolition of the slums? How could we improve our house-building performance? Could we do more for the pensioners? What about the school system? The questions were endless but, of course, the new Labour Government with its programme of nationalisation, the creation of a National Health Service and a social security system provided us with much room for heated arguments. Even more so did the policies of Ernest Bevan, the Foreign Secretary, who was

forging the Western alliance and the Marshall plan. Our greatest pride
was in the new independence being offered to the people of India,
Pakistan and other countries of the British Empire.

My friend Dennis Williams and his wife Ellen lived in one of the
terraced houses. Dennis became my election agent and he has helped
me in every election since, four local government and 12 parliamentary
elections. He was a shop steward in the motor car industry, spending
all his time in sensible negotiations and preventing scores of disputes
from festering and becoming strikes. He represented all that is best in
trade unionism and he has never advanced his own personal situation,
content just to be of service. Together with our colleagues, Jim
Meadows, Frank Price and Albert Benton, who became councillors,
Les Breakwell and others, we would meet in the Williams' household,
plan our campaigns and argue. These gatherings were really seminars,
our substitute for the higher education which none of us had enjoyed.
They covered the whole range of our interests: politics, sport, love and
marriage, war and peace. No subject was taboo on these occasions.

Another meeting place for similar gatherings was the Everyman Café
in a small city centre lane, New Meeting Street, which was owned by
Dan Davis. In 1929 when John Strachey won Aston for Labour, Dan
was his agent. He joined Strachey in flirting with the New Party of
Oswald Moseley after the 1931 debacle but he soon left it when he
discovered the direction it was taking and eventually he opened the
Everyman. The bill of fare was modest but in his two downstairs rooms
we would meet and engage in animated discussion before or after
Party meetings, CBSO concerts at the Town Hall, or visits to the
Birmingham Rep. Often this had to do with political theory, especially
as some of the regular customers prided themselves upon their dialectic,
although they were not Stalinists by a long chalk. Usually our talk
involved the policies of the Labour Government. I thought the Government were doing great things but like so many people reared in years
of Opposition Dan Davis and others judged the reality of office against
standards of perfection founded totally upon expectation. Such com-
pulsions lead to disillusionment as they often did in our circle. But the
arguments were a stimulating experience. Dan Davis would join in,
often with a plate of baked beans in one hand and a Welsh Rarebit in
the other, telling some customer, 'Your opinions are based on ignorance
and are of no value whatsoever'. Never before or since have I seen
customers so addressed by such a proprietor but they always came back
for more. Dan was one of the best-read men I had met at that time,
and if you could hold your own in this circle, then you could hold your
own anywhere.

One of the customers who became a true and valued friend was Tom
Reed, a lifelong member of the Independent Labour Party. A pacifist
who saw active service with the Friends Ambulance Unit in the First
World War, Tom was a great internationalist. He was a contemporary
of Jimmy Maxton, Fenner Brockway and others who were to become

MPs but he himself would never desert his own articles of faith, those of the ILP, which were essentially charged with protecting the soul of the movement. Elected office held no virtues for him but he always came to lend a hand with my own campaigns. In spite of being misunderstood and criticised he would organise a gathering every Sunday afternoon where he entertained German and Italian prisoners of war who were put to work in the Birmingham area. He wanted to introduce them to 'better values than they have known and to show them the futility of war'. While many of us would not go all the way with him we were pleased to help him out with his socials and demonstrate that even in the aftermath of war our socialism too was international in its perception. Another great influence was Tom O'Loughlin. I was introduced to him by Jim Meadows. It was like entering another world. Tom was a large man in every way, nearly 20 stone in weight and dominating in any company. He was the headmaster of a tiny Catholic boys' school, St Mary's, whose old boys adored him. Tom was not only the headteacher and sportsmaster of his school, he was the friend and helper of every single parent who ever sent their son to his academy. He was available to the parents before school, after school and during lessons. The school took on all comers at football, swimming, cricket and boxing. Probably Tom's proudest moment came when this smallest of all schools produced national school boxing and swimming champions and won the District Shield for football and cricket.

Tom married Marie late in life. They had eight children and lived in a large house near the school which doubled up as a youth club. Marie washed all the kit for the school and district teams and together they held 'open house' to all who called upon them, and many there were. A barrel of beer was always kept in the cellar and we would meet in the lounge. No one ever knew who might turn up. There was talking and singing, and only one rule in the household: no one was ever allowed to treat anyone else to a drink. If one of the company wanted a drink they went downstairs and pulled themselves a pint, putting the money in a tin box on the table. Tom had no time for people who could not hold their liquor and believed that no man should be asked to drink beyond his limit. Visitors like me who preferred a cup of tea or coffee were looked after by Marie. Tom's infectious love of sport soon got to me and in no time I found myself refereeing school games and helping out with the Aston schools team, travelling to cricket and athletics meetings, nurturing my belief that all sport is founded upon schools sport and that the teachers who devote themselves to that cause are the true benefactors of British sport. Tom was also a true Labour man. As a young student he had addressed his first meeting on behalf of the unemployed who sent their sons to his school. We became as inseparable in our politics as in our sport. Until he died I never fought in any election without him at my side. We would put our loudspeaker on his car and drive from street to street, rarely talking while the car was travelling which is a waste of effort, but getting out of the car and doing a double act in the roadway. Tom, with his great sense of fun and biting wit, often sang to the audience as well for he had a wonderful voice, drawing the crowd and then introducing me as the candidate. No one ever had a better grounding in community politics than I did nor in the art of relating politics to people. I owe to Tom any skills that I possess in that direction.

COUNCIL WORK

I was soon deep into council committee work, having been appointed a member of the Health, Catering and Establishment committees. In 1946 the Health committee had a vast range of responsibilities, including all aspects of public health enforcement and the management of the city hospitals, numbering about ten, since the National Health Service was still two years away. It was, in all, a plum appointment. I held it throughout my ten years' membership of the council. At the first meeting I was nominated for the Maternity sub-committee and for the committee of a home for unmarried mothers and their children. Alderman Nellie Hyde, the veteran chairman, nearly had a heart attack. 'He is only a lad,' she said, 'what does he know about such matters?' But she soon recovered and proved a wise counsellor.

My appointment to the committee of Dudley Road Hospital formed my interest in hospital work. When it was transferred to the NHS I moved with it as a representative of the city council. Later on I became the chairman of the Hospital committee for some 12 years until I became a Minister. It has proved a lasting relationship, for every year since 1946 I have taken part in the Christmas Eve carol procession around the hospital. We meet in the chapel for a short service then sing our carols around the wards and corridors before having refreshments with the chairman and senior staff. I am home by about midnight, and Christmas has begun! The management of hospitals is all about personal relationships. Successive governments have imposed systems of cost accounting, systems of managerial structure, systems of medical care and systems of nursing hierarchy. In my experience they have all proved to be expensive failures. The greatest disaster was the move in the early 1970s to do away with house committees which, at one stroke, removed the personal touch from hospital administration and replaced it with large scale administration by people who could not possibly identify themselves totally with the life of one hospital.

A remarkable episode occurred when I received a call one day from the matron of the hospital to tell me that the night nurses had gone on strike and were refusing to eat their midnight dinner. Would I return from London to deal with the matter as it would be treated seriously by the General Nursing Council? I drove back in time to find the matron, attended by her deputy, the hospital secretary and the catering officer, describing to the nurses sitting in their dining-hall the most horrendous consequences of such wilful refusal to eat their meals. Realising that all these healthy and extremely hard-working young people would not be refusing to do any such thing unless there was good reason I asked the nurses to select a small deputation to come and see us and explain the problem, giving an assurance that there would be no victimisation of any sort. Even so I had to reinforce my guarantee when the leader of the delegation was described as a 'troublemaker'. It turned out that every night for two weeks the nurses had been served with Irish stew. They were going to eat no more Irish stew. I agreed with them and asked the nurses to eat this meal for the very last time as a favour to me. The next day we called in the Birmingham Civic Catering Department who revolutionised the catering for the whole hospital. They started with a declaration from the general manager that there were no doctors, nurses or patients so far as he was concerned, only customers. Everyone was to be provided with choices for each course. The 'strike' was over, the catering officer took retirement and the meals improved immensely without any addition to cost.

My principal work on the Health committee centred on its Finance and General Purposes committee, of which I became chairman. We were determined to tackle the scourge of slum housing and authorised our officers, then called sanitary inspectors, to visit thousands of houses in the central area of the city. We served 7,000 notices of statutory defects, mainly leaking roofs and defective drains. We soon found that some landlords of large blocks of property would use the rents of other homes to repair another on which we had served a notice. We responded by serving 20 or 30 notices at one time. Many owners asked the council to carry out these essential repairs and this soon became a regular procedure. Meanwhile, the Public Works committee proceeded with a Birmingham Bill giving us powers to acquire most of these properties by compulsory purchase, to make them wind- and weather-proof and afterwards to demolish them. We had to set up a new management department and a Central Areas Improvement and Repairs Service. It was very costly, but it brought new hope to thousands of families. This was a gigantic undertaking. The Bill was bitterly contested and our colleagues spent days attending the committee stage in both the Lords and the Commons, but the Bill became law and five huge development areas were designated. In due course the slum properties all disappeared and the people were housed in new dwellings with fine bathrooms and kitchens. We were thrilled with the success of our elected programme. Alas, our jubilation was short-lived. We allowed ourselves to be talked into high-rise development by architects with more imagination than good sense and they remain to plague us.

My two other areas of health responsibility, smokeless zones and noise abatement, led to an abiding interest in these matters both as an MP and as a Minister. The chairman of the main Health committee was George Corbyn Barrow, who thought we ought to pioneer a smokeless zone. My work on the Dudley Road Hospital committee brought me into touch with Dr George Hearn, one of its senior consultants. He had researched the effects of the air pollution from the Black Country foundries which came to Birmingham with the prevailing south-westerly wind. Our hospital dealt with all the bronchial and asthmatic cases from the north-west of the city and Sutton Coldfield, and we found we had a heavier load of these cases than any other hospital in Birmingham. Consequently the proposal to introduce the first smokeless zone in the country had all my support and I got down to obtaining the necessary powers and implementing them. After some initial problems over smokeless fuel had been overcome we proceeded to designate other zones and to extend the provision across the city. It was a remarkably successful programme as far as domestic houses were concerned but left a great void for industrial premises. I was soon to return to this matter in the Commons.

The effect of noise pollution came to my attention in a very dramatic way. Within 30 yards of my home in Guildford Street some empty premises were bought by a plating firm. They installed extraction fans which discharged their fumes directly into a row of terraced houses. These fans operated day and night and made an awful noise, so much so that two people were made very ill, one of them requiring admission to a mental hospital. A third resident committed suicide. All my attempts to get the health inspectors to stop this nuisance failed. They were frustrated by a senior medical officer responsible for these services who kept advising my committee that he needed medical evidence of the harm to health. Apparently, one suicide and two serious illnesses were not enough for him! The committee agreed to my proposal that his objections should be overruled and the case passed to a very junior solicitor for action. He was John Methvin, later to become the director of the CBI. He was much more enthusiastic and I set about obtaining the evidence he told me he would need. First I visited the local doctor of one of the victims and found that he too had been trying to get the matter dealt with by the Health Department. He said he would be pleased to give evidence in Court. Then we had a stroke of luck. I mentioned the matter to the general manager of the Midland Fan Company where I worked and he remembered that we had had an enquiry from the offending firm about a possible installation. We looked it up and to our pleasure found that our reply contained a guarantee 'to install fans that will be to the satisfaction of your neighbours'. We provided a copy of this letter to our barrister, and without declaring his hand he soon trapped the managing director of the company into admitting that he had sought quotations from various firms. He did not have them with him, but the Court adjourned so that he could go and get them. Once he returned the case was over in five minutes, the new fans installed, and peace restored to my neighbour's terrace. Twenty years later when I became Minister I was to add noise pollution to the Control of Pollution Act 1976 which I was to pilot through Parliament. Regrettably, the provision to create noise abatement zones has to be brought into action by an order in council and no such order has yet been made.

Membership of the Catering committee provided an altogether different and most exciting challenge. During the war Lord Woolton had been put in charge of feeding the nation. Rations were low so he encouraged local authorities to open up cafeterias in old schools, church halls and similar premises. They became known as British Restaurants and served some very good, reasonably priced fare. Apart from fish and chips their main menu consisted of Irish stew, shepherd's pie, cottage pie and similar meals. When the war ended the food situation did not improve – if anything it grew worse. So most local authorities took over the restaurants and the Birmingham Civic Catering Department was created. We inherited 39 restaurants spread across the city. With its usual civic enterprise Birmingham set about transforming them into good permanent ventures, but when I joined the committee the honeymoon was over and the catering trade was beginning to agitate for their closure. After consultation with the Government we were given authority to maintain this new service provided we made a profit over three years and were no charge on the rates. This was not easy, since we had to operate with wage rates that were based on local authority scales and not the Catering Wages Act, a difference of some 30 shillings a week on basic rates, quite a sum in those days. Within a year or so of joining the committee I became the chairman and found myself competing with private enterprise on more than unequal terms. We cut out the unprofitable restaurants and opened a most successful outdoor catering division which was a novelty in the Midlands. Soon a number of industrial businesses invited us to run their factory canteens, and we operated more than 40 of them.

We built a few permanent restaurants and soon we were prepared to do battle with our competitors, political as well as industrial, on the basis of my declaration that 'no one buys a cup of tea in our restaurants except of their own free will; we maintain our standards, give a good service, pay higher wages, and it does not cost the ratepayer a penny'. Municipal socialism in action! It was opposed by many of the Conservatives but was vintage Chamberlain in its practice. Our success was based on two remarkable men: a professional caterer, Richard Pitts, who became our general manager after his predecessor was discovered one Friday night leaving our premises with quantities of food destined for a café in the Cotswolds owned by his wife! John Newbury, his deputy, was trained in the Town Clerk's department. He kept telling Dick Pitts what the rules were for the local government service, and developed great skills in catering management himself. The highlight of my time was to provide the meal at the opening of the Claerwen Dam, part of the city's great mid-Wales waterworks. The opening was performed by HM The Queen and was a most spectacular affair. She was kind enough to make special mention of the meal, all of which had been cooked in mobile kitchens transported from Birmingham.

As we took on more and more industrial canteens so the public criticisms of the Tories grew fewer and fewer. Our finest moment came when Sir Ernest Canning, a leading right wing Conservative alderman, telephoned to say that his own canteen at W. Canning & Co had run into trouble and would we come and manage it? It took me no more than 30 seconds to authorise the arrangements and Sir Ernest ever after paid tribute to us whenever we came under attack. One of Sir Ernest's arch-enemies on the city council was Alderman Norman Tiptaft, who started out as socialist immediately after the First World War, but who drifted more and more to the right. Norman was quite a character. During the Second World War he served as Lord Mayor and spent the whole of his year engaged in public hostility to Lord Dudley and George Lindgren who were the Regional and Deputy Regional Commissioners. Soon he officially left the Conservatives but contributed controversial columns to the *Birmingham Mail* for many years. One day Tiptaft decided to move a resolution deploring the growth of civic socialism and calling for the closure of the Civil Restaurant Department. I was put up to reply, so I took myself off to our reference library to do some research. I came across one of Tiptaft's early pamphlets – *Socialism for Commercial Travellers* – and found just the quotation I needed: 'The small provider, the individual firm, is out of date, expensive, inefficient – and he must go. Production, distribution, and exchange can be done more efficiently and less expensively by the larger combination. It must come to it.' No one laughed more at my quotation than Canning but Tiptaft had the right of reply: 'My Lord Mayor, when I wrote that I was as young then as Councillor Howell is today'.

The Establishment committee was a great power base from which to influence both colleagues and chief officers. The work mainly consisted of deciding the strength of various council departments, an important matter for colleagues with expansionist ideas, and to determine salary grades. I was amazed at the intensity with which good Labour councillors with the most mundane jobs would fight for the salaries of their chief officers in the belief that only money could determine status. The chief officers agreed with them.

Halfway through my city council service I became a member of the Watch committee which controlled the police force. It was a most sought-after appointment, not least because members were invariably saluted by any policeman who recognised them. Sir Edward Dodd was our Chief Constable, a man of great eminence who later became HM Chief Inspector of Constabulary. Ted Dodd was a fine public servant and a very strong chief officer. I found that the committee ate out of his hand and rarely questioned his judgment; however, when I did so over two issues I discovered that he welcomed the controversy. The first incident was right up my street for it concerned a police constable who had been sent off the field for misconduct during a soccer match. Sir Edward recommended to the committee that he should be discharged from the force. He was astonished when I opposed the proposal on the grounds that the man should not be punished twice, and that furthermore, if a policeman were to lose his job as a result of action taken by a referee, no referee would ever again send a policeman off the field. The chief was undermining our authority as referees. My argument carried the day and Dodd graciously accepted it. The second incident followed a disciplinary hearing we had to conduct into the involvement of a police sergeant with a bookmaker. In those days street bookmaking was illegal and very occasionally an officer would be tempted to show a favour, no doubt because the law was generally being broken. Ted Dodd thought the law should be enforced. I thought it should be changed and gambling legalised. After a lively debate Ted advised the committee that if we supported the legalising of street betting we should send a formal resolution to the Home Secretary recommending it. We did so and I believe we were the first Watch Committee to do so. The sergeant was sacked, but we helped to change the law and to end one piece of humbug in our society.

LABOUR GROUP SECRETARY

After a few years of learning my trade on the back benches the opportunity came in 1950 to achieve a signal promotion to the position of the city council Labour Group secretary. The leader of the Labour Group chaired its meetings and led for us in the council and on the main committees. He did not involve himself in the administration of the Group, in liaison with the city Party machine, in the whipping arrangements or in detailed discussions with the opposition or council officials. Most of that was the responsibility of the secretary. It was a powerful position to hold – effectively the organiser of the Party in all city policy matters. I followed Teg Bowen, who was of Welsh mining stock and who possessed the most engaging vocabulary I have ever come across. He would blind the opposition with verbal science, very often inventing a new word in mid-sentence.

When Teg became our Group leader I was delighted to be nominated and elected as secretary, young as I was. Apart from convening all the meetings and liaising with the local Party on policy and organisational matters I was responsible for a whole range of negotiations with outside bodies. Within the Group the real power came through a small sub-committee of the General Purposes committee – the Nomination sub – which virtually decided which committee members would serve upon it and who would be chairman. It was this experience that taught me the importance and the power of patronage!

Our most important meeting was held on the day after the annual city council elections. Birmingham always followed the sensible practice of making up its committees in proportion to the political strength of the parties on the council. We decided the election of aldermen and nomination of the Lord Mayor by a similar rule – it saved much wrangling. The only difficulty that I experienced in operating the procedure was the aldermanic posts whose incumbents were elected by the council itself to serve six years. Often one side would 'owe' the other side an alderman until the opportunity arose to correct the situation. But in my experience this never stopped either side from controlling the council if it had a majority. It was the exercise of gentlemanly relations and no worse for that.

The Tories with whom the leader and I would negotiate on these occasions were Sir Theodore Pritchett, a distinguished solicitor of the 'old school' and his own Group secretary, either Alderman Eric Mole or John Lewis. Lewis was devoted to the task of keeping all his members on their committees whatever the result of the elections but after some forceful discussion Pritchett would tire of the argument and state firmly to his secretary, 'to the victor the spoils'. When Eric retired from work and from politics he became a Church of England clergyman. I was not surprised, for even in his political days his approach was ethical as well as practical. Both of them were men I respected and I like to think that this was reciprocated. We fought tough political battles but it never affected our personal relationships nor got in the way of our policy decisions. On the policy side I found myself immersed in developing Group strategies and conducting public debates. It was fascinating: I enjoyed every minute of it but I think it was here, in the realisation of policy, that I began to learn the difference between advocacy and achievement. Both are important but the real satisfaction comes from creation, from putting policies into practice and providing a new service or improved opportunities. I had already experienced such feelings of satisfaction in my committee work, especially in the development of the Civic Catering Department, and when we decided to establish new day nurseries for children with genuine social need, I felt I was really getting something done.

In 1947 we lost control of the city in an election which came to be known as the 'bacon election'. Only a few days before polling the Minister of Food, John Strachey, announced the reduction of bacon rations from two ounces to one ounce per person. I can still vividly recall housewives rushing to the polls brandishing their ration cards. It was a year or more before we regained control so my term of office as Group secretary began in opposition. I was determined that we would be an effective opposition. In this I was greatly helped by the Conservatives, who knew nothing about the dangers of a wafer-thin majority. Their first mistake was to challenge our policy for carrying out the emergency 'wind- and weather-proofing' of all the thousands of slum houses we had taken over as a result of the legislation we had steered through Parliament with the support of the Government. Since we could not demolish all these houses in one go and mount a house-building programme big enough to rehouse everyone we had established priorities. These were to cover the roofs of whole blocks of property where necessary, to repair drains and so on. The Conservatives set up a committee to decide which houses in a terrace or a block would be repaired, demolished or left as they were. The result was chaotic and provided me with the opportunity to develop an ability to ridicule in debate which I much enjoyed.

Another success came when the Fire Brigade Union came to see me, complaining that an attempt was being made to establish a rival union with the support of leading members of the committee and chief officers. I went off to consult Mr Walter Bloor, the Clerk to the Council, who taught me more about local government than any other person. Bloor was proud of the fact that he had never had any legal training but he was more knowledgeable than most Town Clerks or their staffs. He didn't like my idea of requisitioning a special meeting of the city council so that we could propose a motion disapproving the actions of the Fire Brigade Committee, largely on the grounds that 'we don't normally do this sort of thing in Birmingham.' However, when he realised that I was determined to do so, like any good officer he advised me on how to proceed and helped me draft the necessary notice and motion. Meanwhile, the lads in the FBU had scrutinised all the log books in the city fire stations and supplied me with some wonderful material. When I proposed my motion I was able to state that 'fire engines in this city have been used as taxi cabs to collect officers and take them to a meeting in order to set up an unofficial trade union!'. I supported this statement by reading out the details from the logs. The poor chairman was speechless when he came to reply. We lost the vote of censure but no more was heard of any official endorsement for the alternative union and the newspapers had a field day. More important for us, our supporters were greatly encouraged.

Meanwhile the Boundary Commission had been active. The West Birmingham constituency was disbanded and split up and I found myself a member of the Aston Labour Party where Woodrow Wyatt was the sitting MP. I was soon to become its chairman, with my friend Jim Meadows continuing as secretary. We met at Ruskin Hall, Aston, where we used to talk for hours in the club after meetings and where new friendships developed. One particular friend was Harry Watton, later to become a first-class leader of the Labour Group. In those days Harry was more left wing than I but out of our discussions we drew up a policy for providing old age pensioners with free travel on our buses in off-peak periods. Harry took the initiative in proposing this revolutionary idea to various policy conferences, and as the Group secretary I used all the influence of my office to encourage its adoption. We succeeded in spite of all the traditional arguments. We were told that we ought to pay pensioners a sufficient pension for them to meet all their needs. We countered by supporting this concept but stating that it would not arrive in our lifetime and that until it did there were overwhelming social arguments for encouraging pensioners to keep mobile and to visit family and friends. We backed this up by drawing attention to the high cost of old age for the social services and the economic benefits likely to result from the scheme.

The policy was a winner from the start. We put it at the forefront of our campaign and the votes rolled in. By 1951 we had recovered control of the city and I found myself secretary of the majority party. We were determined to implement our 'free travel' policy. Here we began to run into difficulties with our new Town Clerk. Mr Frank Gregg, a young and very able lawyer, had been appointed following the premature death of his predecessor, who had committed suicide in his office. Gregg was young to be deputy Town Clerk so his promotion was quite astonishing. He knew his law very well but he was not quite as accomplished in handling his councillors, certainly not his Labour councillors. He advised us that the city had no powers to implement such a scheme and that we ought to take Counsel's opinion. We went to a leading local government silk, Arthur Rowe QC, who advised that such a scheme could not be charged to the transport users but could be paid for by the general ratepayers. The Town Clerk did not think much of this opinion. He persuaded us to seek a second opinion from a Mr Fox Andrews, Recorder of Bournemouth, where Gregg had been deputy Town Clerk. Mr Fox Andrews had no doubt that such a scheme would be unlawful but the chances of the adoption of his opinion were not helped by a widely-reported encounter between himself and Aneurin Bevan at White's Club in London, when Bevan was pushed down the steps. We were damned if we were going to prefer the opinion of someone who had behaved in this way to a hero of a Labour Government! We preferred the opinion of a QC who had advised us that we could implement our scheme. The inevitable happened: we were advised to consult a third leading Counsel. Bless my soul if this opinion did not tell us that in certain circumstances the scheme would be legal but in other circumstances it would be illegal! At an acrimonious meeting in the Town Clerk's office I informed him that we had now won three elections on this issue and that we intended to proceed with its implementation. Gregg was adamant that we had no power to do so and he could not allow us to proceed. I regarded this as a major challenge and, being young and impetuous, as well as seeing myself as the keeper of our collective conscience, I told him that in that case we would need a new Town Clerk. He replied that under the Public Health Act of 1938 we had to have a Town Clerk and therefore we could not remove him, to which I responded by quoting the case of the Mayor and Councillors of Erith versus their Town Clerk, the effect of which meant that we did indeed have to have a Town Clerk, but it did not have to be him. He was given proper warning and told he could record his adverse advice to the council if he wished, but we were going to proceed with the scheme.

But opposition was not over. An aggrieved ratepayer, Mr Gregory Prescott, started to raise funds to seek an injunction against us in the Chancery Courts, in spite of having been defeated on the issue by 915 votes to 78 at a town's meeting and also in a subsequent town's poll.

According to the law, new policy initiatives and new Parliamentary Bills were put to the electors for their endorsement, first at a town's meeting, and then by means of a town's poll of all electors, which was in essence a referendum, much despised by politicians. We won the poll as easily as we had won the vote at the town's meeting. Both these archaic anomalies have long since gone. Prescott is a large man in every way and had been one of the leading pillars of the Public Opinion Action Association. He attracted much support but also provided us with a political bogey man on which to focus our propaganda. Prescott briefed a young barrister named Frank Blennerhasset, now a High Court judge, and we engaged Mr Arthur Rowe QC, who had provided us with our first favourable opinion on the legality of such a scheme. Mr Justice Vaisey reserved judgment and both parties travelled down to hear it on the same train. Everyone seemed to be agreed on the basis of the judge's comments during the course of the hearing that we were going to win. The reverse was the case. Since we were already providing the service now declared to be unlawful it did not take many minutes to decide upon an appeal. The Town Clerk had been vindicated but he cheered us up on the return journey by telling us that this particular judge probably had more of his judgments overturned on appeal than any other. However, the judgment was upheld. We had no alternative but to announce the end of our free travel scheme. But we did so leaving no doubt that we would resume our political campaign to obtain the necessary powers to restore free travel for senior citizens, who were naturally incensed at their loss.

By now we were approaching the General Election of 1955. The Conservative Government was quick to see the dangers of allowing what until then had been a localised campaign to develop into a national issue. They introduced the Public Service Vehicle (Travel Concessions) Act of 1955 which was an extraordinary piece of legislation. It said in effect that those authorities which had implemented such schemes in the belief that they were lawful, even though now declared unlawful, should be given legal authority to reinstate them. We did so, much to the joy of the elderly citizens of Birmingham. In due course legislation was enacted which provided every local authority with powers to provide such a service to the advantage of millions of pensioners. It was a momentous victory and, for me, vivid and encouraging.

In those days the road system of Birmingham was acknowledged throughout the land to be impossible, so much so that it was the butt of every comedian who ever visited the city. Comprehensive development of the city centre including the road system was necessary. We were fortunate to have a city engineer of outstanding vision, Sir Herbert Manzoni, who also had the ability to translate his plans into practical achievement. Great credit must also be given to Frank Price, a young man whom I first met on the terraces of the Birmingham City Football Club and whom I persuaded to stand for election to the council in my own ward of St Paul's, where Frank also lived, in one of the terraced houses we were determined to demolish. They made an excellent team and no city in the country achieved such a spectacular success in its city centre redevelopment. Birmingham is a motor car city; in my opinion we are still the only city that has redeveloped to adequately accommodate the requirement of a car-owning population.

There were controversies about all these developments, the most political of which was our determination to acquire sufficient land on each side of the new highways to ensure that the 'betterment value' created by our investment was accorded to the citizens who had provided it. Most Brummies are proud of the newly-developed city centre but most believe that two mistakes were made. The first was to turn round our famous Bull Ring. When we were youngsters the Bull Ring was a place of unending fascination. It ran vertically uphill to join New Street and High Street at its top end and it contained market traders on the whole of the stretch running down to St Martin's, the parish church at the lower end. Off the Bull Ring was our famous Market Hall and also our fruit, meat and fish markets and our rag market. A visit to the Bull Ring was sheer magic, a voyage of discovery for us children, especially on Christmas Eve when we always bought our mother a crab – her special favourite. The Bull Ring was also the centre of open air oratory, and I went as often as I could to listen to speakers on every subject under the sun. The leading orator was Ernest McCulloch, a welfare worker with a local firm, who would mount his rostrum twice at weekday lunch-times and three times on Sunday. He was a card – he entertained the crowd with a mixture of good political sense and ribald humour. His handling of his audience, especially when it was being critical, or even hostile, was masterly. I would return to the Bull Ring again and again to watch his technique and to enjoy myself. All that I know about the skills of platform speaking and of the arts of relating to an audience I owe to two men – Jim Simmons and Ernie McCulloch. When the Public Works Committee decided to turn the Bull Ring round so that it ran horizontally instead of vertically it was the end of an era. Why we allowed it to happen I cannot begin to comprehend, but we did. I fervently hope that new thinking will restore this national landmark to its former glory.

The second mistake of our redevelopment was the decision to build pedestrian subways in our new motorway system. They have been a disaster for the elderly and for mothers with prams and have provided a refuge for muggers. Frank Price and Herbert Manzoni wanted to put the cars under subways leaving the pedestrians on the surface but the officials of the Transport Ministry insisted that they knew best and would not authorise the expenditure unless Birmingham did their bidding. So that calamity has to be laid at the door of the Whitehall warriors who very rarely, in my experience, know better than local government. However, there can be no doubt about the debt which Birmingham owes to Manzoni and Price, both of whom were deservedly knighted.

SUPPORTING THE ARTS

My maiden speech on the council expressed my concern at the lack of sporting facilities, particularly in our public parks. I described in detail the changing-rooms with holes in the roof and no lighting, the absence of water for washing or showering and the football pitches where touch-lines were marked by ruts dug into the ground, and goal-posts without nets. I even gave a detailed account of my own experience as a referee, of having to change in the losing team's dressing-rooms after a 90-minute mudlark ending acrimoniously. The rain was pouring through the ceiling and there was no light. I mistakenly put on a pair of trousers belonging to one of the players with whom I shared the 'dressing-room'. That speech marked the beginning of my interest in leisure services.

I also became a regular visitor to Town Hall concerts given by the City of Birmingham Symphony Orchestra in the company of Brenda Willson. My devotion to the Birmingham Repertory Theatre also continued to be a source of great pleasure. I was determined that something should be done to bring all these activities together as a proper object of civic patronage. My position as the Group secretary provided the opportunity and I was able to propose that the General Purposes committee should establish an Entertainments sub-committee. I found myself serving on this and had no difficulty in getting myself elected to the chair. Applications for grants soon began to arrive. By far the two most important and significant came from the Symphony Orchestra who had extremely modest support and from the Repertory Theatre, which up to then had received no assistance from the council at all. On the great day when my new committee met in 1952 to consider these applications the CBSO was the first to be interviewed. We studied their accounts, their audience figures and their financial prospects. They were not altogether reassuring but of greater interest to me was their plan to enlarge the orchestra and enhance its reputation. I had no problem with the committee about agreeing to the principle of extending their grant but I could not move them beyond the sum of £25,000. Still, in those days, this was a significant figure. To try to improve upon it I raised the possibility of musical education in the schools, which had come up in our discussions. We soon agreed upon an additional sum of £11,000 a year to enable groups of the orchestra to tour schools, leading to full orchestral concerts in the Town Hall. It is interesting to note that in 1987 the city was contributing £484,000 to the upkeep of the orchestra, still with widespread agreement and with great pride in its excellence.

Next into the committee room came Sir Barry Jackson and his colleagues from the Birmingham Rep. Sir Barry was a very old friend of my boss, Hubert Humphreys, and a long-time associate of George Bernard Shaw and his contemporaries. I had never met him but I knew all about him from Hubert and much admired the way he had kept the theatre going for years out of his own pocket. Sir Barry explained how the ravages of war had not been repaired and that the theatre needed urgent refurbishment. We examined the plans which he laid before us. It was obvious that he found the whole experience of applying for support in this way a painful business. He looked startled when I remarked, 'Sir Barry, I am afraid I cannot agree to these proposals. You are intending to reupholster all the seats in the stalls but you are doing nothing about the gallery'. 'Is this some form of socialism?' he asked. 'Well,' I replied, 'you could say that, but the gallery is where I sit and I don't understand why we should improve the seating in the stalls and not in the gallery.' 'Ah,' he replied, 'I understand. All the true theatre-lovers sit in the gallery.' So we agreed that if he came back with a new estimate to cover the whole of the theatre we would provide some £7,000 to meet the costs. The council subsequently approved an annual grant of £3,000 towards the running costs. It was an exhilarating day which still gives me a feeling of great satisfaction.

The opposition was led by Tory Alderman Jim Williams who was a builder and a cricketer of no mean ability. Jim was a good man but he could not see why the ratepayers' money should be used for subsidising the arts. I am glad to say he did not speak for the Conservative Group as a whole, although most agreed with him. Conservative support for the new policy was led by Councillor Stephen Lloyd. Stephen is married to Dorothy, the daughter of Neville Chamberlain, who has never been over-active in Birmingham political life but modestly and actively supports many good causes in the city, none more enthusiastically than the CBSO. Stephen was chairman of the orchestra for many years and deserves great credit for his contribution to its success.

The Birmingham tradition is that much of our inspiration and objective is truly bipartisan. I first realised the importance of this when we faced up to the opposition for our proposals to support the Rep and the Orchestra all those years ago, and it has repeatedly proved to be the case. This was illustrated once more in 1986 when the city bid to host the Olympic Games. Where others have seen the need to emphasise political divisions, Birmingham has always shown itself ready to unite on matters that transcend party political considerations. And so it proved on the day that Councillor Williams declared, 'My Lord Mayor, when I settle down in front of my fire with my pint of beer and my bread and cheese, I like nothing better than to put on my records and enjoy my music. We don't need an orchestra!'. He suggested that we might have a flag day for the orchestra. He was very effectively put down by his Conservative colleague Stephen Lloyd. The Birmingham press gave us great support and my speech led the front page of the *Birmingham Mail*. The attack had concentrated upon the CBSO grant, and I declared, 'If the CBSO goes down we are removing one of the most outstanding cultural provisions in this city. Our reputation will be universally reduced throughout the world'.

The Entertainments sub was charged with responsibility for another outstanding event in the life of the city: the celebrations marking the coronation of HM The Queen in June 1953. We were determined to ensure that the whole city was *en fête* and I think we succeeded admirably. Musical events and entertainments were organised by the city, and parties were held in hundreds of streets, residents competing against each other in decorating their streets with bunting. Our greatest success was to negotiate for many of the regiments and bands that had been on parade in London to come to Birmingham and join in a great procession. Thousands of our citizens turned out to line the streets, most of whom had never seen such a parade in their lives. The whole programme was a great triumph.

BIRMINGHAM CONTROVERSIES

In the early 1950s I became embroiled in several controversies which stretched beyond party politics. I wanted to speak out for Birmingham while remaining absolutely loyal to the Labour Party, which meant everything to me and was the mainspring of my being. I committed myself to causes dear to my heart with complete conviction and enthusiasm. One such was the attempt to change the character of the Birmingham Blue Coat School, another was the decision of the Warwickshire County Cricket Club to terminate the services of its faithful servant, Charles Grove, its opening seam bowler.

The Blue Coat School is an institute created in 1894 for the purpose of educating the sons of people without means, many of them orphans or the children of widows. It has a first-class reputation. One of its former pupils is my close friend Kenneth Purnell, who entered the legal profession as a barrister's clerk. In 1951 when this controversy broke one of his barristers was Julius Silverman, who continued to practice while he was a Birmingham MP. Kenneth rang me in great distress to tell me that his old school was proposing to change its character and to move away from its founding concept. Would I assist in his fight to preserve the original concept of the school? I could not resist the challenge. It seemed that the Rev Richard Lunt, headmaster of King Edward's Boys' School, had become the chairman of the governors and together with the Rev Harry Clarke, Archdeacon of Birmingham, who was Lunt's brother-in-law, they had just proposed that the Blue Coat School should become a prep school for King Edward's. This distressed many old boys and others and so they had suggested that it became a fee-paying school, to equal dismay. Finally, it was proposed to turn it into a cathedral school helping to provide members for the choir. The old boys, led by Kenneth, joined an old schools' association and asked me to help their campaign.

A well-known Birmingham estate agent, Mr Leonard Carver, offered his support and provided two men who spent about six to eight weeks examining all the investments of the foundation in great detail. He reported to us that the various assets were more than adequate to meet the deficits and that there was no financial case for changing the status of the school to meet a loss of some £23,000 a year. Ken Purnell and his friends quickly mobilised public opinion and soon we had a petition bearing some 26,000 signatures. We placed our objections to the new proposals before Sir Edward Boyle, who was not only a Birmingham MP but a most liberal-minded and widely-respected Education Minister. For the hearing of the objections Purnell had recruited Sir Frank Soskice MP, who had served as the Solicitor General in the Labour Government, to lead our team, along with Julius Silverman. I appeared in the role of public representative. We were helped by the fact that Ken Purnell and I had challenged the chairman and governors to a public debate in the Town Hall which they had declined to accept. Instead, the governors invited us to meet them. When Ken Purnell and I sat down at their table they asked us what we had to say. We replied that we had accepted their invitation to hear what they had to say, to which they replied 'nothing'. We left what must have been the shortest meeting ever held. Edward Boyle threw out their proposals and after more sensible negotiations the governors proposed a voluntary scheme of fee-paying while guaranteeing to preserve places for children representing the original purpose of the foundation. Later on Ken Purnell joined the governors, representing the old scholars, and in the last five years they have sold their ground rents, which were bringing in some £26,000 a year, and realised funds of more than £3 million.

Another great controversy concerned the Warwickshire County Cricket Club. One Sunday morning Ted Hampton, the Warwickshire statistician, knocked on my door accompanied by my great hero, Eric Hollies. They looked shattered. 'They've sacked Charlie Grove', they told me. 'Something has to be done about it, will you help?' I had been a member of Warwickshire since the war and few things in sport have given me more pleasure than watching Tom Dollery's side win the County Championship. Tom was the first professional to captain any county and his success thrilled us all. Eric Hollies was a tremendous Black Country character with a pronounced accent, an ever-present smile and a great sense of humour. He was one of the finest of leg-spinners. Charlie Grove and New Zealander Tom Pritchett were our opening pace bowlers, both of great ability. I considered Grove to be one of the unluckiest of players never to play for England. His performance in 1950 when he took 8 wickets for 38 runs in 26.4 overs, of which 8 were maidens, against the West Indies was quite superb. In all, playing for Warwickshire over nine seasons, interrupted by six years of wartime activity, he took 697 wickets at a cost of 15,484 runs. Considering that he was 40 years of age in his last season these are quite remarkable figures. How could anyone resist Eric's invitation to fight on behalf of Charlie? Ted Hampton assured me that many members had been in touch to pledge their support. They needed someone to lead the resistance to Alex Hastilow, the club chairman, and, as a councillor and a constant supporter, they looked to me.

At that first meeting they had no idea how to proceed and they had not brought with them any copy of the club rules. We went to Grove's house to get his support for the action I proposed, which was to convene a special annual general meeting and to move a motion of no confidence. Hampton went off to collect a copy of the rules and joined us later. As I had assumed, the rules provided for such a special meeting. It had to be requisitioned by 20 members. The recruiting of 20 willing signatures was done with a few telephone calls in a matter of minutes. In the next few days we drafted the motion, attached the signatures and delivered it to the club. We held a couple of meetings to decide tactics and to obtain agreement to the proposition that I should move the motion, and support quickly became apparent from all sections of the membership.

The meeting was held in the Grand Hotel, Birmingham, presided over by Alderman Cyril Yates, a club vice-president and a former Lord Mayor who had approached me days earlier to ask if I would have any objection if he presided rather than Dr Thwaites, the president. I guessed that Thwaites might be sympathetic to our cause but I certainly had no objection. The meeting was packed. It was impossible to get a seat in the main hall two hours before the meeting was due to begin. Latecomers from the offices and factories crowded the corridors and proceedings were relayed to them. As I opened our case I could hear distinct cries of 'Six!' or 'Four!' or 'How's that!' as I made a telling point. My case had been well assembled by Ted Hampton and I let his figures tell the story of Charlie Grove's contribution to Warwickshire cricket. When I sat down I received a generous reception from everyone, whichever side they were taking in the dispute. In their heart of hearts they all thought that such a wonderful servant should have been allowed to end his playing days with the only county he had ever served. Hastilow began his reply by commenting that the motion had been put skilfully by an 'experienced local politician'. This back-handed compliment didn't get him off to a good start. He also made much of the fact that if our motion was carried the whole committee, including the captain, would have to resign. After an exciting debate the chairman proceeded to a vote and asked me whether I wanted a paper vote or whether I would be satisfied by a show of hands. I hastily consulted my colleagues. They were divided but a majority agreed with me that a hand vote would suit us even though most of our supporters were outside the hall in the corridors and couldn't be seen. In any case, most of us did not want to take over the administration of the club; we thought we had won the argument and that was good enough. Voting in the hall was about five to two against us but I have no reason to doubt the view of many of our friends that had we been able to count the vote outside we should have won the day easily. I accepted the vote.

There was an extraordinary postscript when Edgar Hiley, a committee member, jumped to his feet and moved the expulsion from the club of the '20 dissidents' who had caused such costs to fall upon the club. I replied briefly that whatever side the members had voted for I hoped they would all support our democratic right to express our view in a proper manner as provided for in the club rules, and that they would show their contempt for this attempt to discipline members who had behaved constitutionally. The members showed by loud applause that they had no difficulty with this proposition and the proposal was hastily withdrawn on advice from the chair. Charlie Grove moved on to play a season or two for Worcestershire but we were all delighted when he and the club were reconciled and he finished his days as the club scorer.

STANDING FOR PARLIAMENT

My years as a member of the city council saw two important General Elections and I was totally immersed in both of them. Effectively 1950 was the end of the great Attlee administration, but not yet its death knell. A Government which had transformed society, and had introduced the National Health Service and the Welfare State, against all the odds, only just managed to survive. Its greatest achievement was to transform the country from a wartime to a peacetime economy and to carry out its revolution while providing full employment for all our people. There was more besides, notably the unprecedented act of granting freedom to India, Pakistan and other colonies. Boundary redistribution had transferred me into the Aston constituency and as chairman of the Labour Party I gave every possible moment to the campaign of Woodrow Wyatt and to his agent, Jim Meadows. We did extremely well but we never fully appreciated, as we canvassed and campaigned in the streets and the courtyards, that elections are about the future, and rightly so. Gratitude is not a sentiment that the British people exercise on polling day. Attlee just scraped home. Another election became inevitable as age took its toll of the leading members of his administration: it came in the following year.

In 1950 Albert Bradbeer, former Lord Mayor and leader of the Birmingham Labour Group, had been the candidate and polled 21,715 votes in a three-cornered contest. But he indicated that he did not want to run again the following year against Geoffrey Lloyd, who had defeated him by 5,890 votes. I was nominated for the Conservative stronghold of Kings Norton and I was comfortably chosen to be the candidate. The weather was glorious but we had no chance. The only thing to do was to enjoy ourselves and this we did with gusto. The local Co-op lent us a van and a driver and off we went touring the constituency. Naturally, Labour was defending its tiny majority and as the recently created radio programme *The Archers* was all the vogue we decided that this would provide good material for our campaign:

'The sun is shining, everyone is at work. Dan Archer has got his harvest in and even Walter Gabriel has nothing to complain about. Vote Labour'.

George Strauss, the Minister responsible for the steel industry, came down to speak for me and together we addressed two meetings. One of these was in a strong Labour area and the other in a Tory stronghold. I spoke first in the Tory heartland without any interruption and Alderman Teg Bowen took over while Strauss and myself changed over. The meeting changed its character when Teg, an old miner, defended the nationalisation of the mines. Someone shouted out, 'What about Geoffrey Lloyd?' to which Bowen replied: 'I am talking about miners, the workers; Geoffrey Lloyd has never done a hard day's work in his life'. This throwaway line seemed to cause Geoffrey Lloyd grave offence. It appears that he had already been upset by a remark of mine when I said that he was travelling the constituency accompanied by his two lap dogs, PLUTO and FIDO. This was a reference to his own constant theme that he had served in Churchill's Government and introduced the Pipe Line Under The Ocean, and the Fog Disposal System. He complained bitterly about this at the counting of the votes. I had already wrong-footed him earlier in the campaign, which was dominated by the *Daily Mirror* slogan 'Whose finger on the trigger?'. He now accused me of declaring from my van on the evening before nomination day that if the Tories won the elections 'bombs would be raining down'. I was able to dismiss this out of hand on the grounds that on that night we were enveloped in fog, and that I had been talking for only a few moments on the subject of the Health Service when we had to abandon the meeting: he should therefore withdraw this grave charge. I immediately made some enquiries of my van driver who told me that on the previous Saturday one of the local councillors had referred to the *Daily Mirror* story in rather extravagant language and I directed that he was not to speak again except in my presence. Lloyd responded that he had rechecked his information and he corrected the day upon which he alleged the offence had taken place. This enabled me to bring the incident to a close by saying, 'It is typical of the Tories to make such inaccurate charges and that, when challenged, they immediately shift their ground, in this case from Monday to Saturday!'

Lloyd was very sore about all this when we counted the votes, but having heard the first few results, which clearly showed that the Labour Government would lose office, I was able to tell him that he would no doubt be a Cabinet Minister next morning and he really ought not to worry unduly about such matters. So it proved. It was a straight fight this time and I actually put up our vote to 22,325, but the majority against us was also up at 8,131. As so often happens in politics, this encounter led to Geoffrey and myself becoming quite good friends. Later on, as Minister for Education, he invited me to serve upon the Albermarle Committee to recommend upon the future of the Youth

Service. I was pleased to accept. My political apprenticeship was now complete and an opportunity to serve in Parliament came more quickly than I expected, but nothing has ever removed the debt I owe to my Birmingham local government days.

4

'INTO PARLIAMENT HE MUST GO'

ELECTION 1955

The year of 1955 proved to be the most significant of my life. Within the space of three months I had entered Parliament and married Brenda and these two events have subsequently dominated my life. I have rejoiced in both ever since. My entry into Parliament was really determined by the boundary commissioners but it was full of trauma. I was still the chairman of Aston Constituency Party when boundary changes abolished the seat but created a new one, All Saints, which was largely made up of the old Chamberlainite seat of West Birmingham plus the Soho ward. The Aston seat was no part of it, and therefore Woodrow Wyatt, our MP, had no claim upon it, but together with many of his friends I believed that he would be selected to contest All Saints. Woodrow had served as a Junior Defence Minister in the Attlee Government and had played an influential part in the Cripps mission to India which led to the independence of that country and to the creation of Pakistan. He was also a good constituency member. However, a few months before the selection procedure began he made a controversial speech about the Russian threat in Europe. He called for the establishment of a European Army including in its membership a re-armed Germany. The left decided to make this an issue to campaign against. The *Daily Worker* and the Communist Party issued leaflets outside the GEC and other factories alleging that Wyatt was prepared to see Birmingham destroyed. Within hours, we were locked into the consequences of a fierce political campaign.

I was attending a Labour Party summer school in Bangor. Jim Meadows, our agent, rang me and gave a full account of the reaction he was facing, including a requisition to hold an emergency meeting of the Management committee, which he would present to me on my return at the weekend. In the meantime, Wyatt had consulted his solicitor, Barnett Janner, another Labour MP, and issued a writ for libel. I took my own legal advice and ruled that the matter was sub-judice and that therefore we could not hold an emergency meeting to discuss a motion of no confidence. We did hold a normal meeting of the party. It proved to be helpful. Members then agreed to leave the matter until after the forthcoming Court proceedings, which never materialised. The *Daily Worker* briefed D.N. Pitt QC, a former MP, to act for them. It was clear that if the case came to Court it was going to be a long, drawn-out affair. Eventually, the case was settled out of Court on terms which vindicated Woodrow Wyatt.

While all this was going on, the selection procedure for the All Saints constituency had to be got underway. Nominations were called for. The membership of the new constituency was equally divided between centre right supporters, who looked to the leadership of Hugh Gaitskell, and the left, who followed that of Aneurin Bevan. Woodrow Wyatt was soon nominated as expected, but it became apparent that a gruelling contest lay ahead when Ted Castle, husband of Barbara, was nominated as the standard-bearer of the Bevanites. The secretary, Bill Manders, in the centre of the Party, came to see me. He had taken careful soundings and he was convinced that there was no way that Woodrow could win the nomination. Even most of the people he could normally rely upon would not support his candidature because of his German re-armament speech. If we wanted to win the seat for the Gaitskellite cause another candidate had to be found. As I was a councillor for St Paul's ward, I was the obvious candidate. Would I agree to run? Bill Manders himself came from the All Saints ward. He reasoned that I could carry most of the St Paul's delegates, he could carry many of the All Saints delegates, but most of the Soho ward would support Castle. If I ran, he thought I could win, otherwise he was very pessimistic. Never have I faced such a dilemma. I had worked with Woodrow Wyatt for many years; we were friends, I had an obligation of loyalty to him but also to what we both believed in. I agreed to consider the matter seriously and if I came to the conclusion that Bill Manders' assessment was correct I would take advice about it. My contact with friendly delegates left me in no doubt that Bill Manders' conclusions were more than justified. I decided to ring Hugh Gaitskell and seek his advice. He was extremely understanding and realistic. He wanted Woodrow to be in the next Parliament but in his view the divisions within the Party made it essential that the seat must not be lost to the Bevanite cause. At the end of a long telephone conversation he summed up his advice: 'If you are quite satisfied that Woodrow Wyatt cannot win the seat then it is your duty to stand. Only you are in a position to make that judgment.' I decided to stand.

After weeks of high-pressure campaigning by all sides and considerable press speculation, the selection conference assembled one Sunday afternoon at Handsworth New Road School. Woodrow obviously found the proceedings distasteful and sat in his car reading *Winnie the Pooh*! Ted Castle was an extremely friendly man and while the other speakers were addressing the conference we paced up and down in the playground and chatted about Birmingham politics. This nearly proved to be a fatal mistake for me when he told me that as a youngster he had spent a lot of time with an aunt in Birmingham who took him to the Bull Ring to hear a well-known socialist whose name he couldn't remember. 'That must have been Ernie McCulloch', I commented. I had drawn the first place and Ted was last which was an advantage for him. One of my supporters asked him the obvious question, 'As this is going to be a close contest with the Tory, and local connections are likely to be very important, what connections do you have with Birmingham?'. 'Ah,' said Ted, 'I received a lot of my early political education here in Birmingham. My aunt took me to the Bull Ring. I used to listen to the local spell-binder – I think he was Ernie McCulloch'!

Most of the questions to me concerned defence and the issues upon which I would fight the election if I was chosen as the candidate. In my speech I had laid great stress upon my record in the Party and in local government. At question time I was intent upon setting out the 'Gaitskellite' position but equally positive that I was not going to allow defence questions to dominate the traditional domestic issues on which we should fight. My supporters seemed to be happy enough but I realised that they had to sit there for another two hours before they voted. I was full of apprehension. We paced the playground once more and after what seemed an eternity Bill Manders came out and ushered us in to hear the result, managing to give me a sly wink in the process. What a relief! We went off for a celebration drink and there we heard the full story. Woodrow had a handful of votes with Ted Castle just leading me on the first ballot. One of my supporters, who played the drums in a jazz band, said he had an engagement that night and as it was seven o'clock he could wait no longer. Bill Manders told him no one could leave between the first and second round of ballot papers. This was now a straight fight between Ted Castle and myself. He cast his vote for me and left. I beat Ted Castle by one vote! The following day Cassandra, the *Daily Mirror* columnist, wrote a trenchant piece. Ted Castle worked for the *Mirror* and Woodrow Wyatt wrote for the Mirror Group. Cassandra gave his opinion: 'If the Labour Party is going to choose an unknown local worthy over experienced politicians like Castle and Wyatt there is no hope for it'. Years later he stood me a meal in atonement.

After all this the election itself was an anti-climax. My Tory opponent was Julian Williams, who later on became the rather independent chairman of the Cornwall County Council. Nowadays when I holiday in Cornwall we often meet for a drink and a chat about the 1955 campaign and about the current political scene. Our friendship was never in doubt after we confronted each other at about eight o'clock, an hour before the close of poll, in Lodge Road, Hockley. This is a long road with two hills running in opposite directions to the Duke of Devonshire pub. Julian came down one hill and I came down the other, loudspeakers blaring. We met at the Duke of Devonshire and after a few friendly exchanges, cheered on by the clientele who assured us that they had all voted, we decided to join them for well-earned refreshment. Two or three hours later, Harry Parkinson, the deputy Town Clerk, another longstanding friend whom we also still meet in Cornwall, announced the result: D. Howell (Labour) 18,867; J. Williams (Conservative) 17,560; Majority 1,307. The result confirmed our impression that this was indeed a marginal seat. I could look forward to several years of continuous and hard constituency work.

TAKING THE OATH

It was an interesting experience to enter the House for the first time as of right. I felt an enormous sense of awe as I entered the building. In the cloisters, where I hung my coat, every place is marked with the name of the Member and every coathanger has its red ribbon tied into a loop where the Member should leave his sword before proceeding into the Chamber. I went upstairs to the Members' Lobby and bumped into Julius Silverman, who kindly took me on a tour of the corridors, the Chamber, the tea room and the smoke room. I felt submerged in the history of the building and the great political battles of days gone by. Thirty years on I still feel that same sense of wonder.

I went to the Post Office and collected my first bundle of letters. It was enormous. Advised by Julius I took it off to the Library and found a desk where I could work. My post included some surprising letters: a welcome from Tony Greenwood, a Labour front bench Member and a member of the Party's National Executive Committee, whom I had never met; more excitingly, an invitation from Bill Griffiths, who had been Parliamentary Private Secretary to Aneurin Bevan, to go to a party at his house where Nye and Jennie would look in. It was clear to me that new Members were to be assiduously courted. I could not resist the invitation. The only business of my first day was to elect the Speaker and take the oath. Every Member will tell you that all subsequent Speakers are to be judged against your first Speaker. Mine was Mr Shakespeare 'Shakes' Morrison, a tall Scot with a wonderful accent whose manner of rolling his 'r's was a great fascination. He spoke of his feelings of humility but he certainly didn't show any.

I had taken my seat on the third bench for no other reason than it sat me opposite and slightly above the new Prime Minister, Sir Anthony Eden. It seemed to be a good place from which to view the parliamentary pageant and so it was. I found myself sitting next to Roy Mason, then a young miners' MP for Barnsley, who very helpfully explained the proceedings. During the next few years he was to be a source of much help and advice as we often sat together. I looked across the Chamber. Winston Churchill sat on the first bench next to the gangway, not saying a word but peering all around him looking perplexed. His presence seemed to dominate the place. The Cabinet appeared to me to be a quite ordinary set of people except for Sir Walter Monckton, who carried an air of great learning and competence. The Prime Minister arrived to a rapturous reception. He looked debonair, well-groomed, and impatient to get on with the proceedings.

I was however more overwhelmed by the presence of the people sitting on our own front bench. Clem Attlee, our leader, whose speech at the Aston by-election had impressed me so much and who represented all the decencies that his Government meant to our party; Herbert Morrison, Hugh Dalton, Jim Griffiths, Hugh Gaitskell, Philip Noel-Baker, Harold Wilson, Emanuel Shinwell and, standing alongside the Speaker's chair, Aneurin Bevan. All were giants to me. I felt a great sense of foreboding. How on earth was I going to justify myself amid all this talent?

After his formal election and reply Mr Speaker proceeded to give out the order in which Members would take the oath. The third row above the gangway was almost at the end of his list. I went out to await my turn – for the first time since I entered the building I was on my own. I did a little tour. A policeman came over to greet me in a most respectful manner and to enquire my name and constituency. I could hear him passing on the news to his colleagues: 'That is Howell – Birmingham, All Saints'. They never enquired again. Coming down the long Library corridor I saw the huge figure of Hugh Dalton at the far end. He gave me a warm greeting and bellowed at me, 'Hello, my boy, you must be Denis Howell. I have been looking you up, you are a grammar school boy. There is only one piece of advice I can give you, find out where all the lavatories are'. It was good advice since none of the appropriate doors indicated any such location.

I looked into the Chamber and found that my turn was still a long way off so I went back into the Members' Lobby and enquired the way to the bar which seemed the only thing to do. There I found just two Members enjoying a reunion drink, Fred Peart and Bob Mellish. 'Who are you?' they asked. I told them and they bought me a drink with the comment that it was a great change for anyone from Birmingham to come into the bar. I would be very welcome. Thinking this over I realised that most of my colleagues were virtual teetotallers and the others, Roy Jenkins and Donald Chapman, were not likely to visit a bar very often. Fred Peart and Bob Mellish, having discovered that, like them, I was a trade union MP, were a fount of information. I felt that I had made good friends and so it turned out. I went out on to the terrace for the first time. It looked to me then as it always has since, the most civilised part of the House. I found Stanley Evans walking up and down. He was the very independent Member for Wednesbury, with whom I was acquainted as he had owned Birmingham's Labour paper, the *Town Crier*, for which I had written and been a director. Stanley had served as a Parliamentary Secretary to the Ministry of Food in the Attlee Government and had taken on the farmers. He became known as 'featherbed Evans' in consequence but when he described the Ministry of Agriculture as 'the Whitehall branch of the National Farmers' Union' Attlee sacked him. He had two pieces of advice for me: 'Get out of this place as often as you can. It is a political hothouse, quite suffocating. If you can't escape come out here and stretch your legs'. His second piece of advice was even more trenchant. 'Never tell anyone here what you are thinking of doing and certainly not what you intend to say. No confidence is safe here.'

I took the oath, shook hands with Mr Speaker and left for my hotel, completely overwhelmed by the experience of my first day as a new Member.

On the evening of day two I went to the Griffiths'. It was pleasant, and there were some dozen or so new Members in attendance. Nye and Jennie embraced us all in their conversation, the hospitality was generous and the talk took in the political issues in the Party and the forthcoming vote for the Shadow Cabinet. It was interesting to observe the art of befriending new Members, overwhelmed by their new station in life, and seeking to attach them to your bandwagon. After a few days adjournment the official opening of the new Parliament provided my first taste of the pomp and ceremony. I wanted Brenda to be with me and applied for a seat in the Royal Gallery, through which the Queen's procession passes on its way to and from the Lords' Chamber.

Brenda travelled down from Birmingham by the first train and I met her at Euston. We didn't have much time and it was only when we were on our way in a taxi that I took out of my pocket the very large invitation card of the Lord Great Chamberlain bearing the instruction 'Ladies must wear hats'. Brenda had never worn a hat in her life. Panic. I asked the taxi driver to re-route to Marshall and Snelgrove and kept him waiting while we rushed inside, bought a piece of black straw headgear and resumed our journey. Alas, we arrived too late. Admission to the Royal Gallery was closed. Knowing that Black Rod would come to summons the faithful Commons and believing that, as in the Birmingham City Council, Members could actually command seats in the Gallery for their wives and fiancées, I took Brenda up to the Gallery and sat her there, alone, not an attendant in sight. There soon was, for as the Speaker's procession approached for 'Prayers' during which no one is allowed into the Chamber except Members, the Speaker and the Serjeant at Arms, Members looked up at Brenda and started waving and shouting 'Get out! Get out!. A kindly attendant rescued her and put her in the Central Lobby where she could watch Black Rod proceed to the Commons and witness the procession of Members to and from the Lords for the Queen's speech, so some sense of the occasion was rescued. Sad to say that for the next 30 years Brenda has shown no desire to take a seat in the Royal Gallery!

MAIDEN SPEECH

A new Member gets far too much advice as to when to make his maiden speech, and it is usually quite contradictory. Two schools of thought predominate. The first says 'get it over quickly', which then entitles you to feel a fully-fledged member of the 'club', interrupting other Members in their speeches and being subjected to similar treatment in return. The opposite school counsels delay: 'Wait until you have absorbed the atmosphere', they say, believing that the mystique of the House will then be understood and incorporated into words of wisdom.

For my part I followed neither course. I decided to speak in the first debate I thought I knew something about. It came quite soon. In 1955 the nation had endured a railway strike, in itself a rare occurrence, and the Government wished to introduce new proposals in the field of industrial relations and so a debate was arranged. Walter Monckton was the Minister of Labour and Harold Watkinson his Parliamentary Secretary and the debate, on 23 June, turned out to be very wide ranging. The dispute had been caused by the old problem of differentials following an award by the official referee to the footplate men which created a problem for other railwaymen organised by the National Union of Railwaymen. There was also another dispute in progress in the docks and the debate was timely. It was obviously the one for me. As an active member of my union, then the Clerical and Administrative Workers' Union, later to become APEX, I felt that industrial relations ought to be one of my specialist subjects in the House. The Clerical Workers' Union had made me one of their few sponsored Members which meant that they paid 80 per cent of my election expenses and I reasoned that they would expect me to take part in such a debate. I also had strong views about the settlement of disputes. Contrary to the popular view, few trade unionists want to strike. They have no more desire than the next man to deprive their families of much-needed income. They strike when they can see no other means of obtaining redress for their grievances or reaching an honourable settlement of their dispute. I believed in the 'industrial Courts' which the Government now wanted to disband. These Courts had a fine record of reconciliation and they had built up an enormous amount of case law. The desire to abolish them seemed to me then to be madness, and has since led to far more disputes than to any improvement in industrial relations. Governments to this day have proved to be just as provocative as ultra left wingers, who also want to use industry for a political purpose.

On advice from the Whips I informed the Speaker that I would like to make my maiden speech in this debate and, full of nerves, I sat through the opening speeches. My throat was dry and I remember longing for a packet of mints. Worse, new points emerged which I had not thought of and I had to restrain a great desire to rewrite my speech there and then. After some two to three hours, my stomach was decidedly empty for I had missed lunch and certainly hadn't taken liquid. The Whips brought bad news: there were three new boys on our side all waiting to make their maidens and I was third in line. Although by tradition maidens could expect some preference, the other two had to be congratulated by the other side of the House and other speakers had to be interspersed. I could expect delay. 'Go out and get something to eat', was the welcome advice I was given, so I went down to the cafeteria and ordered myself a plate of bacon, eggs and sausage. No sooner had I sat down than one of the Whips came racing in. 'The Speaker has returned to the chair and he is going to call you next, come back to the Chamber!' I had no time for nerves now, just plain anxiety, and I found myself on my feet in no time at all.

I made the customary references to the City of Birmingham and to my trade union and talked about the growing dangers to society of excessive overtime and to family reliance upon two incomes. I also deplored the growing movement among employers towards taking on part-timers at the expense of full-time jobs. Referring to the shortage of labour in Birmingham's local authority services, I deplored the fact that our collective bargaining arrangements prevented the city from setting its own wage rates and explained that when we decided to do so by just one penny an hour extra we were expelled from these organisations. Lastly, I returned to my two main points, which dealt with the need to attract young people into the commercial side of industry as well as into the areas of production and explaining my experience in trying to get disputes settled peacefully and speedily. I illustrated the last point by reference to the 'York' agreement, in force since 1920, which set out procedures for conciliation.

After my 15-minute speech the ordeal was over. Nigel Fisher was the Tory called to follow me. His congratulations seemed to be very sincere and my ego was well polished when he described my speech as 'most distinguished and fluent'. He went on to refer to Birmingham as a nursery of 'such politicians' and over-generously added my name to that list! Alf Robens, who was another trade union Member – his union was USDAW – followed from our side of the House and Harold Watkinson, the Junior Minister at the Ministry of Labour, spoke for the Government. They were both equally kind in their references. It was with a feeling of great relief that I took myself home.

Almost immediately I had good reason to make another speech, for Birmingham had decided to promote a Bill to extend its water operations in Wales. This led to my appointment to serve upon my first Standing Committee which reviewed the Bill in detail. There was much controversy about building another reservoir in Wales, but it was an excellent introduction to the role and the possibilities, which are endless, of the Standing Committee procedures. In effect Members can table as many amendments as they wish as the Bill is examined clause by clause and they can make as many speeches as they like, for the chairman always calls them in the end. Chairmen are very reluctant to accept a closure motion to even the most insignificant amendment, unless it has had a two-hour debate. The possibilities are endless for new Members learning their trade by framing amendments, making speeches, challenging Ministers and developing their skills. No Member is likely to become an experienced parliamentarian unless he has served a good apprenticeship on a Standing Committee and I soon determined that I was going to take full advantage of such opportunities.

THE FLUNKEY

As soon as I could I organised my constituency surgeries, or advice bureaux as we called them in those days. We arranged one in each of the three wards. These were advertised in the local press and by leaflet distribution. I could never have anticipated the avalanche of publicity that arose from one of the cases I encountered at my earliest bureau in August.

Into my interviewing room came an extremely pleasant and smart young man, Brian Holland. He said that he had just been demobbed from the RAF at Halton in Buckinghamshire. He and his friends had made a pact that the first one of them to be discharged would go to his MP and register a complaint about the duties they had been forced to undertake, which they strongly resented. It fell to him to do so. It seemed that they had to act as domestic servants to the wives of officers. They were detailed to do the housework and washing, to run errands and to do all the domestic chores. 'I was a skivvy for officers' wives', he told me. The final indignation was the Officers' Ball, held at nearby Hitchen, where six men had to act as wine waiters. They were required to dress up as 'flunkies' in full gear and to wait upon the officers, their wives and guests. He described the scene to me with great indignation: 'I wore a silver wig, lace cravat, green frock coat, knickerbocker trousers, white silk stockings and buckled shoes'.

It was an astonishing story but I had no doubt that it was true. Brian Holland was an impressive young man, very refreshing and obviously anxious to carry out his obligations to his comrades. I told him that if I took up the case there would be a lot of publicity and that his former colleagues, as well as himself, could expect to be exposed to the limelight. He assured me that they had discussed this eventuality and they wanted to bring these abuses to an end. He placed the matter entirely in my hands and said he would tell his friends that he had done so. I spent the weekend thinking about how to handle the case. It seemed to me to be big news for the nationals. If I wrote to the Minister too soon I had no doubt that a blanket of silence would descend upon the RAF School for Technical Training at Halton. I could put down my first parliamentary question, but I might well fail to do the case full justice in those limited circumstances. In any case, I thought that more investigation was called for before I acted.

I decided to visit the Birmingham Press Club, of which I was a member, and to consult Ray Hill, the *Daily Mirror*'s Midlands man, who was an old friend and one of the most respected journalists in the club. He immediately recognised the potential of the story and after talking to his editor guaranteed maximum publicity if the *Mirror* had an exclusive. Brian was agreeable and the *Mirror* got to work. Ray took Brian back to Buckinghamshire and they met some of Brian's colleagues who confirmed the story. The *Mirror* also felt that there were bound to be photographs of the ball and very soon they had located the photographer who had taken them and discovered some showing the 'flunkies' dancing attendance upon the officers. They were in business. The full front page story that appeared in the *Mirror* on 17 August had a far greater impact than I had expected. Other newspapers took up the story, colleagues in the House were amused and complimentary – although I was more than once described as a 'lucky bugger' – and the Air Minister, the Hon. George Ward, was clearly embarrassed when he came to deal with my question in the House. Brian Holland and his friends were very happy with the result of my endeavours. For myself, I could not have arrived on the parliamentary scene with more impact. I began to feel that my existence was justified and it did my confidence a power of good. The House was in recess but the story ran and ran, enabling me to raise it on the floor in October where it was disposed of by a half-hearted defence from the Minister, who relied upon the fact that no airman complained at the time and they had all been volunteers, which was certainly not an accurate description of the situation.

Soon I was back to committee work. The Government had decided to introduce a Clean Air Bill in order to redeem an undertaking to Gerald Nabarro, the extravagant but skilful Conservative backbencher, whose Bill in the previous Parliament had been dropped after assurances from the Government that it would introduce its own Bill. Nabarro paraded around like a peacock and week after week he presided over the fortunes of 'his' Bill from the back bench seat immediately behind the Minister. Nabarro was clearly very well-briefed by various health organisations and he tabled scores of amendments, many of which the Government could not be expected to accept. This was a subject dear to my heart, too, after my own local authority experience in this subject. I too consulted public health advisers in Birmingham and I and my colleagues not only tabled our own amendments but also decided to put our names to all Gerald Nabarro's amendments. We had observed that for all his bluster he was rarely willing to challenge the Government by forcing a vote. This tactic became increasingly successful. As the Committee approached the crunch questions raised by this Bill – whether or not to include the industrial processes within its scope, as we wished, or whether to exclude the emissions of dark smoke and sulphurous discharges – we were determined to commit Gerald Nabarro to vote for his own amendments. Suddenly he was reported to be unwell and unable to attend the Committee. We were surprised to hear that he was being seen around in Kidderminster, his constituency, but it was clear that he would not be embarrassing the Government by his presence as we forced votes on these essential matters. The Bill was an outstanding piece of legislature which rid the country of its fog menace and led on to the cleaning up of our most important buildings.

MARRIAGE

The renewal of my association with the Willson family came about, as I have said, when I went to visit Steve, who had talked me into running as the Labour candidate for the Handsworth ward in 1945. Now, some eight years on, although we had been in touch from time to time, I was shocked by his condition. Not only was he suffering from asthma but he was crippled by arthritis. He was devotedly looked after by his wife, Ruth, and his four children, the youngest of whom was Brenda. Through our mutual love of music we began to go together to the concerts of the City of Birmingham Symphony Orchestra and then to Edinburgh for the Festival. It was a happy courtship but it was usually conducted late at night after the interminable meetings that were the lot of Birmingham Labour leaders.

Brenda was often practising her violin lessons when I arrived and I used to infuriate the family by letting myself into the house and announcing my arrival by singing up the stairs: 'Up in the garret away from the din, I played a tune on my old violin'. Why on earth Brenda agreed to marry me I shall never know but thank God she did. We have been blessed with a wonderful family, Andrew, Michael, Kathryn and David, and my firmest conviction is the importance of family life. I can only speak for myself, but I find the fellowship and affection of the family to be an indispensable part of my public life. Their loyalty and support make all things possible. When I became a Member of Parliament it seemed the sensible thing to advance the date of our marriage to 20 August when, in the Church of the Messiah, the Birmingham Unitarian church which had seen in its membership the Chamberlains and the non-conformist leadership of Birmingham politics, we married. We chose this church because we wanted the ceremony to be conducted by Ronald McGraw, who was then both a Unitarian minister and a Labour councillor. Brenda was given away by her brother William, with all our friends around us, personal, political and sporting. My best man was Ken Ford, schoolmate and life-long friend.

At the reception the constituency secretary, Bill Manders, hired a full 'flunkey' outfit so that he could portray my first great constituency case and welcome all the guests. It was the happiest of occasions and for more than 30 years I have never ceased to count my blessings. Brenda has welcomed everyone who comes to our home. Whoever has knocked on our door, Cabinet Minister or the humblest of constituents, they have had the warmest of welcomes. Our marriage has been a true partnership. Brenda's 'role' of maintaining our home and caring for the family are in every way an equal contribution to all our endeavours.

SUEZ

Suez produced an intensity of passion which I had never expected to find in the British Parliament. Nothing like it had been experienced in the lifetime of most Members, not even in wartime. Nothing like it is likely to be seen again. The House was reflecting the deepest and most genuine divisions of the whole country, feelings in which the morality of peace was set against the emotions of war.

Anthony Eden had succeeded Winston Churchill far too late. We did not know then how ill he must have been. His impatience to assert principles which he had stood for in the pre-war days of appeasement, which he had firmly opposed, led him now into acts of total irrationality, into collusion with Israel and France and into the most bitter opposition of the United Nations, of our closest ally, the United States, and of the Opposition parties here at home, who had no intention of dealing with this crisis in open defiance of the UN.

Confronting Eden was Labour's leader, Hugh Gaitskell. In comparison with Eden Gaitskell had a towering intellect, but he was never the 'desiccated calculating machine' described by Nye Bevan. He had more than a fair share of emotion in his make-up although he controlled it much better than the Prime Minister. At first Gaitskell intimated to Eden that he would support opposition to the nationalisation of the Suez Canal and the threat to British interests but Eden took this as an open cheque, which it could never have been. As the drama unfolded and the suspicions of collusion grew into certainty Gaitskell's anger at this deception fired his parliamentary performance. Gaitskell's election to the Labour leadership to succeed Clem Attlee had been obvious to me from the moment I set foot in the House. The bitterness of the internal divisions between Gaitskell's followers and the Bevanites was talked about in every bar and tea room. Herbert Morrison had a few supporters but there was no doubt that Attlee's decision to stay on as leader after the 1951 election defeat was fatal to him. The result of the leadership election was announced on 14 December: Gaitskell 157; Bevan 70; Morrison 40. In an extraordinary way Suez produced a good working relationship between Gaitskell and Bevan. The old divisions still existed but during Suez they were of no significance. Gaitskell and Bevan won every round against Eden and his Foreign Secretary, Selwyn Lloyd. It was and remains the most overwhelming political experience of my life.

This fateful parliamentary week started on 29 October when Israel invaded the Sinai. The next day Eden used this action as a pretext for issuing a joint Anglo-French demand for withdrawal of all forces to a distance of ten miles, reasoning that we must divide the combatants, although it soon became clear that the collusion between Israel, France and the UK was total. Nasser refused and the British and French began their aerial bombardment. The Opposition tabled its censure motion on 1 November, and the following day the United Nations Assembly called upon us to halt our attacks. On 5 and 6 November the Anglo-French force invaded Egypt by sea and air at Port Said. In an unexpected step the Commons met on a Saturday for a momentous three-hour debate. The Prime Minister was shouted down, the Speaker adjourned the House, the atmosphere was incredible. The Government benches were incensed, first by the belief of the Opposition that they should not automatically support any Government declaration of war about which they had not been consulted and then by the view that all criticism should be silenced while armed forces were engaged in conflict. This was an opinion shared by some Members on our own benches. The sight of Stanley Evans, our colleague who sat for Wednesbury, recalling the slaughter of his comrades in the First World War with tears streaming down his face remains a most vivid memory. For the most part the Opposition was aghast that any Government could unilaterally renounce accepted international morality as represented by the United Nations when it was supported by the entire British Commonwealth and the United States.

However, a further disaster struck. On 4 November the Soviet Union invaded Hungary. The Government of Imre Nagy had announced its withdrawal from the Warsaw Pact. The British and the French were impotent. With the Suez crisis at its height, deserted by our American ally, censured by the United Nations and opposed by most of the Commonwealth, we could only watch with despair as brave and helpless Hungarian citizens confronted the Soviet tanks. Throughout it all public opinion expressed itself in the most direct manner. Members on both sides of the argument were urged on to even greater efforts. I have never received such a postbag. Every parson in my constituency, every church group, every trade union, every ex-service organisation, parents of men in the forces; they all inundated me with their views. I decided to hold a public meeting in my constituency the following Sunday evening. It was the first meeting to be held in Birmingham. People flocked there from all over the city. We couldn't get them all into the hall. I was worried about whether the meeting might reflect the scenes in the House but there was no cause for alarm. I was listened to with obvious support. At the end of my speech I developed the theme that the tragedy of Suez was Hungary. By attacking Egypt without UN support we had provided a cover for the Hungarian invasion and we were powerless to protest. I concluded with Macaulay's words which best expressed my feelings: 'How can any man die better than facing fearful odds,/For the ashes of his fathers, and the temple of his Gods'.

The general atmosphere of the meeting and the enthusiastic reception for my speech told me that Eden could not win. He had failed to carry the nation with him. So it proved. The British forces withdrew and Eden was soon to resign, his health totally failing. Later on I took part in a foreign affairs debate which brought me a word of encouragement from our foreign affairs spokesman, Philip Noel-Baker, whom I had long admired and who was later to receive the Nobel peace prize.

HARVARD

In the Members' Dining-Room I continued to sit at the 'Shadow Cabinet' table, not out of any mistaken ideas of grandeur but because I enjoyed the company of Fred Peart, Bob Mellish, Charlie Pannell and Douglas Houghton who also sat there. There were kindred spirits and fellow trade union members and their company was helpful and convivial. The presence from time to time of Hugh Gaitskell, Chuter Ede, Herbert Morrison and, especially, Hugh Dalton was an added source of great pleasure and education. When Dalton decided to stand down from the Shadow Cabinet he returned to this table for dinner after having informed Hugh Gaitskell of his decision and in a loud voice, for the benefit of 'Manny' Shinwell sitting across the room, he told us, 'I have decided to help Hugh. I have told him that all the old men must go. I will lead the way, the others must follow'. Shinwell had never forgiven Gaitskell for succeeding him in office when he was replaced after the fuel crisis in Attlee's Government.

It would have been impossible to find a more joyful and encouraging senior colleague than Hugh Dalton. It was sheer delight to sit at his table and to share in his gossip and hear his mischievous commentary upon events. He would always enquire 'What are you doing now, my boy?' and offer good advice as to what issues to take up and how to get the Party back into good shape. It was at one of these 'dinner parties' that he asked me if I had considered applying to go to the Harvard International Seminar, a six-week seminar run by Henry Kissinger for emerging people of about 40 years of age, distinguished in the fields of politics, economics and the arts. He promised to provide me with a reference. In due course I was invited to become a member of the seminar in the summer of 1957. The other two British participants were John Wood, who had written most of Eden's speeches in the 1955 election campaign, and Keith Godwin, a very talented sculptor from Battersea College. We were a happy and resourceful team. Among some very talented participants was Yigal Allann, who had led the Israeli forces against Egypt and had captured Nasser. He used to recount his experiences to us over a beer at the end of the day. We loved his stories about how he visited Nasser after he had been taken prisoner and talked to him about war strategy as well as Israeli/Egyptian relations. Another member of the seminar, sharing one of the rooms in our accommodation in Weld Hall, was Nasim Shah, later to become one of the judges who tried President Bhutto of Pakistan and one of the three who produced a guilty verdict.

It was an exhilarating experience but not without its problems. Henry Kissinger invited a US Minister to address the seminar. The three British representatives decided to question him about the tactics of the US nuclear industry in obtaining an order to build a Japanese power station by putting out stories that a British reactor was unsafe. He had clearly not expected such a combined operation on our part and this led to some deterioration in our relations with Kissinger. Another source of difficulty was the director's dinner parties, given once or twice a week at his home. These were most pleasant occasions and Kissinger was obviously enchanted by the company of one of the Italian members, a film producer, whom he invited more than once in the first three weeks of the seminar. I was approached by Nasim Shah who felt strongly about the fact that he had not yet received such an invitation. He wanted me to speak to Kissinger on behalf of the members who had not yet been invited. Being foolhardy, I agreed to do so. Henry told me that he was not going to be told who to invite into his home. I replied by saying that I understood that, but he was the director of the seminar and if he was not going to treat all the members on an equal footing he might well undermine its purpose. Happily, the matter was soon corrected but a coldness remained. On the day before we left Kissinger phoned me and said that we couldn't part with our relationship in this state, and we fixed up a breakfast together next morning where we re-established friendliness.

When I refereed a US soccer tournament in New York in 1960, Henry was working for Rockefeller, soon to run for the governership of New York, and we renewed our acquaintance. He was a keen football follower and when I next visited the States I stayed with Phil Woosnam, an old friend and former captain of Aston Villa with whom I used to train when I was a referee. He was now involved with soccer on behalf of Mr Lamar Hunt, son of the great oil magnate, Joe Hunt. Lamar's interests are in sport, especially tennis, but he became involved in soccer, too. Later on, when Phil took charge of the North American Soccer League, he told me he wanted a president for this newly-emerging sport to add some prestige. I suggested Henry Kissinger and was delighted when he accepted the position.

Another special and lasting friendship which I established at Harvard was with Carol and Steve Robinson. Carol was on the secretarial staff of the seminar and Steve was then a newly-qualified intern who has gone on to become a distinguished medical researcher in the field of blood disorders, especially leukaemia, and to serve as secretary of the US Institute of Haematology. Steve is now a Professor of Medicine at Harvard.

THE PARLIAMENTARY ROUND

Early in 1958 I found myself caught up in a most dramatic parliamentary incident. A local practitioner, Dr Jain, knocked on my door one Sunday morning in a state of great agitation. He had been treating a patient for many years by prescribing a whole series of drugs. The man became chronically depressed, and on Christmas Eve he had gone to a local pub and got into an argument with a barman. As a result he had gone home to collect a wartime gun and then returned to shoot the barman dead. Dr Jain explained that throughout his trial the patient refused to allow his Counsel to raise the medical facts in his defence. It was an historic case because it was the first to be heard in which a plea of diminished responsibility could be pleaded as a defence to a charge of capital murder. This defence was only available for a restricted number of crimes. The Attorney General had refused to issue his fiat for the case to go to the Lords, and as a result the man was due to be executed in a few days' time.

I decided to table an emergency question under the Standing Orders and it was down to be answered on 23 January. The Speaker called my name in a full House which had assembled to hear Prime Minister's Questions and for a major debate due to follow. The moment the House realised that I was pleading for a man's life there was total silence which heightened my nervous condition but which did the House great credit. Reggie Manningham-Buller, the Attorney General, explained that he could not grant his fiat as he did not believe that the case involved an exceptional point of law which would justify such a course, even if it was the first case under the new law. Patrick Gordon-Walker from the front bench and Leslie Hale from the Labour back benches intervened to support my submission but without success. However, as the Attorney General sat down he looked across at me to indicate that he would like a word behind the Speaker's chair. There he thanked me for drawing the case to his attention and said that everyone knew the effect of alcohol combined with the drugs the man had been taking. He was amazed this had not been raised during the trial and he was going back to his office to telephone the Home Secretary to recommend a reprieve. Never has a Member felt such a sense of relief: I telephoned the news to Dr Jain who was overcome. It was only then that I fully realised the measure of responsibility which I had carried for this man's life. I can only hope that no other young Member is ever faced with such a burden.

My intention to become a campaigning MP was easily satisfied during my first Parliament. Issues seemed to turn up every day. I was soon wading into the Government over the creation of hospital pay beds, claiming for example that at the Birmingham Ear, Nose and Throat Hospital some 12 per cent of the beds were reserved for private patients. My long association with the Health Service continued in Parliament and I became embroiled in the condition of our mental hospitals thanks to my friend Frank Leiath, Midland area secretary of my union. Frank was a hospital committee member in his native Shrewsbury. Alarmed by the stories he told me I decided to visit some of these hospitals. At Shelton Hospital in Shrewsbury I found appalling conditions. There was gross overcrowding and the staff were faced with impossible conditions in which to work. I described the accommodation for the nursing and domestic staff as 'primitive'. It was obvious that no proper funding of this hospital had taken place for years. I called a press conference to announce my findings prior to taking the campaign to the House. The hospital chairman responded by complaining that my visit to his hospital was 'not announced to his Management Committee in advance'. This was true but intentional – I had arranged it with the medical superintendent who totally supported my campaign.

Later on I made a second visit to the hospital to check upon any improvements. About £12,000 had been spent in the interim and I made a statement saying that 'any improvements I can see are entirely due to the efforts of the staff'. This time the chairman replied: 'I do not like the problem of mental hospitals being turned into stamping grounds for politics'.

Nevertheless, it was clear to me that unless politicians did stamp around the mental hospitals we were never going to attract the resources they needed. So I set off to visit the All Saints Hospital in my own constituency, where conditions were equally bad. The staff took me up a winding iron staircase to an attic room in the roof where 20 or more ladies were housed in a ward without water, toilets or fire escape. My outrage was intense. Public response was immediate and supportive: the ward was closed down within days. Next Hatton Hospital in Warwick had been told to expect a visit from me. This was intended as a precautionary warning but I found that the young medical superintendent clearly regarded me as an ally in the ceaseless fight to improve the awful conditions the hospitals had to endure. Next I visited Hollymoor and Rubery Hospitals where another trade union colleague, David Rhydderch, was the chairman. He welcomed my visit with open arms and gave me every encouragement, for he saw his role as a pioneer chairman pursuing the Regional Hospital Board for equality of funding for the hospitals. He was himself a member of the Board and no doubt his unconventional approach to the duties of chairman upset many people, not least the medical staff who thought he was interfering in their spheres of influence. Their anger was so great that later on they prompted the Minister of Health, Enoch Powell, to set up an Enquiry into David's conduct. I determined to force a debate in the Commons and denounced both the chairman of the Enquiry and Enoch Powell. I had no doubt that we won the argument but Rhydderch was relieved of his chairmanship. It was a victory for medical trade unionism, which had prepared and represented the doctors' case, over a pragmatic trade unionist who was single-handedly pursuing his social obligations.

Having had a very successful campaign to draw attention to the deficiency of the Health Service I turned my attention to education and toured the schools in my constituency to demand the end of the 11 Plus examination and to discover what school life was about. I was able to speak in an Education Debate and to deplore the fact that 'entrance to the arts, the professions, the civil service and the universities, indeed the whole future of a child's life, is now geared to whether he or she gets through an examination which they sit for two days only during one week of their life'. Warming to my theme, I described many large schools as 'educational sausage factories' and deplored the fact that it was often not possible for 'headteachers to know their own staff, let alone the children'. I announced my findings in an article I wrote for the *Birmingham Mail,* calling not only for smaller classes but smaller schools, too; more opportunities for the children, and more pay for the teachers whose wages I described as 'scandalous'. One headteacher had told me that the window-cleaner earned £3 per week more than he did, and at Warwickshire Cricket Ground I found teachers doing part-time work as ice-cream salesmen and builders' labourers! Their place in the nation's order of social values has not changed much 30 years on. I still have no doubt that it is in this area of educational deprivation that the Government might discover the cause of any educational decline in the classroom.

Another subject needing my attention in this Parliament arose from a sudden rash of estate agent businesses collapsing in Birmingham, one of the most spectacular being in my own constituency. I was inundated by people who were distressed by the plight of those affected and I spent almost a year investigating the disasters. I found that in 12 months in Birmingham 2,000 families had lost their deposits, which amounted to a sum of £250,000. 'Rab' Butler, the Home Secretary, responded by informing me that he would prepare legislation to deal with estate agents. I found much support from reputable estate agents for my two-pronged proposal calling for compulsory registration and for the lodging of all deposits in a frozen account, subject to audit. This was specifically supported by the West Midlands branch of the Incorporated Society of Auctioneers and Landed Property Agents.

My most sustained campaign in this Parliament was my attempt to change the Sunday observance laws so that sport could be played on Sundays without the subterfuge and hypocrisy that was necessary to charge for admission. I was aided by a stroke of good fortune, for I drew first place in the ballot for Private Members' motions for 14 March 1958 and proposed that 'a Select Committee be appointed to consider the Sunday observance legislation; and to make recommendations as to any alterations that are necessary in present-day conditions'. I soon found that this was not an altogether popular initiative. Not because of the merits or demerits of my proposals, but because of the extra work such a controversial issue brings for one's colleagues.

Members told me that the last time the issue had been debated, in January 1953, they had been inundated with correspondence. One colleague told me: 'I had to reply to 270 letters, and we still have to pay for our own postage'.

We soon strayed on to Welsh matters arising out of the 1958 Empire Games in Cardiff. I trailed my coat a bit because George Thomas, one of the Cardiff Labour Members who was also a Methodist lay preacher and who enjoyed great stature in the House – later on he became one of our finest Speakers – was sitting in front of me, ready to oppose. When I said that I would like to visit his constituency for the Games and I hoped he would offer me some Sabbath day hospitality, it was too much for George. 'Does my Hon. Friend really think that to have the pleasure of his company at the Empire Games, Wales ought to alter the whole of its licensing laws? Is that his modest opinion?', he asked. 'Indeed,' he sang with the greatest indignation. John Parker, the Member for Dagenham, later to become the father of the House, came to my aid. He had taken this cause to his heart and pursued it through several Parliaments. 'Would my Hon. Friend the Member for Cardiff West like to take his Hon. Friend to a Conservative Club in Cardiff so that he may have a drink on Sunday?' I moved on from Wales to theology as I knew I would be followed by an attack on religious grounds. The main essence of my argument was the question of individual conscience: 'We as legislators ought not to exercise our consciences in this Chamber in such a way as to prevent any person outside from exercising their conscience'. George Thomas intervened again. 'If our constituents do not like the way we exercise our consciences they have every opportunity to reject us at the next General Election.'

I had prepared myself for such an attack. I preferred, I said, to take my theology from Archbishop William Temple. I quoted his words on this very subject: 'It is worthwhile to notice how absolute was Christ's respect for the freedom of personal choice. He would never bribe nor coerce men to become followers. Judas must be allowed to betray Him if he so determined. Not even to save a man from that will the Lord override his freedom. For on freedom all spiritual life utterly depends. It is astonishing and terrifying that the Church has so often failed to understand this'. Sir Hugh Lucas-Tooth intervened from the Government back benches to ask me how I would resolve a conflict between two of my constituents who exercised opposing consciences. 'The answer is simple', I replied, 'I do not have to satisfy them. They have to satisfy themselves.' After my speech, which lasted some 40 minutes, my motion was seconded by Peter Kirk, whose father had been Bishop of Oxford. When George Thomas's turn came he stood firm in the belief that Sunday sport would change the character of the Sabbath in spite of the intervention during his speech of some of the most powerful speakers in the House, but he got himself in terrible trouble when he announced that after church he went home to watch a television play.

It was a fascinating debate. There have been few better Private Members' debates in my experience. The wind-up for my motion was undertaken by Reg Sorenson, a Unitarian minister who had put himself out to come down to the House on the very day he was to receive the Freedom of his Borough. He traced the changing character of our festivals from pagan times through to our present Christian days of worship, showing how even these have changed their meaning over the years and concluding that this was certainly true about the way in which we observed both Christmas Day and the Sabbath, which he found not to be in conflict with his own deeply-held religious truth. When the time came to vote on the question that my motion be put to the House we won by 54 votes to 31, but that was not enough. Standing Orders required that at least 100 Members be present in the Aye lobby. So the matter had to wait another day. Thirty years on I am still involved in campaigning on the same issue. In the meantime, more and more Sunday sport takes place which Parliament prefers to ignore.

THE THURSO BOY CASE

My interest in Sunday entertainments brought about my involvement in the case of John Waters – the 'Thurso Boy Case' – as it came to be known. I became involved as the result of a remarkable coincidence early in 1959. Three orders came before the House late at night extending the provisions of the Sunday Cinematograph Entertainments orders to three small district councils. I had stayed on to listen to the discussion on these. They were in fact approved without any debate. The House emptied leaving just one elderly Member, Sir David Robertson, MP for Caithness and Sutherland, and the Lord Advocate for Scotland, W.R. Milligan MP. Just the three of us sat there for the adjournment debate. There was something about David Robertson's concern, almost anguish, which attracted my attention. I had never had a conversation with him but I decided to stay on and hear him out. He told a remarkable story.

John Waters was a boy of 15 brutally assaulted by two police officers in Thurso 14 months earlier. David Robertson had been reluctant to take up the case when the boy's father saw him because five months had elapsed but he was impressed by his earnestness, so he asked him to put the case in writing and he decided to investigate the matter. Waters had been to a local cinema and then called in at a local café at about 11 o'clock where he had met some friends. Two police officers, without being asked to do so, entered the café and took John outside, warning him to watch his behaviour. When the boy returned to the café his friends told him that his coat was torn. The boy ran out after the policemen to complain but they took him under their control and marched him down an alleyway. John Waters remembered nothing after 'the first savage blow which knocked me on my back'. Seventeen witnesses told Sir David that they had seen John Waters led into the alleyway and the policemen come out without him. Some of his friends went to find him lying in the alleyway. A Mrs McPhee took him into her home, washed and bathed him, and took him to a Dr Fell who later told Sir David that the boy had 'an upper lip swollen on the right side with abrasions of the mucous membrane; his eyes were bloodshot and the lids swollen and his right ear was tender. He was shaking badly and the left shoulder of his jacket was torn'. The doctor stated that he had had to see the boy twice more and that he was still in a nervous condition. He had brought the boy into the world and described him as 'a very nice boy'. Sir David had obtained further references from the boy's headmaster and the captain of his Boys' Brigade Company and also from his employer. He had never seen 'better references as to the conduct and behaviour of a boy'.

The Member took the case to the Secretary for Scotland. On the night of the assault the boy's father had taken the boy to the police station and lodged a charge against the officers concerned which was accepted by the officer on duty. Mr Waters senior expected the charge to be dealt with in Thurso. It was not. Days later he was referred to Wick, the county town. The Procurator Fiscal told him on his second visit that there was to be no case. It seemed that the Procurator Fiscal had referred the case to Crown Counsel in Edinburgh who had decided to do nothing. Sir David persisted with his enquiries and was then asked by the Solicitor General if he would postpone his actions while they investigated the evidence which he had submitted. He agreed to wait for 14 days. Apparently, the law officers were awaiting the evidence of a Mrs Banks, who was the employer of the boy's mother. It transpired that this lady had put enormous pressure on the Waters family to withdraw the case. The Lord Advocate told the astonished Waters family that although Mrs Banks had been 'unwell and in an Inverness mental institution during the time of the assault' she was in fact a material witness. Robertson had pursued this matter at Question Time and told the House that this lady was never a material witness. She had been introduced into the case after the event.

With commendable restraint Robertson told the House that he was not saying the policemen were guilty, he was saying there must be a case for investigation. The authorities were saying there was not. 'There must be a case', said David, almost pleading that his enquiries demanded one. He was clearly distressed that his personal investigations should be met with a wall of silence. 'This is treating the House of Commons with contempt', he concluded, and so it seemed to me. It was inconceivable that on this evidence the Lord Advocate would do anything other than order an Enquiry. I was in for further astonishment. The Lord Advocate spoke for exactly five minutes to reply to these serious charges. He opened with an academic irrelevance, chiding the Member for saying that the boy had been assaulted instead of saying that 'a boy of 15 years had *said* that he was brutally assaulted'.

Crown Counsel had decided that criminal proceedings would not be justified. The Lord Advocate had read all the statements but was still of the opinion that 'in the circumstances as known to Crown Counsel and myself criminal proceedings would not be justified'. He gave no reasons for the decision as it would have been unsatisfactory to do so if there was no opportunity to cross-examine.

I was incensed that a law officer could take such a stand, to say that he could give no reasons because the opportunity to cross-examine was not available. Milligan had also made a tactical error, for when he sat down he left some six minutes of the half-hour adjournment debate still available to be taken up. Throwing aside all normal protocol about English Members not intervening in domestic Scottish business I decided to occupy the remaining time with all the force I could muster. I told the House that I had served on the Birmingham Watch Committee, so that I was jealous of the good name of the police force. 'Every Chief Constable that I have met would be most anxious to have the fullest enquiry into charges of such gravity as we have heard tonight. The reply of the Lord Advocate was disgraceful, the worst I have heard since I have been in the House. The safety of the subject is paramount.' In English law, I told the House, there would be three courses open in such a case. A prosecution of the police officers concerned, if there were prima facie evidence. Anyone who had heard this evidence and said there was no prima facie evidence placed himself in the category of a nitwit. Secondly, there could be civil proceedings. In view of the ridiculous, indeed impossible reply to which we had just listened I hoped the Hon. Member would tell the family there was no alternative but to take proceedings and to press for the maximum damages. The third course was to press for the holding of a Judicial Enquiry. I had sat on many such Watch Committee enquiries in Birmingham dealing with allegations against the police and my experience was that the Chief Constable was always most anxious to have the fullest investigation to clear the good name of his force.

I then turned my attention to the shameful treatment of the Hon. Member and the disgraceful manner in which the House was now being treated: 'One cannot escape the conclusion that there is a great covering up going on which is a disgrace to the good name of Government in this country and to the good name of the law of this land'. My indignation knew no bounds. The Lord Advocate retreated from the Chamber, desperately avoiding his colleague David Robertson. David was overcome with gratitude. He told me that in all these months I was the only person to give him support. 'What are we to do now?' he said. I thought we must meet on the following day and draft a motion calling for an Enquiry. He would collect Conservative signatures and I would collect Labour.

The newspapers were full of the case. In Scotland my intervention was given almost sensational treatment and David's case, for the first time, obtained national coverage. We quickly collected signatures for our motion. Members were anxious to support us. With record speed the Government were soon back-tracking. Harold Macmillan, the Prime Minister, intervened personally and within a few days a Tribunal of Enquiry was announced. This was to be an impressive Enquiry chaired by Lord Schon. The extent of the concern now felt throughout the country can be judged by the Members who supported the Prime Minister's announcement: Hugh Gaitskell, Sir Lynn Ungoed-Thomas QC, later to become a High Court judge; Chuter Ede, a former Home Secretary; and Sidney Silverman. At last justice could be done. David Robertson, whom I had now grown to like enormously as a gentleman of the old school, representing all the decencies of life, was vindicated. His personal gratitude for my intervention was very touching. However, we were nowhere near the end of the affair. Caithness and Sutherland had long been a Liberal seat, represented by their leader, Sir Archibald Sinclair. David Robertson had won the seat from them. The Liberals decided to make an issue of the Enquiry, stating that their Member's actions had brought about an Enquiry which would have to be financed by the ratepayers. They mounted a fierce attack upon him. Robertson felt he had to call a meeting to justify his actions, he needed support, would I agree to go to Thurso and speak for him on a non-party basis? Of course, there could be only one answer.

When we landed in our tiny aircraft at the local airport we were met by the chairman of the Constituency Labour Party. He thanked me for coming and assured me that on this issue they supported Sir David and wished us well for the meeting that night to which I was assured people would travel from all parts of both counties. So it proved. We walked from our hotel through deserted streets to the main square, which was full. People not able to get into the hall occupied the staircase. We struggled through to reach the platform. A neutral chairman had been found and I was listened to, with attention, as I denounced the local Liberals for daring to suggest that justice for any citizen could not be available if the cost to the ratepayer was too high. John Waters had travelled down to London to meet me. I had found him to be a quite remarkable boy, intelligent and courageous, with delightful manners. I paid my tribute to their Member and left the rest of the meeting to David. He did very well in his gentlemanly way. The Liberals present made their points but they attracted little support in the hall, certainly not as much as they had apparently attracted from a friendly newspaper. We returned to our hotel to meet many of the people who had travelled far to be with us. All of them were very appreciative of my support and my presence there.

The Tribunal Report was published one year to the day after it had been established. It did a thorough job although some of the authors' impressions of young Waters were certainly not those that I had formed. They found that the boys in the café had been cheeky and sarcastic, leading one of the constables to remark: 'If there is any more cheek I'll mark you for life', which the Tribunal found to be 'highly improper'.

However, they accepted the evidence that Waters had made an 'obscene and offensive' remark and that he had done so again when he pursued the officers to complain about his torn jacket. They had therefore taken him into the alley to tick him off out of the public view. His injuries occurred when the boy tried to run out of the alley. One of the constables put out his arm to stop him and caught him with his wrist. The Tribunal concluded that the constable had in fact struck Waters 'an impulsive blow' after having been exasperated. The Tribunal went on to find that Waters was not 'in any way a bad or vicious boy' but that his behaviour and language was 'shocking'. They then went on to a further finding which was that a relative of one of the officers, a district nurse, had called at the Waters' home and offered to provide a new suit of clothing if the Waters family dropped their complaint. The Tribunal also found other evidence of an attempt to get Waters senior to drop the case in return for money. Finally, Lord Schon and his colleagues investigated the actions of the Caithness police and its chief officers and concluded that they had conducted themselves perfectly properly. Undoubtedly Parliament thought that the Report was competent and acceptable. That was the end of this particular affair, although by now David Robertson had retired and I had temporarily lost my seat in Parliament so there was no debate. But the case had much bearing on the decision to establish a Royal Commission on police procedures which was set up later on.

In this my first Parliament my involvement in three separate cases, that of the 'Flunkey', that of the Birmingham man reprieved from the capital sentence and that of the Thurso Boy all made an abiding impression on me as to the role of Parliament in the defence of the interests of every single citizen. The House of Commons is at its very best when it concerns itself with the fate of the individual citizen. Nothing since has caused me to change that view and I was privileged, in my first Parliament, to find myself engrossed in three such cases.

ELECTION 1959

As this Parliament drew towards its end I was well satisfied with my four years as the Member for All Saints. I felt that I had made my mark in the House. I had borne my fair share of committee work and established a good reputation with my colleagues. I had worked hard to represent Birmingham in Parliament and I could claim to have been very conscientious in the constituency, holding at least three surgeries every month, well advertised, so that I could easily be located. In addition my refereeing in the Football League had attracted much more national publicity and often provided a source of interesting conversation when I called at the clubs and pubs, talk which stretched across the party lines. I was happy with these personal achievements, with my contribution to Labour's cause and with the happy relationships I enjoyed with my constituents.

Our home life was a source of great strength. Brenda was totally supportive of all my endeavours and we now had two sons, Andrew, born in 1957, and Michael, born in 1959, who were a great joy to us. We kept open house and our officers, supporters and councillors were made welcome at all times. We developed a happy team spirit in the Party and were increasingly confident as the election approached.

The national picture was not so rosy. Harold Macmillan had emerged as a great showman. He contrived the answer 'You've never had it so good' to a planted question and this was psychologically damaging to our chances. Even more telling was the campaign against our proposals for further nationalisation, especially of insurance. On doorstep after doorstep we found that the man from the 'Pru' and the other companies were pursuing their own line of propaganda. It was a classic case of political policy being presented without any thought to the hostile forces that would be unleashed and with no consideration given to means of rebutting such tactics. We left ourselves open to sucker punches. Another cause of concern was the London bus strike of the TGWU led by Frank Cousins. After seven weeks of getting nowhere the strike collapsed, causing more political damage. Just before polling day we had reason for some optimism. Personally, Hugh Gaitskell was having a good campaign. One national newspaper reported that the Tory lead in the polls had evaporated but that there were far too many 'don't knows'. In the last three days, however, these voters came off the perch in droves and settled for the Tories. My party workers were confident to the end. They thought we could hold All Saints. Brenda, who is the best canvasser I know, knew better. She always knocks on the doors very assiduously, chats to the voters and makes her own assessment. She is unfailingly accurate. 'I don't like the smell of this election', she told me.

Polling day proved to be disastrous for our organisation. Early in the day a photographer from the *Evening Despatch* called at our committee room and wanted a good 'front page picture' for the newspaper. We had a very elderly voter, a lady in her 90s, who agreed to be photographed with me at the polling station. My agent wanted me to be exclusively on the loudspeaker and refused to listen to reason about the need to be seen on thousands of front pages. I went off to get the picture and when I returned he had disappeared, where to I never discovered. I had no choice but to alter my plans and assume control of the central committee room until an officer of the Constituency Party arrived at tea time and was amazed to find himself placed in charge with a list of instructions for the knockers-up as they reported for duty, leaving me to tour the streets. My election address was one of the best I have ever produced. The back page was taken up with a picture of me in refereeing kit, designed to illustrate my sporting interests. One or two of my opponents toured the public houses saying 'It is no good voting for him, he is never here, he is always away playing football'. It had some effect among the incredulous. Finally, and most damaging of all, on polling night BBC television ran the last instalment of *Spy Catcher*, a thriller serial watched by half the nation. All would be revealed. It ran from 7.30 until 8.15 and the polls closed at nine o'clock. At school after school I had reports of queues of people who had watched the serial and then gone out to vote. Scores of them were locked out at nine, unable to cast their votes.

After the polls closed I returned home for a quick bath and for something to eat before going to the count at the Council House. When I got there I found that my agent had agreed to the disqualification of 76 spoiled papers. I asked to see them: at least 60 were marked in my favour with the figure 1 against my name, the figure 2 for my opponent, John Hollingsworth, instead of with an X. It was too late to complain, the decision had been taken. I lost by 20 votes after two recounts and several checks. At first I was losing by 6, then I was winning by 2, then losing by 8, then 12, then 20. On the advice of Harold Nash, Birmingham's most astute political organiser, I decided to call it a day. The official result was: J.H. Hollingsworth (Conservative) 17,235; D. Howell (Labour) 17,215; Majority 20; Spoiled papers 76. Thoughts of Kipling sprang to mind: 'If you can meet with triumph and disaster ...' How true, how true! They may be impostors but they are also very real.

We went back to our headquarters and tried to comfort our supporters. They were shattered. Brenda and I did our best to console them and to assure them that they could not have done more, which was their main cause of concern – 'Just another 20 votes', they kept saying, 'we should have got them out'. We returned home to lick our wounds and to contemplate the future; a family suddenly bereft of income, with no redundancy pay of any sort and the need to rebuild a new career until another opportunity presented itself to get me back into Parliament.

After a few hours' rest, I received two early morning calls. The first was from Woodrow Wyatt, whom I had displaced four years earlier. He showed a genuine concern, and told me 'You must not reproach yourself, this defeat is in no way your fault'. We were very touched by this kind gesture. The second call was from the *Birmingham Mail* asking me to write an article for early publication analysing why we had lost and where the Party went from here. It was a depressing task but one that needed to be undertaken. It seems to me nearly 30 years on, after three electoral defeats, that I was saying much the same then as Neil Kinnock is saying now: 'How can we readjust our approach to meet a continuing prosperity, a rising generation who demand ever-higher standards from life and yet at the same time project a sense of moral purpose which, in this country at any rate, should be the basis of all political thought?'

As we reflected upon our situation we were naturally anxious for I now had no income of any sort and very little immediate prospects of work, and we had a mortgage to meet and a family to keep. The bank manager wrote a letter drawing our attention to the fact and telling us that we should not cash any more cheques until we had met. We never met – I changed our account to another bank with a more understanding manager. Brenda received a couple of nasty telephone calls but in the main the Party and the good people of Birmingham, whatever their politics, were kind and sympathetic. During the weekend I received an appreciative and understanding call from Hugh Gaitskell, to whom I had written expressing my strong belief that his leadership in the campaign deserved much better than the result we had provided for him. He was coming to Cannock in a few days to speak at their rally and wondered if I would meet him in Birmingham off the train and ferry him to and from Cannock. This gave us the opportunity to discuss the underlying reasons for the Party's defeat and I told him what I had found on the doorstep. Macmillan's 'You've never had it so good' had been a winning slogan while our proposal to nationalise insurance had turned every insurance collector into a Tory canvasser, backed by the absurd interpretation by friend and foe alike of Clause 4 of the Party Constitution: 'To secure for the workers by hand or by brain the full fruits of their industry and the most equitable distribution thereof that may be possible upon the basis of the common ownership of the means of production, distribution and exchange, and the best obtainable system of popular administration and control of each industry or service'. We allowed our opponents to use it for bogey man purposes as though we intended to take over every business in the land and our extreme left wing to use it as a symbol of their political virility.

Hugh was much concerned about our personal situation and told me that he would give some thought to the matter and see if he could come up with any ideas. It was not until the publication of Hugh Dalton's private diaries that I discovered that he had indeed already done so. Dalton records a conversation with Roy Jenkins during the weekend after the election which indicates that Hugh Gaitskell was thinking along the lines of appointing me as the Party's Youth Officer or, possibly, the Secretary of the Parliamentary Labour Party. However, within two or three weeks I was relieved to receive a visit from an Indian businessman who owned a plastics factory. He wanted some-one to assume responsibility for his business and invited me to take up the position. It was a very generous gesture and I accepted but it was obvious from the start that there were going to be difficulties. The business had no proper sales organisation, and orders from the motor car trade were very haphazard. The production side was efficient but there was no co-ordination with the administration. It was very much a personal business and I soon discovered that there was little chance of the owner handing over any of his powers. After two or three months I decided to resign.

This caused me to undergo a deep personal appraisal of my situation, and of any qualities I thought I possessed which might be useful in the business of earning a living. I decided to enter the world of public relations creating an organisation which I could operate from my home, and made a public announcement to this effect. Soon I had taken on three clients. The first of these was Mr Joe Wheeler, the local book-maker. He arrived in a large car wearing an enormous fur coat. Joe was a very respected and warm-hearted man. He told me, 'For 30 years I have been illegitimate but now Parliament has decided to make betting lawful I want someone to tell me how to go legal'. He was my first client and I have been grateful to him ever since. Then I got a call from Gerry Hooke, who had a successful advertising agency specialising in house sales. I was very impressed with the quality of his work and we decided to form a partnership, to be called Howell-Hooke Public Relations, to run alongside my own newly-created business. The third approach I received was from a long-time friend, Neil Nolan, who was a housing developer and he wanted to retain my services for his firm, Alumwell Properties.

Thus established I applied for membership of the Institute of Public Relations and energetically entered into my new world of business activity. Our personal financial crisis was over and I could begin to take a slightly more detached view of politics from the vantage point of a more secure financial position. Whatever the future was to hold I was determined that never again would I expose my family to the dangers of being left with no means of support other than a par-liamentary salary. I have never regretted that decision. It has provided me with the constant reassurance that political life is best conducted with a degree of financial independence. At the same time it has con-firmed my belief that where MPs have to be totally dependent upon their parliamentary salaries then they must be adequately paid, reason-ably provided for in the event of political misfortune, with adequate arrangements for retirement pensions and widows' benefits. Politics is an honourable pursuit and the financial payments for MPs should always reflect that.

5

THE GAITSKELL YEARS

CAMPAIGN FOR DEMOCRATIC SOCIALISM

Hugh Gaitskell's death in 1962 was a devastating blow for all his friends and for the Labour Party. I believe he would have been an outstanding Prime Minister. He possessed all those qualities of intellect and integrity that would have attracted the respect of the whole country, friend and foe alike. Indeed, even though he died two years before the election triumph of 1964, the mark he had made upon the Labour Party and the renewed public support he attracted enabled Harold Wilson and Labour to be returned to office.

From his own friends, personal and political, he drew an intense loyalty and affection. He gave it back in good measure. He also had political nous as well as great clout. Those of us who came to be called 'Gaitskellites' were proud to carry that badge of identification. We would have accepted his leadership through thick and thin, even though there were times when we had reservations. For some people this was over his determination to change Clause 4 of the Labour Party Constitution. Not because they took the ridiculous view that the common ownership of all the means of production, distribution and exchange had to mean nationalisation, which was never the intention of the founding fathers anyway, but because they thought it better to leave well alone. They would have ignored the clause and made policy on a pragmatic basis. Gaitskell believed that he ought to try to change it because any attempt to attract wide support to the Party would be severely handicapped if such a commitment remained in the Constitution, a gift to our opponents. Others, including myself, were shocked when he abandoned the European cause in which we strongly believed. He did it almost overnight and without consulting any of us. It was pretty clear that although he had no great feel for Europe, and was very much a Commonwealth man, he was also repairing bridges with many trade unionists, particularly Frank Cousins, the general secretary of the Transport and General Workers' Union. They made common cause to good cause to good effect in terms of Hugh's leadership but it was a rare mistake of judgment. It had taken the Party 25 years to realise that our membership of the European Community was inevitable and that we had better come to terms with it.

We were never slavish in our devotion to Hugh but we knew he represented everything in which we believed, everything that could be called democratic socialism. As he was to show over the defence issue he would never desert the movement. He would stay and fight in the moments of dark despair.

So we formed the Campaign for Democratic Socialism, or CDS as it became known. The first intimation I received was a telephone call from Roy Jenkins telling me that some of Hugh's friends had got together and talked over the disastrous 1960 Party Conference decision to go unilateral. This was the conference at which Gaitskell had made his great 'fight and fight again to save the Party we love' speech. It remains the most courageous and inspiring speech of my time in politics. Gaitskell knew the block votes would defeat him but he refused to rest until the decision was reversed. Roy asked me to help. I agreed without hesitation. The meeting to establish the organisation took place on a Sunday morning at a public house in Chelsea. The small upstairs room was packed. Together with Roy there was a full turn-out of Gaitskell's friends: Tony Crosland, Patrick Gordon-Walker, Douglas Jay, Jack Diamond as well as Frank Pickstock and Ron Davis from Oxford, Bill Rodgers and Dick Taverne. The name of our group was soon decided and after some debate we agreed that we needed a 'manifesto' upon which we could campaign. Philip Williams, a Fellow of Nuffield College, took charge and he and a few of the group soon produced an excellent draft which was signed by 20 of us chosen to represent a broad cross-section of the movement. We became known as the 'Manifesto Group'.

A little later the left wing of the Party formally announced the creation of their 'Victory for Socialism' group to which we retorted that we represented victory for sanity! They were considerably annoyed.

Jack Diamond took on the fund-raising and as the response to our manifesto came flooding in we realised that our initiative was meeting a widespread need. Offices were found in Red Lion Square and Bill Rodgers was asked to take on the responsibility of becoming the central organiser. I was asked if I would also work for CDS, organising throughout the country. Since my own new-found business was beginning to grow, I was happy to do so. Hugh Gaitskell invited me to come down to London and with Bill Rodgers sitting in the rear of his car we drove round and round Hyde Park and Regent's Park discussing the prospects. We then moved on to meet Bill Webber, the general secretary of the Transport and Salaried Staff Association, at their headquarters, and Webber agreed to take on responsibility for the trade union side of CDS. We were in business. A newsletter, *Campaign*, was launched, and as Party members and trade unionists joined us we soon had a nationwide list of supporters anxious to help and to become active. These were to become the assault troops of our fight-back. Bill Rodgers did a superb job at headquarters and I travelled the country establishing support groups and meeting trade unionists, urging them to take action to reverse the unilateralist decision.

At Edinburgh Willie Hannah got together an excellent group. I met them in an hotel and by coincidence Sarah Barker, the first-class national agent of the Labour Party, was also staying there, meeting the executive of the Scottish Party. She told me, 'I don't know whether I ought to be seen with you in public', but her smile and good wishes expressed a sense of relief that at last something was being done to maintain the Party as an effective electoral force. The Scottish group became our most active and successful unit. In Birmingham news came through that the metal mechanics were doubtful. I met their executive one Sunday morning after one of their meetings. We talked in a pub about the fate of the armed forces facing an enemy who possessed nuclear weapons if we did not, a question raised by one of their number who had a son who was serving in the forces. The discussion concentrated our talk upon the fundamental issue before the Party and when we broke up I knew they would vote for Gaitskell, as they did.

Around the country, at meeting after meeting, both in the Party itself and at regional gatherings of the unions we organised fringe meetings and other discussions with regional officers of the unions, as well as with friendly regional secretaries of the Party such as Jim Cattermole in Nottingham. By these means we built up our list of supporters – we did not have any membership – and Bill Rodgers kept in regular touch with them. The most loyal and coherent group of members came from the ranks of Labour councillors right across the country. They really were splendid in their support and their involvement in our cause. They knew all the constituency activists who we could rely upon and those we could not. Putting all this together we were able to predict constituency by constituency, union by union, how the vote would go at Party Conference.

As dramatic as the 1960 conference had been, our success in the following year by overturning that decision turned despair into relief. We had in fact 'saved the Party we loved'. On the day of decision our cause was tremendously assisted by Aneurin Bevan, now the Party foreign affairs spokesman, who made a vital and courageous speech in which he asked the dramatic question: 'Do you want to send me naked into the conference chamber?'. It turned out to be his last great speech to the Party Conference. Many of his friends were distraught but it was a tremendous contribution towards the Party's future success. It resulted in many of us becoming new admirers.

SMALL HEATH BY-ELECTION

During the year of bitter controversy over the unilateral issue a parliamentary vacancy arose in Birmingham when Ted Wheeldon, the
Member for Small Heath, died after a long illness. Labour's fortunes
could hardly have been at a lower ebb. There was an immediate speculation as to whether we would be fielding a multilateralist or a unilateralist as our candidate. A good loyal moderate, Jack Davis, was
chairman of the constituency. The secretary, however, was a member
of the Co-operative Party, as Ted Wheeldon had been, and was certainly to the left of Jack Davis. As soon as news of a pending by-
election broke, Gaitskellite members began to call upon the chairman,
suggesting that in view of my narrow defeat at All Saints, my leading
role in the CDS and my prominence in Birmingham politics, I was the
natural candidate for the seat. Active among these was the chairman of
the Youth Section, Graham Rea. As the seat had been sponsored by
the Co-operative Party since the war and they had ploughed much
money into it their members understandably believed that they had
claim to the candidature. They too had to make a choice between
putting forward a unilateralist or multilateralist candidate.

A key person in all these deliberations was Harold Nash, the agent
for the Birmingham Borough party. He was easily the most experienced
organiser in the city's political life and extremely shrewd. Harold had
another great virtue, a determination to win elections. He was soon
expressing the view, to Gaitskell among others, that he believed in
'horses for courses'. Although he and I did not always see eye to eye
he was firmly of the opinion that I would be the best Gaitskellite
candidate around and, in his view, a multilateralist candidate was
essential if we were to retain the seat after all the political turmoil
suffered by the Party. Hugh Gaitskell discussed all this with me on the
telephone. I told him that I thought we had enough support to win the
seat but the one danger would be if the Co-operative Party fielded a
candidate who was a unilateralist. Although most of their members
were multilateral, they might well feel themselves to be committed to
their man, whoever he was. Hugh was obviously concerned about this
and promised to discuss the situation with Jim Peddie, the Co-operative
Party chairman. When they made their choice it turned out to be Arthur
Palmer, who had also lost his seat in the 1959 election. He was certainly
no unilateralist. The Harold Wilson wing of the Party was represented
by Arthur Bottomley, also a previous Member who had been defeated
in the 1959 election. The choice lay between us three.

There was a very full turn-out of the delegates for the selection
conference, with many more trade unionists attending than was normally the case in Birmingham. The interest and commitment of everyone present created an atmosphere of considerable tension since this
by-election was to be the first major test of Gaitskell's leadership
following the Party Conference. I was delighted to get a majority of

votes over all the other candidates on the first ballot. I had told the conference that if they selected me I would fight on a straight Gaitskell ticket of multilateralism and moderation, but I would also fight an energetic campaign on other issues of immediate importance to the electors: housing, education, health and social services. I knew that I carried with me the hopes of all those who believed in the party that Hugh Gaitskell led. It was a big responsibility.

Following my selection as a candidate there was a lot of speculation within Birmingham as to how Harold Nash and I would team up. We were both known to have forthright views as to how campaigns should be conducted even though we usually managed to reconcile them. Harold Nash soon raised these issues with me. 'You are well-known for wanting to be the agent as well as the candidate', he told me. 'That's not going to work in this election!' I told him that I had never been fortunate enough to have an agent like him and that I had no problems about leaving the organisation totally in his hands, but as he also had strong views on political subjects I hoped he would be happy to leave me in charge of that area of the campaign. The deal was done and we shook hands on it; each of us would stick to our last, and so we did.

When Harold Nash and I sat down to plan the campaign we soon decided that although I was going to fight a down-the-line Gaitskell campaign we also had to unify the Party as far as we possibly could. We would present a broad platform at a wide range of public meetings. The left would be represented by friends such as Julius Silverman, the Member for Erdington, whose views differed widely from mine on foreign policy and defence but with whom I had shared a long personal friendship. Julius spoke at our first public meeting. In those days it was not the practice of party leaders to appear at by-elections but I had a photograph taken with Hugh Gaitskell which was to be one of the main features of my election literature so that no one had any doubt as to my own political stance. We agreed that the presence of Harold Wilson would be of considerable help. He came and his meeting succeeded admirably in achieving a unified campaign.

My two opponents were Bernard Williams (Conservative) and William Kirk (Liberal). When polling day was fixed for 23 March we were soon locked into an energetic election. The Liberal concentrated on voters who lived in very poor homes. These were the first municipal flats to be built in Birmingham and had well outlived their usefulness. The Tory made what he could of the defence issue and then started to develop the theme of immigration, the first time that this issue had been raised in an electoral context. My father, who was well into his 80s, was taken ill and admitted to hospital almost as soon as the campaign proper got underway. I visited him for a short time every day and he died some eight days before polling. Bill Kirk, the Liberal candidate, immediately announced that as a mark of respect he would cease to campaign until after my father's funeral and this was followed by a similar announcement from the Conservative, gestures which represented the best side of political life. The campaign came back to life for the last five days. When we resumed I began to get questions on the immigration issue. I was able to counter these by telling how my own father in his final illness had been wonderfully cared for by his nurses – all of them on his ward had been black – as had every other patient there. This line of questioning soon petered out.

Polling day dawned with our confidence riding high. The voters seemed to be responding well to our Gaitskell campaign although we had no opinion poll to tell us the result before it happened. This is a practice, incidentally, of which I do not approve – I am convinced that it does affect the course of elections and detracts from serious consideration of the issues. Harold Nash's organisation was superb: every house had been canvassed at least twice and on the day he had an agent for each ward supervising an agent for each polling district. All of these were full-time Labour agents. Oh, that the Party could field such a team these days! Party workers came in from every part of the country, my own union bringing in several busloads. I doubt whether any supporters not yet recorded as having voted by our checkers on the schools were knocked up less than three times. It was an absolute copy-book campaign. The result met all our expectations. Harry Parkinson, the deputy Town Clerk who had declared my defeat in 1959 had a different song to sing this time when, accompanied by the Lord Mayor, he announced the result: D. Howell (Labour) 12,182; B. Williams (Conservative) 5,923; W. Kirk (Liberal) 2,476; Majority 6,259. In spite of all the activity it was a low poll – 42 per cent – no doubt representing the hesitations of many of our people to return to the fold. The immigration issue also had a bearing but, in fact, I had increased our majority.

We returned to the city where Harold had arranged a 'victory party' for the workers. They were jubilant, all their energies and devotions justified. As I walked through the door Hugh Gaitskell rang; in a voice full of emotion he said, 'My dear boy, what a wonderful result, you have turned the tide'. There was little that I could say, for I was too full of emotion to speak. It was a very short conversation but a most moving moment for me. I returned to the celebrations and the interviews and finally to Brenda, who had splendidly combined the job of campaigning with that of caring for Andrew and Michael, visiting my father in hospital and helping to comfort my mother. Later on Harold Wilson was to declare that 'The Small Heath election was the first step towards success at the 1964 General Election'. It was a tribute to the whole of our campaign team.

The following Tuesday, accompanied by Brenda and my mother, I left Birmingham to take my seat. The photographers were busy; it was very different from 1955 for this time I had two sponsors and we all had to rehearse our parts for the moment Mr Speaker called, 'New Members desirous of taking the Oath come forward'. Supported by

Roy Jenkins and Charles Howell (no relation), the Member for Perry Barr, Birmingham and the West Midlands regional Whip, I was welcomed back.

The opinion polls began to show gathering support for the Party and these were helped by two more Gaitskellite by-election victories, both won by prominent CDS candidates. We rallied round in both to reproduce the enthusiasms and the success of my own campaign, and I spent weeks working in each constituency. At Lincoln, Dick Taverne was our standard-bearer and he proved an ideal candidate for the cathedral city. At Stockton, Bill Rodgers was selected and here again he achieved a considerable victory in spite of a strong unilateral element within his party. Like me, both Dick and Bill owed much to Hugh Gaitskell and to the Party and they made a fine contribution towards our future success. It is sad that 20 years on they did not find it possible to emulate Gaitskell's own precept to 'fight and fight again to save the Party we love'.

TRAGEDY

The Party was now approaching the possibility of Government. Three by-election victories were doing wonders for our morale. By contrast the Tories were running into difficulties. There was a long way to go but we had the feeling that we were on the move. My return to Parliament brought an unexpected invitation from Gaitskell to make my first front bench speech. It was a debate on sport, the Wolfenden Committee's Report. The Wolfenden Committee had been set up by the Central Council for Physical Recreation and its principal proposal was that a Sports Council should be established by the Government. The debate took place on 28 April 1961. That day determined that for the next 30 years I would be leading from either the Opposition or the Government front bench whenever questions of sport were before the House. I talked about the importance of developing a philosophy for sport and leisure provision, welcomed the proposal for creating a Sports Council and dealt with a number of current controversies affecting sport. My speech took some 30 minutes. I have always felt a great sense of satisfaction that this major signpost in my political life was given to me by my hero, Hugh Gaitskell.

However, for Hugh and for Nye Bevan, fate was taking a very different turn. Increasingly they were becoming a formidable team; although they remained very different in style and convictions, they worked well together in the House and in the country. Tragedy struck. First Nye Bevan developed a terrible stomach cancer from which he never recovered. We were all distressed: whether we agreed with him or not, and even though his extravagant behaviour sometimes caused dismay, he was a giant of the movement. The void he left was only fully appreciated when we came to elect his successor. This caused much heart-searching but eventually George Brown was chosen as the safest of candidates. But worse was to follow. Hugh Gaitskell was struck down with a mystery illness. He began to look terrible. A spell in the Manor House Hospital where Dr Dick Mabon MP was on the staff produced little improvement and no diagnosis. Gaitskell was due to go to Russia. It was arranged that Mabon would accompany him but the trip was cancelled. Hugh's condition deteriorated and he was admitted to the Middlesex Hospital where he died some days later. After his death it was disclosed that he had suffered from Lupus disease, which attacks all the organs of the body. Massive doses of steroids failed to halt the spread of this disease and his death became inevitable. A true friend and mentor and a great leader was gone.

The campaign to elect a new party leader was traumatic. George Brown was the favoured candidate of the right. His campaign was managed by Gerry Reynolds MP, who had been the local party government officer until entering Parliament, assisted by Patrick Gordon-Walker and myself. There were considerable doubts among some of the CDS supporters, both inside and outside the House. George was not overwhelmingly attractive to many of our friends, his weaknesses being too well-known, but he had one of the best brains I have ever encountered in politics, untrained but precise and decisive. He was totally demanding of his friends and unforgiving of his opponents and largely unforgiven by them. The principal challenge came from Harold Wilson, whose mastery of parliamentary debate and of economic matters had added to the reputation he had gained as Attlee's youngest Cabinet Minister. He was, however, not trusted on our side – a legacy from Hugh Gaitskell's known views – but in terms of all possible leaders he was going to take a lot of beating. When he chose George Wigg as his campaign manager we knew we were in for a fight. Wigg was the MP for Dudley who came into Parliament in 1945 straight from service in the Army Education Corps. He was not so much left wing as Machiavellian. He certainly had no time for George Brown and we knew he would be active, not only in organising the election for Harold Wilson, but in exercising his powers of invention, which were considerable. This he did to good effect, keeping us constantly engaged in correcting or counteracting his stories.

Jim Callaghan was the third candidate and he started with the support of many of the Welsh Members. As time went by he gained others and also attracted a following of English and Scottish colleagues. He was aided in this by Wigg, who wanted to switch as many votes as he could to Jim and away from George. Gerry Reynolds, Patrick and I wanted to be left alone to run our campaign, free from George's intervention, but this proved impossible. Brown was rude to the doubters; we would try to get him to go home early but he resisted. However, we did succeed from time to time in getting him to retire to the smoke room where in fact he took very little drink. However, when Wigg saw George there, behaving and drinking perfectly modestly, he would set off after

Callaghan supporters and waverers and say, 'Put your nose in the smoke room, Brown is at it again!'. However, he did suggest to me that the future leadership had to be either Wilson or Brown or the reverse order. It proved to be the former.

LEISURE FOR LIVING

Harold Wilson's leadership started off at a cracking pace as we looked at issues that had rarely been examined before at a political level, technology being the prime example. When he decided to look at leisure provision, especially sport and the arts, I was enthusiastic and readily agreed to join the working party dealing with sport which was chaired by Bill Mallalieu, the Huddersfield MP who won a rugby blue at Oxford, played soccer and was a good cricketer. Bill wrote very well indeed for several newspapers, including a sports column for the *Financial Times*. He married Rita Tinn, the daughter of the famous Portsmouth Football Club manager. Bill, or 'Curly' as he was called, had served in the Navy with a good friend of mine, Bruce Normansell, who entered the Birmingham City Council on the same day as myself and who, later on, joined the board of Aston Villa. Bill did convoy duty on the run to Murmansk and out of that experience he wrote one of the finest war books, *Very Ordinary Seaman*. We started with the Wolfenden Committee Report which we had already debated in the House. This report led on to Government involvement in sport although it took a few years to mature. It helped to produce the rather eccentric announcement that Quintin Hogg, now Lord Hailsham, would answer questions on sport for the Government. As Quintin was responsible for almost everything for which there was no specific ministerial responsibility, such as the North-east, no one expected much from that pronouncement.

Wolfenden had recommended the creation of a Sports Council and Mallalieu was keen to adopt this proposal. I had endorsed this view in the debate, from the front bench, but I was well aware that many of the governing bodies of sport, through the Central Council of Physical Recreation to which they all belonged, might well oppose the idea of any political involvement in their affairs. Bill Mallalieu had no such doubts. I thought it right to drop a note to Harold Wilson explaining the dangers inherent in the proposal. It proved to be a significant letter. The principal aims of the working party were:

1. To establish a Sports Council of Great Britain accountable to Parliament through the Minister of Education with an initial sum of not less than £5 million ... and thereafter such annual sums as would enable it to do its job adequately. The report itself described in some detail what the job would be and laid considerable emphasis upon the social importance of sport.
2. To preserve what remained of the natural beauty of Britain and to

make the enjoyment of it more widely available to all. We quoted the words of W.H. Auden:

> 'The trees encountered on a country stroll
> Reveal a lot about a country's soul . . .
> A culture is no better than its woods.'

3. To increase the power of the National Parks Commission. It would be the chief agency in this urgent task.
4. To take determined action to deal with the serious problem of pollution of rivers and coastal waters. Inland waterways could and would be used more fully for public enjoyment.
5. To take decisions on the out-of-date laws relating to licensing, betting and Sunday observance which inhibited leisure. These matters would, of course, be decided by free votes in Parliament.
6. The arts. The principle of public patronage of the arts had long been accepted and the amount of financial support would be reviewed realistically so that the institutions essential to a civilised community – museums, galleries, opera – could plan ahead for a period of at least five years.
7. Expenditure on the arts was to be increased by at least £3 to £4 million a year and industrial patronage would be encouraged by tax concessions for suitable forms of patronage.
8. A substantial section of 'Leisure for Living' was to be devoted to architectural design and historic buildings (remember that this was some 20 years ahead of current controversies).
9. Theatre, music and cinema depended upon co-operation between Government and local authorities. The next Labour Government would implement the proposal to establish a National Theatre which would be expected to serve the provinces as well as London.

The arts side of the working party was chaired by Tom Driberg, who did an excellent job. The whole 'Leisure for Living' project was chaired by Tony Greenwood, a member of Labour's National Executive. In my judgment 'Leisure for Living' still represents the best political statement about the importance of providing leisure facilities for all of our people, enabling them to exercise choice from the availability of arts, sport, recreation, countryside and water-based amenities. Sometimes when I am pressed to define my socialism I will do so in ethical terms as a Christian socialist and in material terms as a William Morris socialist. That is to say that I believe the provision of warmth and colour and gaiety and choice to be the ultimate expression of a philosophy for life which we should seek to achieve. 'Leisure for Living' comes very close to these ideals.

HOUSE AND HOME

Getting back to work in the House of Commons after my by-election was like a return to a first love. The general atmosphere within the Party was much more cordial and relaxed and it was enjoyable to be an Opposition backbencher in those days. Our policies were looking good and prospects of victory improved hugely after Harold Macmillan had been dispossessed in favour of Alec Douglas-Home who is, as I well know, a very fine person but an indifferent television performer. One issue of considerable importance was the David Rhydderch affair, which involved the chairmanship of two Birmingham hospitals for the mentally ill, Hollymoor and Rubery. Rhydderch was a very good friend of mine, national treasurer of my own trade union and a most dedicated, if aggressive, chairman of these ill-equipped hospitals. He was also a member of the Regional Hospital Board. The nursing staff supported him wholeheartedly. The doctors took a different view. They carried their opposition to the Minister of Health, Enoch Powell, and he ordered an independent Enquiry.

Undoubtedly, the case which brought the whole issue to a head involved a teenaged female patient at Hollymoor who should never have been in hospital at all. There was no medical reason for keeping her locked up there, but there was nowhere else for her to go. David Rhydderch determined to get her transferred to more suitable accommodation but the doctors procrastinated for months. When he found that she was still there Rhydderch exploded. The doctors wanted to have the girl certified as a mental defective. Rhydderch was having none of that, it was 'monstrous', and he had every right to involve himself because the law then placed such a responsibility upon members of the Hospital Management Committee. David Rhydderch achieved publicity for the case with the result that eventually the girl was transferred to a more suitable home and subsequently married happily and brought up a family. David Rhydderch had been right, but his victory rankled with doctors. He was never forgiven and some of them were determined to see him out of office.

The Enquiry lasted weeks and the press was full of details of the dispute. It produced a highly critical and, in my opinion, grotesquely unfair judgment on my friend. Enoch Powell acted to remove Rhydderch from office. We debated the matter in the House in July 1962. The case against Rhydderch was that he had created a supply committee without a member of the medical staff serving upon it; he had built a new dormitory without their approval and that he had built two villas in the hospital grounds as well as a new chiropody department without consulting the medical superintendent. No doubt all this was unwise but it hardly justified a semi-judicial Enquiry sitting four weeks and costing many thousands of pounds. As I said in my contribution to the debate, he was a man who was too big for most of the people around him.

The principal attack on David Rhydderch in this extraordinary debate was led by another Birmingham MP, Leslie Seymour (Sparkbrook) who was also a member of the same hospital committee. He astonished us all by concluding his speech with the statement that he had already offered his services as chairman to replace Rhydderch. I was able to reveal in my own speech that Seymour had been a member of the Regional Hospital Board for many years and had one of the worst attendance records of any member. I described his offer as an 'effrontery'. I disclosed to the House that not all the doctors opposed Rhydderch. The Deputy Medical Officer of Health for Birmingham, Dr Nicol, sat on the hospital committee. He objected to the course that other doctors had taken in their campaign to get rid of their chairman, so the Hollymoor doctors contrived to get rid of him too – and succeeded. Another doctor, Dr Orwin, who also supported Rhydderch, received a letter from the Medical Superintendent, Dr Mathers, telling him 'This is to let you know that unless I hear you have resigned your membership before then I propose to move a resolution at the next meeting of the group medical committee that you no longer be admitted to membership'. I told the House that at the end of the day the Enquiry had to decide whether it preferred the behaviour of Rhydderch or Mathers. It chose the latter, a triumph for conservative medical politics.

The case took up a great deal of my time. I became involved in it through my personal friendship with David Rhydderch and my interest in hospital matters, but I learned one more lesson: it is no good pursuing good causes in Parliament unless you become thoroughly immersed in them. This meant spending a great deal of time with Rhydderch and his colleagues, helping to liaise with his solicitor, George Jonas, who is also my own legal adviser and close friend, and persuading a parliamentary colleague, Arthur Irvine QC, later on to become the Solicitor General, to take on the case. At the end of the day, although the formal verdict went against David Rhydderch, I believe that we won the parliamentary debate and vindicated his reputation.

My other big campaign in this Parliament was the Leasehold Bill which I introduced following my good fortune in drawing first place in the ballot for Private Members' Bills. It was the only occasion throughout my time in Parliament that I have drawn one of the six places which guarantee a whole day of parliamentary time to promote such a Bill. Mr Speaker conducted the draw but I was not present. On my arrival at the House I found myself besieged by messages from representatives of every manner of cause and organisation, pressing me to adopt Bills already drafted for presentation to the lucky Members who could be persuaded to take up their cause. Others assured me that they would provide lawyers and draftsmen if I would take up their campaigns. On these occasions the Members winning such an opportunity can choose one of two courses. They can find out from various Ministries, usually through the Whips' office, if there is any departmental business they cannot get into the Government's own programme, or they can use the full day available for a Second Reading debate to boost some great cause. I did not take long to make my choice. The first alternative often produces some useful Bills which become Acts of Parliament because they have full Government support. However, I always feel that it is rather sharp practice for a Private Member to use such desperately short time to transact Government business. So I chose the second alternative for my Bill, and proposed legislation to tackle the problem of leaseholds.

This was becoming very acute in Birmingham as well as in South Wales. Whole estates built at the latter end of the 19th century were now reaching the end of their 99-year leases. The ground landlords had issued leases for quite small annual ground rents, but not only were the home-owners faced with losing their houses, often having spent a lot of money upon repairs, improvements and renovations, but under the provision of 'dilapidations' they were required to hand back the property to the landlord in its original state. It was a pernicious system and caused great distress. I was getting more and more complaints in my own constituency in the Small Heath, Bordesley Green and Saltley areas and I had made a number of speeches urging that owner occupiers should be granted the right not only to own the house in which they lived but also the land upon which it was built. My theme produced an immediate and enthusiastic response. The position in South Wales at that time was even more critical because their estates had been built just before ours in Birmingham. I announced my intention to introduce my Leasehold Bill to much acclaim from my friends and fierce opposition from those with entrenched vested interests. Letters of support reached avalanche proportions, and I was inundated with requests for articles and radio interviews. My Bill was a source of hope for thousands of victims of this system but it was obvious that I was taking on some of the biggest vested interests in the land. I relished the prospect.

The first task was to find someone to assist me in the planning and drafting of the Bill. There were no funds available for such a purpose. I had the greatest good fortune to enlist the aid of Sir Frank Soskice QC, the Member for Newport, Monmouthshire. He had been Solicitor General in the Attlee Government and a good friend and enthusiast throughout the Gaitskell campaign. Frank was a gentleman and a fine colleague. When I approached him for help on the legal side he never hesitated, although he knew better than I did the amount of detailed work to which he was committing himself. He always waved away my appreciation by saying 'This is for my people in South Wales as well as for yours in Birmingham'. Night after night Frank and I would walk back from the House to his chambers in the Temple. There he would bring up the problems one by one and ask 'What do you want me to say about that?' I would tell him my solution to each problem he raised and we would then discuss it and refine or amend it. Then I would sit quietly while Frank got down to the drafting. It was an excellent experience in itself to be involved in the drafting of such a Bill and my debt to Frank was immense. We tried to provide for every eventuality. Who would have the right to enjoy enfranchisement? How would this right be exercised? What would be the formula for fixing the price? What about the fag end of leases? Did I want to prevent the sharks from moving in to buy up the old leases? Sometimes he did not agree with me and then he would demur quietly and with deference, 'It is your Bill, I will do whatever you wish me to'. Finally, we produced a draft Bill that stated our purpose and which could be presented to the House with sincerity and defended with fervour. I presented the Bill on 21 November and the names of its supporters were impressive: Jim Callaghan, George Thomas and Desmond Donnelly represented Welsh interests along with Frank Soskice, Dick Marsh, Arthur Skeffington, Bob Mellish and Neil MacDermot.

The date I chose for Second Reading was the earliest available to me – Friday 7 December. We did not expect to win: opposition was too entrenched within the Government and too evident on their benches. We intended to awake a national campaign which would lead to a total commitment by a future Labour Government and that is exactly what happened. When Labour fought the 1964 election a commitment to legislate for leasehold enfranchisement had a prominent place in our manifesto and the new Government gave it priority in its programme. In my own constituency thousands of families benefited. I set up residents' associations and introduced lawyers, surveyors and estate agents, to provide advice. It remains one of the most satisfying pieces of social work in which I have been involved.

After leasehold there were many other issues for me to take up. One of my constituents was a serving soldier who had died while abroad. His family wanted him brought home for burial but burial abroad was army policy and the family could not afford the costs. The Minister told me that there had been 245 such cases in previous years and that two-thirds of the families had accepted the policy. We were told we should accept this as part of the 'conditions of service'. I was having none of this. When I pointed out that the Americans returned home the bodies of loved ones to their own families he told us that the Americans used their own service freighters. 'We use air trooping companies and I am advised that there would be considerable difficulty in re-negotiating contracts with them to provide for the carriage of freight'. So much for principle! It was a sorry business but it brought a generous offer from a local trust created by an old friend, Harry Payne, who had built up a chain of shoe repair shops in Birmingham. Harry put much of his profits into the trust, which aided many good causes in Birmingham. He responded readily to my approach and the constituent was returned to the sanctuary of his family.

One of my interests was the planning and building of motorways. During the reign of Ernest Marples as Minister of Transport I had made him angry by telling him that we ought to build four-lane motorways, not three. I said that we were building for 100 years ahead and we should have two slow lanes and two fast lanes in which lorries were banned. Marples obviously thought I was ungrateful for all the energy and imagination he put into these 'magnificent feats of civil engineering'. We are still making the same mistakes today. I was able to get an adjournment debate to raise the question of the M5 motorway, especially the nine-mile stretch leading from the M6 and going through the Black Country towns of Oldbury, Smethwick and West Bromwich. Consultants appointed in 1957 produced a proposal three years later that half of this stretch should be a two-tier system, one carriageway going North, the other South, both built above an existing train track. This was in fact the second proposal; an earlier one had been considered and abandoned. Now, with the election approaching, we had another flurry of motorway announcements. All these announcements put a blight upon property and caused very real problems for house-owners wishing to sell their houses. I quoted one such letter which I had received: 'To the Ministry of Transport, five, ten or even twenty years means a great deal'. I proposed that we adopt the continental system whereby 'when the engineers, surveyors and planners have determined what they think should be the route for a motorway, the objections to it ought only to be on grounds of principle, on broad matters of strategy.' I got no change out of the Minister in his reply but it was a useful exercise in drawing attention to a problem needing new thinking. It still does!

One Bill that occupied a great deal of time at the tail end of this Parliament was the Water Resources Bill, which established a Water Resources Board. As a vice-president of the British Waterways Authority I was asked by them to take a special interest in the measure. It created an entirely new structure for the water industry and there was much work to do in committee. When the Bill returned to the floor of the House for the Third Reading I summed up views as follows: 'What the country needs above all else is a grid system for water in the same way that we have a grid system for electricity and gas . . . the Water Resources Board operating under the Bill has no authority at all to transfer water from one area of the country to another in times of drought and need . . . we should have had a new type of authority, so that, in consequence, droughts would have been a thing of the past'. Some years later I was to have good cause to appreciate the prophetic nature of these observations!

In June 1964, almost immediately before the General Election, Bill Mallalieu managed to get some time in the annual debate on supply. He chose to raise the question of leisure and sport. This turned out to be a discussion based upon our policy document 'Leisure for Living' and a Conservative document drawn up in response to it. It was an interesting debate, comprehensively introduced by Bill Mallalieu supported by Tom Driberg. They both urged for the adoption of our proposal to establish a Sports Council. We had committed a future Labour Government to start it off with £5 million a year and Chris Chataway, the distinguished athlete who was then Parliamentary Secretary for Education, made much of this and virtually accused us of vote-catching, omitting to mention that in their document the Conservatives had made a commitment for exactly the same sum of money!

The debate took in the whole field of leisure provision. Many speakers concentrated upon the arts, but all of them agreed that a Sports Council and an Arts Council were two essential requirements in an age of increased leisure time and resources. I wound up from the Opposition front bench regretting that there was 'no appreciation of the need for a coherent strategy in planning for leisure'. Chris Chataway had suggested, as I put it, that 'it was not the duty of the Government to enable people to enjoy themselves'. This touched upon a philosophical view which I had long held, and still do, that while work should be enjoyable, and that all should contribute to society through the work they do, work is not an end in itself. Work provides the means by which one enjoys the higher things of life including sport and the arts.

Tam Dalyell, always a devoted adherent of sport, had drawn attention to the voluntary contribution to sport made by such agencies as the Central Council for Physical Recreation (CCPR). This gave me the opportunity to assert the case for a regional organisation to plan and provide for at least one Olympic-size swimming pool in each region of the country. I denounced as 'grossly inadequate and parsimonious' the sum of £20,000 made available for the British team at the forthcoming Tokyo Olympics. I was also able to pay a tribute to my old mentor, Hugh Dalton, for his work in planning and so eventually providing the Pennine Way, the long-distance walk along the whole length of the Pennine Mountains, which he had announced in 1951. He expected it to be opened the following year, but here we were 12 years later still awaiting its completion. The debate was replied to by Quintin Hogg who was both lord president of the council and Secretary of State for Education and Science. He complained that I had injected party feelings into 'an important subject that ought to be discussed in a relaxed atmosphere'. He proceeded to demonstrate for some 20 minutes why a relaxed approach to this subject had achieved very little and was unlikely to do more in the near future. The debate proved to be another useful forerunner of the growing appreciation of sport and the arts as subjects of importance requiring the involvement of Government. For me, it was a good note on which to end this session of Parliament because it provided Harold Wilson with food for thought, which would pay dividends should he become Prime Minister.

In Birmingham itself Brenda and I could not have been happier. We were surrounded by family and friends both political and otherwise and it was never necessary to distinguish between them. Andy and

Mick were now at nursery school, Kate was born in July 1962 and we were expecting David when the 1964 election was called.

ELECTION 1964

As we approached the election we were happy and confident. The pleasures of our family were matched by the great comradeship we found in our constituency party, led by chairman Jack Davis, who agreed to act as my election agent. His vice-chairman and another great friend of mine – Jim Srawley, became his deputy. The team of constituency officers was completed by John Llewellyn and his wife Sonia and Graham Rea. All of them brought their families into the campaign. There was no building available for our election head-quarters so we found a piece of land and Ken Purnell generously provided a large hut. As always, I believed in getting out to meet the people. No door was left unknocked, and Tom O'Loughlin and I did eight to ten loudspeaker meetings a night, covering almost every street in the constituency.

The response was enthusiastic. Harold Wilson's Birmingham rally was full to overflowing. The lunch-time factory gate meetings arranged by our trade union colleagues saw a remarkable turn-out. There were only two or three hecklers at the joint meeting I held with my next-door neighbour, Roy Jenkins. Harold Wilson's jibe that the Prime Minister made his economic calculations using matchsticks caught on. But the runaway victory that we expected did not materialise. The Tories made a late surge in the polls when the 'don't knows' came down on their side. This scarcely troubled us in Small Heath. Polling day was a great pleasure. I was ordered to be back at headquarters immediately the factory lunch breaks were over and there I found a great spread of food and drink laid out for all our workers. Jack Davis insisted that we must have an hour off, otherwise we would 'kill ourselves'. How wise, and what a relief to know that we could enjoy such a luxury! The Small Heath result was as we expected: D. Howell (Labour) 17,010; A. Prescott (Conservative) 10,233; G. Jelf (Communist) 926; Majority 6,777. The effect of the absence of a Liberal candidate was difficult to assess – my vote increased by about 5,000 and the Tory by 4,300, but the poll was almost double that of the by-election. My majority was up by 500 votes which was the best news for us.

After a brief look in at the city party gathering we took our own workers back home to eat and drink and await the results. We went to bed believing that a Labour Government would be a certainty. On Friday we were in, but it was much, much closer than we had dreamed – 317 seats. However, it was enough for the Queen to send for Harold Wilson to ask him to form a Government. The 13 wasted years were over but before the technological revolution could take off the full extent of the nation's economic plight was revealed. Yet again Labour had been elected to Government at a time of serious national crisis. Nevertheless, the anticipations of office dispelled our forebodings – it was enough to be back in Government. Harold Wilson had delivered the victory that Hugh Gaitskell had made possible.

6

MP REFEREE

AUTHORITY

My greatest distinction as a football referee is that I am the only Member of Parliament to have refereed Football League matches and I am the only Minister of the Crown to have refereed at Wembley! Referees and politicians need the same quality to achieve success: authority. In that sense my two careers complemented each other. A politician who speaks without authority has no force; a referee who does not display authority has no control. On the football field I always regarded the assertion of my authority, and the need to protect it, as vital in any match I ever refereed, from my early days in the parks of Birmingham to important games in the FA Cup. In Britain, thank goodness, we can all rely upon the integrity of our referees. Although authority is the first essential it must be followed by a well-developed sense of judgment with a dash of humour.

No referee should ever allow his decisions to be questioned. If he does so he has surrendered control of the match. I suppose that over the 20 years or so that I refereed soccer matches I disciplined more players for 'dissent', as this offence is known, than for any other misdemeanour. In my time as a League referee I found it necessary to dismiss only five players from the field, two of them in the same match. Another was a player who had the audacity to argue with me a second time after he had already been cautioned for the first offence! Reputation is an important weapon in the armoury of a referee. I found that after this sending off the number of players wishing to argue with me rapidly diminished. There are some wicked fouls committed on the football field, although not nearly as many as some people would have us believe, but no referee can deal with them if he has allowed his authority to be undermined. Referees also have to develop a relationship with players which is easy and relaxed, thus ensuring that the skills and the pleasures of the game can assert themselves. I also disapprove of other methods of dissent such as taking up a position close to the ball when a free kick has been given instead of moving ten yards away as the rules require. This is cheating, and it needs to be stamped out by the football authorities. I once had three players in succession who did this and when I cautioned the third player he solemnly told me, 'It is my turn to cover the free kick'. The manager had arranged a rota!

More difficult still is how to deal with the defensive wall, where a whole line of players encroach within ten yards and refuse to retreat even when ordered by the referee to do so. This is a clear breach of the laws of the game. Referees should take action by indicating the ten-yard position. If the line of players does not take up a proper position at once, they should be dealt with in spite of the numbers. I would also like to see the introduction of the practice used in rugby football whereby the referee advances ten yards up the field every time there is such an encroachment. Sometimes referees are criticised for taking firm action in these situations, which are not considered important compared with other forms of foul play. This is wrong. Football, like most sports, should be continuous. It is no service to the game or to the entertainment of spectators to allow the flow of the match to be interrupted. A team which has been prevented from benefiting from a quick free kick has every right to feel hard done by. So have the spectators. They have been assured of another dose of the stereotyped football which is slowly suffocating our game. Referees should eliminate this, and observers, be they public or press, should fully support them in the greater interests of the game.

Football, like all sport, is there to be enjoyed. At the highest levels of the game it sets standards of excellence which thrill us all, but these days that pleasure is too often regulated by regimental football and pre-ordained match control. These trends are transforming our game from a sport into something more akin to trench warfare, presided over by card-waving referees officiating according to field regulations. We need to reassert the pleasures of the game: good humour, enjoyment and easy but respectful relationships between players and officials.

My early appointments to professional League football were with the Birmingham League. From these I graduated to the Football League in 1951 as a linesman. This was pretty rapid promotion as I had only taken up the whistle during the war in 1942 when I helped to form the Birmingham Sunday League. When I arrived in the Football League I found that I was running the line to such refereeing giants as Arthur Ellis, Reg Leafe and Mervyn Griffiths, my three refereeing heroes. If I did not have a match myself I would go and watch them referee, as well as other first-class officials such as Bill Ling and Alf Bond, the one-armed referee from Fulham. The most important lesson I learned was that each of them was completely different in style and temperament. This never mattered – they were all in control. Ellis was a happy, home-spun Yorkshireman who traded banter with the players but never lost control. Leafe was a serving member of the RAF when I first came across him and there was always something of the serviceman in his approach to his matches. Griffiths was a typical Welshman, a non-conformist headteacher from Newport. The difference in their personalities stood out for all to see but at the end of the match they always left the same impression, one of great competence, easy authority and quiet humour which enabled them to establish good relationships with the players – or, as they say these days, good 'man-management'.

My favourite of all referees was Jim Wiltshire from Dorset. He had retired by the time I made the grade but in the years immediately before and after the war I saw him many times. He had all the qualities I admired, applied with particularly good humour. His exchanges with the players were a joy to watch. He had a natural and easy relationship with them but he never allowed this to undermine his authority. I once said this on a radio programme and he sent me the last copy, tattered and torn, of his own book on refereeing. It is a most treasured possession.

It does a great disservice to the game to try to reduce personality to a common denominator. Managers have been at it for years and it has always ended disastrously. It is not possible to provide in advance for every situation that may arise on the football field, either for players or referees. If it was so then no one would ever turn up to watch the match. Football is played by human beings, not robots. The really successful teams are those who are clearly enjoying themselves, expressing their personality, improvising and asserting their skills, both collectively and as individuals. Football matches between two such teams represent the highest form of sporting experience possible. From the time that I was appointed to the referees' list of the League in 1956, one year after I had become an MP, and was dubbed the MP Referee, until I finally retired ten years later, I was privileged to enjoy most of the games I refereed, but only a handful provided a feeling of ecstasy.

Two of these matches involved the great Tottenham Hotspur team of the 1960s. In one of them, against Burnley at Turf Moor Tottenham fielded Danny Blanchflower, Dave Mackay and Cliff Jones, while Burnley included Jimmy Adamson and Jimmy McIlroy. It was a superb match. There was hardly a foul for the whole 90 minutes, making it possible for me to play the 'advantage rule' continuously throughout the match. The total commitment of the players to a full attendance of spectators, to the quality of football, as well as to their own teams helped to produce a most memorable experience for me. The result was Burnley 2, Tottenham 0 but it really was of no significance compared to the quality of the game itself. Teddy Eden, the Birmingham county secretary, travelled with me to this match. Teddy had given me much encouragement since my early refereeing days. He had a great sense of humour and his unique broadcasting voice was heard regularly in the early days of the BBC *Sports Report* programme. Another guest at the game was Bill Cox, who was to stage a North American Soccer tournament of 16 clubs, each of which had won their own national titles. His presence, and no doubt Teddy Eden's prompting, produced an invitation for me to referee in New York which I accepted.

Another Spurs match I refereed, against Arsenal at Highbury in 1963, produced a totally different but still glorious memory. The result was quite sensational – Arsenal 4, Tottenham 4. There were more people locked out of the ground than were able to get into it. I have never known such a sensation as I walked on to the field. The noise was deafening. I realised then the meaning of the expression 'I can't hear myself think'. I needed to breathe deeply and to re-discover myself and my sense of command before blowing my whistle to summon the two captains. The fact that I had difficulty in hearing the sound of my own whistle, so great was the noise, added to the feeling of intimidation that sportsmen experience. Certainly no footballer or referee can succeed at the highest levels of the game unless he is able to achieve total control of all his senses under such circumstances. Both teams were at the top of the League. At half-time the visitors were 4–2 in front, but in the second half Arsenal began to come back into the match. Tottenham defended desperately, causing me to add on two minutes for time wasted. A lengthy injury added another two minutes. When the big clock at Highbury showed 90 minutes played I still had another four minutes to go on my watch. The din from the Spurs supporters was incredible when, in the first minute of added time, Arsenal scored again. Still they were a goal behind. Down they swept again to win a corner. Their winger centred the ball towards the penalty spot and as it headed goalwards Bill Brown, the Spurs 'keeper, just got back to turn it over the bar for another corner kick. One minute of time remained, three minutes over time by the Arsenal clock. The second corner was put about a yard further into the field than the earlier one. The goal-keeper came out to it but never reached the ball, this time it was headed into the net. All square at four each, what a match! Afterwards, Tottenham skipper Danny Blanchflower walked the length of the corridor to put his head round my dressing-room door. 'A wonderful match', he said, 'and if it was good for us it must have been good for you.' Coming from a captain who had been three goals up at one point in the match it was a wonderful gesture of sportsmanship. Some years later I received a letter from an old journalist friend, John Goodbody. He told me that he had been thinking about the finest League football match he had ever seen, the 1963 Arsenal-Spurs derby. He had looked out the programme and discovered that I had refereed the match and he just wanted to let me know. What a delight!

SOME MEMORABLE CUP-TIES

I recall many memorable matches. Often they were FA Cup games – there is no substitute for the magic of the Cup. It is always a great thrill to receive the list of Cup-tie appointments sent out from Lancaster Gate and to discover that you have one of the best. There is always an air of expectancy about these matches and one is rarely disappointed. A good Cup run means so much to any team and the sudden-death nature of the competition guarantees excitement and controversy for the referee as much, if not more than, for players, spectators and managers! All these ingredients were there when the amateur side Tooting and Mitcham, who had made remarkable progress through the preliminary stages of the Cup, were drawn at home to Bournemouth. It was a wonderful football occasion, but sad for Bournemouth who were defeated 3–1. Denis Follows, the FA secretary, was an enthusiastic spectator. He told me afterwards, with great relish, that when I gave one decision a spectator near him shouted 'If this referee goes on like this I shall have to vote Labour'. After the match Tooting followed the amateurs' tradition of inviting the referee and linesmen, and everyone else, into their clubhouse. Speeches were made and I was full of admiration for Bournemouth and their manager, Don Welsh of Charlton fame, for their great sportsmanship in this moment of most bitter disappointment. No professional side losing in the Cup to an amateur team could have been more generous.

Another Cup match with a controversial incident and some interesting personalities was Ipswich versus Huddersfield. The fun started off the field. The chairman of Ipswich was John Cobbold. He and his brother Patrick were two of the most respected directors that soccer has known. John had contested the Ipswich parliamentary seat against Dingle Foot QC, a much respected MP and a good friend of mine, and also of John's. When it was announced that I had been appointed to referee the match John immediately invited Dingle to be his guest. The manager of Huddersfield Town was the great Bill Shankly. The day was cold and frosty and the bitter East Anglian wind was not improving the playing surface. A corner kick caused the controversy and as it was taken I was positioned on the edge of the penalty area. I could plainly see the push made by one of the Huddersfield defenders which nudged an Ipswich player off balance and inside the flight of the ball. Dingle Foot told me that as I awarded the penalty kick to Ipswich, John Cobbold stood up in the directors' box, turned to him and said 'That's buggered the next election!'

For three years running, from 1955–56 to 1957–58, Leeds United drew Cardiff City in the Cup, an extraordinary coincidence; furthermore, Cardiff won each time – Leeds 1, Cardiff 2. I refereed the first of these matches. We had suffered a fair amount of snow which raised questions about whether the match could be played. I decided to stay overnight at the house of Arthur Tiley, a Conservative MP for Bradford, who was in fact my parliamentary pair. We had both come into Parliament in 1955 and we got on so well that we decided to share a flat near Parliament so that when our respective families came to London for holidays or at weekends they could use the whole flat. It was a sensible and very happy arrangement. I used to say that we would get up in the morning and over breakfast we would read the newspapers and decide whether we were going down to the House or visiting Sandown Park! An early morning visit to Leeds showed me that the snow had frozen. I believe that frozen snow makes an ideal playing surface so I asked the groundsman to pack it down by rolling and to paint the markings in blue. Other matches all over Yorkshire were off but we had a cracker at Elland Road. The following week I received a letter from Sam Bolton, the Leeds chairman, saying that he was sorry that he had not been able to see me before I left the ground but he wanted to offer me his congratulations. Wonderful sportsmanship from a losing chairman, a man who in his time made a great contribution to the game and who brought me yet another good football friendship.

In the 1963–64 season Leeds drew Cardiff again but this time at Ninian Park, Cardiff, and I again took the match. It is memorable for two incidents which were sad and remarkably coincidental. After about five minutes Freddie Goodwin, one of the Leeds players, went down and I heard the crack which told me he had broken his leg. I turned and called for a stretcher without needing to look for myself. There was a lengthy hold-up while he was cared for and carried off the pitch to hospital. I restarted the match and within five minutes, on exactly the same spot, another player went down, this time Alan McIntosh, a Cardiff player. Another loud crack, another stretcher. It was an extraordinary experience which certainly changed the atmosphere of this Cup-tie. I was glad to get it over with and the result, 1–0 to Leeds, was really of secondary importance so far as all our feelings were concerned.

The Bristol Rovers and Burnley tie to which I was appointed in 1958 had to be replayed at Burnley following a drawn match at Eastville. There was torrential rain for days before the game and I had a call from another delightful man, Bert Tann, the manager of Bristol Rovers, asking me to travel early to inspect the pitch. I arrived at about ten o'clock to find Bert, who had been up half the night directing his ground staff and forking the pitch to get the water away, still hard at work. The pitch looked in a horrible state but the rain had ceased and Bert told me that as a result of all the forking it had improved in the last hour or two. These are always very difficult decisions to take. Obviously, the first consideration is whether or not it is possible to play football and to play it without undue risk of injury. I decided that I would give Bert and his friends more time and urged them to get more forking done. Supporters standing around also produced forks and helped with the work.

Bob Lord, the Burnley chairman, and Harry Potts, their manager, had brought their team down to stay overnight. They were soon on the telephone, concerned at the situation since they were a First Division side. Being drawn away to a Second Division team was difficult enough for them without the added peril of a muddy pitch. It is interesting that good footballing sides like Burnley often prefer to play on sound surfaces but I believe that English football is meant to be played in all kinds of weather and on all manner of surfaces. In any case, as I used to say to my friends, 'Mud reduces the players down to my speed. I am in favour of it'! I went off for an early lunch and returned around midday to find that all the surface water had gone. I took a ball on to the pitch and kicked it about. The ball moved around in the middle, it was difficult but not impossible. 'Let battle commence', I told the waiting reporters and so it did, producing a great Cup-tie which ended in a draw. I was pleased that everyone involved, including the Burnley club, told me that in spite of their doubts the match itself fully justified my decision to play it. So off we went to Burnley for the Tuesday night replay at Turf Moor. This was another great tie, played on a first-class pitch. Bristol Rovers more than held their own and no one had any doubts that the victory for the visitors was fully justified.

The Manchester United versus Bolton Wanderers match June 1962 taught me that you must never relax your vigilance until the final whistle. Two First Division sides and a local derby, too – a certain prescription for drama. Bolton led for much of the game from a goal scored by their centre-forward, Stevens. The 42,200 Old Trafford crowd was tense and worried at the prospect of defeat. Bolton were 2–1 up and deserved their lead. With only minutes to go they conceded a corner on the right-hand side. I was running the right diagonal, which means taking a line from one right corner flag to the other. My linesmen were therefore patrolling the left-wing touch-lines. Before the game I gave them my usual instructions about corner kicks: 'I'll take up a position just inside the 18-yard penalty line so that I have a good view looking through the players, and you come along the goal-line for about 20 yards to act as a goal judge, looking across the goal mouth'. The theory was that between us we had every situation covered. I added, as I always did, 'If the ball is cleared by the defence don't go back to the touch-line until you are certain the ball is not coming back again. I will have moved into the penalty area and I'll cover all off-side situations'.

As predicted, I had walked some ten yards into the box once the corner kick had been taken. I heard the shout 'everyone out' from the Bolton defence and, dutifully, they all moved upfield to create an off-side trap. The ball went to Jimmy Nicholson, the United half-back, and he just lobbed it back into the goal mouth. All that I had to do at that moment, which was the instant that decides an off-side position, was to turn my head, for I was perfectly positioned. Almost all the Bolton defenders had got upfield except for the full-back, Roy Hartle. He had come from the position he had taken up under the cross-bar and he was still concentrating on getting upfield and playing centre-forward David Herd off-side. He was too slow to do so. He ran past Herd as the ball was travelling back into the area, which meant that the centre-forward was clearly on-side, although when the ball reached his feet he looked yards off-side. I had no hesitation in awarding the equalising goal. To my astonishment the linesman, who had not carried out my instructions to stay on the goal-line, was back on his touch-line, waving frantically for off-side. Naturally, Bolton were appealing equally frantically. I had no doubt that a good goal had been scored but it was clear that I had to go across and discuss the situation with the linesman. He confirmed that he was waving for off-side. There was no more to be said so we talked for a few moments about our return travel arrangements until the excitement had died down. The papers made much of my 'consultation' with the linesman. Little did they know! Unfortunately for Bolton the goal revitalised Manchester and with only minutes left they swept down the field again. A long shot, more in hope than expectation by the same Nicholson, was deflected into the net and Bolton were out of the Cup.

When United were drawn at home to Arsenal in the next round of the Cup, the Bolton manager commented that my decision had cost his club 'thousands of pounds'. I would only answer: 'In that case, before I next referee Bolton, I will first consult their bank manager'.

As far as the FA Cup itself is concerned my highest refereeing appointment was the sixth round quarter-final tie in 1963 between Nottingham Forest and Southampton. This match too went to a most sensational replay. In the first match, on the Forest ground, there was too much tension, brought about by the prospect of a semi-final place for the winners. One of my concerns was to keep George Kirby, the Southampton centre-forward, in the game. George and I had met before on a number of occasions resulting in a number of tickings-off being administered by me. George's problems all arose because he was one of the game's most wholehearted and enthusiastic players. Off the field he is an absolute gentleman, well respected by everyone. On the field he was also respected because of his fearless play. He was never dirty in any sense but never wanted courage, either. One of the problems for a referee with this type of player is not only his 100 per cent involvement but the knowledge that he can be provoked by his opponents into doing something silly. It is as much the job of the referee to protect such a player as to keep him in order. I used to take an early opportunity to have a few friendly words with George and ask for his help in keeping him out of trouble, something along the lines of 'I'll look after you if you will look after me. Neither of us want trouble, do we?'. The first match was reasonably uneventful, ending in a 1–1 draw, and it was down to Southampton for the replay.

The Dell was packed for the occasion, and the atmosphere was wonderful. The match was a ding-dong affair with Forest well on top and leading 3–1 until about ten minutes from time. Suddenly, George Kirby began to play like a man inspired. From one centre he headed the ball goalwards and followed it through. As the Forest goal-keeper went for the ball he must have remembered George Kirby: he made the fatal mistake of taking his eye off the ball to look out for the centre-forward. Too late. The ball hit the 'keeper and went into the net. The Dell was now ablaze with excitement. The home supporters roared on

ABOVE LEFT: *The first known photograph of me.*

ABOVE: *My parents, Herbert and Bertha.*

LEFT: *Our backyard in Guildford Street, Lozells, scene of many football and cricket contests.*
Terry Weir

ABOVE: *Launching the 1955 election campaign. Left to Right: Alderman Harry Walton, myself, Birmingham Labour Group leader Sir Albert Bradley, Cllr Mrs Florrie Hammond and Harold Nash, the Birmingham Labour Party secretary and organiser.*

LEFT: *The prospective MP for Birmingham All Saints gets to grips with bill posting.*

ABOVE RIGHT: *Bill Mander, my constituency secretary, dressed as a 'flunkey' to commemorate my first case, greets Brenda and me at our wedding reception in 1955.* Birmingham Post and Mail

RIGHT: *An early Howell family group. Left to Right: Denis and David, Andrew, Brenda, Kate and Michael.*

RIGHT: *Speaking in defence of Charlie Groves at the meeting of Warwickshire CCC.*
Birmingham Gazette & Despatch

BELOW: *Training at Villa Park, encouraged by one of Villa's all-time greats, Ernie 'Mush' Callaghan.*

OPPOSITE: *On the campaign trail.* ABOVE: *Setting out with Reece Thrupp and two of my most longstanding supporters, Cllr Mrs Kath Finnegan and Jack Crawford.* BELOW: *Discussing the litter problem with some of my constituents.* Terry Weir

Hugh Gaitskell welcomes me as a new MP.

OPPOSITE: *The Prime Ministers under whom I have served.*
ABOVE: *Harold Wilson, flanked by Sir Stanley Rous and myself,*
opens the FIFA Congress in 1966 that preceded the World Cup
competition won by England. BELOW: *Jim Callaghan congratulates*
my daughter Kate on her marriage to Michael Molloy in 1984.
Simon Livingstone

Sir Stanley Matthews, football's first knight, on the House of Commons terrace with Stoke MP Ellis Smith and myself after his investiture in 1965. Daily Mail

their team in the few minutes left. The inevitable happened: Southampton scored again to equalise the match. We played extra time without any further score. Afterwards the Forest manager complained that I had not given his goal-keeper sufficient protection but that was nonsense. The 'keeper's difficulty was the reputation of George Kirby. My task was to keep everyone playing within the laws of the game and I was content that I had achieved this. I was attending the annual Konigswinter Conference in Germany the following week and could not accept the replay appointment, so Jack Taylor refereed in my stead and this time there was no doubt: Southampton won 5–0. I permitted myself a wry smile!

I did referee one major Cup final, the Republic of Ireland Cup final at Dalymount Park in Dublin between Dundalk and Shamrock Rovers. This came about because from time to time I would referee matches in Eire on a Sunday if I did not have a League match in England on the preceding day. I also refereed some matches in Northern Ireland. I was very pleased to be invited to referee the semi-final in 1958 between Shamrock Rovers and St Patrick's Athletic. I had a good game and made one decision which turned out to be quite spectacular. As the ball was sent upfield over the head of one of the full-backs, intended for empty space where the winger could pick it up, the defender jumped up to stop it with his hand. 'Foul!', shouted every one of the thousands of referees watching the match. I gave myself the advantage of some 'thinking' time. The full-back fell on the ground and I was able to wave on the winger, now running flat out, shouting 'play on, play on!'. It came off and provided a most exciting moment as the winger collected the ball and sped on towards goal. His shot hit the post but it was the sort of advantage play which helped the match along and made a big impression. I was, however, brought down to earth as regards the advantage rule the very next week in a League match at Colchester in an identical incident. This time when I shouted 'play on' the winger picked up the ball and claimed a foul. It was a foul against him for not playing to the whistle!

After the Irish semi-final I was lying in my bath when in came Joe Wickham, a most charming and respected secretary of the Eire Football Association. He told me that his committee had held an immediate meeting after the match and had decided to invite me back in a few weeks to referee the final, between Shamrock Rovers, which is the most famous club in the Republic and Dundalk, a much less glamorous team from the border town. It was a unique experience. Shamrock were controlled by the Cunningham family who also owned, I believe, a very large bookmaking business. The Rovers were heavy favourites but that did not help their cause in this match: Dundalk well merited their 1–0 win. After the match the chairman of Dundalk invited me to go back with the team, assuring me that celebrations would last 'the whole night through'. I did not think it appropriate to socialise with one side so I declined as politely as I could.

NORTH AMERICAN SOCCER

In my experience many of the difficulties in which I sometimes found myself arose from the fact that players and managers would not allow me to assert my own control upon the match. They become impatient when trouble occurs – sometimes they want to referee the match themselves. Often, this attitude leads to retaliation. Players then complain that they are being penalised when they are not the original sinners. The fact is that when trouble does flare up most referees need a little time to overcome it and to settle the match down again. Players who are not prepared to help the referee by showing a little patience aggravate the situation they are complaining about. I found myself in just such a situation when I refereed in New York in 1960 in the tournament to which I was invited as a result of having refereed the Burnley–Tottenham match. Burnley were present as the English League champions and were due to play Kilmarnock, the Scottish runners-up. I was the only overseas referee in the tournament, all the others were Americans with little experience of big match occasions. Notwithstanding the fact that I was English, as soon as they arrived in New York both clubs requested that I should referee their match.

Difficulties off the field arose as soon as we touched down. The Burnley team had arrived ahead of the main party which included Bob Lord, the Burnley chairman. As their coach was on its way from the airport to the hotel, Lord asked Bill Cox, the organiser, who was sitting next to me, when his team would be getting their money and insisted that Cox should accompany him to the bank to ensure that the cheque was honoured! When we arrived at the hotel, which had its own subway station, extensive facilities and a roof garden overlooking the harbour and the Statue of Liberty, we were given the news that the Burnley players would not stay there as it was not up to the standards they expected! Kilmarnock soon formed the opinion that Burnley wanted to isolate themselves from the rest of the tournament teams, especially Kilmarnock. I realised that I was going to have a difficult match on my hands.

I was appointed to referee the opening match of the competition. It was disconcerting to be approached by the television producer who told me that his commentator, who would be sitting on the roof of the stand, knew little about football, he was a baseball man. Would I help him? My first difficulty arose when the producer asked me how I was going to delay the match from time to time so that the commercials could take place. I explained that the rules of football did not provide for any such eventuality. He could not believe it. 'We must get the commercials in', he told me, 'you must delay the throw-ins and the free kicks.' 'Nothing doing', I replied. 'This match has to be played in accordance with the laws of the game.' I thought he was going to cancel his contract there and then! The match was held in a baseball stadium. Would I first explain the rules of the game to the viewers? No trouble here. Would I arrange a system of signals which the commentator could jot down so that he could translate and explain them to the viewers? This was more difficult. I went through all the fouls I could think of, working out appropriate signals. When I touched my hand it was a foul for handball. When I jerked my elbows it was a foul for elbowing. Waggling my foot meant a foul for tripping. If I pushed my hands forward the foul was for pushing and so on. Then I explained the difference between a direct free kick and an indirect free kick from which a goal cannot be scored. I illustrated this by saying that if I held my hand up it was an indirect free kick. After some repetition I thought the producer understood. His next concern was to transmit official ruling, such as who had scored the goal and who was to be credited with the 'assists', from me on the pitch to the commentator on the roof. There was a telephone at the side of the pitch linked to the commentator, no doubt provided for similar purposes in baseball. Would I nip off the pitch, pick it up and give my decisions? I certainly would not. Would I agree to the linesman doing it? No, he would be getting on with the match. Finally, could he provide a messenger at the side of the pitch who could ask the linesman for a decision? Yes, I thought that was reasonable, but I instructed my linesmen that nothing was to interfere with their positioning at any time. They were to keep up with the play whatever conversations they were having with the messenger.

All went well during the early stages of the match. I gave a foul for hands and the announcer explained in a broad American accent: 'Referee Howell has awarded that foul for handsball. It is a direct free kick. A goal can be scored'. He repeated the phraseology for other fouls regardless of where the foul was being taken and whether or not there was any chance of a goal being scored. Suddenly, there was a bit of a mêlée and I waded in to sort out the problem and to restore order when, to my astonishment, the excited voice of the announcer sounded out: 'Referee Howell says that is a foul for kicking, tripping, pushing and elbows. It is a direct free kick. A goal can be scored'.

I have never experienced such tension in any match as I did in the Burnley versus Kilmarnock match. One of my linesmen had come over from Scotland years before. He had some slight League lining experience in Scotland and he seemed a reliable sort. I soon decided that I had to rely upon him for any assistance I was going to get in this match so I told him to be certain to keep well upfield. I would concentrate a little more than usual on the situation at the other end of the field. The match had hardly started when the Burnley winger, Pilkington, was twice fouled by the full-back. I had intervened on the first occasion but after the second foul, and before I could possibly deal with the situation, the Burnley team exploded. The result was that I now had two problems on my hands: Kilmarnock, who seemed to be softening up the Burnley winger, and Burnley who wanted to take the match into their own hands. Protracted stoppages to sort out such situations do not help the cause of the game. There was much shouting from the Burnley bench. They had to be told to calm down. Then Bob Lord decided to take things in hand. He left his seat in the stand and came down into the arena, stationing himself behind the goal at one end of the ground where the dressing-rooms were also situated. Half-time was approaching. As I blew up for 45 minutes and left the pitch, Lord shouted at me, 'I am going to report you to the Football Association!'. I told him that he was too late. We might be several thousands of miles from home but I was still in charge of the match. He had no right to be there or address me in that way. I would be reporting him and now I was ordering him off the pitch, and if I had any further trouble I would have to order him out of the ground. Before he could react in any way, Joe Barreskill, the secretary of the United States F A, who was standing nearby, intervened. 'Mr Howell, I shall be sending a report to Sir Stanley Rous to support your action. Do you want us to have this man removed?' I replied that I did not think that would be necessary and Lord went off to the dressing-room, not to be seen again.

The result of the match was a victory for Kilmarnock. That night I borrowed the typewriter of Albert Sewell, one of the press men covering the competition, and typed out my report, sending it off to London next morning. Albert's two great companions were Sam Leitch, then of the *Daily Mirror* but later to become Head of Sport for BBC Television, and Malcolm Brodie, the great Belfast sportswriter. All three became great friends – they were journalists of the old school. I am glad to say that later on my friendship with Bob Lord was restored and I think he came to appreciate that referees have to be allowed to sort out situations themselves.

MISCONDUCT

No referee wishes to earn his reputation through over-zealous and officious match control. Most of us try to keep our players on the field. I always believed that if I had to dismiss a player from the field it was a failure on my part, even if it was for some incident totally beyond my power to control. It was the game itself which had been let down. Yet there are occasions when dismissal from the field is inevitable if one is to enforce the laws of the game. Mercifully, in my ten years on the referees' list of the Leagues I was involved in only four such incidents. Two incidents occurred in the 12th minute of an important promotion match between Colchester and Millwall in October 1962. The play proceeded down the left side of the field and the ball went over the goal-line. The two players concerned, Martyn King, the Colchester winger, and Ray Brady, the Millwall full-back, appealed for a goal-kick and a corner respectively. As they threw up their hands to do so they struck each other. Before I could say Jack Solomons or Jarvis

Astaire, I had a fight on my hands which either of these impresarios would have been proud to stage. I went over to the players, asked their names and said, 'Thank you very much, gentlemen, that will be all for today!' They walked off like lambs and for the next 78 minutes we all enjoyed a delightful match.

At Plymouth I had trouble with the captain of Rochdale. He committed fouls which earned a rebuke and he had to be cautioned. Within a minute he brought down another player so off he had to go. The following week I received a letter from a police superintendent at the match congratulating me on my match control. Unfortunately, this was followed by a letter from the Football League to say that both clubs had registered a complaint about me. I told the League of the earlier letter and I heard no more, but some years later a conversation was reported to me by someone who had overheard it to the effect that if the clubs both gave me low marks this might help the player concerned in subsequent disciplinary action. Fortunately, the days when clubs could exert such an influence have long since gone.

By far the most remarkable dismissal in which I was involved occurred at Shrewsbury, who were playing Queen's Park Rangers. It was quite an ordinary game until some minutes before the end. A home team player was injured and I went over to investigate and then called the trainer. The ball had rolled off the pitch and as I looked up a QPR full-back picked it up, walked towards the concrete pill-box in which sat the Shrewsbury manager, Harry Potts, and others, and threw the ball at him. Harry's head went back and hit the wall behind him, which knocked him out. It seemed to me that I had no alternative but to give the player his marching orders. As I did so another QPR player raced across the field and shook his fist at the home team manager. He had to be cautioned. When the match ended the same player raced off the field and down the passage where the home team manager was disappearing. I went after him. A friend at the match told me that he had never seen a referee leave the field so quickly. My senior linesman was Jack Taylor, an old friend who was to go on to referee a World Cup final. Jack had been patrolling that side of the field but he had no idea what had brought on all the trouble. Neither had I. At the enquiry held at the FA offices, Sir Stanley Rous arrived halfway through the proceedings and suggested that as the player sent off had an excellent reputation, and had never been in any trouble, the incident made no sense unless he had been provoked. I replied that this may have been the case but if so it was outside my knowledge and that of my linesman. In any case provocation was no excuse for retaliation. The Commission found that 'they could not deduce from the evidence that the ball had been thrown with deliberate intent' and that the sending-off was sufficient punishment in this case. They may have been right, but I took Jack Taylor and my other linesman to the House of Commons for lunch where we tried to work out how you could throw a ball accidentally!

One other match that led to some extraordinary scenes was the first round of the European Cup in 1960–61 between Barcelona and Real Madrid. I was appointed to be senior linesman to F I F A referee Reg Leafe, my old friend from Nottingham, who refereed the match superbly. The atmosphere at the wonderful Nou Camp stadium was absolutely electric. For the first time I really experienced the feeling that exists between the two cities: the rivalries are something quite beyond anything we know in our own country. Barcelona won 2–1 and with Ray Hodgkinson, my fellow linesman, and Reg I went off to enjoy the banquet. After the meal, the speeches and the presentations, we left the restaurant in the company of the Spanish official designated to look after us. To our surprise the Real Madrid team were lined up outside in two ranks. We had to walk between them as they clapped their hands in unison, shouting in Spanish. Reg walked through the assembled ranks then turned and bowed to them. That did it. They started to attack. My colleague and I did what we could to go to Reg's aid but, fortunately, our Spanish colleague had rumbled that trouble was afoot and had sent for our car. It arrived in the nick of time. We bundled Reg into it and as we made off the players banged on the roof. It was not a pleasant experience.

FOOTBALL FRIENDSHIPS

All sports produce lasting friendships, none more so than football. People who give their time, sometimes their life's devotion, to a football team are worth their weight in gold. I don't approve of teams being financed by the personal money of directors – clubs should be conducted on the same principles as any other business – but I am full of admiration for the people who see their contribution to their own town or city in the context of striving to keep their team going to achieve some success for their community. Many of them have become firm friends over the years. Other lifelong friendships have arisen through refereeing. If anyone took a check they would discover that throughout the length and breadth of the land football is being administered on a voluntary basis by former referees who first controlled matches in local recreational grounds in all weathers and through all kinds of adversity, and who love the game so much that they go on to provide its administration and its stability. Such men are of fine quality. Likewise footballers, and especially footballers who become managers, have a special place in my affections. The service they give to the game is immeasurable, even the most successful of them knows that public acclaim is a fleeting phenomenon. I have a special friendship with Joe Mercer, a delightful man who has used his outstanding talents solely for the benefit of football. When he managed Aston Villa, my own special team, he would ring me up and say, 'Come and referee our practice game today, it will help get you fit for the season'. I did a lot of training with Joe and the Villa team and afterwards we would sit and talk about football situations on the field of play. It was all a great help to me in approaching the refereeing problems of the professional game.

There are other friendships which originate in quite extraordinary ways but which endure through football. One such was that of the MP Bessie Braddock. We became friends when I was first elected to Parliament and Bessie would come down and 'do me a turn' at election time. She was a tremendous draw. Bessie was a staunch Everton fan. Whenever we met she would ask, 'Are you due to referee at Goodison?' and when I had such an appointment she would say, 'Mind you give me a wave'. So when I walked to the centre circle and put the ball down I would turn and give Bessie a little bow. She loved it.

Neighbouring Liverpool was another good ground for me. Tom Williams was a fine chairman of the club. He was succeeded by Sidney Reakes, another gentleman who has remained a firm friend along with Jack Cross, a fellow director. John Smith, a close colleague in sport and a personal friend, is an outstanding club chairman and a respected chairman of the Sports Council. Liverpool has always produced an excellent board of directors – the key to all club success – I have been privileged to travel with them around Europe, enjoying their great companionship. I once rescued Sidney Reakes' wife in my ministerial car along with the wife of Liverpool player Ray Kennedy. The lady was in the advanced stages of pregnancy but could not miss the match. Both were stranded outside the stadium in Rome after a European Cup final, miles away from transport and surrounded by thousands of jubilant supporters. I was glad to be able to return the friendship of their club. Such a board of directors has produced a continuing success story, unequalled in English football. It is no coincidence that they have been served by such fine servants as Peter Robinson, now their secretarial director and a man of unrivalled ability, a great influence, and managers of genius – Bill Shankly, Bob Paisley, Joe Fagan and now Kenny Dalglish.

Stanley Matthews kindly invited me to referee one of his special testimonial games at a wonderful celebration night arranged in his honour by Stoke City. I had refereed when he played for Blackpool. One game, against Newcastle United, was immediately before the end of the season and whichever team lost was to be relegated. The visitors had to play an untried youngster against Stanley, who was at the end of his League career. The youngster was mesmerised and when Stanley told him, 'Watch what you are doing, son, I'm getting on now', the lad stood off the maestro long enough for Matthews to centre the ball and bring about the winning goal which eventually kept Blackpool up and put Newcastle down. Years later I walked into a sports centre in north Nottinghamshire and the fellow in charge, who had not been expecting me, greeted me like an old friend. 'You will not remember me,' he said, 'but you refereed my match when I played for Newcastle against Stan Matthews'!

Another indelible memory remains from a Watford versus Shrewsbury Town match in 1959. Victory for Shrewsbury meant promotion. I knew the Shrewsbury people very well as a result of having officiated at many matches there, particularly Tim Yates, their long-time chairman, and Freddie Williams and Freddie Fry, his fellow directors. In addition Frank Leath, my oldest trade union friend and their long-time hospital broadcaster, was present at this memorable match. In Arthur Rowley, their player-manager, Shrewsbury had an absolute match-winner. Arthur could hit the ball harder than anyone I knew except for Eric Houghton of Aston Villa. At half-time Shrewsbury, 4–1 up, seemed to be home and dry. As I emerged from the dressing-room after the interval I was confronted by an elderly groundsman who stood there, visibly trembling. 'Mr Howell,' he said, 'someone has stolen the fuses, I can't turn the floodlights on.' What had he done about it? Nothing. He told me there had been a burglary at the club, he thought they had been looking for Cup final tickets. There was nothing for it but to ask him to send for the electricity board as a matter of urgency and I went off in search of Arthur Rowley, who was on the field waiting to re-start the match. Arthur was livid. I told him I would play as long as we could in the hope that the electricians would arrive and enable us to finish the match. But it was not to be. When the Shrewsbury goal-keeper stood rooted to the spot as the ball flashed past into the net from 30 yards, I knew that was it. Furthermore, thousands of Shrewsbury supporters had lit their evening newspapers to turn them into torches and an inspector of police was quite rightly showing every concern. The match was abandoned with 16 minutes to go.

It was the last match of the season – what was to be done? Both sets of directors assembled in the Watford boardroom and, to my surprise, they asked me to preside over the gathering as the only neutral present. Alan Hardaker, the League secretary, was eventually contacted and I explained the position. Since the result seemed convincing, he thought the League would allow it to stand, but he asked me not to tell the directors who were all sitting around me! I broke the news to him, as casually as I could, that this match would decide promotion. He took the point at once. 'The match must be replayed', he said. Would I discuss preliminary arrangements and let him know in the morning? We settled on a mid-week replay, and this time Watford fielded quite a few youngsters to take on Rowley and his team, no doubt believing that this would be their moment of glory. However, justice prevailed in the end and Shrewsbury got their victory and their promotion, but I never go to Shrewsbury without reliving the drama of this night with my friends at the club. Years later it was a pleasure to defend their cause in the Commons when the local authority threatened their ground with compulsory purchase in order to build a shopping centre and a new bridge over the Severn. They won that one, too!

My refereeing career effectively ended with my appointment as a

Minister in 1964. It was impossible to train at least twice a week and there was an obvious requirement for any Minister for Sport to attend many Saturday sporting engagements. Alan Hardaker told me that the Management Committee would be delighted to keep my name on their referees' list since it had never previously included that of any Minister of the Crown. I was very appreciative of this kindness and remained on their list as D.H. Howell, not seeking appointments, until I reached the normal retirement age of 47 years then applying to referees. However, I was to referee one further League match, on the opening day of the 1966 season. This came about because Harold Wilson, the Prime Minister, strongly urged me to take up the whistle again. He thought it would be a good idea for one of his Ministers to be refereeing in the League. 'Never been done before', he told me. I foolishly agreed to do so and spent some three weeks getting fit for my first appointment, Cardiff City versus Bury. I was still reasonably fit and had in fact refereed one other match at Wembley, my only appearance at the national stadium in 1965, when I accepted an invitation from the English Schools FA, with whom I had enjoyed a long and happy association, to referee their England versus Scotland international. They too thought it would be an honour to have one of their internationals refereed by a Minister of the Crown and I was delighted to make an appearance at Wembley.

My appearance at Cardiff was not such a happy affair. I had some soup, my normal pre-match food, at Cardiff station before the match and it tasted rather tinny. It certainly made me feel quite ill during the second half. I really ought to have left the field but my ministerial presence had brought the largest gathering of photographers and television crews, from all parts of the world, that I had encountered. They were there to photograph the referee not the match, so I stayed on the field so as not to provide them with a sensational story. My doctor did not like the outline of my symptoms, especially when I told him that throughout the second half my whistle had hung down from my wrist like a piece of lead. He packed me off to Middlesex Hospital for a full medical check-up. I decided to call it a day – I could see no point in being constantly reported on by journalists looking for ministerial controversies.

PART II

MINISTER FOR SPORT

The real ones, the right ones, the straight ones and the true,
The pukka, peerless sportsmen – their numbers are but few;
The men who keep on playing though the sun be in eclipse,
The men who go on losing with a laugh upon their lips.

The True Sportsman
William Henry Ogilvie

7

BUILDING A
MINISTRY

NUMBER TEN

Harold Wilson was back from the Palace, Her Majesty's First Secretary of the Treasury, the Prime Minister. The only thing to do now was to settle down in front of the television, watch the story unfold, and hope that I might have a part to play in it. Our overall majority was very small – just four. Clearly there would be another election soon but we had broken the spell. The 13 years were over and Labour was back. It was an exhilarating time. Our screens showed the giants of the movement entering Number Ten to receive their appointments and then leaving again, all smiles. Later on came the first of the Cabinet appointments. On Saturday night the first list was issued. No major surprises, but an interesting innovation on the home front. George Brown, also the Deputy Prime Minister, headed a new Ministry as First Secretary at the Department of Economic Affairs. At once there was speculation as to how this would work out with a Treasury headed by Jim Callaghan. At the Foreign Office was Patrick Gordon-Walker, even though he had lost his seat at Smethwick in a very racist type of election. Obviously, a by-election would be needed to get Patrick back into the House. Denis Healey, whom I thought best qualified to be our Foreign Secretary, found himself at Defence, a very safe pair of hands there! Frank Soskice was the new Home Secretary and his legal friend, Gerald Gardiner, became Lord Chancellor. Michael Stewart went to Education and Herbert Bowden became Lord President and Leader of the House.

I telephoned George and left a message of congratulations and good luck and later on he returned my call and raised my excitement by telling me that I was on his list for an appointment: 'Harold tells me that he wants you to be in the Government'. He pledged me not to say anything to anyone, except Brenda, and so I had to settle down as patiently as I could, taking congratulatory calls after my own success in Small Heath and beginning the huge task of answering all the many letters which had been arriving since Saturday morning.

Late on Sunday night, when I least expected such a call, the telephone rang. 'Number Ten here,' said the voice. It took me a moment or two to gather my senses. 'The Prime Minister would like to see you at 9.45 in the morning, can you manage that?' Indeed I could. When I put the 'phone down I realised that I would be hard put to get down by train in the morning. There was nothing for it but a very early start in my own car. The chances of sleep were remote and I was up far sooner than necessary to start my journey. I arrived at the House of Commons at about nine o'clock and found one or two colleagues beginning to assemble there although the place was still on holiday and the tea bars closed. I wandered outside to get a coffee and then strolled round to Downing Street, arriving with five minutes to spare.

I was shown into a small waiting area where one or two colleagues were also waiting to see the PM. We waited and waited. Every fifteen minutes another hopeful arrived and soon the place was full to over-flowing. We were next door to the Cabinet Room and we watched in awe as officials went in and out at repeated intervals. We did not know it at the time but the Prime Minister and his senior colleagues were discussing the financial crisis which they had inherited. Upon assuming office the Treasury had presented the PM with a memo showing that our overseas deficit was £800 million in the red. The question was to devalue or not to devalue the pound. That was certainly more pressing than the appointment of junior Ministers. As we subsequently learned they chose not to do so in the belief, which most of us shared, that since the Attlee Government had devalued we could not afford on day one of the new administration to be labelled the party of devaluation. I think this was a justifiable political decision but it proved to be a doubtful economic judgment. Sometime after 12 o'clock the Prime Minister's principal secretary appeared and told us how sorry he was that vitally important business was holding up appointments with the PM. Would all those people who had been asked to come after 10 am please leave now and they would be telephoned later in the day and new appointments made. I never saw such a look of collective aston-ishment and misapprehension but there was nothing for it but for those people to leave with good grace.

It was nearly one o'clock when my turn came to be called into the Cabinet Room. Harold was seated in the middle of the long table and looked quite imperturbable, as if he had been head of Government all his life, as to the manner born. He apologised for the delay with some throwaway lines to the effect that we had inherited a financial mess and then said, 'I would like you to go to Education and look after schools and sport. You will be the first Minister for Sport, it will be very exciting'. I thanked him and said that I was a little surprised as I had written to him setting out all the objections to such an appointment. 'Yes, I know', he said, 'that is why I am appointing you, you know all the dangers and all the nuances. You will accept?'. 'Yes, of course,' I replied, 'I will do my best to justify your confidence.' He then explained that the lists had to be approved by the Queen and that there would be reporters lurking outside Number Ten. I was not to say a word to anyone, except my wife, until after the official announcement. I thought it was time to ask a few questions of my own. 'Since I have not been a Minister before what do I do now? What policy do you want me to follow?' His answers were quite refreshing. 'Well, you go away and get yourself a secretary and an office and start work. You will be working for Michael Stewart, who is the Minister for Education. I leave the policy to you, I think you know what needs to be done otherwise I would not be appointing you.' My next question was, 'Do I have any money?'. 'No,' he said, 'the country's broke, but remember that when you have no money it is a good time to do your thinking!' My brain was racing away by this time as I realised that at this very moment there were two or three matters to be mentioned. I explained that as I had no money and had to work with people, many of whom would be likely to be opposed to a Sports Ministry, it might be a good idea to consider a few honours. 'Yes,' he said, 'a very good idea, go and negotiate yourself a sports list.' I hadn't the faintest idea how to approach such a task but I was well satisfied by that answer. I told Harold that as we were taking office in the middle of the Tokyo Olympics, where we were having great success, we might do something in that area. His response was more than encouraging. 'Yes, you must meet the team home. Has there ever been a reception for sportsmen at Number Ten?' I did not know. 'Well, we will create a precedent. The floors may need strengthening but we will invite them all here. The cost will have to be met by you, out of your departmental vote.'

I was just about to take my leave, full of excitement, when I suddenly remembered my conversations with Denis Follows, the secretary of the Football Association, about the problems of staging the 1966 World Cup. Follows had been to see Quintin Hogg, who had been deputed by Prime Minister Harold Macmillan to answer questions on sport, and had sought Government help to stage the tournament. Denis had told me before the election that all he had got out of that interview was a promise to provide police escorts for the various teams as they drove around the country. I decided to return to the question of money. I told Harold that there was one very important matter that occurred to me: the 1966 World Cup. He asked me what it was all about and I explained that the 16 finest national teams in the world would be here to compete and that much work needed to be done. I said something like 'It is not much use having a Minister for Sport with a World Cup on his hands if he has no money to organise it'.

Harold's response amazed me after what he had just said about money. 'How much do you want?' he asked. I hadn't the faintest idea; there was no one present to consult; I had yet to meet a civil servant or any other adviser, but I knew that I must not let the opportunity go. 'Half a million pounds?' I suggested, which was a lot of money in those days. 'Right,' replied the Prime Minister, 'I will agree to that, but no more.' I thanked him again and, assuring him of my full support, I left Number Ten, astonished at my good fortune and overwhelmed by my interview with the Prime Minister.

All the reporters had gone away, no doubt having encountered my colleagues who had earlier all left in bulk, so I was able to call home and tell Brenda the exciting news and then telephone the Ministry of Education to inform them that I would be arriving after lunch.

BIRTH OF THE SPORTS COUNCIL

At the Ministry in Curzon Street I found that even the porter must have known I was coming long before I did. He greeted me warmly and told me that they had been wondering where I was. He would take me up to my room where I was expected. He did not take me via the private office, but opened the door of my own office where a small, elderly gentleman was sitting in one of the armchairs. He said, 'Good afternoon, Minister. I am Sir John Lang, your principal adviser, please allow me to greet you on your first day in office'. We shook hands and I asked him what he did and how long it took him to do it. He explained that he had been brought back out of retirement and he was doing a few half days a week advising Quintin Hogg. I told him that this was not going to be enough for me, we were going to take sport seriously, could he give me more time? He thought about that and said he would like to do so but under civil service regulations, having retired, he could not work a full week, he thought that he could do four days. I replied that I wanted my principal adviser to work five days a week but if he did not mind doing five days for four days' pay he was hired. It was the most inspired decision I ever took in my ministerial life. Sir John was a classic case of the young man who joined the Admiralty as a clerk and had then progressed through all the ranks to become permanent secretary. He had served Winston Churchill in the war and he could not have been held in higher esteem throughout Whitehall. I knew none of this at that moment, but to have such a senior man at my side as we battled for new policies, new staff and new money, was the key to everything. Wherever Sir John went, at any level of government, he was deferred to. So it was, too, with his reputation outside. For the next six years we were to enjoy the happiest of relationships.

John Lang handed me half a dozen of the thinnest files I have ever seen and told me this represented the previous Government's thinking on sport. Perhaps I would care to read them and he would return the next day to discuss them. As he was leaving he turned to me and, expressing himself as he always did, with an old world charm, he said 'May I say, Minister, that I have read most of your speeches in Opposition. I know that your party is committed to the idea of a Sports

Council. It is not for me at our first meeting to advise you against the idea but I would like the opportunity to present you with a paper setting out all the arguments against the proposal'. I had still not met any other civil servant, so I asked him how long this would take. Three weeks was the answer. I decided that I had better assert a little independence: 'You can have a fortnight', I told him. He accepted this without any difficulty and left through the private office, introducing me to Kay Masters, my principal private secretary, another appointment which I had the great good fortune to inherit. She was a first-class, cheerful secretary who could not have been more welcoming and more helpful for the first year or two of my ministerial office. I went off to pay my respects to Michael Stewart and then returned to meet Sir Herbert Andrews, the permanent secretary of the whole department. He was another person whom I came to like enormously, a small, friendly pipe-smoker who had spent years in the Board of Trade. I gained the impression that this appointment was rather surprising to him and certainly to other civil servants in the department. He never gave much away but a twinkle in his eye would tell me if I was on to a good point. Andrews knew little or nothing about sport, leaving it all to Lang, but he was always helpful. When he eventually retired he took Holy Orders and became a curate somewhere in Yorkshire. This ought not to have surprised me since some of our most interesting conversations were about the purpose and form of religious education, yet I had no idea of his devotion to his religious faith. Kay Masters explained to me some of the workings of the Ministry and we discussed what sort of routine I would like to follow. I left, taking my files with me, to enjoy my first ride home in a ministerial car, full of wonder, delight and expectation.

Day two started with an astonishing surprise. I arrived at the office to find three huge bundles of files on my desk. Kay explained to me that as the Parliamentary Secretary was my official title, I had responsibility for teacher discipline and, on behalf of the Minister, I had to take decisions about 300 or more cases a year. These cases seemed largely to consist of sexual impropriety, often involving pupils, but also adults, and such matters as misappropriation of school funds. It was explained to me that the procedure for considering these cases involved the formulation of a complaint which could originate in many different ways, quite often arising from newspaper reports. These complaints were then put to the teacher concerned and he or she could reply to them in writing or seek a personal hearing conducted by a senior member of the department. The teachers involved could be represented by a union official or could defend themselves. A file was then prepared with a recommendation to the Minister who made the final decision from which there was no appeal. As very little Government business had been transacted over the months leading up to the election there was a great backlog of cases to be determined. I picked up the first file and read the report and all the supporting documentary

evidence. It recommended the removal of the subject from the register
of teachers. It was clearly going to take me some considerable time to
carry out this responsibility in a satisfactory manner – I could not think
of a more serious decision than to remove a teacher from the professional
register. I asked for an immediate meeting with the head of this section
of the Ministry and said I would then start to deal with these cases
overnight. We moved on to more pleasant matters arising from the
Wolfenden Committee (on sport, not the one on homosexuality!), but
not before I learned that my other duties in the educational field
included responsibility for the education of handicapped children,
the schools health service, the school meals service, the education of
immigrant children, the youth service and the library service. Quite a
portfolio.

I discussed all these duties with the appropriate heads of department
who were mostly holding appointments at assistant secretary level.
They gave me a first taste of existing policies and some insight into
how their sections operated. It was time for a second meeting with
John Lang. I took to him immediately. Not only was he long in service
but he was also long in the tooth. We discussed how I could operate as
a Minister for Sport if I accepted his advice not to establish a Sports
Council. This was the most unsatisfactory part of our discussion and
we left the matter until he could produce his paper on the subject. We
turned to the other two matters which I had discussed with the Prime
Minister.

First priority was the triumphant British Olympics team performing
wonders on the athletic track in Tokyo. The press had reported that
the news of my appointment had been cheered in the athletes' village.
I was anxious to send a signal that we were in business and Sir John
advised the despatch of immediate telegrams to medal-winners, which
I readily agreed to. He was soon on the telephone giving the necessary
instructions. We then discussed the proposed reception at Number
Ten and I left him to work out the financial arrangements. The main
question had been resolved by the Prime Minister: he was giving a
Government reception and our job was to implement that decision.
Lang agreed and undertook to make contact with the British Olympic
Association to discover when the team would be returning home. We
thought that we ought to meet the team on arrival at London Airport
and sent a message to Michael Stewart asking him whether he would
wish to join us. He kindly agreed to do so.

I then told John that the Prime Minister had agreed to the award of
some honours for sport and I thought that these Olympic successes
would be a good place to start. In a style that I came greatly to respect
he told me with a degree of hesitation, but with a respectful force of
argument and great clarity of thought, that the next honours list, due
out in the New Year, had long been decided. It might be possible to
get in a few late additions but they would be very few. He would go
off and investigate. I wondered whether any of the names on the New

Year's list were sportsmen or women since they would be announced with a Labour Government in office and might be perceived as carrying our approval. He thought that this would create some considerable difficulty for me. I got the distinct impression that Ministers at my level had nothing to do with such decisions. I made it clear that I wished to be consulted. He took note of that with good grace and agreed to make enquiries.

We turned to football. My news that I had arrived with half a million pounds for the 1966 World Cup was received as a bombshell. Sir John was incredulous. 'The Treasury will never wear it', he told me. 'They will have to,' I replied, 'it has been personally sanctioned by the Prime Minister.' He enquired what ideas I had in mind and I indicated that these would have to be discussed with Denis Follows, the secretary of the Football Association. Lang had met him during the brief meeting with Quintin Hogg and he thought that this was reasonable, but not until he had cleared the lines with the Treasury. He could see minefields ahead. 'Your colleagues will not like it, they are likely to be very difficult. Collective government works on the basis of opposition from individual Ministers who are representing the interests of their departments.' This was an early but important lesson in the place of vested interest in the exercise of our joint responsibilities, and it was not to be lost upon me. I was assured that the departmental finance officer would have to be consulted and he would take steps to talk at once to the permanent secretary, who was the accounting officer, and to the Treasury. Sir John assured me that there was much for him to do as a result of these discussions and he hastily left to do it. I was happy to have started work as I intended to go on, taking initiatives and demonstrating a concern for sport which was relevant to the issues of the day as well as to its future.

I returned to my flat to think over all the events of another exciting day. I decided that I needed to seek the counsel of my friends. At that time I had no special relationship with sporting administrators except for Sir Stanley Rous, Denis Follows and Alan Hardaker, the secretary of the Football League, in which I was refereeing. All these were football men. Stanley was also chairman of the Central Council of Physical Recreation, and although we knew each other we had no close association. The two men that I decided to turn to were David Munrow, head of the PE department at Birmingham University, and his number two, Denis Molyneaux. Birmingham University was the only one to include sport as part of a degree course, and it also required all its students to undertake some sort of sport or recreational activity in their first year. Munrow had a considerable reputation. He had been a member of the Wolfenden Committee on Sport and he was a member of the executive of the Central Council of Physical Recreation. It emerged later that David Munrow and Peter McIntosh were the two members of the CCPR who had strenuously pursued the Wolfenden recommendation that a Sports Council should be created. They had opposed Phyllis Colson, the secretary of the organisation, a dominating woman who considered herself to be the embodiment of the Central Council. This was very near the truth. In consequence she persuaded Stanley Rous, the chairman, and Arthur Gem, his deputy, to line up in opposition to Wolfenden. For their part, Munrow and McIntosh were among the minority pressing for a Sports Council, having been encouraged in this direction by Walter Winterbottom when he succeeded Colson in January 1963. Previously Walter had been director of coaching at the FA and the England team manager. He took a new look at the Wolfenden recommendations and as they began to gain favour he had pursued the idea with Quintin Hogg when he was Lord Privy Seal. Hogg had responded well to the CCPR initiatives and Winterbottom had been able to negotiate with him and Sir John Lang the first Government grants to support the work of the national sports centres. At first Hogg had been inclined to favour a Sports Council but he had been persuaded by the formidable Colson that the proposal ought not to be implemented. Sport would be against it. This was in fact the situation that had caused me to write a cautionary note to Harold Wilson before the election. Dave Munrow was privy to this information which is no doubt the reason for his great delight at being invited to come round and develop his ideas with me on the following Sunday afternoon. I agreed that he could bring Denis Molyneaux with him, providing that complete confidentiality could be assured.

When we met they could not contain their delight that a Labour Government was honouring its election promise and intended to implement its policy document Leisure for Living. The appointment of Jenny Lee as the first Minister for the Arts (improbably located at the Ministry of Public Works) was regarded as another manifestation of good intention. At last sport, the arts and leisure were to be regarded as subjects of serious Government involvement. They were specially pleased with my appointment, both on personal grounds and also because I was a Birmingham man. We could more easily co-operate using the University as a base for our activities. We discussed the type of Sports Council that I would need to create. I did not reveal that I was waiting for a paper setting out the contrary arguments. It was not appropriate to do so, but it was appropriate to take advice as to how I should implement our undertakings, as I intended to do, so that I would be ready to take immediate decisions.

Both David and Denis were resolute that I had to chair the Sports Council myself. David's experience in dealing with the Ministry of Education about matters affecting his PE department and, even more so, his involvement with governmental advisers during his service on the Wolfenden Committee, had obviously left a deep scar. 'We shall never get the Sports Council off the ground unless your ministerial authority is present', was their implacable opinion. We assumed that the Sports Council would be an independent body but that did not alter their view. Why should a Minister not chair such a body? Their arguments were very convincing. The Government did not have much of a majority, and a further election would not be long delayed. My principal achievement in this period of office had to be the launch of the Sports Council as a successful organisation. We had to demonstrate that it was up and going and radically reshaping the sports scene, bringing new hope and encouragement. We moved on to consider the post of chief officer. Here we were in full accord. We considered all the possible names. We kept coming back to that of Walter Winterbottom. He was the secretary of the CCPR, to which every sport in the country was affiliated. This organisation owned and administered the national centres – Lilleshall, Bisham Abbey, Plas-y-Brenin – where they ran courses for public participation and arranged coaching and training for governing bodies. No one else in the country had such an influence. Furthermore, there was the staff to be considered. If Walter was not to have this job how was the new Sports Council going to relate to the CCPR and to its staff? The arguments were overwhelming: it had to be Winterbottom. David Munrow was the only other possible candidate and he totally ruled himself out. He wanted to be involved as a Sports Council member but he did not wish to be seen as an administrator. Walter's position as a former England football manager was not a consideration, but it was a very useful bonus.

We then turned our attention to the names of possible members of the Council. This led us to think about areas of responsibility. Molyneaux put forward the view that what we needed to do was to identify the main areas of interest with which the Council needed to concern itself and develop the structure around them. This was such obvious good sense that we immediately applied our minds to identifying them. We tossed ideas around and agreed that there were four central areas of development upon which we must concentrate. These were: 1. Facilities and Planning; 2. Coaching and Development; 3. International Participation; 4. Research. David Munrow, if he did not wish to leave Birmingham University, seemed to me to be a natural to chair the Coaching and Development Committee. He agreed. We felt that we needed a first-class local authority personality to take on board the Facilities and Planning Committee. We would have to think more about the international field and, in any case, if Walter Winterbottom agreed to become the secretary we would wish to consult him about all these matters before going hard for them. I had one further flash of inspiration: how did the idea sound of persuading Roger Bannister, our most illustrious athlete, now qualified as a medical consultant, to accept the chairmanship of the Research Committee? It sounded good, we would pursue it. Before we broke up I raised the question of what Denis Molyneaux should do. His reaction to the name of Roger Bannister had been one of great enthusiasm, as Denis's own interests were clearly in the area of research. I agreed that if Walter accepted my invitation to take over then I would suggest that Molyneaux should join the staff as one of his deputies, having special responsibility for research. It had been a fascinating meeting. We parted in great excitement, agreeing to meet again when I was ready to proceed.

Having met all my advisers and senior officials and understanding what the department's existing policies were in each of my areas of responsibility, I was able to turn again to immediate questions of sport. The most urgent of these was the British Olympic team. John Lang had already arranged for us to breakfast with them on their return. The Prime Minister's reception would need to be arranged a little later as the team would proceed directly from the airport to their homes. There were two problems. Did we wish to include the team which had represented us at the Winter Olympics in Innsbruck? 'Yes, of course, especially as Tony Nash and Robin Dixon won a bronze in the bob-sleigh event.' Next question: 'Do you realise that although the Prime Minister is hosting this party it is not usual for the department to be asked to pay for it?' No, I did not, but it seemed reasonable to me for a Minister for Sport to do so, even though as yet I did not have a budget. I was sure that when it was negotiated we could take this item on board. John seemed happy with these decisions and left to implement them.

The following week Kay Masters popped in to see me one evening just as I was about to leave. 'You are to meet Sir John tomorrow,' she said. 'He is going to present you with his paper on the Sports Council proposal and I have managed to procure an advance copy. I thought you might like to read it in bed tonight.' Excellent. It was about four pages of well-argued points which seemed to owe a great deal to the previous attitude of the CCPR and to the belief that sport would be hostile to the concept. This was no doubt a legacy of Lang's work as Hogg's adviser and of the influence of Colson. Such opposition was fading rapidly. Another of his points concerned the probable opposition of other Government departments. Again, that might well apply with the old guard but I could not see that new Ministers would wish to start by opposing a development which the Prime Minister had clearly set his heart upon. After reading through the document two or three times I decided that there was nothing here to cause me to hesitate. We would go ahead – the Sports Council was on its way.

When Sir John came into my room the following morning he had the document with him and with his old world charm he addressed me. 'Minister, I have the honour to present to you my paper on the question of a Sports Council.' 'Sir John, I am pleased to say that my admiration for the efficiency of the civil service is already growing. Mrs Masters was able to procure an advance copy of your paper which I read last night.' 'Indeed,' he said, 'in that case may I enquire whether you have reached any conclusion?' 'Yes, I have, notwithstanding all the excellent arguments in your paper as to why we should not establish a Sports Council, I have in fact decided to do so.' Without a moment's hesitation he replied, 'Very good, Minister, in that case allow me to advise you how best to proceed'. It was a classic response. The matter was never

raised again. There and then we sat down to consider the mechanics of
the operation and his advice was invaluable. I told him that I thought
I must take on the chairmanship myself. He thought this would create
difficulties as Ministers do not usually assume the chairmanship of
outside bodies. Here, my earlier discussions about my duties as the
Minister responsible for the Youth Service came to mind. I had been
advised that I would be expected to chair the Youth Service Advisory
Council as my predecessors had done, and that this was a procedure
which was greatly appreciated within the department as it helped to
facilitate the adoption of advice and its translation into policy. I decided
to take this line of argument. If it was sensible for the Youth Service
it would be sensible for sport. To my surprise Lang agreed: he nodded
his head slowly, turning the matter over in his mind. He could not see
how sport could proceed differently from the Youth Service so far as
the Ministry was concerned. 'But what about a deputy chairman?' I
considered this and had an idea. 'Since we believe it right for the
Minister to be chairman of the Sports Council we do not automatically
need to go outside for a deputy chairman. What about you taking on
the office?' Lang could see no problem there, indeed, he seemed to
relish the prospect, no doubt believing that such a position would
enable him to keep tabs on everything.

The remaining question for that meeting concerned the CCPR. John
advised that I should see them at once to discuss our relationship. I
agreed that he should ask Rous to come and see me with a few of his
executive members and Walter Winterbottom, their secretary. This
gave me the opportunity to suggest that we should have an executive
officer suitable for both sport and the Ministry. Walter Winterbottom
seemed a good candidate: he was proving to be a good secretary to the
CCPR; he would be a good man to work with in the office and he
would be a good choice for sport. Lang thought it was an interesting
idea. He told me that he would begin to draft a paper for Cabinet on
the lines we had agreed and left to do so. I went off to report all this to
Michael Stewart, who was very supportive. He told me that he was
quite happy to leave sports policy to me provided that I kept him fully
informed. This made obvious good sense as he had to represent me in
Cabinet. I was very content with my day's work, believing that I had
reached first base.

YEAR'S END

At no other time in my life have I known a period of such sustained
excitement as in the months which immediately followed my appointment as Minister. Every day produced new possibilities for creativity
and action. The pace was terrific. John Lang was caught up in the
atmosphere as much as anyone and although he always counselled
caution and rightly warned me about reactions from the Treasury and

other Ministers, his unrivalled knowledge and experience was a source of great strength. In particular, he made sure very early on that I understood how the official machine worked in relationship to Cabinet government and to Cabinet committees. He taught me that if the Treasury disapproved of any proposal then the sponsoring Minister could reckon that the Treasury line had been fed to all other departments likely to have a Minister present at the crucial meeting. In practice, as far as sport was concerned, this meant that apart from the Treasury I would have to carry my colleagues in the Scottish, Welsh and Northern Ireland Offices, local government, possibly the Home Office, the Economic Development department and so on. It was almost as if I had become a one-man lobby among my ministerial colleagues. Still, it seemed to be working. My colleagues proved on the whole to be extremely co-operative even if their officials were not wholly convinced about our aspiration.

We prepared our paper proposing the setting up of the Sports Council as an advisory body chaired by myself. It met surprisingly little opposition. I had taken good care to ensure that my paper also proposed to establish Sports Councils for Scotland and Wales and that their Secretaries of State should nominate representatives to the Sports Council of Great Britain. Nor was there any concern expressed about my intention to take the chair. I outlined the problems of time in getting the necessary legislation through Parliament if we wanted an executive council and as I soon sensed that Ministers had their own candidates for the legislation programme there was no difficulty on that front. I was able to return to my Ministry with the good news that all was well. I was very much aware that I had been considerably aided by Lang's work with the permanent secretaries.

When I returned to the Cabinet committee with plans for the 1966 World Cup it was not so easy. I faced universal scepticism as Lang had warned me beforehand. I outlined my plans for ground improvement, Government hospitality, media centres and related matters and proposed an expenditure of half a million pounds as agreed by the Prime Minister. The Treasury Minister mentioned the financial restraints facing the Government and departmental colleagues talked of their problems in having restraints imposed upon their own programmes. I had to rely upon the argument which I had briefly put to Harold Wilson, that the World Cup was one of the most important events in the sporting calendar. My appointment would not be taken seriously if on this very first major occasion the Government was not seen to be active and supportive. Not one of my colleagues actually spoke in support of my proposal but Bert Bowden, the lord president, who was in the chair, cut off the discussion by announcing that the committee approved my proposals! Clearly, he had been well briefed beforehand. Harold Wilson had kept his part of the bargain.

Sir John Lang, with the full co-operation of the department's permanent secretary, Sir Herbert Andrews, had put together an enthusiastic team of officials which formed the core of the sports division within the Education Ministry. Almost their first task was to organise the Number Ten reception for our highly successful Tokyo Olympic team. The British Olympic Association naturally wanted to include all the officials and team managers, the doctors, physios and others who had all played their part in a most successful Games. Sandy Duncan, their secretary, and John Lang managed to ensure that all who should be there were invited, altogether some 300 members and officials of the British team. Number Ten was packed out on 7 November when we all enjoyed a spectacular party. There had never been a reception of this size and certainly not of this importance for sport. Led by Tony Nash and Robin Dixon, winners of the bobsleigh event at the Innsbruck games, Mary Rand (long jump), Ken Mathews (20 kilometre walk), Lyn Davies (long jump) and Ann Packer (800 metres), we had six gold medallists, 19 silver and five bronze medallists. It was a well-deserved acknowledgement of an outstanding team triumph. The success of our athletic competitors had caught the imagination of the whole country and the two captains, Robbie Brightwell, who had also won a silver medal in the 400-metre relay, and Mary Peters, who led the women's team, had every right to be proud of their charges as they took Number Ten by storm. The party was a tremendous success. It really marked the new Government's determination to take sport seriously in a manner that was unprecedented and could not have been more emphatic. I was overjoyed. There was an interesting encounter as I arrived for the reception. Lord Exeter, formerly David Burleigh, a gold medal hurdler, was waiting by the door of Number Ten. He was vice-president of the IOC, a dominating figure. 'Hello Minister,' he greeted me, 'I am glad to note you are the Minister *for* Sport, very important that little word.' I understood the emphasis he placed on the word 'for' instead of 'of', which is the title in other countries, but I was intrigued that he chose this night of celebration to make his point. I had been warned!

Following the summer Olympics, Tokyo had also staged the Paraplegic Olympic Games where Britain had achieved spectacular success. These games, for people who had suffered terrible spinal injuries, were the brainchild of Ludwig Guttmann, a doctor of German descent who had inspired the concept of active sport to cope with the disabilities resulting from car accidents and the like. Ludwig was not everybody's cup of tea. Like all great innovators he was controversial – his ideas at the Stoke Mandeville Hospital, where he practised, were not universally applauded. Likewise, his brusque, direct approach did not always endear him to sports administrators. He did not take kindly to criticism but from our very first meeting I adored the man. He had replaced despair with hope, provided a sense of achievement for men and women who previously would have been written off. He told me, 'Until I started this programme of rehabilitation through sport these people would have been cabbages.' The evidence was before our eyes, we had to believe him. It had not taken much effort on my part to convince the Prime Minister that following his reception for the British Olympic team he ought to offer a similar party for our Paraplegic team. Mary Wilson was specially enthusiastic. It was another great 'first', a most joyous and touching occasion and the start of a long association between the Wilsons, Guttmann and Stoke Mandeville. This time the wheel-chairs of the athletes caused some problems at Number Ten but they were all overcome by a staff determined to make this reception every bit as successful as the earlier one.

Guttmann had formed the Paraplegic Sports Endowment Fund in 1955 and from that moment he strove to build a stadium at Stoke Mandeville by a total commitment to fund raising. When he came to see me early in my time as Minister he was some £4,000 short of his target. I did not have that amount in my budget but in the face of great doubts on the part of my officials and the Sports Council officers, I asked him if he would settle for £3,000, which was all I had and more than the maximum grant we had established for individual projects. He burst into tears. It was a most moving moment but I have never been more proud of being able to help any person. He was a true benefactor of mankind through sport. He started work on the Stoke Mandeville stadium and it was a great thrill to attend the opening by the Queen in 1969.

Into December and another piece of good fortune. John Hunt, the Conservative Member for Bromley, drew first place in the ballot for Private Members' Motions. He chose recreation and leisure as his subject, moving that: 'This House, recognising the necessity to channel the enthusiasm of the younger generation into constructive activity, urges Her Majesty's Government to continue to give every encour-agement to the fuller use of leisure time including further support of the arts and improved sports and Youth Service facilities'. I could not have worded the motion better. It has been the principal theme of my life ever since. In fact the debate came a little too early for me – I was still formulating ideas, selling them to my colleagues and negotiating with both the Youth Service and sport. There was going to be little positive that I could say but that mattered far less than the fact that the House was going to give a whole day to the subject and provide me with my first opportunity for a major speech.

Many other colleagues took part. It really was a first-class debate. Christopher Chataway spoke from the Opposition front bench, and as the most recent and distinguished international athlete present I knew that he would be representing the collective views of sport. He deplored the absence of Jenny Lee, the Minister for the Arts, and thought this handicapped the discussion and was discourteous to the three Members who had spoken in the debate mainly about the arts. He had not been particularly reassured, he said, by my intervention giving the news that we would have another debate on leisure in the New Year. He spent quite an amount of his time dealing with the problems of the Youth

Service and then he moved on to sport, offering generous congratulations upon my appointment. However, he quoted a previous speech of mine advocating the appointment of a Cabinet Minister to deal with sport, and asked, quite reasonably, where he was. He contrasted my level with that of Quintin Hogg who had been dealing with sports questions for the previous Government although not designated as a Minister for Sport. He thought I had inherited a good deal and hoped I would keep up the momentum. Finally, he thought we overplayed the importance of international sport as compared with the opportunity for all to enjoy sport and recreation to the full.

It had been a very wide-ranging debate and it was going to be impossible for me to reply to all the points raised. I was somewhat daunted by the task and I probably made the mistake of attempting too much. Certainly I spoke for too long which is definitely one of my failings. In all I took 50 minutes but I dealt with most of the youth and sporting questions and gave trailers of many things to come. I started by referring to the presence of Michael Stewart, the Secretary of State, who would be our voice in the Cabinet. It was then important to assure sport that the Government had no wish or intention to control sport. As far as recreation in the countryside was concerned I was able to announce that the Minister of Land and Natural Resources, Fred Willey, was reviewing the national parks with a view to 'revitalising them and making them greater assets to the country for recreation and leisure'. Next on my list was the almost prohibitive cost of obtaining land for the voluntary bodies of sport. I had already started to think about that problem. In response to Tam Dalyell, I recognised the importance of coaching and of swimming facilities. I took this first opportunity to make an encouraging reference to the National School Sports Association and to reaffirm our commitment to the policy of joint planning and provision in schools so that educational facilities were available for the whole community. This led me on to the importance of local authority parks departments and my failure to understand why so many of them 'shut their parks at five o'clock at night for eight months of the year when most people are coming out of their offices and factories'. Another initiative I touched upon was that of regionalism and I promised an early announcement about regional surveying and planning for sport and recreation, citing the pioneering work being undertaken in the north-east. A major announcement which I was able to make to the House was the decision to purchase a site at Cowes for the creation of a national sailing centre. I then turned my attention to questions about the Youth Service which had been raised in many speeches and I made one final announcement, that Lady Albemarle had accepted my invitation to follow up her famous report by chairing a committee of the Youth Service Development Council to assess the progress made in the five years since her report was published and to chart the lines of future development. I concluded with a declaration of faith in present day youth: 'The majority of our young people are decent and keen and they intend to make a contribution to life. The Government do not think that the young people are going to the dogs. On the contrary, we believe that the quality of the mass of the young people is higher today than it has ever been before'.

As we moved to the New Year Harold Wilson took action on one of my other proposals: sporting honours. I had confirmed that it was not possible to take much action at this late stage since the honours list for the New Year had long been prepared when we came into office. The Prime Minister had obviously taken the proposal seriously and had ideas of his own which he kindly discussed with me. He thought that the wonderful skills of Stanley Matthews and the pleasure he had given to millions of people had never been properly acknowledged by the football establishment. There was wide acclaim when a knighthood was conferred upon him, making him football's first Knight. The list also contained the unique honour of an MBE for a husband and wife, Ann Packer and Robbie Brightwell, representing the achievements of both the men's and women's teams in Tokyo.

When the New Year dawned I had held office for some ten weeks. It had proved to be the most exhilarating ten weeks of my life so far. I was well content that we had created the foundation of a new future for British sport. I could indeed raise my glass to the prospects of a Happy New Year.

SPORTS COUNCIL MEMBERSHIP

When Stanley Rous brought his team to see me they were in no way hostile to the idea of a Sports Council, but as I outlined our thinking on staffing questions they naturally became concerned as to the effects this would have upon their own organisations. They were also anxious about the national centres which they owned and controlled. What influence was the Sports Council to have in these areas? Perfectly proper questions but difficult to answer at this early stage. I could see that there was one other question present in their minds although it was never mentioned: 'Your Government has a tiny majority, if we go overboard for these new ideas what happens to us and to our staff if you lose the next election which cannot be far away?' It was clear to me that I could only make proper progress if I met that unspoken fear. We moved to the questions of the chief officer. I explained that I wanted Walter Winterbottom for the post. They accepted the logic and thought this would give them some reassurance. Walter himself said he would need to think about it although he was very pleased to be considered. However, he did not wish to move to us on a permanent basis – no doubt because of our political situation – but if he came he felt he had to retain some links with the CCPR. Secondment seemed a natural answer and the idea was well received all round when John Lang suggested it.

Within the week the CCPR accepted the idea that Winterbottom should join our staff along with Sheila Hughes, his secretary, who had in fact moved with Walter from his previous post at the Football Association. So our top team was assembled: the Minister, John Lang, Walter Winterbottom and Denis Molyneaux, who became joint deputy director with George McPartland. We settled down to put together the membership of the Sports Council and to determine its structure, which followed exactly the form that had been agreed in my home on that first Sunday afternoon. David Munrow was first confirmed as chairman of the Sports Development and Coaching Committee. Dr Roger Bannister accepted my invitation to come and discuss his possible involvement in the new Sports Council and I was delighted when he agreed to take on the work of the Research Committee with Molyneaux as his principal officer. I explained that it was a great concern that the next Olympic Games would be in Mexico City some 7,500 feet above sea level and we needed good research into the problems of competing at that altitude in order to give advice about preparation. Roger was enthusiastic and thought he could do it now that he was established as a consultant neurologist. Lady Burton – Elaine – had been a colleague in the House who had always taken an interest in sports questions. She had herself been an active sportswoman and I thought it a good idea to have a Member from the upper House. Elaine readily agreed to chair the International Committee. This left the Facilities Planning Committee. I had no doubt that I wanted someone from local government and after a wide trawl my officials reported that Lord Porchester seemed to be perfectly cast for the role. He owned large areas of land in Hampshire and was chairman of the county council; he had pioneered the opening up of access for the public both on his own land and on public land. He came to see me and we got on famously. He immediately accepted my invitation to become chairman of the important Strategy Committee. All of us were now able to think about the rest of the Council and to achieve a balance of interests and experience which could hardly have been broader, both in terms of sport and recreation as well as from a geographical standpoint.

My Scottish ministerial colleagues very helpfully proposed Dr Stewart Mackintosh, the director of education for Glasgow, and Menzies Campbell, a distinguished athlete who was to go on to become a Queen's Counsel and, later, Member of Parliament for Fife North-East. The Welsh Office were equally helpful with their nominations and produced the names of Clive Rowlands, a legend in rugby football, and George Edwards, a fine outside left of the national soccer team and at that time a director of Cardiff City. I was determined to have more than just one woman member and we were very fortunate to obtain the services of Mrs Kathleen Holt, a national figure in the sport of lacrosse. She had two other advantages so far as I was concerned: she came from Lancashire and she was the wife of Arthur Holt, the Liberal MP for

Bolton, thus widening the regional and political interests of the new Council while more than justifying her membership on her own merits. John Disley was another Welshman, then and now domiciled in England, who after a very successful athletics career had taken up a great interest in all sports of a recreational character and had pioneered the new sport of orienteering. John Dower had a fine reputation in the field of community planning and rural affairs, and was also associated with the Dartington Trust. From the regions I chose Dan Smith, who had more imagination and drive than most. He had pioneered the concept of regional arts and regional sport and while he served with us we all valued his contributions.

I wanted one or two younger people who were active sportsmen but who also had a contribution to make through their own professional skills and I was delighted when David Bacon, an accountant and a director of Murrayfield, the developers, agreed to serve, as I was with the acceptance of Bernard Donoghue. I had first met Bernard at Oxford where he was a Fellow of Northfield College and by this time he was lecturing at the London School of Economics. He went on to head the think tank at Number Ten and to become a peer of the realm. Finally, it was my belief that sport had an enormous contribution to make in a multi-racial society. I wanted a personality who could pre-eminently represent that fact. It was my great good fortune to obtain the support of Sir Learie Constantine, the finest all-round cricketer who had thrilled me as a youngster, a legend in his lifetime and a wonderful inspiration for his own people now settled here.

Quintin Hogg for the Opposition and Philip Noel-Baker were warm in their appreciation, specially welcoming the appointment of the director and urging me to keep after the Treasury for more funds. Antony Fell from the Conservative benches wanted an assurance that the new Council 'will not result in any cost to the taxpayer'. He got short shrift. Tam Dalyell enquired as to how the Sports Council would carry out a policy of regional planning and I was able to refer to the role of the CCPR and the lead it had already taken in the creation of regional machinery for the north-east. I also referred to the association we would have with the National Playing Fields Association and the British Olympic Association. Finally, the Earl of Dalkeith asked about the tourist industry, especially Scottish tourism, and I reassured him on the question while making it clear that 'the members are independent people not representing any other interest'.

The announcement was well received. I was satisfied by the warm welcome it was given in the House and later throughout sport as I was by the subsequent media coverage. Here and there a few established voices raised doubts, mostly in muted tone, but there was no doubt that my discussions with Stanley Rous and his colleagues, and Winterbottom's appointment, had been of cardinal importance in producing a helpful and constructive response. John Lang, in co-operation with Herbert Andrews, had done a fine job in assembling an office of civil servants who were as enthusiastic as we were. We had every reason to face the future with confidence.

There was an amusing sequence to my announcement. Lord Porchester asked if he could introduce me to the Duke of Edinburgh whom I had not previously met. HRH Prince Philip was the president of the CCPR and prominently associated with the National Playing Fields Association, and his other wide interests in sport were also well known. He wanted to know my thinking as to how my sports policies would be developed. I agreed without hesitation and an early appointment was arranged. When I entered Prince Philip's study and as soon as the introductions were effected, the Prince proceeded to the heart of the matter with a frankness I have come to admire. 'This Sports Council you have appointed,' he said, 'there isn't one of them who knows his arse from his elbow.' I reflected that if this was to be the level at which our discussions were to be conducted I would be very much at home! In the intervening years we have had many differences of opinion but these have been easily outnumbered by the occasions upon which we have made common cause on sporting matters. Sport is fortunate indeed to have such a formidable and knowledgeable champion fighting on its behalf. On this occasion he was concerned that my appointments were independent of the governing bodies of sport. In particular he mentioned Learie Constantine. I had guessed that one or two people at Lord's would have preferred a more establishment cricketing figure but I explained that Learie was not going to represent them, he would probably represent the genuine club cricketer and many who played at senior level, but all of us admired his great skills and enthusiasm for sport and most cricketers would be glad that he was contributing to the Sports Council. However, none of that was the reason for his appointment, which was to create a bond with the new ethnic generation of youngsters for whom sport is very important. The second name mentioned by Prince Philip was David Munrow. I explained that Dave was no mere academic from Birmingham University: he was actually a member of the CCPR executive and I went on to explain the development of sport at his university under his stewardship. I got the impression that Prince Philip was basing his thoughts on the views of the CCPR secretary, whom Munrow had opposed on the very question of creating a Sports Council, and that therefore this might well be the source of the briefing. Whether or not I was right about this the Prince seemed to accept my explanations and we went on to have a very constructive discussion.

This conversation led me to consider the essential point Prince Philip had made which was whether or not I had included in the membership of the Sports Council sufficient numbers of people from the CCPR who had been elected to represent sport. He clearly did not think that Walter Winterbottom came into this category. I resolved to improve the situation. During the ensuing year I made other appointments because it soon became obvious that we needed more members to man the committees. This also gave me the opportunity to meet Prince Philip's point and to widen the spread of interests. From the CCPR itself I recruited Mary Glen-Haig, who had fenced for Great Britain in three Olympics and who later became a member of the International Olympic Committee; Peter McIntosh, an inspector of education and author of a number of publications on physical education; and Jack Longland, who was director of Derbyshire Education Department and a specialist in outdoor pursuits. His was a good name to have, a much welcomed appointment.

It was soon clear to me that I needed some industrial involvement and these places were taken up by Bob Gibb of ICI, Desmond Brayley, who later became a Labour member of the House of Lords, and Leslie Wood, a member of the TUC General Council. As I strongly believe that such bodies as the Sports Council should represent all shades of political opinion, provided that the persons concerned also possess sporting merit, I was delighted when my friend, Conservative MP Arthur Tiley, accepted my invitation to serve. The other appointments I made ensured that I kept the balance so far as distinguished sports people were concerned. Brian Close was just the type of cricketer whom most young people admired and Cliff Jones of Welsh rugby fame came on to replace Clive Rowlands, who had discovered that membership of the Sports Council was going to be more time-consuming than he had expected. On a visit to Scotland I took note of accomplished Scottish athlete Janet Sinclair, who had spoken with real flair, and I determined to persuade her to join the main Sports Council as well as to serve in Scotland.

By the time we were fully into our stride there were 26 of us serving as members. We proved to be a most harmonious and dedicated team, determined to achieve great things for sport.

WORLD CUP PREPARATION

It was inevitable that the whole of 1965 would be dominated by preparations for the World Cup. I did a lot of other work both in sport and in education but from the outset I was determined that this had to be my first priority. It would be important for the country that this event, second only to the Olympic Games in international prestige, should be staged in a manner which reflected credit on me and on the new ministerial post which I was proud to occupy. I threw myself wholeheartedly into the organisation.

The Football Association had already decided on the grounds where the matches were to be played in the summer of 1966 but Denis Follows could not give me any details as to what needed to be done at each of these grounds in order to make them suitable to host visitors from all over the world. What soon became clear was that the clubs themselves didn't know either – they had no appreciation of the standards we ought to aim for or of the means by which the necessary work was to be financed. John Lang readily agreed with me that we would have to establish our own standards. That meant personal visits to every one of the grounds where matches would take place. I called in Sir Stanley Rous, the president of FIFA. He could not have been more helpful but he had little to contribute on the subject of ground improvements. He did however put down a very important marker on the question of media coverage at each of the centres. We discussed the nations that would be likely to qualify as I realised that this would be important in terms of hospitality. If officials, supporters and even Government Ministers were going to arrive here with their teams then suitable arrangements had to be made. They would be people of substance used to high standards of comfort and they certainly would not tolerate the male-orientated provision which was normal at English football grounds in the mid-1960s.

Alan Hardaker had to join our team. Alan was extremely efficient and the most forceful administrator that football has known. He did not like the FA too much but he spoke for the clubs. He would be the link with them, convincing them that co-operation was essential and emphasising that we would be offering financial assistance towards the necessary work. Walter Winterbottom, now fully established as director of the Sports Council, completed the team. His experience as a previous England team manager was invaluable. We were ready to go and I announced my plans to Parliament. I assembled the full team I had now put together to form the core of this operation: Minister in the chair, Lang (chief adviser and representative of the government machine – especially the Treasury), Walter Winterbottom, Stanley Rous, Denis Follows and Alan Hardaker. First on the agenda were the spectators. Most of our grounds are products of the Industrial Revolution and many of them still needed a great uplift in standards of comfort. A World Cup played in the summer months would require much more seating at the stadia where matches would take place and an enormous improvement in toilet facilities. Then there was the question of women spectators and the wives of VIP visitors – they did not seem to figure in the thinking of most clubs. That would have to be changed.

The Cup draw would, in effect, regionalise the opening rounds of the competition and for this purpose the grounds had been paired off, with the exception of Wembley, which was to stage the opening game, one of the semi-finals and, of course, the final. Wembley would also stage other matches in the group to which the England team had been allocated. The two Midland clubs were to be Sheffield Wednesday, who would also stage one of the quarter-finals, and Aston Villa; the north-west group provided us with Everton, who would host a semi-final, and Manchester United. The north-eastern group contained Sunderland and Newcastle United when we started our planning but a dispute had broken out between Newcastle and their city council about the lease of the land upon which the club was situated. I went to Newcastle and discussed the matter with both sides but I was not able to help resolve it quickly enough. The necessary work had to start at once if it was to be completed in time and the FA rightly decided to transfer these matches from Newcastle to Middlesbrough. To say that there was not a day to spare in this operation was no exaggeration – when I arrived in Middlesbrough on the morning of the first match there I called at the ground, Ayresome Park, and was astonished to see a lorry containing a staircase, backing up to the directors' room. Waiting to receive it was Charles Amer, the Middlesbrough chairman, standing on the landing with a huge roll of carpet, a hammer and some tacks. As soon as the staircase was in position he rolled the carpet down and proceeded to tack it himself! John Lang and I looked on in awe, but, as promised, the job was completed on time.

As we toured the country going from ground to ground we attracted enormous publicity. Everywhere we were met by reporters, photographers, radio men and television cameras. The principal effect of this was to ensure that the whole country became aware of an event which had hardly registered with the public until our 'grand tour'. We went first to Hillsborough, home of Sheffield Wednesday, because chairman Dr Andrew Stephen, who was also the chairman of the FA, and Eric Taylor, recognised as one of the outstanding club secretaries, would be extremely knowledgeable and co-operative people to work with and to help us establish our priorities. A new stand was required if the ground was to provide the number of seats we thought would be necessary. We discussed the hospitality areas for our overseas visitors and Eric Taylor suggested that a new building could be provided which could afterwards be transformed into a gymnasium. Later on a further stand was built behind one of the goals. I was determined that as far as possible we would encourage the clubs to create facilities which would be permanent improvements to their grounds, so that after the World Cup we would have half-a-dozen top class football stadia.

Sheffield also had a first-class county FA secretary in Ernest Kangley. We explained that we needed an efficient and comfortable press centre in the city as well as good facilities at the ground and we charged him with responsibility for locating a suitable building and setting it up. We had also agreed in committee that each of the participating clubs would need to be allocated a training ground for their exclusive use, and a good hotel where they could establish their headquarters. Denis Follows had prime responsibility in this area as it was an FA matter, and he was very confident that Kangley could be relied upon to supervise all this at Sheffield. So it proved. All of us were very pleased with the outcome of our Sheffield visit. We had established a checklist of priorities and we knew that before we made our next visit the football grapevine would alert the other clubs as to what we were looking for and how we intended to proceed.

Sunderland and Middlesbrough are both cramped grounds. The

opportunity for improvement was limited but the clubs were anxious to play their part as well as to take as much advantage as they could of a once-in-a-lifetime offer of a Government grant. They would certainly not experience again a visiting Minister urging them to do more. They were still a little incredulous, mainly because of our inability at the time of the visit to tell them how much help they could expect to receive. At Old Trafford Matt Busby, Manchester United's most successful manager, was ready with a list of proposals and we were able to endorse them. We travelled on to Liverpool where we met John Moores, the chairman of Everton. Goodison Park was second only to Wembley in importance for they would stage both a quarter-final and a semi-final tie as well as matches in the opening rounds of the competition. We had already told the clubs that we wanted a festival atmosphere, that we would expect flags to be flown for all the competing nations, that the stadia had to look good. The Everton chairman was concerned that his club could not provide good entrance facilities since there was a small row of houses which prevented him from doing so. I went and inspected the houses and agreed with him that they ought to go. The difficulty was that the Liverpool City Council had a very acute housing problem, and as old and unsatisfactory as these houses obviously were they could not provide alternative accommodation. John Moores was head of the Littlewoods Football Pools and reported to be very wealthy. I suggested to him that if he bought some houses to rehouse the families living in the properties we wished to demolish I might get the Council to agree to pull them down. Moores was very sceptical. He seemed to think that the city fathers were not too well disposed towards Everton but he agreed to let me negotiate with them. In fact they could not have been more ready to co-operate and so John Moores was able to proceed with the scheme. Apparently the tenants were delighted. Later on, describing the visit to the Prime Minister, Sir Stanley Rous gave an impersonation of the Minister for Sport standing on the terraces, waving his arms in dramatic style and declaring 'the houses must go'. This was at the Guildhall banquet given by the Government to honour the World Cup. Stanley's speech was greeted with great laughter by the guests and by Harold Wilson, who was a local MP. He told me 'I have never been able to get slum houses cleared so quickly!'

Aston Villa was the last of the clubs to be visited on our travels. I knew every cranny of Villa Park and the directors were all friends of mine. Two of them were widowers and two of them were bachelors. When chairman Chris Buckley asked me 'Where would you like to start, Minister?', he was astonished when I told him 'We will visit your ladies' room'. It was clear that he had done no such thing himself, nor had any of his colleagues. We pointed out the importance of the powder room, the need for plenty of mirrors and creature comforts and then toured the rest of Villa Park. It was agreed that a new stand was needed on the Witton Lane side of the ground and I thought that they ought to build another behind the goal at the Witton end of the ground but I could not persuade them to do so. They settled for providing temporary seating on the terraces which everyone agreed was a big improvement but, sadly, this had to go after the competition was over. I received quite a few complaints from supporters who had enjoyed the new amenity. Years later the club built a fine new stand for which, of course, there was no financial grant from the Government.

By late spring Lang was able to inform me that on the basis of the work which we had agreed on our tour he recommended that we fix the level of grant at 50 per cent for substantial work of a permanent nature and 90 per cent for temporary installations, and that he had obtained Treasury approval for such a formula. I agreed, and in May I was able to make my announcement in the House setting out the details.

We were on our way. Denis Follows and his staff had an enormous task to promote and market the event and to supervise the many thousands of ticket sales. He built up a fine team of administrators and volunteers who successfully carried out these responsibilities. Meanwhile, Alf Ramsey was building his squad and developing his team strategy. We had every cause to look to 1966 with confidence.

QUESTIONS OF SPORT

My first year as a Minister excited a considerable interest in sporting questions both inside and outside the House. It was a new opportunity for Members to table questions on sport and my postbag told me that the sporting public were going to take advantage of this situation by urging their MPs to put questions down or to write to the Minister. In February we had a change of senior Minister. Michael Stewart, who had been very supportive of all my endeavours, moved to the Foreign Office after Patrick Gordon-Walker had failed to re-enter the Commons following a disastrous by-election at Leyton. Michael's position as Secretary of State for Education was filled by Antony Crosland. I could not have been more pleased. Tony was a very old Gaitskellite friend with a passionate interest in sport. He left it all to me and whenever I called upon him for advice or for help in Cabinet he was first-class.

In December 1964 Harry Howarth, the Labour Member for Wellingborough, presented a Sports Facilities Bill to regularise the conduct of pool betting for the advancement of football, other sports and recreation. He was supported by six other Members including Jack Dunnett, who was a football club chairman and later became president of the Football League, and Arthur Tiley, who was my Conservative pair. This Bill was a bit of an embarrassment to me. The Treasury was not going to have any of it. The tax on pools betting was 25 per cent, having been reduced the year before from 33 per cent. It was not possible to allow an independent body to regulate a tax on pools which would have been the effect of Harry Howarth's Bill. I persuaded my colleagues that we could not simply oppose the Bill and that there was an obvious need to examine football administration. I took a paper to the appropriate Cabinet committee and obtained their support. Then I negotiated privately with Howarth and he was happy that his initiative had produced the kind of enquiry as I proposed. He withdrew his Bill with the *quid pro quo* that I would make a statement in the House, which I did on 9 February 1965. In fact, this was the first occasion on which I informed the House that the Government would provide financial assistance for the World Cup, so along with my announcement that we intended to establish a Committee of Enquiry into Association Football, it was quite an important occasion for football and for me. Philip Noel-Baker raised a point of order to make the comment 'Is it not fortunate that we have a Government that is prepared to treat these matters as of great public interest?'.

I had problems putting together the members of the Enquiry into Association Football and I was not able to announce its composition and terms of reference until 23 June. It was an excellent team chaired by Dr Norman Chester, the Warden of Nuffield College, Oxford, who was not only a brilliant founding father of the college and a specialist in local government finance but an enthusiastic supporter of the game. His name was suggested to me by Dr Bernard Donaghue, who had been a post-graduate researcher at Nuffield, and Philip Williams, another personal friend from the Gaitskell campaign days, who was a Fellow of the college. I had invited Bernard Donoghue, Dave Munrow and Arthur Tiley to serve as members of the Sports Council. Two economists and financiers of distinction were Clifford Barclay, an accountant and financial manager from the private sector, and Nicholas Davenport, the distinguished financial and political journalist. They were joined by Lewis Hawser QC, a most experienced barrister who was, as I was told by Harold Lever, 'a most formidable cross-examiner', which was what I needed. My Birmingham colleague Brian Walden, MP for All Saints, was very anxious to serve and he and Arthur Tiley kept the party political balance. We also needed two members with experience of playing the game itself but they could not come from within the administration since that was what we were enquiring into. I was fortunate to get Bill Slater, a university physical education man but no mere academic – he was better known as a fine amateur player and captain of England and Wolverhampton Wanderers – and Welshman Mervyn Griffiths, one of the finest football referees I have ever seen. His refereeing in the famous Cup final between Bolton Wanderers and Blackpool – the Stanley Matthews final – was a joy to behold.

I announced the appointment of the committee in a statement to the Commons on 23 June when I also set out the terms of reference: 'To enquire into the state of Association Football at all levels including its organisation, management finance and administration, and the means by which the game can be developed for the public good; and to make recommendations'. The appointment of this committee taught me an important lesson. I had originally intended to appoint Sir John Foster QC as its chairman. He was the Tory MP for Nantwich and his name had been suggested to me by Harold Lever, my ministerial colleague. However, no one had advised me that such an appointment required the personal authority of the Prime Minister. An added difficulty was that Foster or someone else in the know disclosed the matter to his local newspaper and reports appeared. It was these reports which drew the matter to the PM's attention and I was summoned to explain myself. Harold Wilson accepted my account as to how this situation had arisen and said that in these circumstances he would certainly not approve of Foster's appointment. He asked if I had considered anyone else and as soon as I mentioned Norman Chester he declared himself very happy to agree. The Chester Committee did an excellent job of work. It is still referred to as the standard authority on all matters of football organisation and as we shall see, when it reported, its proposals were totally relevant and far-sighted if not wholly acceptable to the Government.

Throughout the first year of my office Members were raising questions on a whole range of sporting issues which must have been exercising their minds long before my appointment provided the opportunity to raise them on the floor of the House. The black market sale of tickets for important sports events was a very early starter: alas, it is still with us. The need for an international rowing course of Olympic standard, built from disused gravel pits, attracted my sympathy and later on I was able to take the lead in providing one in Nottinghamshire. The rating of sports grounds, although concerned with Scotland, still arouses widespread concern throughout the UK, as does the conduct of both players and spectators in the sport of Association Football. We were to hear much more about these subjects over the years ahead. On the need to give financial support to schools sport, especially the English Schools Athletic Association, I announced in May 1965 that one of the first things I had done was to send for the officers of the schools sports associations and advise them that they were to receive practical financial encouragement in their work. On a somewhat different theme Sir John Langford-Holt, the Tory MP for Shrewsbury, wanted me to set up a control body for professional wrestling similar to the one in existence for boxing. I was able to reply: 'It does not fall within my responsibility. I understand that there are about 400 wrestlers and that they have formed a private wrestlers' union, which has very appropriately affiliated to the Variety Artistes Federation'. Albert Murray, the Labour Member for Rochester, wanted me to withdraw my World Cup grant to the FA because that body would not allow the televising of any games except the Cup final!

As an indication of the progress being made, towards the end of my first parliamentary session as a Minister I was able to announce that 33 grants totalling £44,581 had been made to sailing and yachting clubs. Another matter that attracted attention was a difficulty between the

Amateur Swimming Association and the city of Cardiff which in fact arose from a dispute between the BBC and ITV. The dispute was settled on the basis that the BBC would televise the swimming events on Friday evenings and ITV on Saturday afternoons. Honours even! Drug-taking by amateur sportsmen is another continuing question which was first raised with me in July 1965 by Eric Lubbock from the Liberal benches.

The requirements of the British Olympic team competing in the next Games at Mexico City in 1968 had exercised my mind since the day of my appointment. I was able to tell Parliament that an adequate research programme had been initiated with suitable financial support and would be under Dr Roger Bannister's supervision. This announcement set out the ground rules for our Olympic preparation and I believe that it led to a better performance than might otherwise have been the case. An early but important matter requiring my attention was the need for a national recreation centre for Wales to be built in Cardiff. It was strongly supported by the Sports Council and with the support of the Secretary of State I soon told Parliament of the intention of the Government to move in this direction.

The importance of the Commonwealth Games was also raised with me early on with special reference to the participation of all the home countries in the Jamaican 1966 Games. The House was informed that every encouragement would be given by the Government to enable the appropriate bodies to formulate their plans which I would discuss with Ministers and the Sports Council. Another perennial question was the need to get school playing fields opened up to outside organisations, a problem that is still with us 25 years on. As was to be expected I was repeatedly questioned about money and grants for buildings, grounds, and in support of the Sports Council. In March 1965 I disclosed that the direct Exchequer assistance to sport and physical recreation for England and Wales would be increased from £743,000 in 1964–65 to £1,288,000 for 1965–66 and in Scotland from £172,000 to £283,000. This overall increase from £915,000 in 1964–65 to £1,571,000 the following year represented a growth of 70 per cent. Not enough, but a good start.

8

THE VICTORIES OF 1966

OFF TO THE REGIONS

Having put the Sports Council together and established the regional sports councils I was fortunate to persuade a fine collection of diverse characters to accept appointments as regional chairmen. They proved to be a wonderful blend of sporting, industrial and local government people who gave excellent leadership in the formative years of my new policies. The CCPR assigned their regional officers to act as the new regional secretaries and the whole exercise proved to be an exhilarating experience for all of us in sport and in government.

I decided to visit each region and to convene a regional conference made up of representatives of all their sports bodies, every local authority and other interested organisations. The meetings were a great success. There were avalanches of questions. Very few were hostile – everyone recognised the potential of new initiatives. The sporting representatives were however a bit apprehensive about the presence of so many local authority people. We had spent a lot of time thinking this through. I pointed out I was a local authority man myself, as well as a sportsman, and I knew that in terms of sports provision for the people the local authorities were the great providers. There was resistance to the idea that the local authority membership should have a majority on the regional council but I argued that while I wanted sport to be well represented on the council, decisions which called for a lot of expenditure by statutory bodies responsible to the ratepayers had to be seen to be influenced by members serving on local authority bodies. The most convincing argument was the fact that for the first time sport would have a direct influence on planning and provision and, if necessary, calling people to account about progress.

The greatest interest centred on the question of who would represent the sports bodies and how they would be selected. Winterbottom, Lang and I had thought hard about this and we decided that at each conference we would divide the sports people into three groups – indoor sports, outdoor sports and outdoor recreation – and let them elect their own quota of members for the regional council. This removed responsibility from the centre. It proved to be a good balance. Every major local authority was given the right to appoint a representative and the lesser authorities to choose representatives from their ranks. Finally, I reserved for myself the right to appoint half-a-dozen or so 'Minister's representatives' who were usually well-known sportsmen or women. I thought it would give the Council a bit of 'sporting sex appeal' or fill a gap which I might spot when looking at the list of members elected or nominated. These gaps were usually to be found in the need for people experienced in women's sport, major sports, outdoor recreation, country landowners, industry and commerce. The most important and influential decision I took was to create a Regional Planning Committee whose membership consisted of the chief planning officers of each of the county councils and the big cities plus some officers from the minor districts and boroughs. All the progress we achieved stemmed from this decision, rightly urged upon me by my officers. It won the confidence of both local and central government.

We took our 'travelling circus' down to Wales and were received with great enthusiasm. Jim Kegie, the planning officer for Monmouthshire, was the doyen of all Welsh planners and he had great qualities of vision and realism. His warm welcome and support totally eliminated any latent opposition there might have been in the principality as well as any nationalistic objections. All were silent. Harold Oakes had done a first-class job on the Welsh sports bodies and gained their full support and, as I expected, he became a superb secretary of the Welsh Sports Council. Alderman Philip Squires took the chair at this inaugural meeting and I had no hesitation in recommending him to Jim Griffiths, the Secretary of State for Wales, as the chairman. Jim took a great interest in the formation of the new Council and produced some names of his own for consideration as Minister's nominees. His suggestions were based on his own personal acquaintanceship and all the better for that. I never return to Wales without a feeling of great personal satisfaction. On the day of the inauguration of the Council they took me off to see a statue of the ancient King Hyel Dda – Howell of the Good – the great Welsh law-maker who died in the year 950, which stands in the City Hall. He had a peaceful reign of some 40 years, bringing together all the wise men of Wales to promulgate the laws and customs of the land. I adopted him as my great predecessor.

Scotland proved to be a very different proposition. The Scottish Office was worried about Scottish susceptibilities and was much more nationalistic than the Welsh. The Secretary of State for the Scottish Council of Physical Recreation, May Brown, had warned us that we would not have an easy ride. The Scottish Office had clearly put some pressure upon Willie Ross, the Secretary of State, which he conveyed to me in a very reasonable manner, all things considered. I soon gathered that this was a traditional approach towards any 'sassenach' Minister showing pretensions towards Scotland. However, once more, I had to stake my claim in emphatic terms. The Prime Minister had appointed me to be the British Minister for Sport. I would work in the closest co-operation with my Scottish and Welsh colleagues and I would certainly include two representatives of each nation on the Sports Council, but as so much of our international sport is British, that was how it had to be with me. We were to find that some of this nationalistic feeling had seeped through to the sports bodies and I detected that any hostility that existed among them was not directed so much towards me or my Government colleagues as to the institutions, whether central government or British sports administration.

Sensing difficulty, I called upon Learie Constantine, who had agreed to serve upon the Sports Council to help in such an emergency. We met in Edinburgh. The atmosphere was challenging, but there was genuine astonishment that I had brought Learie along. Walter Winterbottom was also well respected throughout sport and John Lang completed our team. Being so senior in civil service terms, Lang was a useful presence. I decided that I had to open the batting myself but that Learie would come in first wicket down. I gave a broad address designed to convince them all that our philosophy was right and very much in the interests of Scotland. Britain had to develop a strategy for sport. Learie was in top form. He told a number of good cricket stories, talked about the importance of sport for 'the kids of the country', as well as about its international significance, and he wound up with kind personal references, saying that he would not have accepted the Prime Minister's invitation to serve unless he had every confidence in my 'ability to perform'. When he sat down the issue was settled. Scottish sport would co-operate. With Dr Stewart Mackintosh, director of education for Glasgow in the chair and Mrs May Brown, a much respected but formidable secretary, we always managed to reconcile any differences of opinion. We returned to our hotel content with the way the conference had gone and our day's work. We now had the nine English regions in place and the Welsh and Scottish Sports Councils in operation. As we celebrated in our hotel Learie paid me a compliment which I cherish to this day. He asked me if I appreciated that I had a 'natural warmth' which brought a ready response. Be that as it may I had no doubt that this was another Constantine spectacular. He had fully justified my decision to include him in the Sports Council on grounds of sporting ability and charisma, and I was confident that he would produce dividends in terms of multi-racial sport.

VICTORY AT THE POLLS

Tony Crosland soon achieved full command of the Educational Ministry. His intellect was a match for any of the officials and quickly earned their respect. His style was quite delightful – relaxed, amused but always to the point. He was far more radical than the left wing of the Labour Party could ever bring themselves to acknowledge. Compared to him they were positively conservative, often reactionary, over the whole range of economic and educational policies. His political judgment proved to be first-class. It was my opinion that Harold Wilson was forced to promote him in spite of initial reluctance to advance the claims of the Gaitskellites. Ability promoted itself. Tony placed great store upon regular meetings with his ministerial team, both to discuss the business of the department and also to 'gossip', as he put it, about political problems. The dividing line between our educational decisions and our political chat was marked by the introduction of drinks which were never handed round while official business was before us.

There was never any doubt that Harold Wilson would get the date of the election right. He was a political Prime Minister to the tip of his fingers. The press went overboard for him and took in everything he had to say about the technological revolution. He scored heavily at the despatch box and the polls moved steadily in our direction. By March 1966 the announcement of the election became inevitable. The hesitations of 1964 had become the certainties of 1966. It was a joy to be one of Harold's Ministers in that campaign, moving about the country to general acclaim and making enjoyable speeches. I took the principal responsibility for the Birmingham campaign committee, sharing this with Julius Silverman and Roy Hattersley. Roy Jenkins had to undertake a major national tour but he took care to be back in the city for the main rally, which was addressed by Harold Wilson to a tumultuous reception.

Jack Davis was again my agent. His confidence was well justified by the Small Heath result. Although my small electorate had been further reduced by some 2,500 compared to 1964 I increased my majority from 6,777 to 10,604, a swing of 8.35 per cent compared with a national swing of 3 per cent to Labour. Birmingham did well for us. Two other constituencies, Roy Jenkins at Stechford and Roy Hattersley at Sparkbrook, also managed a swing of more than 8 per cent. The city as a whole registered a 6.8 per cent swing and so the pendulum returned decisively and more than compensated for our failure to match the rest of the country in 1964. Birmingham led the nation in recording its confidence in the Labour Government. I resumed my post as Under-Secretary of State for Education and Science, receiving just a telephone call from Harold asking me to carry on. I was more than delighted to do so.

WORLD CUP VICTORY

I was left with three months to put the finishing touches to our World Cup preparations. Reports received by John Lang suggested that progress was being maintained at all the grounds. We were not able to offer help for any permanent work at Wembley since the stadium company was not proposing to carry out any structural improvements. However, it was agreed that better facilities were required for overseas visitors and for the large press corps that was expected. We applied our 90 per cent formula for temporary structures and provided a very large marquee for this purpose.

About six weeks before the first match was due to kick off on 11 July a problem arose from a quite unexpected quarter – NATO. Michael Stewart, the Foreign Secretary, asked to see me and to my astonishment told me that his colleagues at the North Atlantic Treaty Organisation had taken exception to the presence of a team representing North Korea in a NATO country. What could be done about it? The answer to that was a very firm 'nothing'. I explained that when a country issues any such invitation for the World Cup, the Commonwealth Games or the Olympic Games it has to provide an undertaking that every member country in good standing will be admitted to the host country. Foreign Office officials seemed a little doubtful as to whether such a guarantee had been sought by the Football Association; they had certainly never expected North Korea to qualify, but they conceded that the Football Association had provided them with a set of the rules for the competition and I maintained that if the previous Conservative Government had made no such objection known it was a bit late now to do so.

Michael accepted that position but then turned to a new line of argument. If North Korea had to play, so be it, but NATO could not agree that their flag should fly or their national anthem be played. I pointed out that if we flew 15 flags at each of the grounds and left one out there would be an uproar. We certainly could not do that at the grounds where North Korea were due to play: Sunderland and Middlesbrough. FIFA would not be able to sustain that position, the World Cup would be called off and NATO would be looking very silly indeed. They would be undermining their principal purpose which was to support our basic freedoms and I couldn't think of a more basic freedom than to play football. The Foreign Secretary agreed to put the point to his colleagues 'as strongly as you have expressed it to me'. We turned to the question of national anthems. I thought I could help him a little. I have always thought that the playing of anthems was overdone on sporting occasions and I knew that Sir Stanley Rous thought so, too. We both felt that international sport ought not to whip up too much nationalistic fervour. England was due to open the competition by playing Uruguay, the Queen would be present and national anthems would be fully justified on that occasion. Her Majesty was due to be present again for the final and our anthem would have to be played as well as those of the two finalists. However, I said I would negotiate with Stanley and find out whether he would agree to do away with anthems at all the other matches. Such a policy would certainly mean, or so I thought at the time, that there would be no danger of having to play the North Korean anthem.

The Foreign Secretary seemed pleased with this suggestion. He had something positive for his NATO colleagues. I left to talk to Stanley Rous. He fell in with the proposal immediately but he did think that if the Queen was to be presented to the teams at the first match then all the other teams had to be presented to at least one official representative. I agreed to find a suitable British Minister to undertake the task. Denis Follows and the Football Association were fully consulted and they too had no objections to these arrangements, Michael Stewart was delighted and although that was the last I heard from NATO, it was not the last of my anxieties on the subject.

The pageantry of the opening ceremony went very well. It always does in Britain. The FA and Wembley organisation came through with flying colours, but the match itself was a bit dull. Too much was at stake for a display of scintillating football. Alf Ramsey's team looked very sound and well organised and we all believed that their performance in this match could be built upon, but there was no denying that a goal-less draw against Uruguay was a disappointment. Optimism, however, was justified after our next two matches in which we defeated first Mexico and then France, both by 2–0. Alf Ramsey's publicly-declared belief that we would win the World Cup seemed a distinct possibility.

The first game for North Korea was the day after England's opening match. I travelled to Middlesbrough to greet the teams on the pitch. Their opponents were the USSR, who were expected to be a formidable team, and indeed won by 3–0. However, the Koreans were a better-looking side than the score suggested and in their next match they drew 1–1 with Chile and then qualified for the quarter-finals by defeating Italy 1–0. This was a sensation but it was nothing compared with the subsequent events at Goodison Park, the Everton ground, where North Korea played Portugal in the knock-out part of the competition. On that day I was sitting in the Royal Box at Wembley where England were playing Argentina. Suddenly the loudspeakers announced that North Korea were 3–0 up on Portugal. A great roar went up, everyone thought it was a great laugh. Not me. I could see North Korea in the final and NATO calling upon us not to play the dreaded national anthem. No one else in the stadium seemed to be aware of the impending crisis. Fortunately, the Portuguese pulled themselves together and ran out winners by 5–3. Disaster had been averted!

But by then we had another crisis, this time on the pitch. Rattin, the Argentinian captain, managed to get himself ordered off the field. This did not surprise me: I had been present at Villa Park when his team had played West Germany and I thought he had been extremely fortunate to stay on the field in that game. Alf Ramsey was naturally upset that his side should encounter such 'violent' tactics. He described the Argentinians as 'worse than animals', which hardly helped to smooth over the after-match situation. England won by the only goal scored and Argentina were out of the Cup. But my problems were just starting for I was due to give a Government reception to the four losing quarter-finalists – Argentina, Uruguay, North Korea and Hungary – the following evening at Lancaster House. At seven o'clock I took up my position at the head of the grand staircase together with the officers of the FA and received three of the teams in traditional fashion. However, there was no sign of the Argentinian side. We waited and waited, accompanied by an army of photographers, no doubt hoping to photograph the Argentine captain being received by a British Minister. The Argentinians were staying at a hotel north of London. They were telephoned and sent a reply that they had been out for the day and were tired, they would not be able to get to the reception in time. Even in those days the Falklands was a very real issue in our dealings with Argentina, and I was not going to allow any suggestion that the British Government was anything other than courteous and hospitable to any of our guests, including Argentina. Nor did I want to provide an opportunity for Argentina to deliver a snub. I sent a message back that this was an official British Government reception, I understood this difficulty of timing but the reception would continue until they were able to arrive and the Minister could receive them, however long it took! It worked. Just before 10 pm their team arrived and was properly received. It was one of the longest Government receptions on record.

The two semi-final matches went well, West Germany gaining a 2–1 victory over the Soviet Union and England winning by the same score against Portugal. An all-European final, England versus West Germany, was something for all to savour and caught the imagination of the whole nation. The final itself justified every expectation. The football was superb. Individual skills abounded but they were always in the interests of the teams, indeed the teamwork made it the most memorable match that I have ever seen; 90 minutes of total excitement and then another half-hour of extra time before England ran out winners by 4–2. In my book *Soccer Referee* I described this match from a referee's viewpoint. Aside from all the footballing skills two refereeing decisions proved to be of cardinal importance. The first of these went against England and in my judgment the referee, Mr Gottfried Dienst of Switzerland, got it wrong. England were leading 2–1 with but a few minutes to go when the German centre-forward backed into Jack Charlton. I thought the foul was against the centre-forward for 'making a back' which Charlton could not avoid but the referee judged it to be the opposite, a foul against Charlton for 'pushing'. No use complaining – the referee's decision is the only one that counts. The

Germans took the free kick and the ball was in the England net, equalling the score and taking the match into extra time. Alf Ramsey is reported to have said to the team as they stood around waiting for the match to re-start 'You have thrown the match away, now go and win it back'. That is certainly what happened. Early in the first period of extra time Geoff Hurst fired a shot, the ball hit the underside of the cross-bar and bounced down and then out. The Russian linesman, Mr Tofik Bakhraamov, was waving his flag, the suspense was enormous but the goal was awarded. Could England hold on now? They did more than that. In the second period of extra time a long ball sent Geoff Hurst away, he seemed to be running the whole length of the field before he put the ball in the net. Four goals to two and for me and for the whole nation the most famous of all victories. All England players were heroes. It would be invidious to single out any one of them. Each of them has to be recalled with admiration: Gordon Banks, Roger Hunt, Ray Wilson, Nobby Stiles, Jack Charlton, Bobby Moore, Geoff Hurst, Martin Peters, Alan Ball, George Cohen, Bobby Charlton.

The Queen presented the trophy and the players ran round the pitch enjoying the acclaim. The Prime Minister beckoned me to join him as we watched the scene. 'We shall need to acknowledge this achievement. Ramsey has done a brilliant job and Bobby Moore has captained his side very well', he said, more by way of a question seeking approval than a statement. I agreed but added, 'If you intend to mark their contribution please do not forget the administration, it has been equally first-class'.

We all went off to the celebrations at the Royal Garden hotel. These were quite remarkable: the banquet was preceded by a final Government reception and as we arrived thousands of people were gathering outside in Knightsbridge. Soon the police were requesting that the team appear on the hotel balcony and, urged on by the Earl of Harewood, the president of the FA, the Prime Minister and I both went to enjoy the scene. In fact the team had to make a number of appearances, the final one representing the last incredible twist at the end of the story. When we got to the balcony, we found Pickles, a dog who had become part of the 1966 World Cup story.

Some three months before the competition began the FA decided to put the Jules Rimet trophy on public display at the Stampex Exhibition at the Central Hall, Westminster. I can still recall the horror on the face of Denis Follows as he came to my office to report that the trophy had been stolen. There was consternation everywhere. Nothing as disastrous had occurred since 1895 when in my own constituency the FA Cup itself, won by Aston Villa, was stolen from the window of a shop owned by William MacGregor, founder of the Football League. This time the publicity was enormous. Within a few days a man was charged with the theft but the trophy was still missing. One week after it was stolen the trophy was found by Pickles, who was said to have sniffed it out in a garden while being exercised by his master! The trophy was wrapped in newspaper. Follows and I could only reflect how fortunate we were to have a dog that knew where to look. Now, on the balcony of the Royal Garden hotel, sharing the adulation of the players, was the same hero. How on earth he ever got into the hotel, much less on to the balcony, was as mysterious as how the trophy was first stolen and then recovered!

It remained for me to report to Parliament the details of the financial aid provided by the Government to the six clubs where all the matches outside Wembley had been staged. Grants: Aston Villa £46,100, Everton £48,360, Manchester United £39,940, Middlesbrough £42,900, Sheffield Wednesday £78,700, Sunderland £61,300. Loans: Aston Villa £9,900, Everton £10,740, Manchester United £9,760, Middlesbrough £30,500, Sheffield Wednesday £17,700, Sunderland £3,600. There was not a word of criticism inside or outside the House – no one dared!

INTERNATIONAL ASSIGNMENTS

Jamaica

My involvement in the World Cup, especially through the close association which I had established with Stanley Rous, marked the beginning of a continuous interest in international sport – and politics – which has remained. Stanley was a remarkable man, a born ambassador. It would be a good thing if every sport produced such a diplomat. Today his style would be described as 'laid back'. He never asserted himself unduly but he attracted great respect. He could be very dismissive, and this form of disapproval was the only one that I ever saw him express. There can be no doubt that his great height and his unfailingly good manners attracted people to him and created confidence. He would command by suggestion rather than by advocacy but he was an attractive speaker. All these skills and this bearing brought him friends in every country where football is played. He introduced me to the members of FIFA assembled in London for the World Cup as a 'young and energetic Minister who is also a football man', a tremendous assistance to me in building up a network of international contacts. I am sure that it helped me to establish a reputation as a sportsman who was involved in politics rather than a politician who was advancing a career through sport.

As soon as the World Cup was won Walter and I were off to Jamaica for the Commonwealth Games. These Games are known as 'the friendly Games', and with good reason. The only time the Commonwealth comes together in a meaningful fashion is when heads of State meet or when sportsmen and women meet. Anyone who believes in the Commonwealth should regard the Games as important. Unlike all other Games they are based upon a political concept. Many people think that is their weakness, but it is also a strength in a multi-racial Commonwealth. The Jamaican Games were the inspiration of a remarkable man, Herbert Macdonald. He had a stadium built and raised the money to stage the Games, with the support of both Government and Opposition. It was an astonishing success story. Sir Arthur Porritt, now Lord Porritt, was the chairman of the Commonwealth Games Federation, a position he filled with both skill and charm. The opening ceremony was one of the most enthusiastic ever seen. I found myself sitting between Alexander Ross, a New Zealander who was to succeed Porritt, and Edward Seaga, the Jamaican Minister for Sport who was later to become Prime Minister.

The England team had outstanding success: 33 gold medals, 24 silver and 23 bronze. We seemed to be constantly engaged in celebrations but I was determined to visit each of the British teams to meet and talk to both athletes and officials. This is the only way to find out what needs to be done and so to develop policies to meet these needs; it is also the way to establish confidence. Whistle-stop visits are treated with derision by sporting people. So I spent most of my time visiting the headquarters of all our teams – England, Scotland, Wales, Northern Ireland, Isle of Man, Jersey, Guernsey – and spending time with them.

The serious business of my trip was to support Edinburgh's intention to host the next Games in 1970. The Edinburgh contingent was led by Herbert Brechin, who became their Lord Provost, and I was delighted when Edinburgh got the vote. It meant another four years of effort to ensure that we would successfully stage another international sporting festival. It was a challenge that I relished. The news of Edinburgh's success was welcomed by the Prime Minister and by Willie Ross, the Scottish Secretary of State, but it soon became clear that there were formidable problems ahead. The Edinburgh City Council was not the easiest local authority to negotiate with and I had some sympathy with Brechin and his colleagues who had been to Jamaica and now had to rouse the city to embrace a festival of sport as enthusiastically as they did the Edinburgh arts festival. The trouble, as always, was money. The city had already built a fine Olympic-size swimming pool but as Brechin had discovered in Jamaica a great deal more had to be built if the Games were to be successfully staged. I wanted to help in all this but I also had my own problem – the Scottish Office. There was talk that my remit did not extend north of the border. I was having none of that. My officials knew that I always insisted upon being described as the Minister for UK sport and that the Sports Council was the appropriate authority to represent British sport. That is why we had Scottish and Welsh people on it. It was necessary for me to remind my colleagues that while we had Scottish sport, Welsh sport and Northern Ireland sport, British sport was my prime responsibility. If they wished to dispute that they could consult the Prime Minister. As far as I know none of them ever did. I resolved to go to Edinburgh as soon as possible and to take the initiative. Facilities had to be built and Government support was essential to encourage those in Edinburgh

The most important need was for the stadium itself at Meadowbank. My good friend in the Scottish brigade, Bruce Millan, who was a junior Minister, proved to be a most helpful colleague. He gave me good advice about how to deal with Willie Ross, his Secretary of State. When Willie himself came to understand that my purpose was to help the Scots to put on a superb Games and not to usurp the Scottish Office we made progress. I presented my proposals to my colleagues and the Government made its offer to grant £700,000 towards the Meadowbank stadium. It had to be explained that since Edinburgh had itself already built the swimming pool the rules against retrospective financing prevented us from providing money for that undertaking. Also, we were able to take two further decisions of importance for the staging of a successful Games. These were urged on me by Edinburgh University when I visited their campus which was to form the Games village. Scottish colleagues were able to speed up the construction of residential buildings so that all the athletes could be accommodated in the village and also the building of the special catering block so necessary if the feeding arrangements and the social and recreational facilities could meet the standards required for a happy Commonwealth gathering. The Edinburgh City Council still seemed in a state of hesitation but I hoped that this firm support from the Government would help to resolve any remaining doubts. Willie Ross carried the grant on his own estimates and that seemed to provide him with a sense of satisfaction which I shared with him and with his Minister of State, Bruce Millan.

Moscow

The 50th anniversary of the Russian Revolution, in 1967, was to be celebrated by the Soviets in a spectacular fashion, starting with a 'Sports Spartakiada'. I was summoned to Number Ten and told by the Prime Minister that he had accepted an invitation for a British Minister to attend and he wanted me to be the Government's representative. I could take Walter Winterbottom with me and I would need to be briefed by security. He had one further piece of advice based on his own personal experience: 'They will try to get you drunk, toasts every few minutes, and each time you will be expected to drain your glass. Make sure that when you sit down at the table you ask for a bottle of water and whenever you can, fill your vodka glass with water'.

The Russians had invited everybody in world sport and many Ministers too from around the world. Avery Brundage, president of the IOC (International Olympic Committee) had special attention; they even provided him with a plane so that he could travel wherever he wished. Brundage was an aristocrat who was said to despise governments and politicians. He was certainly very cool towards me and other Ministers but we soon observed that he had a rather different attitude towards his Soviet hosts. He appeared to relish every moment of adulation. Everyone with a British connection was seated at one large table in the Hotel Russia dining-room, in fact we were the first people to stay there in the only wing of the hotel which had been completed at that time. I found myself seated with Stanley Rous; Colonel Maynard Russell, president of international amateur boxing; Bill Phillips of Australia, president of FINA (the international governing body of swimming) and Alan MacEachen, the Canadian Minister of Health, who said he was there because he was the only Minister in the world with responsibilities for swimming in his title. They all proved to be the most agreeable colleagues but as I sat down I was a little concerned to spot a Union Jack flag in the middle of the table, for I had been told by security that the base of such flags often concealed a tiny microphone. If anyone was detailed to listen to our conversation I hope they enjoyed it, or made head or tail of it, considering the jumble of international folklore and hearty good humour we shared!

On the night Walter Winterbottom and I flew in we were met by the Soviet vice-president of FIFA, who was an old friend of Walter's and a loyal supporter of Stanley Rous. He took us to a separate table in the hotel restaurant and treated us to a special bottle of Georgian wine that he told us was Stalin's favourite. It deserved to be, it was a great wine. The following night Rous installed me as the head of the British table. I decided to treat my friends to the wine I had enjoyed the night before. 'We have no such wine in this hotel', I was told, first by the waiter and then, after a long wait, by the manager. All my protests were in vain. The following morning I was invited to meet the Soviet Minister. It was an extraordinary meeting. As soon as I walked in he asked me to agree to talk about sports exchanges and before I could utter a single word he said, 'We would like Sir Ramsey to come here and coach'. I explained that this would be a little difficult as he was fully engaged. 'However,' I said, 'we have many good coaches of football and if you would like some of them over here I will talk to the Football Association.' 'No,' he replied, 'we want Sir Ramsey. He said England would win the World Cup and England won the World Cup.' I told him this was a remark which Alf had made as a 'leg pull, a jest'. He thought about this and then pronounced: 'In the whole of the Soviet Union we have no such jester'. At this meeting I learned that the one thing the Soviets appreciated more than anything else is absolute frankness, or realism as they call it. When they are convinced about your frankness they accept your genuineness, and if they make an arrangement with you it is totally honoured. This visit paved the way for 20 years of mutual confidence. As I rose to leave the Minister made the conventional remarks with which we usually greet our guests. 'I do hope you are comfortable. Is there anything I can do for you?' 'Well, as a matter of fact there is', I replied, explaining how much I had enjoyed the Georgian wine and how surprised I was not to be able to order any more. He made a note and I left to return to the hotel not ten minutes' drive away. When I walked into the dining-room there on the table stood four bottles of the wine. Would we enjoy it with the compliments of the Minister? We did, but I saw no more of it!

Harold Wilson's advice proved to be spot-on when I was taken for a meal at a Georgian restaurant in Gorky Street. I had gone down with a Moscow stomach and had not left my bedroom for days when Walter knocked on my door one morning and insisted that I get up and go on a tour of the Moscow baths with some Soviet officials who would guarantee a cure for my Moscow tummy. With great reluctance I did so and I was taken off for a Russian steam bath and a massage. This was followed by a visit to the office where a large ancient safe was opened and from it was taken a crate of eggs and two bottles of vodka. Two raw eggs were broken into a glass and I ate those followed by a glass of vodka. The dose was repeated two or three times. I was cured. Off we went to the restaurant where I was placed at a table with cutlery laid out for at least half-a-dozen courses. I followed the Wilson advice.

The Spartakiada itself was quite spectacular. I had never before seen such an opening ceremony. Tableau after tableau of thousands of young gymnasts and dancers traced the 50-year history of the Soviet Union. The Soviets had set a new standard in opening ceremonies which owed as much if not more to choreography and dramatic production as it did to sport. During the next few days I received a bolt from the blue in the form of a message from the British Embassy. The Edinburgh City Council had met and were contemplating withdrawal from the Games of 1970. I was dumbfounded. I asked the British Ambassador to get Herbert Brechin, now Lord Provost, on the telephone. The Ambassador's reply was even more astonishing. 'That will be difficult, Minister, because he is paying an official visit to the Soviet Union. He is somewhere down in Georgia but he is scheduled to return home via Moscow.' A message was sent to Brechin and a few days later on his way back home we had breakfast together in Moscow. He was very distressed about this turn of events and was determined to try to get the position reversed. I took a tough line. 'When we invite the Commonwealth to come to our country and they accept our invitation then that invitation has to be honoured', I insisted. Brechin was in total agreement. He left to get the show back on the road and, thankfully, though not without difficulty, he succeeded. Whatever I had expected to be doing in Moscow, it had not been saving the Commonwealth Games!

Mexico

In 1968 Mexico hosted the Olympic Games. The moment we touched down an official of the British Embassy was waiting to receive us and we were whisked off to a small luncheon party being given by the Mexican President in honour of Prince Philip, who was present in his capacity as president of the International Equestrian Federation. Afterwards, Lord Rupert Neville, Prince Philip's secretary and, more important on this occasion, chairman of the British Olympic Association, and chef de mission drove us to the Olympic village some miles away so that Walter and I could pay our respects and discuss the first reports of the effects of the altitude. Dr Roger Bannister had commissioned Dr Lionel Pugh of the Medical Research Council to carry out research on the problem. We were relieved that training was going extremely well and that the acclimatisation programme we had helped to finance seemed to be working successfully.

The principal officers of the BOA were Sandy Duncan, the secretary, and Richard Hicks, their fund-raiser. Both had an inherent distrust of governments of all hues, but when they learned that I did not regard it as desirable for a Minister for Sport to be running sport we got on extremely well. When I took office the BOA were among the first people I talked to about the relationship of Government to sport. Rupert Neville, at least, thought that the Government might have a limited role, possibly as an underwriter if one of their public appeals were to fail. I accepted their right to depend upon appeals if that was their wish but I was anxious that the British team should receive at least some pocket money allowance to bring them somewhere closer to the conditions enjoyed by the Americans and others with whom they shared facilities in the Olympic village. After an initial reluctance the Commonwealth Games Association agreed that HM Government should pay them pocket money, modest enough in all conscience, of some ten shillings (50 pence) a day. It was nice to meet members of the team who had taken part in previous Olympics and to be told how much this gesture was appreciated. Years later, in Moscow 1980, when the Prime Minister disapproved of British participation in the Olympic Games because of the Russian involvement in Afghanistan, the Government did all that it could to discourage financial support for the British team. I realised then that the BOA had been right: how foolish it would have been to be totally dependent upon politicians who would withdraw their finance without consultation.

There were some people who thought that the Mexico Games ought to have been cancelled or the British team withdrawn. It was only when I visited the offices of the British Council that this matter was drawn to my attention by some of its staff. They confirmed a dramatic account provided by John Rodda of the *Guardian* who had been present at a student rally in a city square when the students had been attacked from the air by soldiers in helicopters. Rodda himself had been told to lie down in a doorway and described how he was in fear of his life. His was one of the very few accounts to find its way into our press. Rodda believed that the students had been encouraged to assemble in the square so that they could be dealt with before the Games opened. The British Embassy seemed ignorant of the incident. So were the British team officials when I asked them. Whatever the cause of the protest it was put down effectively, if savagely, and the Games themselves proceeded without any apparent public concern.

Walter Winterbottom and I worked out a programme that I have repeated whenever I have attended the Olympic Games. Apart from giving a reception for the British contingent the Minister can learn best and encourage most in the week or so before the competition takes place. A quiet visit to the different training sessions where each of the separate sports – 26 in all – are located provides the best opportunity to talk to the athletes, the coaches and the administrators and to discuss their hopes and their problems. Athletes don't want to talk to Ministers of the Crown when they are about to perform and are in a state of high tension. Walter and I discovered an exception to this rule when we visited the shooting practice the day before the competition. One of the team members we met was Bob Braithwaite, who is a vet by profession and a clay pigeon shooter. He was insistent that we went back the next day to watch him and his colleagues in the actual event. Bob told us: 'Our sport never gets any encouragement, no one bothers about us'. Winterbottom and I assured him that we would come back and we kept our word the next morning. The shooting centre was miles away from our hotel but when we got there we immediately looked at the scoreboard, which revealed that the first round of shooting had just taken place, Bob Braithwaite scoring 22 shots out of 25. It was a good score but many competitors had hit all 25. As we studied these marks Bob spotted us and raced over to express his pleasure that we had turned up. 'How are you doing?' I asked him. 'Fine,' he replied, 'now you have kept your word I shall not miss any more.' He went on to hit the next 175 pigeons to win the gold medal: a fantastic achievement.

Earlier we had been present at the track to cheer on David Hemery as he won his gold medal in the 400 metres hurdles. It was the first gold medal that I had seen won by a British athlete, and it was a tremendous thrill. I shall never forget the sight of Hemery coming off the last bend ahead of his rivals but with the final hurdles in front of him. What moments of apprehension, what a triumph! We had a great celebration the next day in the village and I could only describe David's achievement to television reporters as 'bloody marvellous'. Beforehand our disappointment that Lyn Davies could not repeat his Tokyo gold medal success in the long jump was partly offset by the enormous jump of Bob Beamon of the United States with his very first effort – over 29 feet. The altitude made a great contribution to this record – I doubt that it will ever be beaten at lower levels of competition and it raised all the questions we had feared as to the fairness of competition at so high an altitude. But we were reassured about the British Olympic preparation by Hemery's success.

One of my oldest friends in sport is Harry Llewellyn, a gold medallist himself from the Helsinki Games of 1952 on his wonderful horse Foxhunter. He has been a constant source of encouragement to me in all that I have attempted, as have his colleagues throughout his sport, and it was a very happy visit that I made to the equestrian training centre. Harry, our team manager, was positive about our chances and his optimism was justified by the three-day event team. The previous day Walter and I had walked into the headquarters of the British team. Sandy Duncan was explaining on the telephone that there was no one to go to Acapulco for the yachting competition. The yachting boys were furious, saying that Britain was going to win a gold next day and that someone from HQ should be there to cheer them on. Rodney Patterson and Ian McDonald-Smith were now so far ahead in their class that they had only to finish in the middle order to be certain of taking the gold. There are seven races in the yachting competition and the competitors can each discard one result. This meant that with one race to go Patterson and McDonald-Smith had six wins and unless they were disqualified they looked virtually unbeatable. As all this was explained to Duncan he looked increasingly unhappy. The headquarters staff had obviously made all their arrangements to be present at the three-day event where British fortunes were in the capable hands of Derek Alhusen, Richard Meade, Staff Sergeant Ben Jones and Jane Buller, the first woman to represent us at the Olympics in this event. I decided to intervene. 'Tell the yachting boys that the Minister will come to Acapulco,' I volunteered, 'together with the director of the Sports Council.' Sandy foresaw an insurmountable problem. 'There is only one plane and I know it is full', he explained to me. 'Then we shall have to get the British Ambassador to deal with the matter', I replied. Walter and I made it to Acapulco.

Acapulco proved to be an inspired sporting occasion. The organisation of the British team was superb. The attention to detail of the team manager, Vernon Stratton, as well as his overall vision was outstanding. Vernon invited Walter and myself to attend the early morning briefing session and we were astonished when this started with the most detailed forecast of the winds and the tides that the crews would be likely to encounter. The forecaster was David Houghton, a Met man from Bracknell. He had measured the winds, put bottles in the sea to chart the tides, and seemed to know more about sailing conditions in this part of the Pacific than any other living person. All this information was charted, locked up in his map room and guarded more closely than many a state secret. We were told that the opposition were green with envy. Not content with all this prior intelligence Houghton had already been out that morning and made his early reconnoitre. Now he presented his final forecasts. The race would start with the windspeeds of so many mph, the tides would be running at this speed in that direction, and so on. He went on to say how he expected these details to vary as the race proceeded. It was fascinating stuff. He then left to do a final and last-minute survey which, in accordance with the rules of racing, had to be delivered to our yachtsmen not later than 30 minutes before the starting gun. As the course for the races was a few miles offshore the yachts had to leave the harbour well before the race started. This had initially created a problem: how would the forecast be delivered to the yachts well out to sea within the time allowed by the rules? Vernon Stratton and his back-up team deserved the good fortune their planning had made possible. They appealed to the British community in Mexico. Did anyone own a plane and if so, could it be made available to the British team? Such a patriot was indeed found and he was delighted to make his plane and his services available. Within minutes of the last possible moment when information could be communicated to the competitors the plane dropped brightly-coloured bottles containing all the latest information.

After Houghton had left to complete his mission Vernon Stratton gave his final talk. For Rodney and Ian it was really very simple. 'Keep out of trouble whatever you do. Under no circumstances cross the starting line before the gun, do not give any other competitor the chance to lodge any objection at any stage of the race. Finish in the first dozen or so and you have won the gold'. Both Walter and I could not have been more excited. Nigel Hacking, who had served with Walter on the executive of the CCPR as the representative of the Royal Yachting Association, had met us in Acapulco. Now he was secretary-general of the International Yacht Racing Union. Upon hearing that we were flying in to be present for the final day he had secured permission for us both to join him on 'Yeomana', the official boat. It was a wonderful surprise.

However, there was one further surprise in store for me. As the briefing ended Vernon Stratton turned to me and said, 'I have a job for you today, Minister, you can help us with a bronze medal. Robin Aisher has a good chance of winning a bronze in his event, the 5.5 class, and I don't want anyone to distract him before the race, not even his father'. The parent in question was the remarkable Owen Aisher, owner of Marley Tiles who until that day I had never met. Vernon explained his plan. He would inform Owen Aisher of my presence and ask him to receive me on his yacht. He was sure that Mr Aisher would offer me some hospitality and he wanted me to keep him engaged in conversation until I received a signal that Robin had left the quayside. The plan worked to perfection. When the conversation showed signs of drying up I introduced the question of taxation, implying that the Labour Government's taxation programme couldn't be too bad if we were still able to enjoy such a splendid occasion. Owen certainly responded to that one! Vernon finally gave me the signal, and Robin Aisher and his colleagues Adrian Jardine and Paul Anderson (crew) were on their way to an Olympic bronze which they deservedly won. Whether or not it was ever explained to Owen Aisher how our meeting had come about I do not know, but we remained friends thereafter.

The trip out to sea to watch the race was wonderful and our heroes followed their instructions to the letter. Walter and I were within hailing distance as they sailed over the finishing line. We had a wonderful party that night; I have never been more delighted to order the champagne. We telephoned the headquarters in Mexico City and exchanged joyous tidings, for the three-day eventers had won their gold, too, in spite of atrocious weather conditions.

In these three years the World Cup, Jamaica, Moscow and now Mexico had provided me with an unparalleled insight into international sport, its administration and the people who dominate it. All my subsequent involvement in international sport was built upon this experience and the friendships I had created. I like to think that I used it all for the benefit of British sport and that it still stands me in good stead 20 years on.

9

MINISTERIAL MERRY-GO-ROUND

MINISTERS COME, MINISTERS GO

It was one of Harold Wilson's more pronounced faults that he moved his Ministers around far too often, though I was glad to be an exception to the rule. Harold undertook his Government shuffles for two principal reasons. First, he genuinely believed that Ministers should move upwards, onwards and then out, allowing new blood to come in. Secondly, it was one of his defensive mechanisms when his Government found itself in some difficulty, or he wanted to stir the news from time to time. Government changes provided news and gossip, the spice of political life. The weakness of this approach is that it plays into the hands of the civil service. In my experience civil servants like firm Ministers provided they are rational beings and have some imagination. They do not like Ministers who are not long enough in a post to master their brief and their department. When that happens, the officials are left to make too much of the running, and contrary to common belief, that is not what they desire or appreciate. The Department of Education and Science suffered more than most in my time there.

As I have already explained we started the 1964 Government with Michael Stewart as Secretary of State but very soon Antony Crosland took over. When Tony moved to the Board of Trade he was succeeded by Edward Short, followed by Patrick Gordon-Walker. It was fascinating to compare their styles both at the despatch box and within the department. Michael Stewart is a man of reason. He argues his case with an earnest approach, whether in the House or among his civil servants, appealing to his audience to respect the facts, and he has the ability to relate his facts to his principles. Antony Crosland was altogether a more scintillating type of Minister. Although he sat back, apparently totally relaxed, he felt passionately about issues and about the future of the Party. He was always in command in the House and was respected completely by everyone. He placed great emphasis upon keeping in touch with the backbenchers who he took pains to cultivate. He had great charm and an infallible sense of direction.

Edward Short – 'Ted' to everyone – had been our Chief Whip, a position he occupied with the type of firm resolve that was always the hallmark of that post. It was inevitable that when he took over Education he would bring the same type of mind to our affairs, and as he was a schoolmaster by profession he had a thirst for education. It was a great pleasure to work with him for he had a tidy mind and a determination to make progress along agreed policy directions. In the House Ted operated with a degree of modesty which could be disarming but his greatest asset was his close knowledge of the backbenchers. He relied upon them and they were his source of strength.

When Patrick Gordon-Walker joined the department he was still a little shell-shocked, having suffered the most traumatic experience at Smethwick which he lost in the General Election and a worse one still at Leyton, where he was a Minister seeking re-election at a by-election. He was a longstanding colleague from the old Gaitskell days, when we made common cause in the battles within the party. He had served in the Attlee Government and had also been Foreign Secretary so it could be said that he arrived with more experience than any of the other Ministers. But he never recovered from his first morning in Education. His appointment came with the Government changes of 29 August 1967. It was the recess, and I was the only other Minister on duty in the department. Patrick sent me a message suggesting that if I did not have a lunch appointment we could meet so that I could brief him. As we travelled up Piccadilly in his car he told me that he had taken a decision about the 'Enfield situation'. This concerned the requirement of the Government that each local education authority should prepare a plan for comprehensive education, which some of them did not wish to do. Enfield's attitude was certainly not in sympathy with Labour's policy and challenge in the courts was a serious hazard. Officials and lawyers had waited upon Patrick, requesting a decision before he had even had time to sit at his desk. I was appalled. It was a classic case of rail-roading a new Minister and I begged him to have the advice checked out with the Attorney-General. He later told me that he had done so. My fears proved to be well-founded: the Government lost in the courts and it was a humiliating defeat. Patrick had a natural authority and he was a loyal colleague but he never recovered from this first decision on his first morning in office.

By 1967, after three years as the Under-Secretary of State for Education and Science, and as the Minister for Sport, I was well into the routine of my daily and weekly work. I greeted every day with relish. As the Sports Minister I had a constant avalanche of questions in the House. I presided over the Sports Council which was a joyous experience. The Council worked as a real team, all the time pioneering new initiatives and attracting widespread support. Every weekend found me at some sporting occasion. Those were the days when the people who really run British sport were to be found at their posts. I had long ago recognised that if I wanted to find out what was really going on then, after five days at the Ministry and in Parliament, I needed to be out and about on Saturdays and Sundays. My family could not have been more supportive. We now had four young children and Brenda coped with them admirably, dealing with all the problems of school and leisure without a moment's qualm, other than a well-justified complaint when I could not get to some school function or Sunday School treat. It is quite impossible in the main narrative of this story to deal with the full programme of the Sports Council and I have therefore included many of the details in Appendices 1 and 2.

THE EDUCATION OF IMMIGRANTS

As soon as Antony Crosland came to Education he expressed considerable concern about the provision being made, or rather not being made, for the proper education of the immigrant population. It was understandable that he should ask me to take on responsibility for this since both in Birmingham where I lived, and in Small Heath which I represented, there were increasing numbers of children from Asia and the West Indies who often spoke no English.

The experience of my own family reflects almost exactly the situation that has confronted schools in the places where the new arrivals have settled. When Andrew went to Park Hill primary school in 1964 the percentage of immigrant children was in single figures. Two years later, when Michael enrolled, the percentage had doubled to about 15 or 16 per cent. Kate joined the school in 1967 and the numbers had grown to somewhere near a third but in David's time, 1969–1975, they had become even greater, partly because some of the white parents had moved their children to schools in other districts, often moving house in order to do so. Towards the end of David's time at the school he came home one day and told us with great amusement: 'This has been a great day, another white boy has joined our class, there are now two of us'. I should add that there were one or two girls as well, but the percentage of immigrant children was now well into the 80s. Neither Brenda nor I ever had a moment of concern about Park Hill. It had a fine headteacher, Mr W.G. Labon, and a most caring and professional staff. Andrew and Michael both passed the 11-Plus examination and went on to Grammar School. Kate and David passed what were known as 'aptitude tests' before joining the comprehensive schools. One of our great joys was to watch the cricket and football matches that regularly took place on our lawn on Saturdays and holidays, fielding as multi-racial a mix as it would have been possible to organise, all friends of our children.

I decided to tour the country, visiting different cities and examining their approach to the new problems. Some were impressive, like Bradford and Luton, where my old football colleague Mr I.D. MacMullen, soon to become vice-president of the Football Association, was responsible for a dispersal programme achieved by guided choice. Others, such as Leeds and Birmingham, were far from satisfactory, with teachers making their own decisions when faced with a lack of official guidance. Bradford achieved its results by adopting the requirement that all children should take a medical examination in the term before they went to school. They did this so that they could discuss with the parents which was the best school for them to choose. Not only did this produce a measure of dispersal but they found that the new procedure had considerable medical and social value.

One of the difficulties was that no one could advise me as to what percentage figure I should put in my proposals to represent the maximum of immigrant children it was desirable to have in any one school or in any one class in a school. There was no professional advice available. Finally, late one Friday afternoon, I announced that I was going home to Birmingham and that when I returned on Monday morning I would announce my decision. My staff were astonished when on Monday I told them, 'It is to be one third, write it into the circular'. They asked me how I had arrived at this decision and I told them I had asked a first-class headmaster in whom I had every confidence, and that he had suggested 30 per cent. So I settled for a third. What I had done that morning was to call at Park Hill School to ask Mr Labon the question I thought to be paramount: 'How large a percentage of immigrant children do we have in the school now, and what is the maximum percentage of such children that you can take while still being able to guarantee to parents like me that you can maintain the standards of education for our children?' We discussed the difficulties of five-year-olds with no English and the need to make special teaching provision for them. We considered the growing number of Asian wives now joining their husbands, very desirable on every social ground, but unable to give much help to their children at home since they had no English either. Mr Labon considered all this. He told me now some 30 per cent of his charges were such children and he thought he could maintain standards at that level but he would be very concerned if it went much higher. My officials appeared incredulous when I explained all this to them but they could not produce any challenge on professional grounds so that was that. I was much reassured some months later when the Birmingham branch of the National Union of Teachers carried out a study, which was also accepted by the NUT nationally, proposing a 30 per cent maximum.

What we actually said in our circular was: 'Experience suggests that up to a fifth of immigrant children in any group fit in with reasonable ease, but that if the proportion goes over about one third either in the school as a whole or in any class, serious strains arise'. We went on to advise the redrawing of catchment areas and, if necessary, a policy of dispersal. We placed great importance upon the need to discuss all this with parents in all the communities so that they could see the benefits of the policies we were recommending. The policy we advocated had some short-term success but to my great regret it was soon overwhelmed. Other local authorities failed to take a similar approach on the establishment of multi-racial communities. If we had succeeded, who knows how much better race relations would be in our country today? Even so, I have to report from my own constituency of Small Heath and the district of Moseley, where my family still live, that there is a remarkable degree of tolerance and good living which we all enjoy.

THE COURT LEES AFFAIR

The Court Lees Affair did not reach my desk as it ought to have done by way of a report from my officials upon a serious matter of professional discipline. Instead, I was to read most of the details in the press and learned more by talking to Roy Jenkins, the Home Secretary, who was dealing with the scandal which had exploded around the Court Lees Approved School, first as a result of anonymous information supplied to the *Guardian* newspaper and then as a result of the Enquiry set up by the Home Secretary. I waited and waited for a report but none was submitted to me until I finally demanded to be informed about the matter.

The Court Lees Approved School was a private institution in Surrey. The anonymous information alleged a regime of beatings which went far beyond what even supporters of corporal punishment would have considered tolerable. Photographs supplied to the *Guardian* showed appalling injuries on boys inflicted by means of a thick cane. The school was soon identified as Court Lees and the supplier of the information was a Mr Cook, who was a teacher at odds with the regime at the school and with many of his colleagues. Cook revealed himself as the author of the letters to the *Guardian* and in May 1967 Home Office officials met the Board of Management which was chaired by a Judge Cohen. He had not been chairman at the time of the incidents but had subsequently taken over that position. Roy Jenkins decided to hold an Enquiry. The evidence that emerged at this Enquiry shocked the nation and certainly shocked me. Very severe beatings had taken place, some of them not recorded in the record book as required, some of them late at night upon boys brought back after absconding wearing only pyjamas. Masters were said to have sought out thicker canes and some boys who resisted these punishments had their heads held between the legs of other teachers while they were punished.

When the House subsequently debated the Report of the Enquiry in November Mr Reginald Paget QC, MP (Northampton) put these matters very starkly: 'Canes were obtained which would stand the full strength of Mr Hayden, a quarter-finalist at Wimbledon whose forehand drive used to be famous'. Mr Cook, an avowed opponent of corporal punishment, had taken coloured photographs of some of the boys after their beatings and sent them to the *Guardian*. Mr Cook was not a popular master of the school. He was criticised by the Enquiry chairman, Mr Gibbens QC, and certainly condemned by his colleagues for not having reported his complaints to proper authorities such as the governors or the chaplain and for having instead resorted to anonymous disclosure to the *Guardian*. However, there is no doubt that it was his camera that brought the abuse to light. At the Enquiry two eminent doctors, described by Mr Gibbens as 'medical witnesses of great eminence in their profession', declared that if such cases as those of two of the boys had been brought to them at their hospital they would have felt bound to call for an investigation by the police or other authority.

Within four days of receiving the Gibbens Report the Home Secretary acted. It was the speed with which he acted that roused the wrath of the Opposition. Jenkins was, I know, particularly incensed that even after he had set up his official Enquiry ten more beatings took place at the school. He withdrew the licence of the school, arranged for the 116 pupils to be dispersed and for the affairs of the Court Lees School to become the responsibility of the Surrey County Council. Both Mr Hayden, the headmaster, and his deputy were given six months' notice terminating their employment. Mr Cook took six months' leave of absence with Home Office approval.

That was not the end of the matter as far as I was concerned. I had had no satisfactory explanation as to why I had received no report on these matters which were covered in every newspaper in the land. I called the head of the appropriate department to my office. He astonished me by stating that he did not think that a few whackings needed to be brought to my attention. Obviously, he did not take my view that severe beatings raised questions of professional competence. He did not believe that they compared with the hundreds of cases of sexual impropriety or financial misappropriation that were submitted to me each year. When I asked what view he took about the photographs of the bruisings suffered by the pupils I learned with amazement that the officials had not seen them nor requested the Home Office to make them available. I ordered that they be immediately obtained and made available to me.

When I did see them it took me but a few minutes to agree with the judgment of the doctors. There most certainly was a case to answer and I ordered the department to deal with it in the normal way, that is to say by setting out details of a complaint to the teachers involved, holding an Enquiry at which the teachers could be represented and then presenting me with a full report and recommendations. At this point my head of department declared that he lived in the village of Court Lees; everyone there knew of the situation, he would be extremely embarrassed if he had to conduct this Enquiry, and he asked to be relieved of any further responsibility. By this time I was prepared for almost anything in this sordid case and it was a request to which I agreed with alacrity. When the debate was held in the House, Roy Jenkins asked me to be present and to sit beside him to advise on any questions relating to the educational issues. His instinct proved to be correct. During a powerful speech Quintin Hogg, speaking for the Opposition, attacked Jenkins for not having heard the headmaster: 'I could not, I would not, and I would never concede the possibility that I could condemn a man without a hearing. That is what the Home Secretary has done'. I was able to tell Roy that since Quintin Hogg had been Secretary of State for Education he himself must have removed hundreds of teachers from the register without hearing them – it was normal procedure. They were heard by officials who reported to Ministers. Roy promptly intervened to put the point to Hogg: 'May I ask the Right Hon. and learned gentleman, who held office as Secretary of State for Education, whether during the whole period he held that office, when undoubtedly I am informed, several hundreds of teachers must have been dismissed, he ever saw a single teacher himself in connection with that process?' It was a knock-out blow. Hogg never recovered and the Home Secretary wound up the debate with a devastating speech.

CHESTER COMMITTEE ON FOOTBALL

Sir Norman Chester's committee took just two years to present their Report into 'the state of Association Football at all levels'. I was delighted by their thoroughness and hoped that their wise conclusions would prove to have a lasting benefit for our national game. It is a great mistake to believe that the conclusions of such committees of enquiry will be, or ought to be, immediately implemented. That is never the case. No doubt some of their revelations may lead to instant remedy in appropriate cases but the real value of these reports is that they provide a bench-mark for the future. They cannot be ignored. Whatever happens thereafter, such as in this case, the question that is bound to be asked is 'What did Chester have to say about it?' Therein lies its continuing influence.

The committee proved to be a good team. MP's did not find it possible to attend all the meetings, and this was a disappointment to me. He likes the glamour!' The report contained 36 recommendations covering every aspect of the sport starting with schoolboy football and addressed itself to every conceivable authority including the Government.

The committee wanted to extend the size of the League by six to ten clubs, which has been partly achieved, and to have a system of four up and four down for promotion and relegation which the League has now moved towards. It also proposed raising the dividends of shareholders to 15 per cent and allowing managers of clubs to become paid directors. Both these objectives have been achieved, as has the proposal to establish players' contracts for a definite period of time and to impose a levy on transfer fees. Also accepted by the League was the suggestion that a 'director' or similar official be appointed to assist in the selection and training of referees. It has to be acknowledged that the League has implemented most of the recommendations directed at them and in this respect the leadership of Alan Hardaker played a most important part.

Chester's recommendations to the Football Association have not met with as much success. We still do not have representatives of professional footballers, secretaries or managers serving on the FA Council, nor is there an age limit of 70 years for members. There is now a more effective committee structure although not the 'central policy and planning committee' Chester envisaged.

So far as Government is concerned I have to confess that I was not able to make much progress on the taxation front or in achieving the recommendation that grants should be available for professional clubs as well as amateurs. Grants had of course been made to World Cup grounds, and I was able to use this as a considerable argument in support of a proposal to make funds available to professional clubs for the provision of community-based sports. By far the most far-reaching proposal was to establish a Football Levy Board which imposed a 1 per cent levy on the gross proceeds of all pools betting after taking into account the appropriate pool betting tax. Lewis Hawser and Magnus Williamson signed a minority report proposing a 2 per cent levy. I did my best with this recommendation but the Treasury would have none of it. The fact that horse racing has a levy upon which it is almost totally dependent is the result of a piece of superb parliamentary strategy conducted by George Wigg, then the MP for Dudley, and supported by Chuter Ede MP, who had served as Home Secretary in Attlee's Government. This cut no ice with Treasury Ministers. 'That was a tragic mistake,' I was told, 'it won't happen again'. I suffered another great disadvantage: every time I went to discuss this matter with Treasury colleagues, I seemed to be preceded by the announce-ment of yet another mammoth transfer fee. Faced with this evidence it was difficult to argue the perilous state of football financing especially as the League, at that time, were justifying the existence of the transfer system on the grounds that most of this money found its way down through the League structure to reach the clubs in the lower divisions. I never believed this to be the case but that was what they believed. In my second term of office I was able to initiate the Football Grounds Improvement Trust with the tacit support of the Chancellor of the Exchequer and this has proved to be of enormous value to football.

FURTHER EDUCATION

By 1968 my educational work and my sports work were proceeding side by side. I had been in office for four years but I was surprised one day to receive a visit from the permanent secretary, Sir Herbert Andrews, to discuss one or two matters which would be of interest. These turned out to concern the future of Sir John Lang and myself. John was now over 70 and there could be no doubt that his position within the civil service was anomalous. Andrews wondered how much longer he ought to remain in his post. I was far from willing to support any suggestion of retirement as I was still gaining considerable advantage from Lang's seniority within Whitehall. Andrews could not offer me anyone of equal seniority who could negotiate with Number Ten, the Treasury and other departments. Nor could he suggest anyone who could remotely fill Sir John's shoes as deputy chairman of the Sports Council and the other roles which I had assigned to him. I was able to tell the permanent secretary that until those questions could be answered John Lang was staying put.

We then turned to my own position. Sir Herbert gently suggested, 'We think that when a Minister has been with us for about two years he has usually given us all he has to contribute', and he enquired about my own feelings regarding the future, expressing, I am sure, a genuine concern about my prospects. It had been reported to me earlier by Charles Pannell, a good friend who had been Minister of Works, that John Lang had told him it was time for me to be promoted. All this was a pleasant surprise but embarrassing. It was good to know that people I respected were thinking along these lines but I could not see what I could do or say about such suggestions. I could not be happier than I was in my post as the Sports Minister; it was unique and as far as I could judge I was filling it successfully. The support I received from the Prime Minister certainly led me to believe so and I was conceited enough to believe that the partnership which I had established with British sport was an advantage to the Government. I could only respond to Herbert Andrews by saying that these were matters which were entirely for the Prime Minister. If he wished me to move he would move me. Thinking about it afterwards I realised that what was being raised with me was the question of whether I wished to be a one-subject Minister and, if so, whether I was prepared to continue in sport at the expense of future advancement. I did not feel disposed to suggest any change.

I had new initiatives before me, the two most important of which were a full-scale review of the Youth Service, which I presided over myself as the chairman of the Youth Service Development Council, and a similar review of the adult education service, which Andrews had suggested to me was the only part of the education service that had not been looked at in depth. My worry about the Youth Service was its relevance to the world of today. The age range for which it catered seemed to me to be too restricted and it seemed to have less and less connection with the new leisure service I was promoting through my work in sport and recreation. I decided to approach the subject through two working parties and confine myself to co-ordinating their conclusions to produce a cohesive report. Andrew Fairburn, the Director of Education for Leicestershire, which had a good reputation for its youth work, chaired the working party on 'Youth and the Schools' and the Rev Fred Milson, a Methodist minister who was senior lecturer at Fircroft College, Birmingham, which specialised in training youth leaders, led the second working party thinking on 'Youth and Community Work in the 1970s'. The latter was reasonably well received but whether it was enough to prevent the steady decline of the Youth Service within the community was a very relevant question. Our chief concern was to widen the age range and to recognise that we should be providing for youngsters still at school at the bottom of the age range and making provision for the needs of young adults at the top end.

For the chairmanship of the Enquiry into Adult Education I turned to another man for whom I had enormous respect, Sir Lionel Russell, who had just retired as Director of Education for Birmingham. Lionel was a bachelor who lived for his work and although he had many outside interests they were all connected in one way or another with education. Whenever he came to dine with us at home his great love of children was obvious; we would find him crouching behind an armchair playing hide-and-seek with our young family. His report was presented to Margaret Thatcher as the succeeding Secretary of State for Education and Science in 1972. I expected it to represent Russell's approach to life, in view of his own personality and the eminent people on his committee. These included Clifford Barclay, whose work had so impressed me on the Chester Committee; R.D. Salter Davies, who had been an excellent chief inspector of education for the Youth Service, recently retired; Jim Conway, a much respected trade union leader (AEU); H.D. 'Billy' Hughes of Ruskin College, and others of equal distinction. Russell made 118 recommendations, the most important of which they identified as the creation of a Development Council for Adult Education for England and Wales and a Local Development Council in the area of each local education authority. Other recommendations were that adult education should continue to be provided on a partnership basis between statutory and voluntary bodies, with the latter receiving increased financial support; a request for guidance by the Secretary of State to secure a varied and comprehensive service of creative, intellectual and physical activities; a planned increase in the number of full-time staff, increasing substantially and as quickly as possible; a proper career structure; a service leading to qualifications at all levels; more positive effort towards the disadvantaged; better accommodation; an expanding contribution from the universities and more resources for the Workers Education Association; all this leading to the doubling of numbers of students from two to four million over a period of some five years or so and an expenditure rising from £16 million to £38 million.

I had a big row in my own department about proposals for a new reference library in Birmingham. I supported the proposal and I was right to do so. The department's advice was based upon fears of a substantial backlash. The issue was this: the amount of capital allocation available for the whole nation for the library service was about £4.5 million. Birmingham came up with proposals to build a major new central library and reference library which would take all the money available. Until then the department had recommended that the £4.5 million be divided into small parcels and allocated to various local authorities around the country. There was consternation when I said that it was time the country had at least one major new library. 'You can't do it, Minister', I was told. 'It is in your own constituency, there will be uproar.' As the Prime Minister recounted when he came to perform the opening ceremony some years later, 'The Minister banged the table and settled the matter by declaring "I'm not here to see Birmingham discriminated against!".' In the event Birmingham built a fine central lending and reference library, as befits a population of a million people and the service of two excellent universities and a first-class polytechnic. It also contains the best Shakespearean library in the world. So far as I know not a word of public criticism was ever uttered about the decision which I had been told would bring the world down around my ears. What criticism did arise came much later on from a most unexpected source – Prince Charles. He did not like its appearance which he believed to resemble a pill-box, a concrete monstrosity. That is a matter of taste and he may well be right but I wish he had balanced his remarks by commenting upon the excellence of our library service.

THE AINTREE GRAND NATIONAL

Mrs Mirabelle Topham, the owner of Aintree racecourse, home of the Grand National steeplechase, was one of the most formidable women I have ever met. Her reputation for a sturdy independence, especially where the National Hunt Committee and the Jockey Club were concerned, was legendary. When we met I found her to be a very agreeable lady, if full of possessive prejudice about her beloved Aintree for which, in those days, she received very little financial support. The great race itself was treated equally shabbily where prize-money was concerned. My own view was that the Grand National was the people's classic race. It had merely been tolerated by the racing establishment instead of enthusiastically supported, and I had no doubt that the northern location of the race, near Liverpool, roused little sympathy at Newmarket. I was determined that the Grand National should be supported. The massive betting staked on the race by millions of ordinary punters, many of them placing only one bet a year told its own story.

I had not been in office very long when we began to receive calls from Mrs Topham requesting a meeting to discuss the problems of the course. It was not possible for me to reply as positively as I would have wished as I had run into difficulties with the Home Office, who regarded racing as their prerogative and nothing to do with the Minister for Sport. Their main line of argument was that they were responsible for gambling and the control of betting was so important that it could not be divorced from the control of racing. They supported this line of thinking by saying that the Home Secretary had to fix the betting levy when there was a dispute between the Levy Board, which he also appointed, and the bookmakers. In my judgment there was no reason why these latter functions could not be undertaken by a Minister charged with responsibility for sport, and why this should affect the responsibility for law enforcement which always lies with the police authority I don't know. In any case, I asserted, it did not seem to me that up to now the Home Office had shown any imagination about racing policy or done anything to develop the sport. To me, it was vital to ensure that all sports facilities were opened up for constant public participation and these included racecourses.

It took some time to persuade the Home Office of this new policy and it was not until Roy Jenkins became Home Secretary that I really made much progress. We began to consult each other in such matters as the appointment of George Wigg as the chairman of the Tote Board in November 1967. Unlike many people in racing I had a lot of faith in Wigg's commitment to sport. Many members of the Jockey Club acknowledged this but found him an impossible man to deal with. He was – but like many impossible men that was the reason he achieved so much. I had already admired Wigg's imagination in another aspect of racing, the threat to racecourses which came from developers. They bought up the shares, usually at a small cost because the courses were open spaces, obtained planning consent and then sold them for development. George Wigg took the initiative to bring this threat to an end by convening talks between R.H.S. 'Dick' Crossman, the Minister for Housing and Social Government, and myself. This resulted in Crossman making an announcement listing a number of important racecourses such as Aintree, Cheltenham and others, which he would call in for ministerial decision should there be any planning applications that threatened their future as racecourses. Every one of those courses still exists today. Whatever his faults, and there were solid grounds for criticism, George Wigg probably did more for racing than most of his critics, certainly until the arrival of Woodrow Wyatt to the chairmanship of the Tote Board. This was another of Roy Jenkins' appointments which I was pleased to be consulted about and to support. He has also been an outstanding success.

But all this is to overrun my story. Mirabelle Topham was another of racing's impossible people. Her achievement was to keep Aintree going for the public. I was well aware in those days that the racing establishment would have closed Aintree down and moved the Grand National elsewhere. Haydock Park was suggested to me, so was Cheltenham, but superb as that racecourse undoubtedly is, it already staged the Gold Cup and the Champion Hurdle and I was not supporting any move south for one of the great sporting events of the north. The fact is that the Grand National would not be the Grand National anywhere other than at Aintree. Something had to be done to respond to Mrs Topham's calls. The racecourse itself was terribly run down and starved of cash, and attendances were dwindling, but public support, as measured by betting on the race and the television viewing figures, showed where public opinion stood. I decided that Sir John Lang should go off to meet the lady. They were both old world characters, charmingly polite but forthright. They got on famously. In due course John suggested that it was time for me to accept an invitation to lunch at her Regent's Park house which I did. It was a memorable occasion. There were five of us – Mrs Topham, her niece and nephew, Sir John and myself. We enjoyed four or five courses but for each course we were offered a choice of two or three dishes. It really was a sumptuous affair laced with Mrs T's sparkling, if acid, comments upon all and sundry.

She explained to Sir John and I that she had to sell Aintree, and went on to ask why the Government could not buy it from her and run it on behalf of the nation. I explained that the Government did not have powers to run sport, certainly not racecourses, but that we did have powers to assist others such as local authorities and that was the line of thought I was pursuing.

I had indeed already initiated discussions with all the appropriate authorities, and considering the earlier suggestions made to me about transferring the race elsewhere I made good progress. The Lancashire County Council was Labour-controlled and understood the importance of keeping Aintree as an open space for the whole of Merseyside, which had less open space per 1,000 population than any other urban area in the country. The North-West Sports Council was very keen to build a regional sports centre at Aintree and favoured the idea of having terraced seating on its outside wall from which the public could view the race while the sports centre was used for catering on race days. Unfortunately, the democratic process took its toll and Labour lost control of the county council. The incoming councillors were not prepared to continue discussions and I had to start again. This time I turned to Liverpool itself. When Bill Sefton, later to become Lord Sefton, the leader of the city council came to see me he could not have been more positive and this time, when control here also passed to the Conservatives their leader, Councillor H. MacDonald Stewart, who had served with me as an MP, was equally supportive. They were both attracted to the idea that we could save the race and open space for Merseyside for all time and build a regional sports centre too, and the concept crossed the party lines in Liverpool.

In July 1968 I was able to make my statement to the House reporting on my discussions with Liverpool Corporation, the Turf Authorities, the Horse Racing Betting Levy Board and Messrs Topham. I explained that negotiations would now take place between Liverpool and Tophams for the purchase of the land, and if this was successful Liverpool would lease the racecourse to a non-profit making trust to be chaired by Lord Leverhulme. The trust would develop Aintree as the National Hunt racing centre of the north, a scheme that had the support of the Betting Levy Board. I was able to announce: 'We shall apply the provision of Section 8 of the 1966 Local Government Act in order to make a grant not exceeding 50 per cent in respect of that portion of the site which is to be kept as public open space. It is believed that at a later date the Liverpool Corporation may wish to establish a sports centre on the site in which the North-West Regional Sports Council is much interested'. My statement was welcomed from all sides of the House and I was satisfied that we were now set fair to reach a solution. Yet it was not to be. It had to be explained to Tophams that the maximum price Liverpool could pay was determined by the valuation of the Government's District Valuation Officer. Naturally, this price was based on the open space value of Aintree. Mrs Topham had other ideas. She wanted a price which Liverpool could not pay as a local authority. Negotiations dragged on throughout 1969 and beyond my period in office which ended with the election of 1970. I could understand the earlier despair of the racing authorities in their dealings with Mrs Topham but I was more than ever convinced that my determination to maintain the National and to develop the site as a regional sports centre and public open space was absolutely correct. I was beginning to believe that only a compulsory purchase order, made by Liverpool and confirmed by the Government, would bring this about when such a possibility was removed by our election defeat.

Eventually Mrs Topham found a willing buyer who paid a price which I did not believe could be sustained, given the fact that no serious development could take place. The company who bought the course was owned by Mr William Davis and his quite extraordinary plans seemed to consist of building houses in the middle of the racecourse and running the race around the houses! It never got to the starting line. In 1975 when I was back in office and again contemplating the problem I had a visit from Cyril Stein of Ladbroke's, the bookmakers. He asked what my reaction would be if his firm bought Aintree and secured the Grand National. I was overjoyed. Ladbroke's invested a great deal of effort and imagination as well as money and made the race safe until 1982, when they sold it to the Racecourse Holdings Trust, a subsidiary of the Levy Board. Since then the race has gone from strength to strength. Every spring when Grand National time comes round I still get a feeling of pleasure at having played some part in the campaign to save the National.

MINISTER OF STATE

When the 1969 Government reshuffle took place I received a summons from Harold Wilson. I had not expected it even though I had now been in office for almost five years. The Prime Minister was in a chirpy mood. 'I have been wondering what I should do for you', he told me. 'The solution came to me at the weekend when I was playing golf. I would like you to go to Housing and Local Government as Minister of State and take sport with you from Education to Local Government. You will be the first man in history to take a Ministry with him when he moves.' In fact, Christopher Chataway from the Tory front bench had been advocating that sport should be relocated exactly as the PM now proposed. There were convincing arguments both ways. Generally speaking, sport and recreation was the responsibility of parks and baths departments in most local authorities, but educational sport and the Youth Service were rooted in the educational service.

Whether or not Harold Wilson knew of this and wanted to steal the Tory clothes, a ploy which was not unnatural to Harold, I do not know. Maybe, as Sir Herbert Andrews had suggested earlier, it was time for me to move on, and it was the civil service which had put the idea to the PM. Whatever the reason and if, as I liked to imagine, it came as a result of the satisfaction of a long drive down the fairway, I found myself moving to be number two to Anthony Greenwood. Tony was an agreeable colleague. Back in the early 1960s he had chaired the pioneering working party that recommended the Party to take sport and the arts seriously and to create a Sports Council. And local government was my subject since I had served my apprenticeship on the Birmingham City Council. The move was tailor-made for me. I soon found myself immersed in a whole range of responsibilities – local government finance, rate support grant orders, the betterment levy, Countryside Commission, rating policy and rate relief, the Land Commission, Water Resources, rivers and reservoirs and, of course, sport. The sports department was transferred from education lock, stock and barrel and the Ministry's existing functions in this area were merged with it. I took good care to take Sir John Lang with me and I was pleased that my permanent secretary, Sir James Jones, who I knew reasonably well, was in every way agreeable and supportive.

It proved to be a heavy load and much more controversial than education. The rate support grant orders were always complicated and usually strongly contested. Tony Greenwood's health was beginning to fail and he was absent for quite long periods which meant that I found myself attending more Cabinet committees and accepting more responsibility than I had expected, but it was all very stimulating. One change that could not have been more appreciated was that Ministers of State had their own car and driver. No more did I have a car pool driver who might be anyone, a great inconvenience at weekends when I was off to sporting engagements. Eric Adams volunteered for the job.

He loved sport and as a bachelor he had no difficulties about the weekends. It was a very happy arrangement. He knew his way around better than any other driver I ever encountered. When I went to Wembley and took my seat in the Royal Box I would look down and see Eric waving to me from a seat behind the managers, trainers and substitutes. How on earth he got there I never found out but, unfailingly, he was always there. I think he must have had some arrangement with the police and security but it worked out very well. The private secretary I inherited was Harry Price, who was ready to move on when I arrived but was asked to stay on and to run me in, which he did. He knew the job backwards and fought strenuously to ensure that I toed the departmental line, which I usually, but not always, thought it right to do. My year as Minister of State proved to be an agreeable experience.

BASIL D'OLIVEIRA

If I ever had any doubts about the relationship between sport and politics they were totally removed by the D'Oliveira affair which dominated my activity in the final two years of this Government. Basil D'Oliveira was a young coloured cricketer from the Cape who desperately wanted to play his cricket in England because of the cruel racial discrimination existing in South Africa. His abilities came to the notice of John Arlott, that most distinguished cricket journalist. Arlott championed his cause and pursued it with John Kay of the *Manchester Evening News,* who eventually got him fixed up as professional for Middleton in Lancashire League Cricket, where he prospered. The great Lancashire wicket-keeper George Duckworth included D'Oliveira in one of his touring sides along with Tom Graveney. It did not take long for Tom to recommend Basil to Worcestershire, who quickly signed him up.

D'Oliveira's progress with Worcestershire was meteoric and his selection to play for England became inevitable. England were due to tour South Africa in 1968–69. I was already concerned about that tour and the likely problems of including D'Oliveira in the side before pressure started to build up in Parliament early in the January of 1967. I held discussions with the MCC (Marylebone Cricket Club) who were then the governing body of the sport and responsible for the tour. Their secretary, Mr S.C. 'Billy' Griffiths, a man whose integrity was beyond any question, assured me that the England team would be selected on merit alone and if it proved to be unacceptable to the South African Government then the tour would be called off. This was no more than I expected. I would not dream of interfering with the selection of international teams myself, as the responsible British Minister, and I was damned if we were going to allow South African Ministers to do so. I therefore informed Parliament: 'The MCC have informed the Government that the team to tour South Africa will be chosen on merit and in this respect any preconditions that the host country lays down will be totally disregarded. The Government are confident that if, when the time comes, any player chosen for the touring side were to be rejected then there would be no question but that the MCC would find such a condition wholly unacceptable and the projected tour would be abandoned'. My statement was welcomed on all sides of the House although Geoffrey Rhodes, MP for Ashton-under-Lyme, thought it might embarrass D'Oliveira.

The side touring in England in the summer of 1968 was Australia and when they came to the Oval for the final Test England had to win to square the series. Basil had played in only one previous Test that summer, scoring 87 not out. However, when he was brought into the side for the Oval Test he batted superbly and knocked up 158 runs, a match-winning performance. This meant that he finished the season with a higher Test average than any other player on either side. He scored more runs than all but two of the other England players although he only played in two of the five Tests. His century was also the fastest of the series. The selectors for the South African tour, chaired by Mr D.J. Insole, met during the Oval Test and then announced the tour side to be captained by Colin Cowdrey with Tom Graveney as his vice-captain. There was no Basil D'Oliveira. All hell was let loose.

Tom Graveney, Basil's Worcestershire captain as well as the vice-captain of the proposed touring squad, obviously appreciated the storm which would follow D'Oliveira's non-selection, as well as the deep sense of disappointment he would feel at being left out after his great innings at the Oval. Tom seems to have broken the news to him and sent him home half-an-hour early from the match at Worcester where they were playing and where he had just scored 128. Doug Insole met the barrage of criticism directed at him and his fellow selectors by saying, 'I think we have players rather better than him in the side'. This was an extraordinary statement. D'Oliveira was good enough to be in the side for the Oval Test, he had made a match-winning score – how could he not be good enough to be included in the 16 players chosen to tour South Africa? It was an explanation that satisfied no one that I met and it fuelled belief that D'Oliveira's omission had a political or diplomatic ring to it. No evidence has ever emerged that Insole and his colleagues considered any factor other than cricketing merit but the sceptics abounded. The voting members of the selection committee have never been revealed to me, nor so far as I am aware to anyone else, and as incredible as I found their decision, I have never had cause to doubt that it was taken on cricketing grounds alone. However, there was every reason to doubt the wisdom and judgment, both cricketing and political, of the MCC committee.

The controversy raged. I was inundated with requests to intervene, to give interviews, to reply to letters from parliamentary colleagues. I stood firm on the twin planks of my earlier statement, that it was not my job as Minister to intervene in the selection of the team and that I accepted the MCC's assurance that the team had been selected on cricketing merit alone. The Rev David Sheppard, who announced that he was 'terribly disappointed', took the same line. 'They have made a dreadful mistake, but I know all the selectors, they are friends of mine. They are people of honesty, and they don't suffer from racial prejudice.' Others did not share this view. Sir Learie Constantine was a member of the Race Relations Board, one of my appointees to the Sports Council and the finest all-round cricketer I ever saw. He also had diplomatic experience – he had been his country's High Commissioner in London – and he voiced grave doubts: 'The circumstances of this omission are positively suspicious'. Ivor Richards, MP for Baron's Court, asked the Race Relations Board to 'investigate the affair as a matter of urgency'. Members of South Africa's ruling National Party broke into loud applause when Mr Muller, their Minister of the Interior, interrupted his speech to a Transvaal rally to give them the news of D'Oliveira's omission. Inevitably, members of the MCC, concerned over the course events had taken, decided to call an extraordinary meeting of the club. David Sheppard renewed his opinion that the selectors were 'honest but naïve, not understanding the dynamite that they are holding', but he rightly laid more blame on the MCC committee for not having cleared the ground beforehand than he did upon the selectors. Events were rapidly to endorse that judgment.

First of all D'Oliveira was signed up by the *News of the World* to report the coming tour from the press box. John Vorster, the South African Prime Minister, soon vetoed that, saying 'guests who are sponsored by people with ulterior motives usually find that they are not invited'. Then Tom Cartwright, Warwickshire's fine all-rounder, found it necessary to withdraw from the tour. His original selection had seemed doubtful since he had nursed a troublesome knee throughout the season. On medical advice he withdrew from the England party. There was no escape now from the decision that had to be taken. Almost immediately the MCC announced that Cartwright would be replaced by D'Oliveira. Tom Cartwright was a bowler who could bat whereas Basil D'Oliveira was a batsman who could bowl. There was no doubt that his inclusion in the team was urged by the captain, Colin Cowdrey, and it would certainly have been supported by Tom Graveney. He was rightly in the touring side but from that moment the tour was doomed.

The South African Prime Minister made his views known within the day. 'The team as constituted now is not the team of the MCC. It is the team of the Anti-Apartheid Movement, the team of the South African Non-Racial Olympic Committee and the team of Bishop Reeves, Anglican Bishop of Johannesburg.' (The Bishop had previously been deported for his opposition to apartheid.) He went on to say that D'Oliveira was 'no longer a sportsman but a political cricket ball'. I described Vorster's speech as a 'monstrous libel on the MCC'. Protests poured into my office and I could only regret that Parliament was in recess; it would have been of great value to have Vorster condemned from all sides of the House, as he surely would have been. When Vorster said the touring team as constituted would not be acceptable he actually had the gall to say he was acting on principle. An even more ludicrous comment was made by one of his Ministers to the effect that if D'Oliveira was given out by a white umpire it might provoke a riot! The MCC were informed by the South African Cricket Association that the side was not acceptable for reasons 'outside their control' and the MCC unanimously decided to call off the tour but the recriminations and the disclosures were only just beginning.

The specially convened meeting of the MCC took place at Church House, Westminster in early December. David Sheppard moved the vote of censure 'regretting the committee's mishandling of affairs leading up to the selection of the team for the intended tour of South Africa in 1968–69'. He was protesting against the toleration of racism in cricket and he introduced a new fact which surprised most people: the MCC had changed their policy in the months leading up to the team's selection. In January they had asked the South Africans not to impose any conditions on the team's selection. But in March the committee changed their policy on the advice of 'a prominent professional politician', and this advice 'had been shown to be wrong'. Sheppard did not name the prominent politician but he clearly knew it was Sir Alec Douglas-Home, a most distinguished Foreign Secretary, a former Prime Minister and a great lover of cricket. The establishment carried the day on all the motions before the meeting by something like 4,357 votes to 1,570, with the postal vote being in the order of about 4,000 to 1,250. None of those voting by post heard any of the arguments at the meeting, of course, but, even more astonishingly, none of those present were told anything about the dramatic diplomatic involvement Sheppard had disclosed. Neither was I, as the Minister for Sport, ever afforded the courtesy of being told of the political move which actually involved meetings between the South African Prime Minister and Douglas-Home. It emerged that these meetings were followed up by Lord Cobham, another former MCC president, who was summoned to meet Vorster and to convey to the MCC the message that D'Oliveira, if chosen, would not be allowed to tour South Africa. Lord Cobham – Charles Lyttleton – was himself a fine cricketer who had captained Worcestershire, and he became a diplomat of the highest calibre, serving as a most respected Governor of New Zealand. His behaviour in this affair as in everything else in his life was impeccable.

As it happened, my first inkling that South African politics, or diplomacy, had overtaken cricket came one day in the summer when I happened to bump into Lord Cobham behind the pavilion at Lord's. Cobham simply told me, 'I have had to tell them that Vorster will not let D'Oliveira in if he is selected'. I asked if that was his opinion. 'No, it is a fact', he said. He gave no details and broke no confidence, just stated a fact based upon the message which Vorster had summoned him in March to deliver to the MCC. This now set me thinking. The final Test was still to come, the team was still to be selected, and I had resolutely taken a stand, confident that the MCC would select the team on cricketing merit alone, as they had advised me. At that moment I knew nothing about the involvement of Alec Douglas-Home. I assumed that if there was any political consideration of any sort then the MCC would inform Her Majesty's Government. It was a serious mistake for a Labour Minister to make.

What happened was even more startling, as the MCC had to admit when Lord Cobham made a statement the following April, describing his summons by Vorster and the message he had relayed to them. Shortly before the Cobham message Sir Alec had held discussions with Vorster and as a result he advised the club 'not to press South Africa for an answer on whether there would be a difficulty about D'Oliveira being a member of the touring party'. In effect he was advising the MCC not to press for an answer to the letter they had sent to the South African Cricket Association in January asking that no preconditions would be laid down upon the selection of the touring team. The MCC committee unanimously accepted the advice of Sir Alec Douglas-Home. As Billy Griffiths subsequently told me, 'We took Alec's advice. We did not think we could possibly do better'. So when Lord Cobham brought his message, even though it could not have been more ominous and came direct from the South African Prime Minister, the MCC decided to ignore it. The Cobham message was delivered to Mr A.E.R. Gilligan, the president, and Mr G.O. Allen, the treasurer, who has been a life-long friend of Sir Alec. They decided not to inform the MCC committee and that meant that the selectors could not have had any formal knowledge that D'Oliveira would not be allowed to tour. Whether any of them knew informally, as David Sheppard claimed that he knew the previous August, can only be conjecture.

What is certain is that the crisis brought about by Vorster's imposition of racial politics upon sport, which still has its repercussions 20 years on, was aggravated by what can only be described as a monumental miscalculation – an attempt to appease the South African Prime Minister – and the decision to keep a vital policy decision away from the full committee. So much for democracy. Nor does there seem to have been any thought that the British Government of the day had any standing in the matter, in spite of its importance for sport and for diplomatic relations. And one must assume that Douglas-Home did not see fit to advise the MCC that they had some responsibility towards their own Government. It was an episode from which few could claim credit. The exceptions were Basil D'Oliveira himself, whose bearing throughout could not have been more dignified, and his chosen captain and vice-captain, Colin Cowdrey and Tom Graveney.

This diplomatic saga was not the only South African chicanery in this affair. Even before the team was due for selection an attempt had been made to get Basil D'Oliveira out of the way to make him unavailable for selection. It was brought to my knowledge by Reg Hayter, who owns one of the leading sports agencies in the country, and who was managing D'Oliveira's business affairs. He told me an incredible story and sought my advice. A South African named Tiene Oosthuizen, acting on behalf of the South African Sports Foundation, had approached Basil and offered him an enormous sum of money, some £40,000, and a car if he would immediately take up a coaching job in South Africa. Unknown to Oosthuizen the conversation was taped and when Reg Hayter played the tape through he realised at once that the implication of this quite sensational offer would be that if D'Oliveira were coaching in South Africa he would be unavailable for selection. When Hayter telephoned me we discussed how this situation should be dealt with. I advised full public disclosure. Another storm erupted. The director of the South African Sports Foundation, a Mr Gert Potgeiter, explained that the offer just before the team selection was 'a coincidence'. He also denied any South African Government pressure to make such an offer and went on to say that finance had not been discussed since D'Oliveira had declined the offer. Since the cricketer could hardly have had a greater ambition than to tour the country of his birth as a representative of his adopted country I was quite prepared to believe the stories of the colossal sums said to be on offer. Again, D'Oliveira behaved with total propriety. It may be that his personal ambitions to tour for England contributed to his thinking, but he certainly put the interests of English cricket before his own financial considerations. If only we could say the same today in other cases!

Inevitably, after the D'Oliveira crisis nothing was ever going to be the same again. I again came under pressure to intervene, this time in respect of the forthcoming tour of England by the South African team scheduled for 1970. Questions were asked in Parliament. I discussed the situation with Jim Callaghan, a close friend of mine who was Home Secretary. We decided to allow the Cricket Council, now established as the new governing body of cricket along with the MCC, time to consider the events of the D'Oliveira affair. Surely they would now understand the social and political implications of sport with a country practising apartheid and interfering with national team selection? The cricket authorities maintained an ominous silence. Meanwhile the protests grew, not just from the organisations which would be expected to lead them, but from all sections of our national life. When Sir Edward Boyle, the Conservative MP for Handsworth and an MCC member, announced that he would be joining the largest protest march ever assembled over a sporting controversy it was clear how strong the feelings were against the South Africans.

The protest came to a head in Parliament on 14 May 1970. A day earlier Mr Speaker, Horace King, had astonished the Government by accepting a request from Mr Philip Noel-Baker for an emergency debate on the proposed South African tour. It was an application made under Standing Order Number Nine, that is for a matter of great public urgency requiring priority over all other business. When the Speaker accepted the proposition and put it to the House there was never any doubt that the necessary 40 Members would rise in their places and support the application. The Speaker announced that the debate would take place at 3.30 pm the following day. I was a long way from Westminster when the news reached me in the early evening. I was touring Pembrokeshire inspecting sports facilities, and the only way I could get back to London was by the sleeper car, which was full up. We had to use powers of Government priority to obtain berths and I sent instructions to my office and to the Sports Council to convene an urgent meeting in my office for 10.00 am so that I could consult them before speaking in the debate in the afternoon. When I arrived at my office I was surprised to be told that the Prime Minister had asked the lord president of the council, Dick Crossman, to agree my statement in advance and we arranged a one o'clock meeting. Crossman complained that this was inconvenient but it seemed to me to be the earliest possible moment I could prepare my statement after my consultations with the Sports Council.

I was surprised at the large turn-out at the Sports Council meeting and at the firmness of their position. At an earlier stage they had advised me that they would be considering South African questions on sporting criteria alone although they accepted that there were other considerations which were for the Government of the day. Now they were much more resolved. The D'Oliveira affair had been too much for them, they could not stomach the political interference of the South African Government. They admitted that they had had to face up to the situation as sportsmen and women as well as identifying the political considerations. It was a serious and responsible Council, very sad but realistic. I went off to prepare my statement, the resolution of the Sports Council being the main theme. When I met Crossman I was amazed by his truculence. He tried to cut out or amend all references to the MCC which might lead them to take their own decision along the lines I was hoping for. 'We can't trust these buggers,' he told me, 'you will have to firm it up.' In vain I tried to reason with him and to tell him that there was a dividing line in relationships between sport and government that I had never transgressed. We may have to interfere but that moment was not today. 'Harold will never stand for it', he told me, proceeding to put his pen through sentences he did not like. By this time I had had enough. 'If you are going to alter my speech', I told him, 'you can make it yourself, or Harold can make it. If I am making the speech it is going to be my speech.' He looked nonplussed. Then, throwing my speech up in the air and shouting 'Be it on your own head!' he stormed out of the room. I returned to my own office feeling ready to take on anyone in the debate.

Philip Noel-Baker opened the debate with a powerful review of the history of sport in its relations with South Africa and then he moved on to the issue giving me the greatest concern. What would be the effect of a South African tour on the Commonwealth Games due to be held at Edinburgh later in the year? He told the House that India, Malaysia, Ceylon, Singapore and Pakistan had already declared that they would not come to the Games if a South African team toured England. He quoted the views of Walter Winterbottom, director of the Sports Council, who was most concerned to protect the Games. All this pleased me very much because it was a matter of major concern. I had been urging the Cricket Council to consider their responsibilities to sport as a whole. Noel-Baker was followed by John Boyd-Carpenter, a tough cookie, who believed that to cancel the tour would be to deny a freedom and he compared the South African tour with the visit of the Red Army Choir which we had allowed to come here even though the Soviets had invaded Czechoslovakia. He wondered how many Jews were members of that choir but did not provide any evidence that they were discriminated against either in music or sport. He paid no attention to the main point that it is the discrimination against citizens in sport, because of their colour, which happens nowhere else in the world outside South Africa, that is the root cause of the offence South Africa gives to the world.

I decided to intervene next, much to the consternation of Fred Peart, the Leader of the House, who was sitting next to me. Jim Callaghan, the Home Secretary, sitting on the other side thought I was right to speak early and urged me on. My plan was to have the debate conducted on my terms rather than to wind up a debate conducted in ignorance of the news of the Sports Council's advice which I had to reveal to the House. I took the Red Army Choir point head on, being prepared for it, by quoting a speech of Sir Alec Douglas-Home urging its cancellation and comparing this to the actions of Iain Macleod, who had also demanded the cancellation of the Choir's visit although he had then gone to Twickenham to watch the South Africans play rugby.

I emphasised the importance of Commonwealth sport, making much of the fact that cricket is almost entirely a Commonwealth game. There were four major considerations: the effect of the tour upon racial harmony; the question of law and order; the implications for the Commonwealth Games; and the long-term interests of sport. I dealt with each of these matters in turn and gave the latest count of countries which would withdraw from the Edinburgh Games if the cricket tour went ahead – of 18 countries involved 12 had already indicated they would not be coming, three were uncertain and only three had confirmed their participation. This meant that 600 athletes would not be at the Games. Next, I stressed the fact that it was sport itself that was taking the initiative to exclude South Africa. 'I have always thought it interesting that where we have a genuine governing body it is impossible for South Africa to be a participating member. The Olympic Movement, the Federation of International Football Associations and now Lawn Tennis all find it quite impossible to have a member country which says that half the countries in membership cannot visit it, or can do so only on terms which are quite unacceptable to them'. I proceeded to give to the House the news that I had convened an emergency meeting of the Sports Council that morning. It had received two resolutions, one from the Scottish Commonwealth Games Council and another from the Scottish Sports Council and had then gone on to consider the specific question of the proposed South African cricket tour. I read out to the House the resulting advice of the United Kingdom Sports Council, which I had already despatched to the Cricket Council, urging them to accept its conclusions. The resolution read:

'The Sports Council strongly urges the Cricket Council to withdraw the invitation to the South African Cricket Association for the 1970 tour. It does so because it believes the consequences of the tour taking place will have harmful repercussions on sport, especially multi-racial sport, extending far beyond cricket itself.

'The Sports Council maintains that governing bodies of sport must have autonomy and authority in the control of their own affairs, and therefore recommends that the Government should not intervene directly in this matter.

'The Sports Council has reached these conclusions in the exercise of its responsibilities for all aspects of sport, after taking fully into account the past development of the South African issue and its likely future implications for sport as a whole.

'With regard to the particular question of the Commonwealth Games in Edinburgh, the Sports Council believes that the longer-term interests of multi-racial sport in the Commonwealth transcend all other aspects of the issue. In support of the British Commonwealth Games for Scotland and the Sports Council for Scotland, the Sports Council urges all countries who have already accepted invitations to the Games to send teams to participate.'

When I sat down I had effectively ended the debate, as I had intended. My speech had taken 23 minutes. Jim Callaghan told me, 'It is the best speech I have heard you make', and David Steel also commented that it was 'an excellent speech'. It was certainly a speech which gave me as much satisfaction as any I have made in the House during my 35 years there. Some heavyweights followed – Reginald Maudling, Sir Derek Walker-Smith and Sir Edward Boyle. Boyle made a most courageous speech in which he quoted with approval a passage of my speech in which I had dealt with the changing situation and the growing impatience of the world with the intransigence of the South African Government. 'I agree with the Minister that a tour of this kind seemed to make sense in 1960, it just made sense in 1965 but not now', he said. 'There is nothing extreme or disruptive about holding the view that what seemed just tolerable in 1960 or 1965 no longer makes sense in 1970.' There was nothing more to be said. The resolution of the Sports Council had taken the edge out of the opposition.

Subsequently, the Cricket Council came to see Jim Callaghan at the

Home Office. Their delegation consisted of Mr G.O. 'Gubby' Allen, Mr Billy Griffiths and his assistant, Mr J.C. Allom. Jim told them that the Chief Constables in whose areas the games were to be played were very concerned about serious disorder. The protests were going to be mammoth, and some grounds were in public parks, where protection of the wide open areas of turf would cause a major problem. Even Quintin Hogg was calling for assurances that his constituents living around Lord's would be given adequate protection. The Home Secretary could not provide these assurances; the tour, he said, should be called off for many reasons, not least to protect law and order. And so it was. On 19 May the Cricket Council resolved that there would be no further Test tours with South Africa until teams were selected on a non-racial basis. That information was conveyed to the Home Secretary by Griffiths and Allom, who expressed their concern that the tour might affect the forthcoming Commonwealth Games. They indicated that the Cricket Council would most certainly accept the Government's advice to call off the tour. They were acting honourably but they were also demonstrating, right to the end, that they preferred to rest their decision upon the Government's advice rather than upon an acceptance of sporting responsibility.

I was told later by John Arlott that the view at Lord's was that the Government's position would cost us half a million votes at the forthcoming election. Whether or not that would have been the case is difficult to judge. Another sporting event proved likely to be much more decisive – the defeat of the England football team in the World Cup a few days before polling day!

10

THE FORTUNES OF WAR

DEFEAT

When Harold Wilson finally decided to go to the polls it was with every prospect of success, in spite of all the difficulties produced by Barbara Castle's proposals for trade union reform, 'In place of Strife'. That policy provoked the almost unanimous opposition of the trade union movement and split the Cabinet, the opposition being skilfully led by Jim Callaghan. Finally, the Government backed down from the clauses which could have put trade unionists in prison – an impossible situation for a Labour Government – but the policy had a considerable effect upon the TUC, who later on moved some way towards the Government. The Prime Minister clearly believed that this was enough to counteract the feeling of many voters. He was fortified by the polls. We were 5 per cent ahead with Gallup and 3.5 per cent up with NOP, and most of us believed we could build on this during the campaign, in which Ted Heath would be matched against Harold Wilson.

I was able to report to Wilson when he came to Birmingham that canvassing on the housing estates was going well. We had a fine city rally with an enthusiastic response. It was my job to take up the collection and notes were floating down from the balcony when Harold arrived early and insisted on making his entrance, interrupting our proceedings and bringing the collection to a premature end. This cost our Birmingham campaign much-needed funds. I thought at that time that Wilson looked overwrought, and his speech seemed a little lack-lustre. I believe that the private polls available to him were reflecting a growing unease with economic issues.

A few days later Bob Mellish, the Chief Whip, came to Birmingham and asked me to see him after his day's campaign. I went along to the Albany Hotel and was amazed to be told that if we won I should stay close to the telephone as I could expect a call from the PM. He, Bob, wanted to go to Housing and expected that I would be offered his post as Chief Whip. I could hardly believe this as only four months earlier my private secretary had told me that I was suspected of having leaked a Cabinet committee decision about nurses' pay and that a full scale 'leak' enquiry was going on. Since there was not a word of truth in the accusation I had replied, 'In this administration all leaks emanate from Number Ten!' This amused my department but not, I imagine, the PM's staff working from that illustrious address!

My fears about the way things were going were aroused at a quite dramatic factory-gate meeting that was held jointly – as was our tradition – with Roy Jenkins, on the Monday before the poll, for workers at Metropolitan Cammel and Carriage and other factories at Common Lane, Ward End. Roy decided to speak first but as we waited for the chairman to make his speech, to an audience a thousand strong, he took me to one side to tell me that he had heard from Bill Rodgers, the Minister dealing with civil aviation, that he could not prevent the cost of two giant planes appearing in the next day's balance of payments figures, in spite of the fact that they had only just landed here and had not yet been delivered to the airline. This would mean that instead of being in the black we would be in the red by some £31 million. What was my judgment about the effect of this? I thought that if the presentation was good and the one-off nature of this transaction was fully explained it would not be disastrous. Roy made his speech and was reasonably well received, no one raising any questions about 'In place of Strife', or showing much concern about the economy. They did not even take up Enoch Powell's great mischief-making, in which he had accused Government officials of deliberately falsifying the immigration figures, a charge that was outrageous but bound to affect the prejudiced Labour vote. Instead, they waited for me, and politics were not uppermost in their thoughts. It was England's defeat the day before in the World Cup which dominated their thinking and I was the Minister for Sport. They wanted to know what I thought about it all.

The crisis for English football was of much greater concern to this audience than any political or economic question. Roy looked on, bemused, but I understood their disappointment, especially as we were in the competition as the Cup-holders. We had gone out in a quarter-final match. England were winning 2–1 with 15 minutes of the match remaining when Sir Alf Ramsey decided to take off Bobby Charlton. No doubt Alf thought that Bobby's legs had to be saved for the semi-final match due to be played in a few days' time. It was reasonable thinking. However, everything went wrong for England in the closing moments of the match, just as they went wrong for Labour from that moment onwards. Peter Bonetti, our goal-keeper, made a hash of what should have been a comfortable save and the goal put us out of the Cup. It was also sad because it proved to be Bobby Charlton's last match in an England jersey. No player has ever served his country better. On this Monday lunch-time this disaster was the only thing that mattered. The tabloid newspapers were full of it; I had no doubt that in the factories that morning talk had been of nothing else. I did my best to answer their questions. 'Why did he take Charlton off, Denis?' and other shouts, 'We threw it away!' The questions were good-humoured and I countered in a similar vein. But for the first time I had real doubts – the mood was changing.

The polls published in the final days predicting a swing to Labour had been taken before the bad set of trade figures and certainly before England's World Cup exit. They totally failed to prepare us for defeat but on polling day the omens were bad. Brenda had already told me as a result of her canvassing, 'I don't like the smell of this, it is like 1959', when I lost my seat. On the council estates the wrong people were voting, what I later called the 'woodworm' vote. Many people who had never voted before asked our canvassers how to find the polling booth. They even asked how to record their vote! Many of our voters abstained. Nationally, the late swing against us amounted to 4.7 per cent. In the West Midlands it was even greater, the Powell factor playing its part. Birmingham's results were mixed, the three Ministers doing worse than our back bench colleagues, a situation which reflected some logic, I suppose. At Stechford a 7.1 per cent swing was registered against Roy Jenkins while in Sparkbrook Roy Hattersley recorded 4.5 per cent. My own result showed a majority down from 10,604 to 6,871, a swing of 5.3 per cent on a 2 per cent lower turn-out. At Perry Barr Chris Price, a very good Member, lost his seat. So did the Liberal Wallace Lawler at Ladywood, with a swing to us of 9.6 per cent. Liberalism in Birmingham declined from that moment onwards. Nationally, the long, long night of waiting produced a net loss for Labour of 60 seats, a Tory gain of 68 seats and a majority for Ted Heath of 43 seats over Labour and of 31 seats overall. There was nothing for it but to thank Jack Davis, my wonderful agent, and his faithful band of workers, to eat and drink, and then to collapse into bed contemplating a new back-bench lifestyle.

ALL CHANGE IN SPORT

I waited with some apprehension to discover what the new Prime Minister intended to do about sport. Ted Heath had a well-developed interest in sport. He was a sailor of considerable distinction and a frequent visitor to Wembley for the Cup final. He also went to Wimbledon and other national sporting occasions. I was confident that he would continue the post in his Government. In Opposition his spokesman had been Charles Morrison, the MP for Devizes, with whom I had enjoyed a very constructive relationship. It was not to continue. The appointment of Eldon Griffiths, the Member for Bury St Edmunds, was a great surprise even if his constituency did contain Newmarket with all its racing interest. I learned later that Charles Morrison was told that he had to be left out because Griffiths must be included; he had been close to Ted Heath's office in Opposition. I dropped Eldon a note of good wishes which I reinforced when I saw him in the House. He responded very agreeably by telling me that he had already discovered that I was going to be 'a very hard act to follow'. I offered him my fullest co-operation in all matters in which bi-partisan policies ought to be followed. The offer was never taken up.

The greatest disappointment for me was to be out of office immediately before the staging of the Edinburgh Commonwealth Games. I had put in an enormous amount of effort to help make them a success, taking on the Edinburgh City Council and the Treasury, and establishing good relationships with my Scottish ministerial colleagues. Probably of even greater significance was the firm action taken when the Supreme Council of Sport in Africa threatened to boycott the Games. I had asked the chairman of the Commonwealth Games Federation, Alex Ross, to fly immediately to some of the African Commonwealth countries to assure them that they could have every confidence in Britain's hosting of the Games and of our total opposition to apartheid. Alex Ross did an excellent job and Edinburgh enjoyed the results of that initiative. Willie Carmichael, the director of the organisation, proved to be a supreme organiser of the Games. He certainly recognised my contribution and made all the arrangements for my presence, including allocating to me a car and a driver. The Games were an outstanding success and Edinburgh deserved the fullest congratulations. Alex Ross, who was later to be knighted, a most well-deserved honour, told me that he would have loved to have invited me to present one of the awards but that, of course, he couldn't. He did not explain why this was so and it was certainly never clear to me. I sat in the Royal Box and watched Minister after Minister from the new Government presenting medals. None of them had given any encouragement to my endeavours but I explained to those who enquired that this was how British parliamentary democracy works. No one is more dead than an ex-Minister! But the compensations were enormous. Sports people who knew the story and Scottish friends expressed their personal appreciations. That was more than satisfying for me. The great thing was that after the success of the 1966 World Cup Britain had another triumph in Edinburgh in 1970.

The new Minister lost no time in proceeding with changes which Charles Morrison had indicated when he was shadowing me. However, the proposal for a Royal Charter for the Sports Council had certainly never been suggested or considered by civil servants during my time as Minister. The CCPR was told that such a Royal Charter would guarantee for evermore the independence of the Sports Council from the interference of Government or Ministers, providing a similar status to that of the BBC and the Arts Council. It seemed to me that the presence of the Minister in the chair of the Sports Council had proved to be of great value for sport. He was there to be confronted if necessary and to relate sport to government. When new policy initiatives were being proposed for discussion he was able to follow the thinking of the Council and to raise questions if he was unhappy. As I often explained, the so-called advisory nature of the Council was not a handicap in practice, it meant that the 'advice' given to me and my decision to adopt it was a simultaneous process. I had only differed from the Council on two questions throughout my period in office, first on the South African question, when the Council had tried to divorce the sporting merits of the issue from the political considerations but where they also recognised that the Government must have the ultimate responsibility to take the decisions. Secondly, I had disagreed with the rejection of the proposal to accept tobacco sponsorship in order to build a sports injury clinic at Crystal Palace. Dr Roger Bannister had persuaded the Council to oppose the proposition and I accepted that vote although I thought we desperately needed such a clinic whoever sponsored it. Another factor of great importance was that the CCPR owned and administered the national sports centres of Crystal Palace, Lilleshall, Plas-y-Brenin and Cowes as well as conducting many of the coaching sessions held at these centres. Each of these centres had a unique place in British sports provision: they were 'home' for two generations of our national sporting heroes; they were the means by which the governing bodies of sport prepared to take on the world; they were the indispensable resource upon which British sport depended and they were owned and administered by sport, through the CCPR. It was inconceivable to me that the CCPR, as the democratic assembly of sport in this country, entirely voluntary in character, would surrender their position, but they did!

There was no consultation with me by Eldon Griffiths about the Charter proposal. I decided to seek a meeting with Willie Whitelaw, the lord president of the council, since he was the Minister responsible for Royal Charters. I explained to Willie that in my judgment it would be wrong to create a Royal Charter if it was the controversial step I expected it to be, especially if it did not command the support of HM Opposition, and I had to inform him that this was the position. I proposed to consult the CCPR and to advise them to oppose the granting of the Charter. If they did so I would expect the Government not to proceed with the proposal. Willie took all this down, listened extremely courteously, as he always does, and made no comment of any sort himself. My next step was a meeting with Stanley Rous. I explained my views on the developing situation. By this time I had become aware that not only was the Sports Council going to be hallowed by a Royal Charter but that the CCPR was to be required to hand over all the national sports centres, its entire staff and all its assets to a supposedly independent body entirely appointed by a Minister of the Crown. I was incredulous that a voluntary body of sport would even contemplate such a proposition. Rous listened to me and then said, 'Well, if that is how you feel, you must come and meet the executive and let them know your views'.

The meeting duly took place just before Christmas in 1971, at the

CCPR office in Park Crescent. I was kept waiting for quite a while during which Jack Barry, one of their officials, came out to keep me company. The next surprise was to be told by Jack that Stanley Rous, their chairman, was not present to take the meeting. He had deputed the task to his deputy chairman, Arthur Gem, a former inspector of physical education and now an ageing veteran. I addressed the meeting at length, setting out my arguments leading to the conclusion that it would not be in the interests of sport to relinquish its possession of all the national centres, the staff and the resources of the CCPR. I informed them of my meeting with Willie Whitelaw and told them that if they decided that the Government's proposals were not acceptable to them then I would, on their behalf, proceed with my objections to the granting of a Charter, taking my opposition on to the floor of the House if necessary. I did not see how Ministers could advise Her Majesty to grant a Royal Charter in controversial political circumstances. Indeed, I was mindful of the situation when it had been proposed that a Royal Charter should be granted to the Jockey Club. The then lord president, Richard Crossman, had specifically explained to me that this would not be possible if, as the Minister for Sport, I objected to it. I did not do so even though I was uneasy about the undemocratic nature of the appointment of members to that body. There would not have been much support of consequence from within the sport or the industry of racing for such a view. Naturally, I did not spell this out to the CCPR executive, but it was an important part of my thinking. As an old devotee of the voluntary principle for the control of sport and with six years of experience in operating an important partnership between sport and government I could not believe that such traditionalists as I now saw before me would do anything other than heed my warnings. When I finished I sat down, took out and lit my cigar and waited for the questions and observations I had invited. I was in for another shock – not a word was said by any single member, nor by Walter Winterbottom, their secretary, nor by any of the staff. Without inviting any questions or discussion Arthur Gem turned to me and said, 'It was very good of you, Mr Howell, to make this special journey down here on the eve of Christmas. I do hope you have a pleasant journey back home and a happy Christmas with your family'! I was flabbergasted that the CCPR executive did not apparently have a single doubt in their collective mind about the fate that was about to overtake them. Nor did their staff, apparently overwhelmed by the prospect of civil servant status.

I was later told by Charles de Beaumont, the doyen of British fencing, who was present, that he fully shared my fears but that the executive had been instructed by the chair, immediately before I entered the meeting, to listen to me but not to ask any questions or to enter into any discussion. With no support of any kind, and apparently without any questioning from the leaders of British sport, there was no alternative but to allow the Royal Charter to proceed. When I later saw the minutes of this meeting, I found that two members of long standing, both much respected, had expressed themselves in my support. Charles de Beaumont sympathised with my point of view. He felt that 'the executive decision had been taken before sufficient knowledge had been acquired on the structure of the Sports Council'. He feared the possibility of the growth of Government control of sport as had happened in France and West Germany. Mr Ernest Clynes, representing the Amateur Athletics Association, drew attention to the fact that I had asked to meet the officers in July and it was now December. He said that 'many members of the Council felt they had been rushed into a decision to go into liquidation without adequate information'. Kenneth Martin of swimming is also known to have declared great unease at all these developments. After these brief contributions the Council had passed on to next business, believing that the die was cast, that it was too late to think again, and also that the staff approved of this translation to permanent civil service status. That was not entirely true – Emlyn Jones, then director of Crystal Palace, among others had raised substantial doubts.

An interesting consequence of all this was that Miss Phyllis Colson, the real founder and longstanding secretary of the CCPR, added a codicil to her Will, revoking a generous bequest which she had been intending to leave to the CCPR. The first time that some members seemed to realise that they were being rail-roaded by the Government into creating a Sports Council far removed from the voluntary concept was when a new, young, solicitor from the CCPR lawyers, Farrer and Co, Charles Woodhouse, attended his first meeting. He has since shown enormous dedication to the importance of the voluntary principle in sport which right from the start he seemed to understand better than his clients. Woodhouse actually arrived at his first meeting with a draft resolution to put the CCPR into voluntary liquidation. He thought these were his instructions, but he drew the attention of all concerned to two basic facts. The first was that the CCPR was a members' organisation. It could only vote itself out of existence if the members themselves did so. In essence, Walter Winterbottom, the secretary of the CCPR and also the director of the Sports Council, was negotiating with himself! The second fact was that the CCPR was a charity. It was not possible for it to hand over its contents and its assets to a statutory body like the Sports Council. This second opinion caused some consternation to the senior civil servants sent to oversee the deal. Their eyes glazed over when Woodhouse explained to them that they could not take over such a charity, so a new device was thought up: the Sports Council Trust. The nation's sports centres do not to this day belong to the Sports Council, they belong to the Sports Council Trust. That Trust can have as trustees all the members of the Sports Council but it must always have three trustees appointed by the CCPR. When the Minister seeks to reduce the membership and the role of the CCPR within the Sports Council (as Moynihan is doing as I write) he would be well-advised to remember that the CCPR still has substantial rights in respect of all the national centres. Charles Woodhouse was establishing a fundamental point that some Ministers and the Sports Council itself have either never fully understood or preferred to ignore. That is that no Government, nor any statutory body, can override or supplant the essential voluntary nature of British sport.

Twenty years on all my misgivings are being justified. It is not only the Sports Council but also the BBC and the Arts Council which are finding out that the protection of their Royal Charter is meaningless when the appointment of their entire membership, and most of their funding, is entirely at the disposal of the Government of the day and controlled by a Government which is determined to exercise its patronage to achieve its own policy objectives.

PRINCE PHILIP INTERVENES

The merger – as it was constantly called – between the Sports Council and the CCPR took place on 17 April 1972. In the late summer of that year I received a call from Buckingham Palace asking me if I would call upon Prince Philip, the president of the CCPR, to discuss the affairs of the Council and, of course, I was pleased to do so. The meeting took place in late September and it was an extremely agreeable occasion. Prince Philip had obviously followed developments with growing concern. I got the impression that he had not been consulted in any meaningful way, if at all. We both held identical views about the situation and I judged that he had no intention of presiding over a body which had 'merged' itself out of existence. New leadership was needed to take them on. Would I agree to become the CCPR chairman? With the support of such a president behind me I relished the task but I had one caveat to make: I could not accept appointment to such a position, I must be elected by the executive or the members. Prince Philip did not think that would cause a moment's difficulty. 'I will be in the chair', he told me. 'I do not anticipate any difficulty.' What I did not know at that moment was that while I was awaiting my audience, Prince Philip was interviewing Peter Lawson, a young CCPR technical officer who had worked in the Leeds office and who had been appointed secretary of the moribund organisation when Walter Winterbottom left for full-time work with the Sports Council. Lawson had obviously been selected to run the CCPR down as fast as he could. I understand that it had been made clear to him that another job was waiting for him at the Sports Council, something to do with Sport for All. If that was the intention no greater misjudgment could ever have been made in the history of sports politics! At Lawson's meeting with Prince Philip the situation of the chairmanship was raised by the president. Who did Lawson think could take on the job in view of the battles ahead and the fact that Stanley Rous was now too old to continue in these new circumstances? Peter Lawson expressed his view that the job needed political experience, and he thought I was the best person to provide it. 'I agree', said Prince Philip, without disclosing that I was in the next room waiting to be invited. When Lawson got back to his office he was just in time to take a telephone call informing him: 'Howell has agreed to take it on', and asking him to do all that he could to help bring it about.

The Annual General Meeting of the CCPR took place some months later in April 1973. Prince Philip was in the chair. Immediately after the central executive meeting I was unanimously elected the chairman and Mary Glen-Haig the vice-chairman. We set about the creation of a new role for the organisation and within a month we had agreed our new objectives:

1. While wishing at all times to co-operate fully with the Sports Council, the collective voice of sport and recreation must be independent and the CCPR as the National Association of Sport and Physical Recreation should work towards complete independence from the Sports Council.

2. There should be a developing partnership through consultation with the Sports Council, and the CCPR should aim at constructively critical appraisals of the developing policies of the Sports Council.

3. Firm links should be established with regional associations of sport which should be brought under the CCPR umbrella. These regional associations of sport should be represented on the CCPR and have a place on the central executive committee.

4. The CCPR should be able to express a British voice on matters of European and international concern in sport, and should seek contracts with other national counterparts.

Another question to be resolved as a matter of urgency was the status of our secretary. It was not acceptable to me nor to my executive that Peter Lawson should continue on a seconded basis. We decided to advertise and I was relieved that Lawson interviewed well. His abilities were already apparent and so there was no doubt in any of our minds that his position should be confirmed. Having got ourselves a secretary we then turned our attention to the 'Heads of Agreement' which had been signed by the CCPR, the Sports Council and the Sports Council for Wales to become effective on 1 June 1972. We now had to work within it as we developed our new strategy. When it became clear that I had become chairman in order to rescue the CCPR from oblivion the shock to many people was considerable. 'Good God, you are going to re-start the CCPR', said one astonished member of the Sports Council staff. Everything depended upon how Article 6 of the Heads of Agreement was to be interpreted. It still does today. Article 6 reads: 'The Sports Council agrees that (so long as the CCPR is a body representing national organisations of sport and physical recreation as a whole) the Sports Council will make such resources and facilities available to the CCPR without cost to the CCPR as may reasonably be required by the CCPR for the carrying out and implementation of the objects of the CCPR as amended by Special Resolution Number Two which was duly passed at the Extraordinary Meeting of the CCPR on 17 April 1972'.

At the CCPR we spent hours of our time examining that clause and relating it to the four objectives we had already agreed upon. We had no doubt that we could require the Sports Council to finance any activity within the four objectives that we thought to be reasonable and the Sports Council could only refuse to do so if they could demonstrate the unreasonableness of our proposals. We were further encouraged in this view by the knowledge that when the first draft of this agreement was produced by Charles Woodhouse he had included the words 'and so long as the Minister for Sport approves'. Philip Noel-Baker happened to be present at the meeting and upon hearing these words he addressed Charles Woodhouse, 'Young man, if you give a Minister that power he will use it, take it out'.

Regrettably, difficulties soon began to arise over our new relationship with the executive Sports Council and the interpretation which we put upon the Heads of Agreement. The first indication of these came when Roger Bannister, the new chairman of the Sports Council, told me that they had acquired plush new offices in the IBA building at Brompton Road, almost opposite Harrods. We were asked to inspect the building where the Sports Council were offering to provide the CCPR with accommodation and to inspect a floor which might be suitable for our offices. Peter Lawson and I went down to view them. When we were viewing a very nice oak-panelled room which I observed 'would make an excellent committee room and chairman's office', we were told by the officer accompanying us that he was instructed to inform us that this room was not available to us. After I had forcibly expressed myself the room did become available to us. It was a very insignificant incident but it proved to be a straw in the wind.

More important issues soon presented themselves. These concerned the number of staff the CCPR would be allowed to appoint, the fact that the Sports Council believed they should have a greater involvement in the appointment of our secretary, the salaries we decided to pay our staff and, an important matter of policy, our rights to pursue our fourth objective 'to seek contacts with other national counterparts'. This last matter arose because the CCPR central executive wished to establish relationships with kindred bodies around the world – usually known in other countries as Federations of Sport – in order to discuss the vital question of how political control of international sport was being exercised against the interests of the free world. The simple fact was that no organisations existed to match the close working arrangements of the Soviet bloc. As the Commonwealth Games were about to be staged in Christchurch, New Zealand, that was the obvious place to start. Our executive authorised Lawson and myself to make the necessary initial contacts and to arrange for such a meeting. In particular Bill

McEwen, who was then chairman of the Canadian Sports Federation, Graham Brockett, a New Zealand barrister, and Les Martin of Australia expressed enthusiastic support for such a gathering and Brockett undertook to organise the meeting. The Sports Council reacted negatively to all of this. They would not approve the salary we had fixed for our secretary, nor authorise adequate staffing posts and they adamantly declined to pay for Lawson and myself to travel to New Zealand to consult our fellow sports bodies about these matters of serious concern. They were also hostile to the idea that we should bring the regional standing conferences for sport into a formal relationship with our new organisation. At every turn we seemed to be on a collision course. The final point of absurdity came during our move from Park Crescent to Brompton Road when even the portraits of HM The Queen, our patron, and HRH Prince Philip, our president, were removed by Sports Council staff. I described this as 'nationalisation without compensation, something which even the party to which I belong would not attempt in its wildest moments'. The portraits were soon returned. I kept Prince Philip aware of all these developments and he replied, 'Your correspondence should be published in *Punch*'. In a letter to Dr Bannister in August 1973 I set out our views as to how this situation ought to be resolved:

'The General Purposes Committee spent considerable time in determining an appropriate salary scale for the general secretary of the organisation. The committee carefully considered all the salaries being paid in sport, both within Government machinery and within governing bodies in relation to their chief officers. They also considered salaries of comparable posts outside sport such as the Association of River Authorities and other positions in the commercial world.

'As a result of these deliberations, it was unanimously agreed that the only salary scale which would reflect the importance to which we attached the post of general secretary but which would not in any way embarrass the position of director of the Sports Council would be a scale equivalent to that of senior principal officer within the civil service'.

Accordingly, I informed the Sports Council:

'The committee were well aware that for the immediate future the whole burden of this salary would of necessity fall upon the Sports Council, but I should point out that it was the unanimous view of the committee that this salary scale was, in their view, in full accordance with paragraph 6 of the Heads of Agreement between the CCPR and the Sports Council and should be regarded as a reasonable requirement of the CCPR for the carrying out of its new objects.

'As you know, it is our intention to devise an equitable and realistic affiliation fee and to introduce other schemes for producing an income for the CCPR. When this comes into effect, it is our intention to meet you again to discuss and agree upon a system of grant aid, thus relieving you of the full burden of the running costs of the CCPR.

'You will also wish to know that it is the intention of the CCPR additionally to appoint two administrative/executive officers to facilitate the running of the organisation, the first appointment hopefully to take place immediately after the position of general secretary has been filled. We shall of course also require an adequate supporting secretarial staff and we shall be in touch with you again about this aspect of our proposals.

'You will be interested, I am sure, to know that our recent conference of CCPR members fully endorsed my proposal that there was no justification for any duplication at regional level of staff or offices to service the regional standing conferences of sport. We are quite happy for the present arrangements to continue as long as the independence and freedom of expression of view of these associations of sport is fully guaranteed, and I was sure that this was something you would want to preserve.

'We trust that after consideration you will find that these proposals are acceptable and I look forward to a long period of co-operation between our two organisations'.

With no money and no assets Peter Lawson showed commendable enterprise in raising the funds to pay for our visit to New Zealand from the BBC, which wanted to do a television piece about the future of sport and to interview Roger Bannister and myself against the background of a sports festival being held at Lytham St Annes. He negotiated a facilities fee which was sufficient to pay for our travel. The executive decided that sponsorship of the CCPR was the immediate answer to our financial problems and Nigel Hacking of yachting and David Nation of water-skiing did great work in creating our Sponsors of Sport organisation by which companies made a donation of £500 a year to become members. The idea was warmly approved by Prince Philip, who told me he would be delighted to offer a Buckingham Palace reception to the sponsors. The scheme was an immediate success. We were able at last to open a new bank account.

Owing to the political situation brought about by the miners' strike and the possibility of an early General Election Lawson travelled on ahead of me to Christchurch. When it seemed that there would be no election I followed on via Los Angeles, the Pacific, Australia and the North Island of New Zealand, finally arriving in Christchurch totally exhausted. Peter was waiting to greet me with the news that my friend Joe Waldon, the New Zealand Minister for Sport, had arranged excellent seats for us immediately behind the Royal Box. As David Bedford was about to race we should go to the stadium at once, even though I was asleep on my feet. As we sat down, Prince Philip arrived accompanied by Lord Rupert Neville, his secretary, who was also chairman of the British Olympic Association. When Rupert saw us he drew the Prince's attention to our presence saying, 'They're here, they're here'. Prince Philip kindly turned and raised his hat. We were invited to lunch with him next day on the Royal Yacht where we were joined by

Prince Charles, whose ship had just arrived in port. It was a delightfully relaxed occasion and we were able to provide Prince Philip with details of the new international organisation we proposed to create and he indicated his support. The meeting duly took place and the wide basis of representatives from both the old Commonwealth and the new were enthusiastic. Only the Australian delegate wondered whether he had authority to commit his country to the project at this early stage. The International Assembly of National Confederations of Sport was formally established two or three years later at a meeting in Australia under Prince Philip's chairmanship with Wayne Reed, the Australian tennis supremo, as president and Peter Lawson the secretary.

The General Election was called while I was still in New Zealand. I had become very friendly with Norman Kirk, the popular and able New Zealand Prime Minister, who invited me to fly back to Wellington with Joe Waldon in his personal plane. When I arrived home the campaign was underway. The election took place on 28 February 1974 and I resumed my old job as Minister for Sport on 4 March.

We had all been striving hard to find a way to overcome the differences between the Sports Council and the CCPR about the arrangements for financial support. Following discussions between our respective legal advisers, I believed there might now be a basis for settlement without recourse to arbitration and we worked out a way in which we could implement Clause 6 of the Heads of Agreement.

My term of office as chairman had been brief but exhilarating; the new CCPR was firmly established and its future funding agreed on an acceptable basis. My mission was accomplished. The CCPR was beyond the destruction of the Government. I resumed occupation of my Minister's office to the astonishment of some but the delight of others, ready to recreate the partnership between sport and Government which I believed to be our fundamental purpose.

PARLIAMENTARY BUSINESS

The excitement of conducting the 'save the CCPR' campaign had to be arranged around my normal parliamentary duties, which were heavy. The 1970–74 Parliament was full of new legislation, all change everywhere. I had been appointed again to the Opposition front bench to shadow Sport and Environment. One of my jobs was to lead for the Opposition on the Water Resources Bill. This required a great deal of attention. The Bill proposed to give the Minister more direct powers over river authorities and it provided for more public rights to object to the building of reservoirs, especially in national parks and areas of natural beauty. This was a result of the opposition of Lady Sayer, a doughty fighter for the protection of Dartmoor, strongly supported by words from Prince Philip, to an earlier proposal to build a new reservoir on Dartmoor. In my speech of welcome for the Bill I cast a prophetic glance upon a subject that was to have special significance for me: 'It is verging upon the ridiculous that in a country completely surrounded by water, and with an average rainfall of $18\frac{1}{2}$ inches per annum, we should from time to time experience drought, with considerable difficulties in various parts of the country'. The great drought was still five years away! I went on to propose a grid system of water aimed at transferring water from areas of plenty – Scotland and Wales – across and down the country to areas of shortage, the south and east. We still await such a scheme.

A month after that debate sport's ever-faithful MP, Tam Dalyell, managed to initiate a debate on sport and recreation at 7.25 in the morning after an all-night sitting. He started with a rousing denunciation of the English and Scottish Rugby Unions for persisting in excluding players who had taken part in Rugby League football. He suggested that the Rugby Union grants might be withheld. He had a novel illustration to make his point: he had heard about a prisoner committed for murder who was allowed to play Rugby Union in prison, a permission which was withdrawn when he was found to have taken part in Rugby League football. Tam's main concern was to discover what steps the Government proposed to take to implement the Chester Committee Report on football, which I had myself set up. In particular he wanted to implement the proposal that a Football Levy Board be created and he was critical of me for not having brought it about in my time as Minister. A 1 per cent levy on all pools betting had now been proposed to be used for the development of football. The Treasury would have none of it. To them it was the 'hypothecation of taxation' which they said went out with Lloyd George and his road tax. Never more would a tax be levied for a special purpose; all taxes would go into the Exchequer for use as the Chancellor and Parliament saw fit. The fact that George Wigg had got Parliament to agree on such a levy for horse racing was an aberration, not to be repeated. 'One George Wigg is enough', I was told by a Treasury colleague.

In the 1972 session of Parliament I had the good luck to draw another prime position in the ballot for Private Members' Bills. Like my earlier Bill to provide for Leasehold Enfranchisement I decided to opt for a Bill which would raise important questions of policy, rather than a minor Bill which was really only a convenience for a Government department. As I was the national president of my trade union, APEX, I decided upon a Bill that we had long campaigned for to bring about earlier retirement and I introduced my Employment (Holiday Extension and Early Retirement) Bill in February 1972. I had no difficulty this time in arranging for the drafting to be professionally provided by the union. Like my earlier Bill I found that this measure also caught the public imagination. Letters poured in by every post, all of them in favour. There was one of particular note, from a correspondent in the north of Scotland, fully supporting my proposal for earlier retirement as 'our MP ought to have been retired years ago'! The overwhelming number of letters I received were very sad, from widows stating again and again how their husbands had worked all their lives and were looking forward to a few years of happy retirement only to die just before or just after retirement. There was also a strong plea for preparation for retirement. 'He just gets in my way' was a repeated cry from wives with retired husbands in the house. This reinforced my interest in pre-retirement education and counselling; not only in the management of a reduced family income, in tackling the problems of boredom and unfulfilled leisure time, but also in human relationships – how to learn to live with the wife after 40 years of marriage! In discussions with my extremely able union general secretary, fellow Brummie Roy Grantham, we decided not to include in the Bill any specific date for retirement. We wanted the age to come down progressively and thought that the male retirement age of 65 could immediately be reduced by two years as a first step. In his reply the Minister, Paul Dean, told the House that this would cost £250 million a year and would mean an extra 2 pence a week in contributions for a man on £20 per week, and 25 pence for a £42-a-week man, and that the second stage reduction to the age of 60 would cost a further £700 million a year and would have to be financed by a 5 pence and a 60 pence per week contribution increase respectively for the £20 and £40 weekly wage earner. He thought that our scheme not to write in any specific age but to leave the Government to do so from time to time was 'ingenious' but not a responsibility the Government wanted to accept. This was a remarkable abstinence for any Government to display. We also discovered from the Minister's speech that the expectation of life at the point of retirement was 12 years for men of 65 and 19 years for women of 60. He fully accepted that most people wanted to get rid of compulsory retirement. Every speaker in the debate upheld the principle of voluntary retirement and we had some very powerful speakers in support. From our side of the House Bob Edwards (Bilson) and my old friend and trade union colleague, general secretary of the Chemical Workers Union, John Golding (Newcastle-under-Lyme); Reg Prentice (East Ham North) and Edward Lyons (Bradford East). On the Government side they were matched by John Selwyn Gummer (Lewisham West) and Nick Scott (Paddington South), who later became not only a Social Services Minister but a good friend and my regular pair. John Tilney (Liverpool Warentree) also wanted flexible retirement and he strongly took up one of my main themes that the new technological revolution would produce technological unemployment necessitating retraining, earlier retirement and more leisure. On the other hand Robert McCrindle (Billericay) described his own speech as 'reactionary', and Ivor Standbrook (Orpington) described the Bill as 'a typical piece of airy fairy, wishy washy, sentimental socialist nonsense'!

My other proposals were to legislate for a minimum of four weeks' annual holiday which I justified by reference to the fact that civil servants and local government employees already enjoyed such a benefit and that Belgium, France, Italy, Holland and Germany were preparing for it. Bank holidays have a fascination for the British. We have fewer than most other countries where saints' days are the rule. This was raised in the debate, one member even suggesting a 'Saint Denis' Day! I wanted eight days of bank holidays, an increase of two, one of which would be New Year's Day, the other might be May Day, which is usually observed as international labour day. We did indeed achieve both these objectives later, although the New Year's Day holiday had already been anticipated by most people! Michael Foot, when Minister of Labour, added May Day to the list but I was disappointed that it was not on 1 May itself, but the first Monday of the month. This is very sad. May Day is May Day.

In my introduction to the debate I made much of my admiration for the philosophy of William Morris, who believed that there was no virtue in work for its own sake but that it was 'a means by which to enjoy the rich possibilities of life'. William Morris believed that we should have a society of warmth and colour and infinite possibility. Mankind should have the opportunity for work that was 'worthwhile and satisfying', which was important for the human personality, but he never believed that work was an end in itself. The debate was good but few Members followed me in discussing the purpose of life on this planet. When we moved that the vote be taken no one voted against but only 54 Members supported me. We needed 100 to get a vote on the Bill itself. Still, among my supporters that day were Neil Kinnock and Roy Hattersley. Who knows, another day, a new possibility?

As 1973 drew to its close we were well into the miners' strike. Power cuts were operating everywhere and the Government used emergency powers to close down activities which they believed to be non-essential. The floodlighting of football matches was on the list. This caused me to protest that theatres and concert halls had been exempt from the cuts and that this was a discrimination against football. The Minister replied that both theatres and football belonged to the nation but he did not attempt to justify the different treatment proposed for each activity. The discussions Eldon Griffiths held with the football authorities carried over into the New Year and the election was upon us before they came to any decision. When Parliament resumed after the Christmas recess we were immediately into the Safety of Sports Grounds Bill and rumour was rife that Ted Heath was going to the country on the issue of 'who is governing the country, the Government or the miners?'. It was doubted whether the Bill would complete its passage before Parliament was dissolved. I had another reason to be anxious since I was due to be in Christchurch, New Zealand for the Commonwealth Games. The Bill was the result of the report of Lord John Wheatley, a Scottish judge and father-in-law of Tam Dalyell, who had been appointed to enquire into the Glasgow Rangers disaster in which 66 people lost their lives and another 140 people were injured. The tragedy occurred when thousands of spectators, who were leaving

near the end of the match by some steep steps, heard a great shout
indicating a late goal and turned back. They were met by an overwhelming crowd coming the other way, with disastrous result. Most
of the dead were trampled underfoot. It was the worst tragedy suffered
at a British football ground until then. Previously, there had been a
very serious incident in 1946 at a Cup tie at Bolton Wanderers when
33 people died and 500 were injured. In 1985 an even more devastating
tragedy took place when the main stand caught fire at Bradford City,
leaving 56 dead and 200 injured. Since then, the FA Cup semi-final at
Hillsborough in 1989 resulted in 95 deaths and hundreds of injured.
My support for the Bill on behalf of the Opposition contained two
criticisms. The first was that the new measures would be implemented
on a gradual basis starting at First Division grounds – I thought that
lower order grounds, and non-league grounds staging Cup ties, might
well prove to be more vulnerable. The second was financial: no money
would be forthcoming to assist clubs with the expensive work required
and many clubs would be in considerable difficulties. There was, of
course, a determination on all sides to enact the legislation. When Ted
Heath seemed to pull out from the prospect of a General Election I set
off post-haste for Christchurch.

VICTORY 1974

The Christchurch Commonwealth Games were among the happiest I
have attended. They well justified the description of 'the friendly
Games'. Peter Lawson and I were able to hold many useful meetings
with administrators from all over the Commonwealth. We concentrated, as we intended, upon the political unity in sport of the Warsaw
Pact countries and their increasing success in securing the leading
positions throughout international sport. We also found a large measure
of agreement among our Commonwealth friends on the twin dangers
of state scholarships in sport on the one hand and the award of bogus
university sports scholarships on the other. There was general agreement that we had to come together and make common cause to tackle
both these menaces. It was not possible to pursue them further in
Christchurch since the General Election was called as the Games were
nearing their conclusion. Peter Lawson cancelled some lecture engagements he had arranged for me in the US on my way home and we made
emergency arrangements to get back as soon as we could.

It was a great comfort to know that the organisation in Small Heath
was in fine fettle and that I could have every confidence in the team
that were setting up the election machine in my absence. We were
sharing a full-time agent with Yardley constituency, a former Kent
miner, Jim Smy. He had the chairman of one of my wards, Reece
Thrupp, operating under him in Small Heath. It proved to be an
excellent arrangement. The ward agents were also longstanding friends

and supporters I knew I could rely on. George and Marion Smith in Small Heath ward were also chairman and secretary of the constituency party and towers of strength. In Duddeston ward my agent, Jack Crawford, was known to almost every elector. He had a great ability to 'smell out' the election, to predict the effect of issues as they arose, and to get the result right within a very narrow margin. In Newtown ward we had Jimmy Greaves in charge, a quieter but enthusiastic colleague who was ably supported by Les Thomas, one of the few prison officers to be active on behalf of the Party. By 1974 we had a sizeable Asian vote on the register and Urdu language leaflets were essential, as was a distinct organisation to canvass and knock up these voters, many of whom, especially the women, did not speak English. We had some tremendously enthusiastic leadership from among the ethnic community: Mohammed Afzal and Lachman Singh in Newtown; Bashir Khan in Saltley and Mohammed Chishty and Mohd Aslam and others in Small Heath. Another tower of strength was Tony Huq, who became the first black headteacher in Birmingham and is now the Bangladesh ambassador in Paris.

I spent much of the plane journey home writing up my election address and other literature. It was a one-issue election. Edward Heath had made two miscalculations: first, he had dithered about calling the election; second, he had failed to appreciate the fickleness of the electorate. Heath had a clear majority of people who supported his stand on the Government versus the miners union issue, but when they had suffered days and days of power cuts and general inconvenience the mood changed dramatically. A negotiated settlement on the best terms possible became a realistic battle cry.

The election in Small Heath was a hectic affair. The Liberal candidate was a local councillor, Dennis Minnis, who always worked like a Trojan, taking up every case he could lay his hands on. He increased the Liberal share of the vote from 7.7 per cent in 1970 to 22.1 per cent while my own share of the vote improved and my majority jumped from 6,871 to 11,878, which represented 35.2 per cent of the poll. I was well satisfied.

RETURN TO OFFICE

Four days after the General Election, which had been held on the last day of February, I was called to see the Prime Minister. I arrived at Number Ten wondering whether I would be asked to resume my responsibilities for sport or whether some new position was in the offing. I need not have bothered too much about these prospects. As soon as I saw Harold Wilson he made it clear that there was to be only one holder of the post of Minister for Sport. He then astonished me by saying that he thought that the Sports Ministry should be separated from other Government departments. 'I think we would find you a nice residence to take over,' he said, 'somewhere like Belgrave Square where you could have your own staff and offices.' Once more I was faced with a most vital decision with no one to consult. I promptly expressed my doubts. What was to be the level of my chief civil servant? What access would I have to the Cabinet and the Treasury? There seemed to be no satisfactory answers to these questions so I told Harold that I thought it would be a mistake; I would prefer to be attached to a department with a Secretary of State representing me in Cabinet and with a permanent secretary and an establishment carrying clout in Whitehall. He smiled and said that he understood. 'Where would you like to go?' As the Department of the Environment had been created since my previous period in office and since Tony Crosland had been appointed its Secretary of State I had no hesitation in answering that question. We discussed how I would like to operate and the PM agreed with my suggestion that what would make sense would be to bring together all those branches of the Ministry which dealt with what can be described as the 'quality of life', a strategy which I had long advocated. Harold ended the interview by telling me to go off to see Tony and to 'carve yourself an empire'.

I left Downing Street just before seven o'clock and decided I would go straight to my new Ministry. As I had not been to the place since it had opened I hailed a cab and set off, being put down at the wrong tower block in Marsham Street. Ministers were housed in the north tower but I did not know that at the time. I enquired of the porter where I could find the Secretary of State and he told me that Mr Crosland was in his room on the 16th floor but he did not know which room it was. I took the lift and got out to find a long deserted corridor in front of me, not a soul in sight. There was nothing for it but to investigate. I set off down the corridor knocking on doors and opening them. The first three were empty but the fourth revealed Tony Crosland sitting at his desk. To say that he looked surprised would be an understatement. 'Hello Tony, I am your new Minister of State. I have been told by the PM to come and talk to you.' Tony soon recovered his sang-froid and discussed the various possibilities which could go alongside my sports portfolio. As we were discussing these the door burst open and in came the permanent secretary, Sir James Jones. 'I have just heard from Number Ten, Mr Howell is coming here . . .' he began. Stopping dead in his tracks at the sight of me he could only say, 'Good God, he's already here'! Tony had already suggested as one option that I took responsibility for the branches that interested me: Countryside Commission, Nature Conservancy Council, National Parks, Control of Pollution (for which a major Act of Parliament was imminent), and working upon water resources with John Silkin, who was our second Cabinet Minister. I was also asked to oversee the work of the former Ministry of Public Works, which included the Royal parks and the Property Services Agency which I passed on to Ken Marks, MP for Ardwick, when he became Under-Secretary of State.

Sir James could see no snags in this allocation of duties and took me off to see the suite of rooms available for the Minister of State. I chose one there and then and returned to my flat to telephone Brenda with all the news.

At nine the following morning Eric Adams arrived at my flat to announce that he was my ministerial driver. He was a sports enthusiast, a single man available at weekends when I would be very active, and in every way a splendid choice. He was welcomed into my family, which is the only successful way to conduct a private office, and for the next five years we enjoyed a first-class relationship. He knew everything and everybody – the drivers' mafia – and he was a source of much information, usually extremely accurate. I soon found that I had been bequeathed a very fine private office and a very competent sports department. The second permanent secretary was Sir Robert Marshall. The Sports, Countryside and Nature Conservancy branch was headed by Alan Leavett, who was specially dedicated to his area countryside responsibilities. It was soon decided that his deputy, David Sharpe, would be number one at Sport leaving Alan Leavett to take charge of countryside, national parks, nature conservancy and related matters. Tony Fairclough headed the side dealing with pollution control before moving off to represent us at Brussels in our EEC negotiations. My private secretary was Jerry Rendell, a quiet and unassuming person, very pleasant to work with and also very competent. Chris Jones, his number two, was one of the most hard-working private office staff I ever encountered. Brenda Pym maintained high and pleasant standards as my diary secretary. Vic Shroot from the press office was a great find and an outstanding and loyal press officer. I had a little trouble about his appointment. The press office did not like a press officer to be allocated full-time to a specific Minister. They wanted to allocate a member of their staff for each specific issue but I would have none of it. Also, in the case of sport, it was important that he should develop close relationships with sports journalists. They wanted to ring up someone they knew and trusted, not an anonymous individual in the press office. After much argument I got my way. When later on the Government ran into trouble and Ministers were complaining about their press coverage, as they inevitably do in such periods of ill fortune, Tony Crosland asked me to review our press office arrangements and I recommended that the system that suited me so well should be adopted for all other Ministers, and this was agreed.

Finally, I reinherited the old firm of Sir John Lang and Walter Winterbottom as principal adviser and director of the Sports Council respectively. Although they must have been involved in all the plans to change the status of the Sports Council to that of an 'independent' chartered council, of which I strongly disapproved, I did not have any hesitation in welcoming them back. On day one of my new administration I was happy and content with my team. There was much to do, and I was raring to go.

11

Man for all Seasons

NORMAL SERVICE RESUMED

My return to office presented me with a challenge. I was pleased to renew my relationships with John Lang and Walter Winterbottom and I knew they must have been involved in the decision to grant the Sports Council a Royal Charter and, in theory, to take it outside the Government as an independent body. This was a problem for me. The rules of government prevent an incoming Minister from having access to the files and the thinking of the previous administration. My officials had a problem too. They knew that I had strong views as chairman of the CCPR and that I was not going to depart from my stated position on the importance of the voluntary bodies – the governing bodies of sport – now that I was restored as Minister. My main concern was about relationships with Roger Bannister, who had served me loyally and well when I was previously in office and chaired the Sports Council. He had now occupied the chair of the Council for some three to four years and had developed a new style of leadership. He knew that I was not the man for passive leadership. These difficulties had to be resolved, and quickly. A Government such as ours with a tiny majority was bound to be back on the hustings sooner rather than later. I had other wise counsel: Jerry Rendell was a fine private secretary, calm and rational, who knew I could be impatient and headstrong. In contrast he expressed himself very quietly but persuasively. He never let me take decisions without ensuring that the other point of view was considered. Sir Robert 'Bob' Marshall, the second permanent secretary, was something of an extrovert and he did not hesitate to tell me when I was wrong, but he had a great Whitehall knowledge and after a difficult start we became good friends.

A problem arose on day one when I had something of an altercation with the deputy secretary. I received a paper containing advice which I took one look at and rejected. The deputy secretary wanted to discuss the matter with me but I was determined not to be bounced on my first day back in office. He told me that as the senior civil servant he had the right to discuss departmental policy with me. I reminded him that I had been the Minister previously. In civil service terms I had set all the precedents. What the department had done was to change them all while I had been out of office! We were now returning to the principles set down when I was the Minister before. Months later Tony Crosland told me that soon after this incident Bob Marshall had been to see him and told him that he would have to go and ask the Prime Minister to move me as they found me 'impossible'. Tony replied that if there was one Minister in this Government who was not going to be moved by the Prime Minister it was me! They had better establish a better relationship. He was telling me this, he said, because the civil servants had just been back to tell him they had misunderstood how to handle me – 'we are now getting on famously, all is well'. I assured him that I had no complaints at all and we both enjoyed the joke.

As I expected the status of the Sports Council became my first problem. I was firmly advised that now that it had a Royal Charter it would be inappropriate for me to resume the chairmanship; worse still, there would be difficulties about my attending its meetings! If I wanted to get rid of a Royal Charter it would require an Act of Parliament. I asked one question: 'What is the role of a Minister for Sport who has surrendered all his authority to the Sports Council?' That was certainly not to be my style of Ministry. I sought the advice of the Government's business managers and I was left in no doubt that there was not going to be any place in our legislative programme for a Bill to annul the Royal Charter. Other alternatives would have to be considered. Roger Bannister was clearly going to hang on to the new structure of the Sports Council at all costs. He appreciated the relationship – once removed from the Sports Council – that Eldon Griffiths had developed with him. When I asked Roger what he thought my role should be he replied to the effect that my job was to fight the Treasury for as much money as possible and to make this available for the Sports Council to distribute as they determined. I had to tell him that as he knew from previous experience, this was not how I operated.

The matter came to a head in a remarkable way. I had already told my officials that I believed it to be important that we should be seen to achieve something in each term of Government. This Government, with its tiny majority, would not be long-lived. We needed a project that could be quickly achieved. No ideas were forthcoming. I then started to think about grumbles I had heard about from some of our athletes concerning Crystal Palace. It really was not good enough to have a national athletics stadium that was just a one-sided track. The athletes had told me that when the stands were full they left the cheering behind as they approached the back straight and it really was like running 'into Siberia'. The more I thought it over the more I liked the idea of building a new stand at Crystal Palace as the one announcement that I could make in the summer indicating that I was back in business. The Sports Council officers were decidedly less enthusiastic so I consulted Emlyn Jones, an outstanding director of the Crystal Palace national sports centre and a good friend of mine. We discussed the matter during the AAA Championships. Emlyn was in touch with officers of the Greater London Council who had provided the national sports centre and they had to approve any new construction. Emlyn reported that something like a quarter of a million pounds would be required for the first stage of the project.

The next stop was the money. That meant Tom Caulcott, the department's finance officer. As always with Tom, he laughed when I told him to find the money. 'Minister, there is no money', he said. I had already found out from Emlyn and Walter Winterbottom that we could not expect to do more than make a start on the new stand in the financial year. Caulcott told me that if he found enough money to make a start on the design and to purchase materials there could be no guarantee of follow-up money for the construction. My view was that if we made a start this year the following years would take care of themselves; no Government could start such a project and then cut it off. Tom went away and did his sums or his readjustments and soon reported back that he could just about manage £250,000 for the first phase, this year, of the new stand. In a few days' time at the Hilton Hotel I was due to address what was probably the largest gathering of sports administrators ever held in our country with Prince Philip, president of the CCPR, in the chair. The occasion was the Phyllis Colson Memorial lecture. The conference had been planned by Peter Lawson and myself while I was still chairman of the central council. It was the natural place for me to make my announcement. When I told Roger Bannister that I had good news about this additional money and that I would be making my announcement next day he astonished me by saying that he could not accept the money on those terms. It was my job to give him the money and for the Sports Council to decide how it should be spent. I pointed out that these were additional funds. He was really saying that the Minister could not take an initiative. I could understand that he would take issue with any instruction from me to rearrange existing finances, already approved, but this was quite different. Bannister was adamant. So was I. He was to speak after me and if he wished, he could announce that he could not accept the proposal for the new stand after I had made my announcement. In the event he did not do so but the following week he came to see me and expressed his regret that he could not go along with my style of Ministry. He had decided that he ought to give up the chairmanship of the Sports Council. It was an honourable resignation.

My speech was well received. I described it as one of my 'football speeches' – 45 minutes each way with extra time if necessary! Having convened the conference as chairman of the CCPR I spent the first half outlining my struggles in that capacity with the Sports Council, upholding the important principles inherent in maintaining the voluntary nature of the government of British sport, especially in its relationships with HM Government, and then I announced that we had reached half-time. I was now the Minister for Sport announcing my acceptance, as policy, of the proposals urged upon me by the former chairman of the CCPR! It was all good fun, but a declaration which I regarded as of prime importance.

The task of finding a successor to Roger Bannister did not take long. I wanted a chairman with whom I could do business and who understood the position I had taken up. The obvious choice was Sir Robin Brook, already a member of the Council and a long serving and respected treasurer of the CCPR. Robin understood that I would have liked to have resumed the chairmanship of the Sports Council and readily agreed to the compromise suggested by John Lang and Walter Winterbottom that I would attend meetings of the Sports Council whenever I wished or could be represented as the occasion required. It was not a satisfactory formula for me, but it worked reasonably well for the next five years. In spite of this I still think it would have been better if I had chaired the Sports Council myself.

Meanwhile, Bob Marshall had talked with Lang and Winterbottom and came up with an idea that I ought to produce a Government White Paper on Sport and Recreation setting out my policy on a whole range of issues and proposing new initiatives. There had never been a White Paper on sport until now. We were breaking new ground. We spent many hours thinking it through and arguing out ideas, an exhilarating experience. It was published by Command of Her Majesty in August 1975 and remains the only White Paper on the subject of sport ever to be published by the Government. It became the blueprint for my second tenure of office as Minister for Sport, in 1974–79. Preparation for the White Paper was interrupted by the inevitable General Election called in October 1974. My own result was eminently satisfactory: Howell (Labour) 19,703; O'Connor (Conservative) 5,648; Caney (Liberal) 4,260; Majority 14,055. The total vote was 4,000 down – an old register had something to do with it – but my share of the vote was up by 9 per cent, a swing of 5.3 per cent. The Government's position improved in the West Midlands as a whole; we had caught up with the rest of the country's February situation. The final outcome, however, showed only slight improvement for the Government – we had a majority of three. There was nothing for it but to soldier on as a slimline Government, but we were all determined to make it work.

THE BOMBS

The new Parliament was elected in October. In accordance with his normal practice the Prime Minister gave a party for all his Ministers at six pm the night before the State opening. Harold Wilson read out to us the speech Her Majesty was to deliver from the throne the following day; he accompanied his speech with some light-hearted comments as specific items from the speech were read out. It was an extremely pleasant occasion. We had every reason for good cheer apart from the mining crisis and other pressing political and economic matters, with which we clearly believed it was well within our competence to deal. We broke up just before nine and Eric Adams was waiting to drive me to my flat a couple of miles away.

As I entered the flat I turned on the television for the nine o'clock news. Before the picture even came on I heard the news-reader say: 'We can now confirm that the bomb which has gone off in Birmingham tonight was at the home of the Minister for Sport, Mr Denis Howell'. It is impossible to describe my feelings. I was struck dumb, rooted to the spot. My first thoughts were for my family and how I could get to Birmingham at this hour of night. My confusion was brought to an abrupt end by the ringing of the telephone and, almost simultaneously, of the doorbell. The telephone call was from my sister-in-law and secretary, Jackie Howell. She had heard an earlier announcement on the news saying that a bomb had gone off in Moseley, Birmingham, where we lived. There had been two or three bombs planted under cars of prominent Birmingham citizens in the days immediately beforehand. An IRA campaign was clearly underway. Jackie realised the significance of the announcement. She immediately rang our home, confirming her worst fears. The policeman who took her call asked her to please find me, wherever I was, and to let me know that Brenda and David, our youngest son, who were in the car when the bomb went off, were alive, though badly shaken, and bearing up well. She was lucky to get me with her very first call. At the door was Eric Adams, who had heard the news on his car radio as he left me. Without hesitation he had turned round and come to fetch me. 'You will want to go to Birmingham, sir,' he said. 'The bastards. I will get you there well before midnight.' I told Jackie we were on our way. It was a nightmare journey.

No Government car has ever been driven up the M1 at such speed. Eric was a wonderful man to have with me at such a time. We listened to every news bulletin. There was no news about Brenda or David. I wondered how they would be and said a silent prayer. Eric's language cannot be recorded here. In under two hours we had reached Moor Green Lane which was sealed off, full of arc lights, police cars and fire engines. My mangled car was still on the driveway, debris everywhere, windows blown out, not only at our home but those of our neighbours. Policemen were searching through it all, looking for any minute piece of evidence. In charge was an old friend and former football referee Harry Robinson. He was the chief superintendent in charge of the CID and later on he was appointed assistant chief constable. He was reassuring. 'Don't worry, she is all right, we have got her away with Ken Purnell. The doctor has seen Brenda and David and Ken is waiting for you at his home.' The house was full of good people all anxious to help. They made us a cup of tea and a sandwich and I was pleased to notice that my whisky was serving its proper purpose. Manning the telephone was the Rev Rex Crawford, minister of the local Presbyterian church where all our children attended Sunday School. He had come straight round upon hearing the news and the telephone was his special duty. The first call he took was from the Prime Minister! Before I left to go to the Purnell home Harry Robinson told me that Brenda would never know how lucky she was to be alive. 'But you must not tell her, just try to settle her down.' One of our family doctors, Michael Massey, had turned out and examined them both, prescribed some medicine and agreed that they should both leave with Ken. Ken is not a man to be stopped from reaching his destination by any sealed off road and he soon had Brenda and David safely in his own house. Our daughter Kate had been with friends in the next road. Brenda and David were going to collect her from there when the bomb went off. Our other two boys, Andrew and Michael, who were inside the house, behaved exactly as boys might be expected to behave. When they heard the explosion they raced outside to meet their mother shouting, 'The windows have gone!'. They then stayed outside the house observing all the excitement and were not allowed back by the police, so they took themselves off to join Kate. Ken Purnell was able to put me up for the night and we sent Eric Adams off to find a hotel that would take him without luggage or spare clothing.

The next morning brought a new insight into the industry which exists to service such emergencies, from the man who came round offering to board up windows to reporters, broadcasters and a host of others. Television soon discovered our whereabouts and from the bedroom window we could see the media gathering. I talked it over with Brenda, suggesting that if she felt up to it it would be better for us to give the interviews in Ken's garden and get them over and done with. It was a wise decision. I discovered that the previous night the local radio had arrived at our home before the police or the fire brigade. We have never found out how they knew so soon where to come, even allowing for the situation in Birmingham, whereby a bomb a night went off at that time. The local police station at King's Heath heard the bomb go off and got their police patrol cars on the move, waiting for the call which would tell them where to go. When Harry Robinson explained to me what had happened I could only endorse his judgment that someone 'up there' was looking kindly upon Brenda.

During the late afternoon Brenda had fetched David and Kate from school and dropped off Kate at her friends'. We have a small semi-circular drive with two entrances, and as my secretary had her car parked in the middle of it Brenda parked just inside the drive. It was about 8.45 when she got into the car with David to fetch Kate. Of course, my secretary had long since driven home in her own car, leaving the drive free. But instead of going forwards, although it was now dark, Brenda decided to back out and over the bomb that was planted underneath the car, attached to it by a piece of fishing line. When the fishing line broke it released the detonator, and as the bomb was now at the front of the car this part took the full force of the explosion. Had she driven forward and out of the drive, which most of us would have done, the bomb would have exploded under the petrol tank. I always say that her life was saved because she is a woman driver. She told me that she was momentarily stunned and the car was engulfed with smoke and dust, but she was brought back to reality by the voice of young David: 'Come on, Mom, let's get the hell out of here!'.

We received masses of letters and messages and were touched by them all, especially those from Prince Philip and Ted Heath, the outgoing Prime Minister, as well as from Harold Wilson and many other colleagues. The police offered us special protection but after talking it over we asked them to keep a close watch on our road but not to provide any personal guard for us or the children. We were anxious for life to return to normal as soon as possible. Our troubles were soon to be put into perspective. The following week saw the two Birmingham pub bombings which left 19 dead and 200 injured. I travelled up to Birmingham with Roy Jenkins, the Home Secretary, who was also a Birmingham Member. The devastation and the deaths were heart-breaking. The anger of the people could be felt, indeed it was expressed, as we walked between the ruins and talked to the heroic policemen, firemen and others who had carried out their duties of rescue and recovery with the utmost devotion. Roy and I parted for separate visits to the two hospitals which had taken in the injured. It was a gruesome task but wonderfully relieved by the cheerfulness of the survivors and the dedication of surgeons, doctors and nurses, and all the other staff upon whom a hospital depends.

Roy Jenkins went off to visit the Roman Catholic Archbishop of Birmingham, George Patrick Dwyer, a very fine man, and other church leaders. If ever there was a time when the peace of God had to express a common purpose this was it, denominations seemed irrelevant. One or two lunatics started to throw home-made bombs into Irish clubs. Since I have three such clubs in my constituency I visited them as soon as I could. There was no doubt that the Catholic population was fearful. At both the Emerald Club and the Rosary Club I was applauded just for walking in, and again after my few words of reassurance and support. They knew that my own family experience was being shared with them. It was very moving. Eight of the dead from the pub bombings turned out to be constituents. I visited all their homes and many of the injured. Two of those killed were brothers who had met for an evening out. Their funeral service was conducted by Archbishop Dwyer, hundreds of people attending the church. Their deaths united us all: perhaps that is the only service violence offers but it is a terrible price to pay.

WHITE PAPER 'SPORT AND RECREATION'

My White Paper, Sport and Recreation, was published in August 1975. I was extremely pleased with its proposals, many of which still serve sport well, and I remain grateful to the excellent team of officials who helped put it together, led by Sir Robert Marshall, Sir John Lang, Walter Winterbottom and David Sharpe, who now headed the sports branch of the Ministry. The White Paper proposed many innovations, and it remains an achievement which still provides great satisfaction. The White Paper was the logical consequence of the announcement made in the House by the Prime Minister on 16 July 1974. Harold Wilson gave the Government's response to the House of Lords Select Committee report on Sports and Recreation. 'The time has come ... to place a leading responsibility for the co-ordination of policies and the promotion of research in the field of active recreation.' He went on to announce my new designation as Minister of State for Sport and Recreation but he was careful to stress that cultural recreation – the arts, libraries, museums and galleries, and adult and further education, remained with the Minister for the Arts. The announcement took us a long way towards the creation of a leisure service which remains a desperate need in our society, but yet again it failed to merge sport and the arts in one department of State. The arts establishment have always succeeded in their rearguard actions. In essence, sport is a cultural pursuit. It provides the same sense of exhilaration for me when performed at its highest level as does great music, dance, drama and the visual arts, and the same sense of satisfaction in participation. One day the nation will provide for the cultural needs of all its people without discrimination or division. This was not yet to be. A disappointment, but one I had to live with. The challenge for me was to take us as far as I could along that road with the authority of my new designation.

The White Paper took exactly a year to produce and it first set out the principles of policy that Government would follow. These recognised the growing importance of leisure provision and activity and its relationship to the health of the nation. A United Kingdom affairs committee was to be set up from the four Sports Councils, a long overdue step needed to combat the inherent nationalistic approach which is still rife. As I write I cannot say that we are any nearer that goal; for example, we still do not compete in the Olympic Games in football with a Great Britain team. However, Ted Croker, the retiring secretary of the Football Association, is beginning a new initiative in that direction. Thank goodness that many sports do appreciate the importance of creating a British framework, which is essential for world and Olympic competitions. The gold medal won by the Great Britain hockey team in Seoul in 1988 with a most praiseworthy performance is a striking example of such a success.

The announcement was made that the Royal Charter would remain but that I would be attending meetings of the Sports Council whenever I wished and that Sir Robin Brook's appointment was confirmed. He had in fact been the acting chairman since the resignation of Sir Roger Bannister, who had been very properly and worthily recognised in the Queen's honours list. I was pleased that our differences of opinion did not in any way cloud a proper recognition of his great services to British sport. But I was also able to announce that seven places on the Sports Council would be reserved for representatives of the CCPR – one quarter of the membership – and I made it quite clear outside the White Paper that I would accept their nominations for these positions. The civil servants wanted me to retain the right to pick and choose from a list supplied by the CCPR, but I was having none of that. Turning to the structure of government and the co-ordination of all the agencies – Countryside Commission, tourist boards, water authorities, British Waterways Board, Forestry Commission, Nature Conservancy Council, Ancient Monuments and Historic Buildings and the local authorities – I announced three important developments. First, I was to chair regular meetings of my ministerial colleagues responsible for all these various services in England, Scotland, Wales and Northern Ireland. This proved to be a most successful and harmonious committee. Secondly, I would also chair a matching committee of the chairmen and directors of all the agencies represented at the Ministers' committee. Thirdly, the regional councils would, like me, have the designation 'Sport and Recreation' in their title, and they would take as their first priority the creation of regional planning, which involved much wider co-ordination with the local authorities and the voluntary bodies. As so often is the case Wales, having one Secretary of State responsible for all services, was already way ahead of us.

We were able to report some good progress on a number of fronts. Following the provisions in the Local Government Act of 1974 which gave powers to pay grants to local authorities, more and more recreational provision was coming into service. Capital expenditure had already doubled from £23 million in 1968–69 to £56 million in 1972–73. Good progress had also been made since 1968 with the creation of 97 country parks and 136 picnic sites. Voluntary clubs, on which all our sport and recreation so heavily depend, needed encouragement. We strongly recommended that local authorities should give them 50 per cent rate relief. I would have liked to have made this a compulsory relief but I could not carry my colleagues that far and, with a legislative programme and a very tight parliamentary situation, it was not on.

The White Paper made firm proposals for the creation and management of recreation in the urban areas. Joint use and joint provision by the local authorities, the educational authorities and the voluntary bodies was to be the basis of the new policy initiatives and top priority was to be given to areas of environmental and recreational deprivation.

I was determined to recognise the value of happy, informal sport for our young people and this led me to demand the provision of adequate 'kick-about areas' for our youngsters. Thus my own childhood experiences found their way into Government pronouncements, a special source of pleasure! I went on to make a speech reminding local authorities of the importance of walls. I complained that we were knocking down all the walls and called for them to be rebuilt, reflecting the hours of fun and of developing skills I had enjoyed by kicking balls or hitting them with bats and rackets against walls. I am sorry to say that we have not made much progress. One wall, built outside the home of one of my greatest friends and best ward agents, Jack Crawford, had a short life – it became the recipient of all the graffiti in the neighbourhood. Jack led the campaign to get it demolished. It was a sad blow. And the basic skills of British sport still decline! Other services were also commended and encouraged. I insisted upon recognising the importance of allotments, now called leisure gardens. Most important was the work of the Countryside Commission and the local authorities in co-operation with the country landowners in protecting the urban fringe and providing access to countryside and the undeveloped coastline. The long-distance footpaths of our national parks and coasts were commended for special support. Later on, in May 1978, it gave me special pleasure to open the Somerset and North Devon coast path, which completed the South-west Peninsula coast path, a total length of 830 kilometres, more than twice that of the first long-distance walk established as the Pennine Way in 1965.

At the suggestion of Sir John Cripps, chairman, and Reg Hookway, the director, I visited a number of national parks to look at the work of the warden service and I hope I was able to give them every encouragement. In all this work the need for improved management services and a proper career structure for the leisure service was obvious and we recommended accordingly. Local authorities took up these proposals with enthusiasm. A youth sports programme would be launched involving joint use and joint provision in the schools. PE teachers would have a special role linking their work in the schools with the needs of the community. The gap between so much physical activity in the schools and the lack of it which follows for many youngsters when they leave is a special cause of concern. The White Paper made the point with commendable clarity: 'Schools and the community must not be set apart from one another'. Our survey also took in the needs for appropriate sport and recreational provision for the retired and disabled which should provide 'social confidence and a sense of fulfillment', and this was illustrated by reference to the outstanding success of the World Paraplegic Games at Stoke Mandeville in 1974.

Finally, we turned our attention to the needs of the gifted sports people, the development of excellence. Universities and colleges should give these matters special attention. Bursaries should be provided for the gifted encouraged by business and commerce. This recommendation led to the creation of the Sports Aid Foundation. All in all, my White Paper was a satisfying document, certainly a landmark in the development of Government philosophy for sport and recreation – a leisure service. Most of the White Paper was written by my team of officials but I wrote the conclusions myself. For good or ill they state a philosophy in the field of sport and leisure which represents my long-held views. It was good to get them endorsed by colleagues and published as a proper aim of Government:

'The Government believes that sport and recreation provide enormous benefits for the individual in society, and recognises the part that they can play in the enhancement of personality. The social stresses on many young people today are enormous, especially in the big cities. If we delay too long in tackling the causes of these stresses constructively, the problems that arise from them will be magnified, and the cost of dealing with their results greatly increased. The need to provide for people to make the best of their leisure must be seen in this context.

'Where the community neglects its responsibilities for providing the individual with opportunities and choice in the provision of sports and recreational facilities, it will rarely escape the long-term consequences of this neglect. Where life becomes meaningful for the individual then the whole community is enriched'.

SPORTS AID FOUNDATION

There was no doubt in my mind that Britain was taking on the world in sport while shackled with self-imposed handicaps. I had seen for myself the concentration of resources in eastern Europe which enabled men and women of great sporting potential to be provided with all the resources of the State and maintained as State employees so that they could compete as amateurs. Technically that description could not be challenged – they received no payment for their sporting pursuits yet we all knew that they were full-time sports people. On one occasion in Moscow, Walter Winterbottom and I asked a very good international player, now getting on a bit, how long he expected to be studying at the Lenin University. Even we were surprised by his frankness: 'As long as I continue to represent my country at sport'. On the other hand we had also seen first-hand evidence of bogus university scholarships provided by some American universities in order to get promising talent on to their campus and into their sports teams. Talent scouts were attracting many more developing internationals to the sunshine of the States where universities could provide wonderful facilities, first-class coaching and attractive scholarships. We had to make a response and it had to represent traditional British values. After months of discussion with the Sports Council members and officers, the Sports Aid Foundation was born. This was to look at the needs of individuals put up to us by the governing bodies, upon the recommendation of the national coaches as men and women of outstanding potential, and to assess what financial help they required for study, subsistence, travel, equipment and so on.

The co-operation of the governing bodies was essential. When they understood that the scheme was to embrace their authority and that any names to be submitted would need to be endorsed by them and their national coaches their initial hesitations were overcome. I proceeded to assemble the names of the first Foundation governors and thought they would carry confidence with sport as well as with the public and the business community to whom they would have to appeal for funds. The names of the SAF governors were announced on 2 March 1976. They were Peter Cadbury, chairman, Lord Rupert Neville of the British Olympic Association, Mrs Mary Glen-Haig of the CCPR, Sir Robin Brook from the Sports Council, David Nation, Paul Zetter, Harry Cressman of the American Chamber of Commerce and Tony Stratton-Smith, a former sports journalist and extremely successful musical entrepreneur. Mr Cadbury's name came from the officials. They had consulted the list of the 'great and the good' kept by Cabinet Office for just such a purpose. He was a rather dynamic businessman, chairman of Western Television and the ticket agency Keith Prowse. When I met him I had no doubt that he would be a go-getter who could raise funds and get the show on the road. When I introduced him to his fellow members all went well. The media launch was successful. To my astonishment, then, within a day or so he was telling me that he could not work with his fellow governors. I would have to get rid of them. This message arrived in time for the first meeting of the governors, which I was planning to attend as a result of an earlier message from Cadbury requesting that I do so. He arrived late because of some difficulty with his private plane and I took the opportunity to tell his fellow governors of the demand which I had received. The governors were dumbstruck and sat in embarrassed silence as we waited for the great man to come. When he did so he got to the point with commendable speed. He wanted to be a one-man organisation and obviously he was not impressed by his fellow governors, they would have to go. This was an astonishing request in view of their eminence and expertise. I pointed out to him that I could hardly sack people whose appointment I had only just announced and who had not yet met. Apart from that consideration the governors appointed to represent sport had been nominated by sport at my invitation. I did not have the authority to remove them and it was essential that sport had confidence in the Foundation. Cadbury seemed to be adamant so I had to tell him that there was no way that I was going to accede to his request and I suggested that he had better go away and 'consider his position'. He did so and in record time he tendered his resignation. It was an extraordinary episode. I consulted the governors and they were unanimous that Paul Zetter should be persuaded to take up the post. Paul was chairman of Zetters Pools and he was now willing to take on voluntary work for sport which I encouraged. He was a little reluctant to take the chair but he recognised the potential crisis facing us and agreed to serve. It was an inspired choice and he provided enthusiastic leadership for many years, establishing the Sports Aid Foundation as an essential part of our sports provision.

All the governors made very valuable contributions but on the money-raising side David Nation proved to be a genius. I have only ever met one other man like him at the fund-raising business, my friend Ken Purnell in Birmingham. They were two of a kind – persuasive, persistent, encouraging, totally dedicated to the cause at hand and irrepressible. David raised more money for sport than any other man I have ever met. He would ring me up in the middle of the night with his latest brainwave. He persuaded Leslie Porter of Tesco to allow collections to be made at the check-out points of their stores in parts of the south-east. His greatest coup was to propose to the Sports Council, of which he was also a member, that when they found themselves in danger of being underspent in one financial year they should make a grant of that sum to the Sports Aid Foundation for international preparation. He was advised that this could not be done, so he left the meeting and telephoned me at the Ministry. 'Will you disapprove if we do this?' 'No', I said, having always thought that the greatest of all sins for a Minister is to underspend his budget and return it to the Treasury. David returned to inform the astonished Sports Council that 'the Minister agrees'. It was a decision of mine which I had to defend vigorously to the Treasury, but they could not deny that international preparation was one of the approved objectives of the Sports Council and they had the right to take the decision if they thought it appropriate. The Treasury soon tightened up that regulation but the grant of £425,000 really did establish the SAF as a going concern. David had a number of heart attacks, all generated by his non-stop devotion to the cause of sport. When he died prematurely a few years later, and I was privileged to give an address at his memorial service, I began, 'David Nation was an impossible man, that is why he achieved so much'. I have never spoken words of greater truth.

Alan Weeks was appointed the first director and was succeeded by Brigadier Noel Nagel. Paul Zetter, together with David Nation, David Coleman and Tony Stratton-Smith, formed the nucleus of the early fund-raising machine. Later on Eddie Kulu Kuadis followed Paul Zetter as chairman and among those who gave their time as governors were such people as Sir Leslie Porter, Robin Butlin, Anita Lonsbrough, Adrian Metcalfe, Raymond Miquel, Bill Slater, John Smith, Tony Gubba and Denis Thatcher. There were still problems. I went to an important rowing event at the Holme Pierrepont national water centre a year after the Foundation was underway and was confronted by Chris Baillieu, the successful Olympic oarsman, who told me how his team-mates had had to finance themselves in their international preparation. He was astonished when I explained the purpose of the SAF and how it operated. It seemed that no one in their sport had consulted the internationals nor sought to put forward any names for consideration. Gradually, however, all this passive resistance was overcome and the governors were able to report solid progress, going on to create regional organisations about which I had some doubts. In the event some regions succeeded admirably, although others were always struggling even though they could support their cause with some attractive names. Few national and international companies seem to leave their regional management with sufficient resources and independence to make effective contributions.

However, the Sports Aid Foundation can truly claim credit for an impressive performance over its 12 years of existence. More than 5,000 international athletes of great potential in more than 50 different sports have been assisted, a remarkable record involving some £567 million, a considerable feat of fund-raising justifying all my hopes. Among the success stories are personalities who have thrilled the nation: swimmers David Wilkie and Duncan Goodhew, Malcolm Cooper (shooting), Richard Fox (pentathlon), Mike Hazelwood (water-skiing), Robin Cousins, Jane Torvill and Christopher Dean (ice-skating), and from athletics, Alan Wells, Fatima Whitbread, Tessa Sanderson, Seb Coe and Daley Thompson. In all, 48 Britons assisted by the SAF returned from the 1988 Seoul Olympics with medals. This number includes all our gold medallists. It was a great success story born out of controversy, as so often happens in our country, but the SAF is now accepted as an indispensable feature of our sports provision.

MINISTER FOR DROUGHT

On the morning of 16 March 1976 Vic Shroot, my press officer, informed me that the Prime Minister had announced his retirement. It was a bolt from the blue. We were all dumbfounded. My close friend Bernard Donoghue, the head of the Number Ten 'think tank' told me later that he knew that immediately after the October 1974 election Harold had promised his wife Mary he would retire at this time. I have no doubt that losing in 1970 was a bitter blow to Harold. He wanted to retire as the undefeated champion and regaining the title had served his purpose. When I had got my breath back I picked up the telephone and rang Ron Pollard, the genius of Ladbroke's, who had a great fascination with politics and was responsible for their political bookmaking. He was equally astonished as he had not heard the news and could not quote me any odds on a successor. Who did I want to back? '£20 on Jim Callaghan' was my reply. 'Done,' he said, 'I will give you the best odds offered today.' When I went into the division lobby that night Jim was the first person I bumped into and I told him that I had put my money on him to win. Ever the realist, and no doubt realising that both Roy Jenkins and Tony Crosland might well be standing, Jim responded in characteristic style. 'I'd sooner have your vote', he told me. I assured him that whatever I did with my first vote he would certainly get my second, which was the one that would matter. In the event, after terrible heart-searching, I voted for Roy Jenkins because he was my neighbour and colleague in Birmingham. It was a loyalty vote. When Roy left the Party it caused me great distress, especially since I have no doubt that Tony Crosland would have stayed and fought for the sensible moderate and democratic socialist values so desperately needed in the Party and the unions and which I believe to be in the interests of the country. Never, for one moment, did I contemplate deserting the Party.

When Jim Callaghan asked me to assume responsibility for the serious water shortage affecting the country in 1976 it was not as surprising an appointment as most people thought. I was the Minister responsible for the water industry as well as for sport, countryside and recreation. When my family arrived in the West Country for our traditional August holiday we found notices everywhere warning of the serious drought and urging everyone not to use water unless it was essential. Baths in the small family hotel where we stayed were already banned. I was well aware of the situation because John Silkin, my immediate superior Minister, and I had spent time drafting emergency legislation which John had steered through Parliament. Among other things this reduced the planning procedures necessary to obtain access to land for the purpose of laying water pipes from a period of many months down to five days. My family always stayed at this same hotel in the middle two weeks of August because so many of our holiday friends did the same. The children were tremendous friends with all the other children. From the moment we drew up in our car friendships were renewed and each day we would meet over breakfast and decide whether to go on a picnic to Dartmoor or to organise a dads versus lads cricket or football match on the beach. It was great fun. On the Saturday morning we were about to set off when the proprietor ran after me. 'There is a telephone call', he said. 'Someone says that Number Ten wants to speak to you but I think it is one of those silly so-and-sos having you on.' I went inside to take the call followed by half the hotel. When my friends heard my side of the conversation they were convinced it was a great hoax. The PM wanted to know where I was and after telling him that I was at Goodington Sands, which I doubted whether he would ever have heard of, he assured me he knew it well. 'Halfway between Torquay and Brixham', he said. 'Have you been on a pilgrimage to number eight Coastguard Cottages, Berry Head Road, Brixham? That is where we lived when my father was a coastguard.' I repeated the address out loud and said I would make a pilgrimage, by which time the listening audience were convinced it was all a leg-pull. However, it was indeed a serious matter, and after I had been granted a little privacy Jim told me that the water situation was getting very bad – in some parts of the country we were down to 35 days' supply – and he wanted me to take charge of the situation, to get the public to save water and to get emergency supplies organised where necessary. He had called a special meeting of colleagues at Number Ten for the following Tuesday morning when he would announce my appointment and he would send the necessary papers to Birmingham the following day so that I could study them in advance of the meeting. My holiday ended, I returned home to receive the detailed situation papers.

Having read them I contacted Bob Marshall, the second permanent secretary, to tell him the news. He was astonished and immediately asked if John Silkin knew about the pending appointment. I had to confess that I did not know and left him to find out. Bob immediately advised that if I wanted to make the maximum public impact I should establish an emergency headquarters in the department and he assured me that the necessary telephones, equipment and staff could be in place by midday on Tuesday. It was a tremendous feat of organisation. John Silkin was indeed concerned about his position but when he raised it with Jim he was comforted with the news that he would soon be in the Cabinet as Minister for Agriculture. When I arrived at Number Ten on the Tuesday morning it was obvious that the press had been told that action was to be taken to deal with the serious drought situation and that a Minister was to be appointed to take charge. I have never seen so many photographers assembled at one time. They took photographs of almost all the Ministers arriving but very few of me. When we came out it was a different story! Inside the Cabinet room we discussed all the reports from water authorities and local authorities and agreed that the country was now facing a critical situation. The Prime Minister then announced that he thought the time had come when it was necessary to appoint a lead Minister to co-ordinate all necessary action and that I was 'a natural person' for this task. My colleagues agreed to provide the maximum co-operation and I left to generate the maximum publicity.

In the preceding 24 hours my officials had provided me with excellent advice. I had already decided upon priorities: people first, especially babies who would need supplies of pure water, followed by livestock, then market gardeners and other agricultural users. We considered an action plan to be brought into effect immediately my appointment had been confirmed. This plan would be the creation of regional emergency centres manned continuously in all regions. We decided to go immediately to the regions at the greatest risk to urge the public not to use water unless it was essential, to plan emergency procedures for the transportation of water and, if necessary, to use the new emergency planning procedures provided by Parliament. It did not take two minutes' consideration to decide that the first region to be visited must be the West Country. Their main centres of population – Plymouth and Exeter – were down to 35 days' supply which would be reduced by five days if the new planning procedures had to be invoked before emergency water pipes could be laid upon the land of objecting owners. My office was also reorganised in the course of a single afternoon. Jerry Rendell, my private secretary, was touring the highlands of Scotland and was incommunicado. Bob Marshall advised me to make a new appointment immediately and told me that he had three possible candidates in mind. One of these was John Noulton, who had come into the service a little late and thought he had missed his chance of serving in a Minister's private office. He was also interested in sport so I arranged to have him up for a drink later on. I told him that I was sure he would not have been recommended to me unless he was very suitable. We had no time for niceties. I only had two questions. Sport and the job we were about to do both required a lot of time away from home, was that OK with his wife? And would he get upset if I swore from time to time? He said 'yes' to the first, 'no' to the second so we had a drink, toasted our future relationship and got started on the tasks ahead. It was an excellent appointment. Vic Shroot was another invaluable companion as well as first-class press officer, while Chris Jones, my office number two, and Brenda Pym and Mike Rowlands, my diary secretaries, completed the team in my private office. Head of the water department was Andrew Semple, who commanded a team of excellent technical ability including Dennis Musgrove, our chief water engineer.

All told, about eight or nine of us travelled down to Devon. Accommodation would be impossible, I was told, but I did not think so. John Perry, a very old friend of mine and a director of Torquay United, owned the two Livermead hotels, and John Noulton was soon able to tell me that John had responded by making sufficient bedrooms available, even in the middle of a scorching midsummer month. Some of the team actually slept in his own bungalow. I met the water surveyors and engineers for the first time at Paddington in the dining-car we had taken over both for eating and also as a travelling conference centre. Maps were provided and the serious situation confirmed. The obvious question was where was the nearest supply of available water and how could we get it to Exeter and Plymouth? The answer was Bristol, some 90 miles away, but how could we transport it? No one present knew the answer to my question about how many miles of pipes had been stored away for civil defence purposes and how many pumps. Chris Jones was detailed to leave the train at Reading to find out and to let us have the answer at Bristol where the information – enough pipes and pumps to lay two six-inch pipelines between Bristol and Exeter – was delivered by a stationmaster in full uniform, accompanied by the regional directors of environment and agriculture who both joined us on the train. That raised the next question. How could we get it all in place and activate the new planning procedures? While we were discussing this the train passed over the M5 motorway, and I realised immediately that since the Government owned the motorway we could lay the pipeline down the fast lane and so save the five planning days, as well as providing a much more satisfactory solution to our problem from the engineering point of view.

The Livermead House hotel was equal to all our demands and next morning we were in conference with the National Farmers' Union, the agricultural workers, the local authorities, police and other emergency services. They were all totally co-operative. Preliminary work on the pipeline was authorised and we then turned our attention to Plymouth and north Devon. The regional agricultural officer had an excellent idea for getting water to Plymouth, albeit in the very limited quantities needed in extreme emergency. Milk trains transported the Milk Marketing Board's supplies to London and trains then returned empty to Devon and Cornwall. They could return with supplies of water. Barnstaple and north Devon proved more difficult because of the terrain but some tankers were available. Another idea was put forward: a small entrepreneur had developed floating tanks which could be towed across the Bristol Channel. Monmouthshire was also suffering from severe drought but Pembrokeshire had good supplies. We could transport water if we had to in this way, enough to meet the absolute minimum needs of the health service and the children. I authorised contingency planning on all these matters. The next day was devoted entirely to public presentation of the emergency – I travelled around Devon and Cornwall by helicopter, viewing empty reservoirs from the air. We put down to talk to local authorities and MPs, including Jeremy Thorpe, as we had to demand the absolute maximum saving of water by the resident population and the tens of thousands of holidaymakers. The reservoirs were virtually empty, and buildings that had been submerged for years were clearly visible. At the most there was only a few days' water remaining. I was left in no doubt about the crisis facing us. The reservoirs were very small. I was told that they filled quickly. I could only silently contemplate the desperately needed additional capacity which had been opposed and delayed by various groups exercising their undoubted right to do so while carrying no responsibility to provide adequate water supplies. The publicity was enormous but the real value of this exercise was to establish a workable plan of action which could be transmitted to the other badly-affected regions. As I travelled the country, I found that much time had been saved. All the necessary factual information was awaiting my arrival, together with proposals based on the work we had done in Devon and Cornwall.

We moved on to South Wales, to Monmouthshire, the old name which I much prefer. After Devon and Cornwall this was the country's area of greatest shortage. Michael Foot urged me to visit the steelworks at Ebbw Vale which used great quantities of water, and where there seemed to be some fear that my declared priorities of human and animal life might jeopardise industrial production. I was anxious to make such a visit to assess their needs and I was impressed with their case. Travelling on to the headquarters of the Welsh Water Authority I broke my journey at Bedwellty to look at the acute difficulties there and to discuss the situation with their MP, Neil Kinnock, who backed my 'save water' pleas. Neil took us to inspect a disused pumping station which might be brought back into operation. This meant travelling up and up across an overgrown tip to Cwm Nant Yu Haern, above Blackwood, where the village of Manmoel stood at the top of the mountain. Neil was wearing a natty lightweight suit when we started but by the time we arrived, after ploughing through the dust and debris, he looked far from elegant. I was not surprised that the excessively dry spell produced the same conditions here for him and his friends. At least they had the refuge of a welcoming pub. I had to travel on to meet Lord Brecon, chairman of the Welsh Water Authority, and his team. In advance of our meeting I had already heard from Lord Brecon that he wanted the Severn–Trent Water Authority to make more water available in the river Severn from the reservoirs I knew well in mid-Wales, the Elan, Claerwen and associated reservoirs built by the far-seeing citizens of Birmingham, which had been nationalised by the Tories without a penny of compensation and placed under the control of the Severn–Trent Authority. At the time of writing this insult is to be further compounded by the proposal to sell off the undertaking to a private enterprise in order to provide profits, but not competition, which will increase the price to the consumer. What nonsense!

Sir William 'Bill' Dugdale, the chairman of the Severn–Trent Authority, was an old friend whose qualities I much admired in spite of his deep attachment to the Tory party. He is a former chairman of Aston Villa FC and treasurer of the Birmingham Church of England diocese. His term of office was about to expire when I became the Minister and in spite of loud noises of opposition I had no hesitation in re-appointing him. He was a first-class chairman and served me loyally. When we met Bill lost no time in telling me, and Lord Brecon, that if I asked him to do so he would release more water into the Severn although his obligation was to provide for the needs of his many millions of consumers stretching right across the middle of England from the Welsh border to the Anglian and Yorkshire water authorities. However, he demanded to know of Lord Brecon, 'How many millions of gallons of water are flowing down the Wye and into the sea, and is it all going to waste?'. The only counter to this reasonable question was that the river Usk was in danger of drying up, and I knew that water had to be pumped from the Wye to the Usk, which the engineers assured me was quite feasible. So the issue was whether it was necessary to take water from the Severn and put it into the Wye for onward transportation to the Usk and then into the reservoir which served Ebbw Vale and Monmouthshire. The unreasonable counter to Bill's question provided by Lord Brecon was that if he took any more water from the Wye it would interfere with the quality of the salmon fishing! I thought Sir William was going to have apoplexy. I was able to authorise work on the Wye to Usk scheme and to ask Bill Dugdale to prepare contingency plans. Later on it was found that the severe two-year drought had caused cracks in the bed of the river Severn so that the river was losing water and emptying itself. The Thames Water Authority suffered similar losses from their river. Bill Dugdale had flown down to the meeting in his private two-seater plane and he kindly flew me back to Birmingham where I could change my clothes and receive a delegation of my Muslim constituents who wished to pray for rain, a kind offer that I was glad to encourage. After a night at home I set off for East Anglia via the London emergency headquarters.

The most dramatic decision to be taken on that trip was to reverse the flow of the river Ouse, which was achieved by damming it up and letting it flow backwards. This proved to be a success. When I had time to think about the lessons of all this at the end of seven or eight days and to talk it all over with officials I became more than ever convinced that the country needed a national grid system similar to that in operation for gas and electricity. The river system of England and Wales lends itself to such a development. There is no shortage of water whatsoever in Great Britain, the problem is transporting it from areas of quantity to areas of shortage. In practice that means from the north to the south and the west to the east. This would serve the south-west by pumping water from a point near Bristol across Somerset and into rivers which flow to the coasts of Devon. The Severn could also provide supplies to flow across the country via the Trent and on to the Humber. Likewise, the Thames flows eastwards from the Cotswolds to Essex and Kent. The Scottish supply could also be made available for pumping south into England. The engineers and the water authorities agreed to work on the scheme. Later on it was reported to me that the water authorities were content to create their own regional grid systems which would make each of them self-sufficient and that they saw no need for a national grid system. I hope the future proves them right. My own view remains that the water supply of every regional water authority should be connected to that of every other water authority with whom it shares a common boundary. If that happened there need never again be any water shortage in this country.

It is widely believed that the rains came immediately upon my appointment as 'Minister for Drought' – and that it has never stopped raining since! The fact is that we went a further ten days without rain and in the West Country we were then down to 25 days' supply. The situation was growing desperate in parts of Yorkshire and it was arranged that I would travel there for a ceremonial turning-on of a standpipe put up on one of the housing estates, which was the only supply of water to be available for the residents. This would certainly emphasise the need to preserve water. My concern was that arrangements were made to carry water to the sick and elderly. The local authority and the Yorkshire and Humberside Water Authority both impressed me by the detailed planning they had undertaken and by the voluntary organisations they had recruited for the task. As I turned on the stopcock the rains came, only a few spots at first, but soon we were deluged. The reservoirs were empty and the ground was dried up. It was going to take weeks for the water to soak through the earth and fill the rivers and reservoirs. My appeals for continued water-saving, delivered as I stood in the pouring rain, were amusing but necessary. We had got through a crisis far more serious than most people appreciated. However, the emergency measures we had embarked upon did not need to be brought into operation so we were never able to test the efficiency of a two-line pipe system laid down the fast lane of the M5 motorway.

The nation was relieved as well as amused. The fun was good-natured, even if at my expense. I learned to live with it and to build some of my after-dinner stories around the folklore. Two of my stories were true. On a visit to Tashkent and Samarkand in the central Asian region of the Soviet Union I arrived to find the temperature at an all-time high, certainly higher than anything I have ever experienced. The heat was unbearable. I was taken off for a luncheon in my honour given by the State Sports Ministry. Upon arriving at the hotel we had to go through the main dining-room which was full of people sitting at tables bearing the Union Jack. I was immediately recognised and greeted, 'Hello Denis, how nice to see you here, are you going to bring us any rain?'. The Uzbekistan Minister for Sport who accompanied me was amazed at this. He told me that he would never be recognised like this by his own people in his own state, much less many thousands of miles from home. He asked why it was and I told him that in our country I was recognised as the miracle man, I brought the rains. He told me that in Tashkent they had had no rain for two years, would it rain because I was here? I could only reply that anything could happen. That night we had one of the worst electric storms experienced in those parts. The lightning struck the electricity works and plunged the town into darkness, including our hotel. Patrick Cheney, my chief researcher, was with me and we had to walk down 12 storeys in pitch darkness with many others seeking the refuge of the lower floors. The rain poured down. It was quite an experience but it did wonders for my reputation in the Soviet Union!

It worked the other way, too. One day at Cheltenham races I lunched in the Royal Box and the Queen Mother very graciously asked me to accompany her into the parade ring to look at the horses for the big race, the Champion Hurdle. It was raining heavily and a large umbrella was provided for us but the moment we set foot in the parade ring the rain ceased. The Queen Mother told me that had she not seen this for herself she would never have believed it! After the races Her Majesty asked me if I was coming next day to see the Gold Cup. I had to say that this was not possible as I was due to answer questions in the House. 'What will the weather do tomorrow?' When dawn broke next morning the whole of Cheltenham was covered with several inches of snow. The Gold Cup had to be postponed!

Following the rain, inevitably, came the floods, flash floods brought about because the earth was rock-hard and unable to absorb the heavy rains. The Prime Minister called me into action for a second time but it was nothing like as dramatic as the drought. The local authorities and the water authorities were prepared for the eventuality and, indeed, we had taken the precaution of urging them to be ready for such flooding. They all coped extremely well. The floods were contained but a great deal of damage had been done in the worst-hit areas.

... AND BLIZZARDS

The winter of 1977 brought far more snow in far less time than usual. The blizzards were severe, drifts of 18 feet or more were reported on Dartmoor and Exmoor and conditions were very difficult right across the country. Whole communities were cut off and sheep and cattle were submerged. It was clear that a Minister was required to co-ordinate the emergency actions needed to be taken by several Ministries and by the local authorities. Once more I was pressed into service. There was much speculation as to how long I would take to produce a thaw. The *Daily Mirror* reported that William Hill had opened a book and offered odds on the prospects. I was able to authorise the department to repeat the successful action taken during the drought and to establish emergency headquarters at the Department of the Environment, with the regional offices also being re-activated. As main roads and railway lines were blocked across the country Sir Robert Marshall, John Noulton and I soon decided that a helicopter was essential if I was to get to the worst-affected regions. These turned out to be almost the very same counties I had visited during the drought – Devon, Wiltshire, East Anglia and Yorkshire. The helicopter arrived in Birmingham to pick me up but the weather was so severe that it was grounded and I was lucky to find a train that managed to get me to London. The reports from the regions soon led us to the conclusion that a massive co-ordination effort was required by the Government involving the armed forces, the police and fire services, local government and voluntary agencies. The Ministry of Agriculture regional offices played essential roles and they performed excellently.

The local authorities were soon asking who was going to fund these operations and my officials and the Treasury quickly came up with the 'Howell formula', which was that the local authorities should meet the costs up to a penny rate and everything above that would be met by the Government. Central Government also met the costs of the armed forces, a big item. The National Farmers' Union were pressing for emergency supplies of animal feed to be delivered by helicopter or to be got through by the army, and since there was no time for collective consultation with colleagues I decided that where it was necessary to provide such a service the farmers would pay the costs of the foodstuff and we would deliver it free. All these arrangements worked out well in practice although it was inevitable that as I toured the country county council after county council asked for more. They were all Conservative or independent and they certainly had not yet embraced the Thatcher philosophy of cutting back on public expenditure! However, we got on remarkably well and my own faith in local government was reinforced.

When the situation reports came in it was clear that my first visit had to be to Devon. All the roads from the south of the county to the north were blocked and whole communities were cut off. Milk and food, medical services, supplies and animal foodstuffs were soon established as national priorities while in some parts of the country – Yorkshire in particular – the army was needed to help open up the motorways and get traffic moving. We had to travel to Devon by train as the freezing blizzard still prevented the use of helicopters. Once more John and Pat Perry were able to provide our West Country headquarters at their Livermead hotels in Torquay. Later on this became quite an office joke. John Noulton told me one day that a ship had run aground off the Shetlands – 'I've booked a suite at the Livermead'. When the train reached Bristol we were met by a posse of reporters, radio and television people who had set off to meet my helicopter only to be re-routed to the station. At Bristol the stationmaster greeted me and asked if I would mind doing interviews on the platform and I did so while the train awaited my return. I was pleased to note that my fellow passengers seemed fascinated by all this and accepted the delay without complaint. At Exeter I was met by another old friend, Jack Tarr, the deputy chief constable, who provided me with a police car and escorts. He had also detailed as my driver a football referee colleague, Lester Shapter, later to become one of the most proficient of our national referees. At County Hall we were briefed on the latest crisis position and I provided information about the Government's financial position. All the armed services responded magnificently. Teams of servicemen cleared the roads to remote farms and communities or carried food and emergency supplies to isolated villages. My chief concern was for elderly people, infirm or housebound, who might be in great need and cut off from neighbours. I made a special point of mentioning this in all my statements. The local authorities and the voluntary bodies did excellent work in drawing up lists of people at risk and getting them visited. The telephone line engineeers worked night and day in appalling conditions to restore communications and the police service used its own radio system to great effect. I decided to make a visit to one isolated farm high up on Dartmoor. Lester Shapter told me he could get me there and so he did, a considerable feat of driving. We were warmly welcomed but the main concern was for animals buried in the snow drifts and anxiety about how to get milk deliveries from the farm to the nearest depot of the Milk Marketing Board.

At Taunton I found the officers of the Somerset County Council to be extremely efficient and this proved to be the case wherever I went – Wiltshire, Dorset, Kent, Essex, Norfolk and Sheffield. As a man who himself graduated from the local government school I had good cause to appreciate its worth in these emergencies. Any central government that wishes to weaken its resources or undermine its structure will indeed be placing at risk the essential services upon which our people depend in times of crisis. The thaw came after about a week. The nation returned to normal and I reported to the Prime Minister how well everyone had performed. Jim Callaghan was very interested in all the details and asked me to provide a full report of all that we had done and of the role performed by the armed forces, the agencies and local government. He thought it was important to have such an account filed away in the Cabinet Office where, I suppose, it remains.

The cartoonists had another field day at my expense but it was all good-humoured stuff. I told Jim Callaghan that I now hoped to retire from these exploits the undefeated champ! In fact, he did call upon me on one further occasion when the Amoco Cadiz went aground off the French coast and spilt thousands of tons of oil into the English Channel. The oil was reported to be flowing towards the English coast and emergency action seemed necessary to protect our beaches. Jim's call came through one Sunday lunch-time and he told me that Stanley Clinton Davis, my ministerial colleague responsible for shipping matters, would be in charge of that aspect of the emergency. Within the hour Stanley was on the telephone asking my agreement to bomb the ship. I had to reply that I was not able to agree to any such course of action at three o'clock on a Sunday afternoon without any advice being available to me. Our partnership proved to be short-lived. As we set off for the cliffs of Kent the winds changed and blew the oil back to France! I returned to the rather mundane tasks of sport and the environment leaving Stanley to cope with the more intractable problem of a grounded oil tanker breaking up in heavy seas.

12

MINISTERIAL CONTROVERSY

SPORTS COUNCIL DIRECTOR

Towards the end of 1977 Walter Winterbottom announced that he intended to retire from office the following March when he reached the age of 65. While everyone should have been prepared for such an eventuality the fact was that they were not. Walter is the sort of man that you automatically expect to be a permanent fixture. He has always filled controversial posts – manager of the English football team, secretary of the General Council of Physical Recreation and director of the Sports Council – and he coped well with every eventuality and survived every crisis. Of all the men I know the description 'he has a safe pair of hands' fits him the best. And he had to contend with difficulties other than job performance. He brought a new intellectual strength to the coaching and team management of English football and at times he faced an avalanche of press criticism but he sustained his authority and that of the Football Association throughout it all. I know that in spite of the bad patches his influence was enormous and much praised by people I admire like Joe Mercer and Ron Greenwood. At the CCPR he was brought in from outside by Sir Stanley Rous when the formidable Phyllis Colson was due to retire, and after Walter failed to get the FA secretaryship, which was due more to a reaction against Rous's long and somewhat autocratic reign than to any shortcomings of Winterbottom. I knew of all this when in 1964 I invited him to become the first director of the Sports Council; there were still lingering if muted hostilities in some quarters but I never had a moment's doubt that I had taken the right decision. After 14 years with the Sports Council, watching its development and Walter's relationships mature with both the governing bodies and the public it was a considerable satisfaction to reaffirm my first judgment. We had differences of opinion from time to time, most seriously when he was serving new masters after I left office in 1970, but we always kept our friendship in good

repair and it was a delight to find his great services to sport acknowledged by the award of a knighthood, so richly deserved. I may add
that throughout all his public service Walter enjoyed the wonderful
support of his wife Anne and British sport has much cause to be grateful
for that, too.

With his resignation tendered, speculation began as to who would
succeed Walter. Favourite was John Coghlan, who was deputy to
Winterbottom. I thought these odds well justified, for John had been
an outstandingly successful secretary of the West Midlands Regional
Council for Sport where I had admired his work at close quarters and
had encouraged his appointment to the post of deputy director. I had
every reason to believe he was performing well there because Sir Robin
Brook, the Council's chairman, told me so. Other possible contenders
were John Wheatley, the regional secretary in the south-west and
Emlyn Jones, a most successful director of the Crystal Palace national
sports centre. However, although I read all this speculation in the press
no one came to talk to me about it. What information came my way
was conveyed by my officials, who attended all the meetings of the
Sports Council. This was the practical effect of the Royal Charter
which guaranteed the independence of the Sports Council, but it certainly rankled with me. Apart from the courtesies of the matter
I thought it unwise that members of the Sports Council did not
seek my views about the appointment since the new director would
need to work closely with me and my officials. We discussed this
in the office but I decided against direct intervention, as I did not
wish to be accused of ministerial interference. The shortlist was drawn
up and candidates interviewed, yet still there was no reference to
me. I was astonished. I did not know who had been chosen. As it
turned out two future directors of the Sports Council who applied
for the post – Emlyn Jones and John Wheatley – had not even been
interviewed.

I attended the Chrismas lunch of the Sports Council held immediately before its December meeting and sat next to Robin Brook. The
first I knew of the impending crisis came towards the end of the lunch
when Brook turned to me and said, 'I intend to start the meeting by
announcing the name of our new director. I think you will be amused'.
I took out one of my large cigars and puffed away in contemplation as
I waited for the bombshell. Sir Robin opened the meeting by welcoming
me and then said that he had an additional item of business. The
recommendation was to appoint the Rev Nicholas Stacey, currently
director of Kent County Council social services department. Members
of the Council seemed to me to be shell-shocked. One or two had not
yet arrived at the meeting and took their seats during the two minutes'
silence that we seemed to be observing. I still said nothing. Robin asked
for any comments and one or two doubts began to emerge, hesitantly
but quite definitely. 'Laddie' Lucas, a former Tory MP and a fine
golfer, was the first to object, and Bill Hicks, a former sports editor of

the old *News Chronicle* and the *Daily Mail* was another. I took note since they were both men whose judgment I respected. Furthermore, Laddie Lucas had been a member of the selection committee. His opposition was the first indication that the selection had not been unanimous. It later emerged that the proposal to support Stacey had been made by John Disley, one of the two vice-chairmen and an old Oxford fellow athlete of Stacey's. I made my first comment to the effect that Nicholas Stacey seemed to me to have had a lot of jobs since leaving the Church. So far as I could judge there was not the degree of enthusiasm among the members that I would have expected for such an appointment. No vote was taken, Sir Robin collected voices and announced that there seemed to be a majority in favour of Stacey. He then turned to Sheila Hughes, who was effectively the secretary of the Sports Council, and asked her to go and convey the news to Stacey and to see whether he could come over and meet the Council. Since he could not possibly come in from Kent it seemed obvious that he must be waiting nearby. Sheila moved towards the door. I decided that the time had arrived for direct intervention. I stopped Sheila in her tracks and reminded the chairman that in accordance with the terms of the Royal Charter this appointment required the endorsement of the Secretary of State which for all practical purposes was me. Sir Robin replied that as I was present could I signify my approval. 'I am afraid not', was my answer, 'I shall need time to consider this matter, and you certainly can't make any announcement until I have done so.' I returned to the department.

My first call was to Tony Crosland, who was as astonished as I was but left the matter to me. My next call was to my own vicar at St Paul's Church in Birmingham, Canon Ralph Stevens. Ralph had been an Oxford athletics blue in his day – he had been chosen to participate in the Olympic Games in Berlin but was prevented from doing so by an illness. He knew sport but more to the point he had known Nicholas Stacey when Stacey was chaplain to Leonard Wilson, Bishop of Birmingham. I explained the situation and my hesitations. Ralph Stevens immediately confirmed me in my doubts. He did not think that Stacey was the man for this post. All my leading officials were still at the Sports Council meeting but when they returned we discussed Stacey's CV and all the posts he had held, which included responsibility for a London churches housing association as well as Oxfam and Kent social services. I was reinforced in my view that he seemed to move from post to post rather too often. Neither did there seem to be any immediate explanation as to why Nick Stacey had given up his vocation in the Church. I sat and thought about the action I was about to take, realising that if I vetoed the appointment there would be a major public controversy. I would be accused of political interference in the government of the Sports Council but I concluded that there was no point in having this safeguard written into the Charter if I did not use it when necessary. It was essential for me to have a director with whom I could work with

ONE IN THE EYE

ABOVE: *Franklin's cartoon for the* Daily Mirror *depicts the outcome of the D'Oliveira affair in 1967.*

BELOW: *My role as Minister for Drought and Blizzards inspired this characterisation of Howell as snowman and continues to provide scope for jokes.*

..'If Howell comes, can spring be far behind'?

The Minister for Sport attempts to demonstrate his footballing skills in a London classroom.   Photosource

'Plant a Tree in '73, Plant Some More in '74.' Launching the 1974 campaign as Minister of State for the Environment.
Department of the Environment

Presiding over APEX in 1983.

The Sports Council holds a press conference in 1966 to report on its first year's work. S & G Press Agency Ltd

Introducing former England rugby captain Dickie Jeeps as the new chairman of the Sports Council in 1978. Photosource

Receiving the president, HRH the Duke of Edinburgh, with Sir Stanley Rous and Arthur Gear at the AGM of the CCPR. Fox Photos

The Howell family, Christmas 1982. Left to Right: Mick, David,
Andrew and Ceri; Denis and Brenda; Kate and Patch.   Terry Weir

There were times of distress and grief, too. ABOVE: *Brenda is escorted from our home by Ken Purnell on the night the IRA bombed our car.* BELOW: *Our beloved son David, who lost his life after a car accident in 1986 at the age of 21.*

OPPOSITE:

ABOVE: *Jimmy Munn and I receive HRH Princess Anne at the Birmingham Olympic gala dinner. Looking on is Frank Greaves (right), president of the Birmingham Chamber of Commerce.*   Simon Livingstone

BELOW: *Delivering Birmingham's Olympic bid to IOC president H. E. Juan Antonio Samaranch and Raymond Gafner in Lausanne in 1986.*

Celebrating 25 years of front bench service in 1989 with the Canoldir Choir (above) and celebrity guests David Coleman, Cliff Morgan and Bobby Charlton (below).   Birmingham Post & Mail

every confidence. I had serious doubts, and my mind was made up – I was not going to endorse this appointment.

Hardly had I reached this conclusion than Laddie Lucas arrived at my office. I agreed to see him. He urged me not to agree to the appointment on grounds that centred upon Mr Stacey's administrative qualities, which had caused him some concern. He also felt that there was too much Oxford athletics influence at work. I thanked him but did not disclose that my mind was already made up. He was immediately followed by the arrival of Robin Brook and Bernard Atha, the second vice-chairman of the Sports Council. They had come to find out if I had yet decided to accept their decision. I told them that my mind was indeed made up and the appointment was not acceptable. Robin Brook now wanted me to take the matter to Tony Crosland and seemed crestfallen when I replied that I had already done so. Bernard Atha, a Labour councillor from Leeds with very considerable ability, took up the arguments but I was not going to budge. As they left a telephone call came through from John Rodda of the *Guardian*, who seemed to have the story. So did Ian Wooldridge of the *Daily Mail*. I suspected that Bill Hicks had been in touch with them and although I did not want to make my announcement in this way I confirmed their information rather than fire speculation which might lead to considerable public controversy and pressures about a matter I had now decided. This turned out to be a wise move. All the press comment centred on my judgment and my right to impose it. Sporting opinion turned out to be almost entirely on my side.

In the next few days press comment was quite vociferous and all sides were heard on the radio. The controversy was effectively ended by a trenchant piece from Ian Wooldridge in the *Daily Mail*. He was obviously well briefed and all his facts were spot on. He had, of course, interviewed Nicholas Stacey and he then rang me with some obvious trepidation, telling me that he had to put to me an embarrassing matter he had learned from that source. Nick Stacey had told him that he believed the reason for my action was that he had turned down my brother for an appointment in the Kent social services department. I could hardly contain my amusement and informed Ian that at that moment my brother, Stan Howell, was happily driving his post office van around Birmingham collecting the Royal Mail. No thoughts of becoming a social worker had ever entered his head! What had happened was that a former Birmingham City councillor also by the name of Howell, and by coincidence also a former cleric, but no relation of my family, had asked me to provide him with a reference as he was job seeking in the social field. I had been happy to do so, as he had been a very good councillor. Apparently he had used my reference in applying for a post with Kent County Council. Nick Stacey had got the wrong man and Wooldridge duly reported all this. It was the last I heard of the matter and the whole procedure had to start again. This time the Sports Council did consult me. I told them that the correct way to proceed was to draw up a shortlist and bring it to me for my approval. At that stage Ministers should be able to agree to the shortlist or to indicate non-acceptance. This they did. I found all the names acceptable. I would confirm whichever person they chose from this list which included Emlyn Jones, not interviewed on the earlier occasion. It really was between him and John Coghlan, who were my two preferences. They chose Emlyn, whose close working relationships with sports people proved to be decisive. It was a happy choice, and Emlyn certainly justified it during the five years he held that office.

However, the departure from office of Emlyn Jones was another traumatic and quite disgraceful event. Neil Macfarlane became the Sports Minister in late 1982, succeeding Hector Munro. Macfarlane was a good club cricketer and took a passing interest in sports politics but he never really understood how sport is governed. I believe that he harboured resentments or suspicions about Emlyn's relationship with me. In fact it could not have been based upon a greater sense of rectitude. I could not understand these disapprovals by my successor. When I was the Minister I had regular and pleasant discussions with my opposite numbers, first Charles Morrison and then Hector Munro. I used to tell the directors of the Sports Council, Walter Winterbottom and Emlyn Jones, that it was their business to keep in touch with the Opposition. It made good sense – as far as possible I wanted sport to have all-party support. Hector Munro became Minister in the new Conservative Government of 1979 and continued friendly discussions with me, but when he left office all that changed. Emlyn Jones, Gerald Coghlan and Vic Shroot all seemed to suffer the consequences of their continuing friendship with me. Shroot actually served for two years as press officer to Hector Munro and there was no difficulty of any sort. They both got on extremely well. His troubles started when Munro left office in 1980 after the Moscow Olympics fiasco. I became so concerned about these matters that I requested an appointment with George Moseley, permanent secretary of the department, to explain the position and to protect the careers of all my former colleagues. I was left in no doubt that the position was fully understood and I need have no worries on that score. Emlyn's bombshell was dropped on him when his chairman, Dickie Jeeps, returned from a meeting with Macfarlane and said something to the effect that the Minister wanted him out by Christmas. Jones had 40 years' service behind him, and although he was shocked by the statement he immediately resigned. He fully appreciated that his position would be untenable if he stayed. He consulted me the next day and I could only say that in my opinion he was wrong to do so. The Royal Charter was there to protect him and the Sports Council from ministerial interference. Only the Sports Council, not even the Minister, could demand his resignation.

The incident raised serious constitutional questions. I decided to request a meeting with the full Sports Council membership. It did not get off to a good start. There was no one available to greet me and I sat outside the meeting room, where I was provided with a cup of tea by a young lady who thought I should be offered one, and who then put her head inside the meeting room to tell people that I was waiting outside. After another ten minutes or so I decided to announce my own presence by knocking on the door loudly, entering the room and wishing the assembled company 'good morning'. I then withdrew and waited for the summons which came a little more quickly than might otherwise have been the case. The introduction by Jeeps contained no welcome, just a cursory 'you all know Denis, he has something to say to you' or something to that effect. I told the members in straight language that they should not allow their chief officer to be treated like this; they were in effect allowing their director to be removed without any reference to their own independence. The situation was even worse for their deputy director, John Coghlan, who had also been forced out, again without reference to the Sports Council. I knew that the effect of the Royal Charter under which they operated was designed to protect their independent position from all ministerial interference. Most of the members observed a shrouded silence. Jones did indeed start legal proceedings against Jeeps but after an exchange of correspondence it fizzled out. I put down questions to the Minister to get the record straight in *Hansard*. Macfarlane replied that he was made aware 'of the possibilities of the resignation of the director general before it was formally announced'. It was a sorry business, the saddest part being the Sports Council's abject surrender of their sovereignty. They should have created hell.

FOOTBALL TRAUMA

It is estimated that some 5 million people attend football matches from time to time. At least 1 million do so on a regular basis. Any national sport which holds this attraction for so many citizens is bound to provide constant activity for any Minister for Sport. I did not, of course, need to be stimulated by any sense of ministerial responsibility: for me football matters are a labour of love. They could never again reach the high point of World Cup success such as we enjoyed in 1966, but football still provides me with so much exhilaration and fascination. The game is a potent factor in the social life of the country. I believe that is because a football club expresses the aspirations of the community it serves and represents. Football belongs to the people, not just to the shareholders and directors of any one club; theirs is the privilege of holding their club in trust on behalf of the people. Given this social purpose the sport is bound to reflect the social strains of our society and the problems they create as well as the delights of success which unite all supporters. When we are confronted with problems at football grounds or in their vicinity they are the problems of society. We cannot isolate the evils of human behaviour as they may express themselves from time to time in the society from which they emerge. When governments try to do so it becomes a self-defeating exercise. These problems are vital problems. They have to be addressed in the interests of good order in the whole community. The consequence of this must be that football supporters also enjoy the same rights and civil liberties as those claimed by any other members of the public. And the duty of government is to assure those rights just as much as it protects those who exercise them in going about the lawful occasions of sport. These were the principles which governed my second term of ministerial office during which football matters were rarely off my desk.

Lord Wheatley had conducted a masterly enquiry into the tragedy at Glasgow Rangers. His analysis and recommendations led to the Safety of Sports Grounds Act for which I had major responsibility along with my Home Office and Scottish Office colleagues. The Bill was introduced into Parliament in 1974. It was welcomed on all sides and received a swift passage on to the statute book. The main provision of the Bill designated all grounds with accommodation for more than 10,000 spectators. This allowed the Secretary of State to estimate how many spectators should be allowed in any such ground and to obtain any information he required about the ground. The clubs were required to obtain a safety certificate from the local authority who had wide powers controlling numbers, access and dispersement within the grounds and responsibility for approving every aspect of ground safety.

It was quite right to place upon football the same stringent requirements to ensure the safety of its patrons as already existed in other related entertainments such as theatres and cinemas, but I knew well the financial burden that would result for many of the smaller clubs. There was no prospect of Government grant given the perilous state of the country's financial situation. Then, one day I had a request from Alan Hardaker, the secretary of the Football League, asking me if he could bring Mr Cecil Moores of Littlewoods Pools to meet me in order to discuss the crippling effect of pools tax upon their business. It is indefensible to my mind to impose a tax of 42.5 per cent on pools betting, the working men's pleasure, compared with a tax upon horse racing betting of 8 per cent off course. Cecil Moores' great worry was that the Chancellor might start to tax the pools' Spot the Ball competition which was tax free. Alan Hardaker's concern was to protect the income the League received from the pools. This came from the copyright of their fixtures and would be reduced further if additional increases were imposed upon pools betting. Secondly, he was trying to get the pools to provide more income to help with the cost of the sports grounds safety legislation by making a contribution from Spot the Ball. I told Cecil Moores that his difficulty was that he had no friends in Whitehall. When increases in taxation were being considered there was no one to put the case against raising the pools betting. I advised him that he needed a Minister with an interest to argue his case. 'If I can get the Chancellor to agree not to tax Spot the Ball', I asked, 'how much will you offer for football ground safety?' He told me that I could depend upon at least 7.5 per cent of their turnover, but that he would have to talk to the other pools companies, Vernons and Zetters. I went off to sound out my colleague the Chancellor, Denis Healey. Denis had no hesitation in telling me that he could not provide any funds to meet the needs of the new legislation. When I told him I thought I could get money out of Spot the Ball if I could assure the pools companies that he had no proposals to tax these competitions, he looked at his officials and confirmed that this was the situation. I was delighted and immediately sent for Moores and Hardaker to tell them the news. We struck a deal in record time. A trust would be set up and the pools would make an initial contribution of 10 per cent. We agreed the three objects of the trust would be to provide assistance towards the cost of ground safety; grants towards ground improvements and spectator comfort; grants to extend the role of football clubs within the community.

The rest is history. Since 1979 the pools promoters have made a voluntary contribution to football totalling some £68 million, and the trust has enabled every ground in the country to meet the requirements of the Safety of Sports Grounds Act. When the need arose for further measures such as video cameras to identify troublemakers inside the grounds the money was forthcoming – something like £2.8 million has been spent on this one measure alone with considerable success. I am now urging the Football Trust to give higher priority to the creature comforts of their customers. Many of our grounds have facilities which are quite unacceptable. Many toilet facilities are disgraceful or non-existent. Refreshment rooms, family rooms and comfortable seating are all obvious priorities. The Spot the Ball levy is now running at 21 per cent of turnover, producing an annual income of some £9.5 million. It is a great tribute to the pools promoters that they have more than honoured their deal with me. The first chairman of the trust was the late Sir Norman Chester, who ensured that its guidelines and procedures were well-founded. Today Lord Aberdare chairs the trust and Richard Faulkner is its secretary, the other members coming from the English and Scottish football authorities. They make up a most successful team. Looking back I cannot think of a happier day's work than when I met Cecil Moores and Alan Hardaker and achieved the ready co-operation of the Chancellor of the Exchequer.

However, troubles soon mounted on the football front. Visiting supporters from some clubs were obviously looking for trouble. Home supporters sometimes reacted or anticipated trouble, attacking peaceful visitors. There were increasing problems outside grounds, in shopping centres, on trains, in coaches, at motorway service stations. Three clubs in particular had supporters who caused me great concern, Manchester United, Chelsea and Leeds United. In May 1975 I travelled to Paris to see the European final between Leeds United and Bayern Munich.

One could sense the trouble well away from the ground. Inside the stadium the French police lined up on the surrounding track facing the crowd, unlike in our own system of policing where officers are on the terraces among the spectators. Given a free run some Leeds fans behaved quite disgracefully. When the French riot police – the notorious CRS – arrived and started to take out some of the troublemakers by dragging them across the ground, near pandemonium broke out. Seats were torn from their fixtures and rained down on the police below. There was nothing to restrain the hooligans. It was a terrible disgrace and I have never felt so humiliated or distressed, seated as I was in the presidential box, as I attempted to apologise to the French Prime Minister and my colleague the French Minister for Sport. The match was largely irrelevant, the German team winning by 2–0. I returned home to report to colleagues and determined to take steps to prevent a repetition of such shameful behaviour.

One of the problems facing us was the amount of publicity this hooliganism generated. Violence clearly breeds violence and is fuelled by publicity, a dilemma in any democracy. No one could suggest that these outbreaks were not news or that the news should be suppressed. I decided that any action I had to take must have the fullest support of the football legislators. I set up a committee which met weekly in my office. It included the principal officers of the FA and the League, Sir Harold Thompson, Denis Follows, Lord Westwood and Alan Hardaker, together with the police, British Rail and the coach operators, the Association of Football Supporters' Clubs and government departments. We produced a code of conduct which was accepted throughout football by police, rail and coach transporters and other services.

Several of our recommendations were crucial and totally unprecedented. The segregation of home supporters from visitors was essential if the game was going to be preserved. Supporters had to be prevented from trespassing on to the playing area by fences or other means. Personally I favoured the dry moats used by most continental grounds but only Arsenal provided one. We proposed that no alcoholic drink should be available on coaches or trains, no stops should be allowed at public houses, and visiting supporters should not arrive at home grounds earlier than one hour before kick-off time. We had splendid co-operation from all the clubs and supporters' associations which helped gradually to improve the situation.

Where serious trouble persisted and needed urgent action and where intelligence reports had to be assessed and acted upon I relied on my 'inner cabinet', consisting of Philip Knights the Chief Constable of the West Midlands, Lord Westwood and Alan Hardaker of the League and Andrew Stephens and Denis Follows of the FA, later succeeded by Ted Croker. We took many decisions that were unprecedented but we were dealing with an unprecedented situation. Manchester United and Chelsea away matches were declared to be all-ticket. Club or supporters' club stewards were required to travel in every coach and to accept responsibility for the behaviour of the fans in their charge. We were able to do a great deal of advanced planning. Each time we met we reviewed future fixtures and recommended action that we believed to be appropriate. By this time I had become the principal European Minister for Sport, chairing all the 23 Ministers in membership of the Council of Europe. This was largely attributable to the esteem in which Walter Winterbottom was held within the Council, where he was undoubtedly seen as one of Europe's leading sporting administrators. My European colleagues took up the issue of violence in sport both on and off the field and we enjoyed remarkable co-operation. This was never seen to better effect than when my working party expected trouble at a European club match in Belgium. Intelligence reports caused us concern. We decided that supporters arriving without match tickets or with no reserved accommodation would be a risk. I was advised that as legislation then existed we could not prevent them leaving the country. That meant that the solution to the problem was to prevent them gaining entry into Belgium. I telephoned my ministerial friend and explained the situation. We saw to it that no drink was available on the ship and when it put into port all those supporters without match tickets or accommodation were refused entry into Belgium, put back on the boat and returned to England. The match took place without any problems.

In May 1977 Liverpool played Borussia Munchengladbach in the final of the European Cup. I travelled to Rome for the match, and as I expected the Liverpool organisation was first-class under the active direction of chairman John Smith and his fellow directors and secretary Peter Robinson. They took many thousands of supporters, all observing the terms of the code of conduct and returned home safely, bringing with them the European Cup which they had deservedly won by 3–1. Bob Paisley, their modest genius of a manager, deserved every congratulation on a great team success. Another pleasure was to observe him receiving the congratulations of his legendary predecessor, the great Bill Shankly. It was a wonderful party we had that night. It proved that British clubs could compete in Europe with dignity. I felt a great sense of relief that all the planning had succeeded so well.

Combined vigilance on all fronts was improving the situation enormously. By 1979 we were able to remove the restrictions on the visiting fans of Manchester United and Chelsea and we had high hopes that we were moving back into a normal situation. Tragically, the committee I established has never met since the day I left office, a fact much lamented and commented upon by those who served upon it. All of them believed that our consultations led to effective action being taken and to a considerable improvement in crowd control and behaviour. It was wrong of the incoming Tory Government to drop its guard, and I have no doubt that this lessening of vigilance contributed to the resurgence of the problem.

Having left office in 1979 I had a welcome opportunity to become involved in the organisational problems of crowd control at important matches through the great European success of my own team Aston Villa, who won the European Cup in 1982. They qualified as the English representatives in that competition by winning the English League Championship in the previous season, 1981–82. They were a well-disciplined side brought together by manager Ron Saunders. When he left, the momentum was maintained by Tony Barton, who succeeded him to excellent effect and achieved a harmonious relationship with both the team and their supporters. The chairman at this time was an ailing Ron Bendall, who was the majority shareholder and controlled the club with his son Donald. When the Villa played Anderlecht an unfortunate incident occurred. Two soldiers stationed with the Army of the Rhine took some leave and attended the match, buying tickets from the home club Anderlecht. They were in a section of the crowd well away from the Aston Villa supporters and could not in any way be said to be the responsibility of the club, yet when they misbehaved by jumping over the perimeter fence and causing the game to be held up Aston Villa were held to be responsible. Villa was hauled up before UEFA, the European Football Association, to account for the incident. The arrangements for this match were ridiculous and quite contrary to the code of conduct I had established when Minister for Sport, and which I had urged upon UEFA and its secretary, Herr Bangeter, from my ministerial office. Under my chairmanship, the Council of Europe Ministers had also urged the code of conduct upon Bangeter. This would have prevented the problems which confronted Villa, and in my view it should have been UEFA who were in the dock for allowing such unsatisfactory arrangements.

I entered the scene when I received an urgent telephone call from Donald Bendall and the club secretary Steve Stride asking me if I would help to represent the club at the hearing in Zurich. There were two reasons for concern. First, the pitch invasion by the two soldiers for which Villa were being held responsible, and second, the argument from Anderlecht that the stoppage of the match affected the result. They claimed that they were about to score a goal and therefore that the match should either be awarded to them or at least a replay should be ordered. After the soldiers had been removed the match had continued, resulting in a goal-less draw. Villa won by the one goal scored in the first leg. At the hearing we argued that Aston Villa could have no responsibility for the soldiers. The argument was not accepted. UEFA was exonerating itself and Anderlecht by making Aston Villa the scapegoat. Anderlecht's second demand was more worrying. I decided to use my knowledge of the rules of the game to deal with the situation. When the chairman of the hearing invited us to ask questions of the referee I suprised him by asking him to explain at which point on the field he had restarted the match after the disruption. He indicated a spot near the centre circle which was correct. I was then able to ask my follow-up question, more by way of an observation, 'In accordance with the laws of the game you restarted the match, of course, at the place where the ball was in play when you stopped it?'. The answer had to be yes as that is what the laws require. I then argued that as the play was in the midfield when the stoppage occurred the incident could not have affected the result which must stand. The commission agreed and Villa proceeded to the final tie against Bayern Munich which was played at Rotterdam.

Donald Bendall, Steve Stride and I flew direct from Zurich to Rotterdam to inspect the ground for the final, to hold discussions with the club and the Dutch police and to decide the transport arrangements for the thousands of supporters of Aston Villa who would travel to the final. The arrangements carried out by the club were superb. The West Midlands police, with the agreement of Sir Philip Knights, Chief Constable, and through the organisation of chief superintendent Jack Bagley and a very enterprising sergeant, Mick Marshall, arranged for two off-duty police officers to be present in every coach of supporters. Those travelling by air would also be carefully supervised. All these supporters were marshalled through and escorted home on the return journey. There was not a single untoward incident and the club and its supporters received the warm commendation of all the Dutch authorities. It was an organisational feat which deserved this praise and demonstrated how English clubs can participate in European football with credit. What a disaster that the succeeding Government learned no lessons from any of this. Instead, seven years on, the Government tried to introduce its Football Spectators Bill which relied upon prohibitions, registrations and an assault upon the civil liberties of football supporters who were to be subjected to computer surveillance every time they wished to watch a football match. The Villa story ended on a glorious note with victory over Bayern Munich in the final by a single goal scored by Peter Withe.

THE APEX YEARS

I can never understand the hostility to the principle of trade unionism which is often expressed by people who are themselves immersed in and protected by acts of collective interest or bargaining. Lawyers and doctors are obvious examples but it extends far beyond their boundaries. Most employers band together to negotiate wages and to represent their interests to government about a whole range of matters involving taxation, and import and export controls. Increasingly they seek to influence government about European legislation which affects their trading situation and establishes social conditions which they have to observe. That is the role of the Confederation of British Industries, the Chamber of Commerce and other bodies. I hazard a guess that there is not a single citizen in the land who is not affected by the agreements made by these employers' organisations. Free trade unions are also the essential right of every working person whether they be professional associations or organisations for those who labour by hand or brain. In any well-ordered society this is understood and accepted. All the best employers I know have the best records of industrial relationships.

Good industrial relationships require a partnership between employers and trade unions. That is not to say that trade unions should usurp the functions of management. They cannot carry out their own responsibilities if they do so. But they certainly must involve themselves in the future prosperity of the companies that employ their members. For 12 years I was president of APEX and often I would need to resist those delegates at our annual conference who would attack profits as if they were obscene. I used to reply by referring the delegates to those representatives present whose firms had collapsed or needed to be rescued by government. There was a long list including such well-known companies as Upper Clyde Shipbuilders, Rolls Royce, British Leyland and many more. All these companies were represented by APEX on the staff side. I would urge our delegates to go back home, meet their managements and ensure that their companies had a future of profitability. What we should be arguing about is our share of the profits which we have helped to bring about. Now that we are firmly embedded in the European Community – and APEX has always been a wholehearted supporter of British membership – this approach will become increasingly relevant because it reflects the style and purpose of our sister unions in Europe who conduct their negotiations with employers on this basis. These principles in turn are accepted by their governments as the normal basis for their industrial relations policies. Britain will have no option but to accept them here if it wishes to remain in membership of the EEC and there is no future for our country now outside Europe. For these reasons free trade unionism will be just as relevant in the future as it has ever been. It is disappointing that our present Government does not understand this and expresses as much hostility to the unions as do the irresponsible left, who do not want to understand. As I once said in one of my presidential addresses, 'to understand is the beginning of all civilisation'. Not original I am afraid, but true.

I joined the union as a clerk earning seven shillings and sixpence a week at Hercules Cycle Company. I was following in my father's tradition. Both at Hercules and then at Higgs Motors, I started work as the only clerk in membership of a trade union. Since those days I have held almost every possible post in the union, branch secretary and chairman, area council executive member, and national president member of the executive council. I like to think that this form of public service is as valuable as any other. It is vital to uphold the democratic traditions of the trade union movement. Active trade unionists spend long hours at inconvenient times attending mundane meetings, often doing so in order to protect the union from infiltration and take-over by those who would drive normal people away from attendance. I often tell employers that if they had any sense they would encourage unions to meet in work time and give their employees facilities to attend. I do not regret any of it. I have had the honour of being chosen by the vote of a 150,000 membership to be their president. I have had the opportunity to give service in a field as important, or more so, than any other. And I have been supported by my union as one of its sponsored MPs throughout the whole of my parliamentary career.

Before I became president of the union I was elected to be a member of its standing orders committee and for 21 years I was its chairman, controlling the business of the conference, deciding what was in order or out of order, arranging the debates, protecting the union. In those 21 years I never lost a single challenge to the authority of the standing orders committee and sometimes the challenges were fierce indeed. When I joined the union there was a strong left wing, communist influence, nearly domination. Some great people fought that battle: Helene Walker from the Midlands and Bill Elgar, Bob Scouller and David Currie, all from Scotland, who were presidents of the union and my predecessors. They had fine intellects, great debating skills and real passion. I learned from them most of the skills I possess. Then we had David Rhydderch, our general treasurer for more than 30 years, who came to the Midlands from the Welsh valleys where he had been a contemporary of Aneurin Bevan, both of them being sent by the miners to the Labour College as part of their education. The administrative arm of the union produced general secretaries of exceptional talent such as George Elvin, Fred Woods, Dame Anne Godwin, Henry Chapman, and Roy Grantham. In the Midlands we also had an outstanding area secretary, Arthur Lummis Gibson, who was a most successful Lord Mayor of Birmingham. He was followed by Roy Grantham and then Frank Leath, my close friend and associate in many of these battles. There were many more, unknown and unsung, but they were our comrades in the fight. They fought for the union but they did so because they realised the vital importance of free responsible unions in the life of the Labour movement.

APEX is a moderate union but we have never shirked an issue when it has needed to be faced. The Grunwick strike was the most traumatic dispute in which we have ever been involved. It started with every justification but its tragedy was that extreme forces sought to wrest control of the strike from the responsible members of the union's executive committee. By pursuing confrontation they played into the hands of the Conservatives. Those so called left wing activists who welcomed confrontation, including Arthur Scargill, the miners' leader, and the supporters of the Brent Trades Council, have a great deal to answer for. They helped more than most to turn Labour out in 1979 and to keep us in the wilderness since that time.

On 23 August 1976 35 employees of Grunwick and 35 students

walked out of the film processing firm based at Willesden. In subsequent days they totalled 137. They were not members of a trade union and they were complaining about all manner of conditions inside the factory and of extremely low wages, £25 for a 35-hour week and £28 for one of 40 hours. Many of the people involved were immigrant workers. The matter came to a head when one of them refused to continue to supervise student workers taken on to cope with the heavy load of summer film processing. He was then dismissed for going slow. The workers rang up the TUC to ask for help and were referred to the London area of APEX. Our senior official, Len Gristy, took them into membership, having advised them that he would seek union representation on their behalf to which they were entitled under the Employment Protection Act of 1975, Section 11. The firm refused to recognise APEX and within a month 137 workers were out on strike. It was the only time in the history of our union that we have recruited workers who were already on strike but in view of their Asian origin, their grievances and their low pay we believed we had a moral duty to offer them protection. Then entered the National Association of Freedom, a far right organisation established to challenge the unions among other things. Without a doubt they were spoiling for a fight. They advised the company against any recognition of the union and settlement of the dispute. All correspondence from Roy Grantham, couched in the most conciliatory terms, went without response. The union executive offered a no-strike agreement accompanied by arbitration in the event of a dispute to protect the company against stoppages at the height of their season. No response. For eight months this strike lingered on entirely peacefully with no trouble of any sort. The union was becoming more and more frustrated. Legislation passed by Parliament to grant basic rights in exactly this situation was being flagrantly ignored. The company sacked the striking workforce and declared that there were no union members to negotiate about. The dispute was referred to ACAS, the organisation established by Parliament to mediate in such matters. They could get no response from Grunwick so finally, and after endless delays, they decided to proceed with a ballot of the workforce as required by the Act to discover if the employees wished to have union representation and, if so, which union. Grunwick refused to provide the names and addresses of their workers so ACAS balloted the workers on strike, holding that they could not be deemed to have left the company's employment if they were legitimately on strike. The vote was overwhelming, 91 out of 93 voted to be represented by APEX. Grunwick challenged the ACAS procedure and the declaration in our favour and gave evidence before Lord Widgery the Lord Chief Justice. APEX won the case. Inevitably, an appeal was lodged by the company on a point of law and upheld both in the Appeal Court and the House of Lords. The substance of the appeal was to the effect that even though Grunwick had refused to release the names and addresses of its workers to ACAS they should have taken part in the ballot and it was therefore null and void. The whole trade union movement believed that if that was the law then the law was an ass. How could ACAS include in a ballot people whose names were not known to them and refused by the company? Anger was rising.

During the long peaceful period of the strike I visited the picket line as president of the union to offer what moral support I could. The union's financial support was beyond anything I have known. APEX, like other unions, has sponsored MPs, in our case people of great moderation holding ministerial office. At the suggestion of Shirley Williams, who wanted to give support to the Asian women on strike, Fred Mulley, Shirley and I agreed to visit the picket line, believing that we had more than an ordinary sense of duty to support members of our own union. With hindsight it was a mistake. It removed the focus of attention from a very legitimate grievance and transferred it to the public action of three Ministers. Shirley Williams and I were both sued for comments we made on the visit, even though they might be thought to be mild in the circumstances, and we had to settle. The BBC and newspapers who reported us also had to pay up. Meanwhile the call for a mass picket to break the deadlock gained support with great speed. It was impossible to contain and to discipline, and given the police tactics of refusing to allow more than six pickets on duty, for which no legal requirement then existed, serious problems became inevitable. Busloads of trade unionists travelled to the scene daily, incensed at the affront to trade union rights. Some of the most decent people in the trade union movement fell foul of tough police action. Mass picketing turned out to be a tactical error and was abused by those who wanted confrontation not settlement. The Brent Trades Council usurped the position of the union's executive, which was in near despair at the frustration it felt at having every peaceful approach rejected. Arthur Scargill, without any reference to the APEX executive council, decided to bring down his Yorkshire miners. At this point we ought to have called off the dispute; it was no longer our dispute. Scargill and the Brent Trades Council tried to provide an alternative leadership which we could not countenance. Len Murray was ill and Roy Grantham was also out of action for a period so the union sent its deputy general secretary, Tudor Thomas, to meet Norman Willis, number two at the TUC. It was their view that emotions throughout the country were now so high that only a massive and peaceful opportunity for the trade union movement to demonstrate support for the Grunwick strikers could help redeem the situation. In all, 377 people had been arrested on the picket line and 243 policemen had been injured. Scurrilous newspapers and television paid large sums of money to neighbouring residents to hire bedrooms to photograph the confrontations which they themselves were actively encouraging. The peaceful march under the control of the TUC was fixed for 17 June. The details were worked out between Tudor Thomas, Norman Willis and the assistant commissioner of police. Scargill was seen in London by Thomas and agreed not to get his miners on the picket line before the march. He said he would 'hold them on the motorway' but this did not happen. Early trouble on the picket line was a gift to the press and television people. The march itself was a most peaceful and impressive display of trade union solidarity, decent people demonstrating their basic beliefs in the right to free association. Some 1,500 people marched, led by brass bands, efficiently marshalled and wonderfully impressive. The congratulations offered afterwards by the senior police officers involved were very sincere and certainly appreciated.

Albert Booth, the Secretary of State for Employment, was constantly urged by me and Roy Grantham to establish a committee of enquiry as the only means now to find any sensible way of bringing the dispute to an end. Lord Justice Scarman agreed to chair the enquiry. Thankfully, the APEX executive responded by immediately announcing the end of all picketing other than for six official pickets. In his report Lord Scarman said: 'The union was fully justified in raising the dispute at the TUC and invoking the support of the trade union movement as a whole. It was fully justified in referring on 15 October 1976 a recognition issue to ACAS'. Justification in full but not a victory. In July 1978 the union finally called off the strike. There were hardly any strikers left to support, they had mostly given up the strike and found other jobs. The strike cost the union nearly half a million pounds. We made errors of judgment in our tactical and strategic handling of the strike but it was a great comfort to know that two of the most respected judges in the land had found for us on the issues of principle we were pursuing. No other trade union could have given its members more support.

Happily, the 12 years of my union presidency were marked by many successes and much solid achievement. I can only hope that history will be kind to us when it weighs these in the balance against the failure of Grunwick. Early in my presidency I found the union in the Courts defending an entirely different type of action in which victory emerged from defeat. A quite extraordinary situation arose from the desire of SAGA, the Staff Association of the General Accident insurance company, to merge with APEX. Our rivals were ASTMS, led by Clive Jenkins, a man who had plenty of experience in the union take-over field. He did not savour defeat and a complaint was lodged with the TUC that we had breached the Bridlington Agreement under which unions are not allowed to poach each others' members. SAGA members were not affiliated to the TUC and we could see no legal or trade union argument as to why we should not take them into membership. To our surprise, the disputes committee chaired by Joe Gormley, the miners' leader, found against APEX on the grounds that as SAGA was not an affiliated union they were outside the TUC, and so could not be trade unionists. Accordingly, he reasoned that the protection the TUC gives to unions against other unions interfering in a merger did not apply in this case. The disputes committee awarded that APEX must exclude the members of SAGA.

We regarded this as quite ludicrous and our legal advice was that it would never stand up in Court. We were not proposing the recruitment of new members but a transfer of engagements from a non-affiliated organisation to an affiliated union, which was also justified as SAGA had more members than ASTMS. Thus advised, we had to inform the TUC of our position. Len Murray came to see me and argued forcibly that by convention member unions always accepted the decisions of dispute committees. If this was not so the whole procedure would fall into disrepute. We did not want to challenge that principle and after an agitated session the union executive agreed to accept the verdict. As we expected the SAGA executive, who had seen our legal advice, promptly challenged our decision to expel them in the Courts and won. The TUC had to change its rules, a considerable achievement, and in the end the General Accident staff became a section of APEX. This stand cost Roy Grantham his seat on the general council of the TUC, an act of petty vindictiveness. He was not restored until APEX, GMB and NALGO won another campaign to provide an automatic seat on the general council for every union having more than 100,000 members. Once more we had helped to modernise the machinery of the TUC and to provide for proper democratic representation.

Later on we achieved a further amalgamation which has been an outstanding success, namely the 7,500 staff of the Automobile Association, including the patrolmen. By 1989 we were looking for a new home ourselves and found it with the GMB. APEX has become the staff section of the new union taking in some 70,000 staff workers already within the GMB. This restores the membership back to the high level it achieved under my presidency. I was delighted, especially as in John Edmunds, the general secretary, we have one of the most impressive leaders the movement has produced.

These structural matters played only a small part in the work of the union. We were determined to pioneer research and to campaign in new areas which we judged to be in the interests of our own members but which would also raise the whole profile of the union. We had a considerable success. Pension rights and the investment of our members' funds were an early subject for campaigning. In one of my presidential speeches I drew attention to the fact that the pension funds of trade unionists were being invested without consultation, and in ways that could decide the future of British industry. This could actually result in members' pension funds being used to put them out of work!

Job evaluation procedures were another area we pioneered. We published two books on the subject and negotiated more job evaluation agreements with companies than any other union in the country. The rapid advance of technology in the office called for special attention.

The union established a technology committee whose reports were much sought-after and appreciated by employers' organisations. These were used as the basis of special debates which we organised at our annual conference and did much to inform a wider audience than our own members. We took the line that technological change was inevitable and desirable but that changes had to be negotiated with us so that our members might enjoy their share of the benefits. We also drew attention to the health hazards, especially to the eyesight, posture and wrists of operators of word processors and computers. This concern has alerted the public to the dangers.

APEX has a significant women's membership, and it was natural that we should give a special place to their needs and to the issues of equal pay and women's rights. We fought and continue to fight for equal grading for men and women doing equal work. Again, we paid much attention to health issues such as cancer screening and health and safety standards. Throughout its history the union has always enjoyed a major contribution from its women members. So far as I know we are the only union ever to have had a woman president – Helene Walker – and general secretary – Dame Anne Godwin – in office at the same time. They made a formidable team. Helene was a Yorkshirewoman who had settled in Birmingham. She spoke at conference with great force of argument and total command of procedure and of the rule book. Anne Godwin had a brilliant intellect, a sceptical mind and a formidable presence. At the time of the recent amalgamation with the GMB the executive council had four women members serving upon it, two of whom were vice-presidents, all of them elected on their merit.

Probably, the most significant political role of APEX during my term in office was in respect of Europe. No other union can boast such a record. We met the opposition head on and Roy Grantham and I would never waver in our belief in the fundamental importance of British membership of the European Community. We carried our conference with us year after year, the first union so to do, in spite of vigorous left wing opposition. We had to go through all the trauma of discussing food mountains, wine lakes and the absurdities of the common agricultural policy. Usually we would take our membership industry by industry, pointing out the dangers of being left isolated outside Europe. Jobs and investment, we argued, were more important than prices. We moved resolutions at the TUC and the Labour Party Conference, where Roy and I both spoke with great feeling. On the political flank of the movement we sustained our principles by fighting within the Party and not by deserting it, as did other colleagues who had enjoyed great support from APEX for which they did not appear to be over-grateful. When many of them left the Labour Party to form the Social Democratic Party they left the Labour Committee for Europe en bloc. I was pressed into service as its chairman, Roy Grantham became treasurer, Geoffrey Drain of NALGO the vice-chairman, later joined by my former parliamentary colleague Arthur Palmer. With Jim Cattermole as our director we kept the flag flying and now that our European membership is no longer challenged we can enjoy a considerable sense of satisfaction. Justified or not, I view my presidency of APEX in the same light.

MINISTER FOR THE ENVIRONMENT

My duties as Minister of State for the Environment were many and varied. Obeying my own precepts I ensured that all my appointments to the Sports Council, Countryside Commission, Nature Conservancy and the water authorities had a political balance. This approach sometimes landed me in trouble, especially in the appointments of regional water authority chairmen. I insisted upon reappointing Sir William Dugdale to the chair of the Severn–Trent authority and retained other leading Conservatives such as Sir Ralph Carr-Ellison in Northumbria, Sir John Wills in Wessex and Peter Liddell in the north-west, later succeeded by a good Labour local government man, George Mann. I was also able to appoint some first-class Labour men as chairmen: Len Hill in the south-west, Dennis Mathews in Yorkshire, succeeding J. C. Brown, an industrialist of sturdy independence. Over in Anglia, where I had encountered problems, I appointed as chairman Alex Morrison, who had been a most impressive chief executive of the Thames Water Authority. He brought a lifetime's experience into the chairmen's discussions and was also a political independent so far as his public position was concerned.

One of my appointments as a member of the Severn–Trent Water Authority was certainly a political supporter of mine. Edna Sadler has a fine intellect and is a former president of the Students' Union at Cardiff – and she is black. She also has a wonderful sense of humour. During her first meeting on the Severn–Trent her presence must have created a stir and she rang me to tell me, in case I was embarrassed, that she had been followed into the ladies' loo by a Tory lady member and asked how she came to be appointed as the Minister's representative. 'Well, you see ladies, every Napoleon must have his Josephine', was the crushing reply! Lord 'Dick' Nugent, a former Tory Minister, was chairman of the National Water Council. I never had a moment's difficulty in working with him and the water industry certainly has good cause to appreciate his contribution.

The countryside and nature conservancy work in which I became involved was a sheer joy and I regret that I was not able to give more time to it. The protection of otters came up early on, and I was keen to help. I was urged to do so by Philip Wayne, who was my chairman of the Eastern Regional Council for Sport and Recreation. Philip had done excellent pioneering work by establishing the Otter Trust to safeguard this endangered species, and in 1978 I was able to use the provision of the Conservation and Wild Creatures Act 1975 to ensure that the otter had full protection. The Nature Conservancy Council worked with the joint Otter Group and the Society for the Promotion of Nature Conservancy to carry out a specific survey of otters. Their report in 1981 underlined the importance of the steps which I had taken. There was a steep decline in the numbers of the otter population. Evidence of their existence could be found on only 6 per cent of the sites visited in England, 20 per cent in Wales and 73 per cent in Scotland.

In a 1977 statement I drew attention to the need to protect wildlife and safeguard the beauty of the landscape. I went on to demand that we 'facilitate the recreational aims of national parks by opening up paths, drives and trails, or wider areas with suitable picnic areas and other facilities for such activities as fishing, sailing or canoeing'. I was encouraged by the enthusiasm and dedication of my official team which handled countryside matters, led by Alan Leavett. During this time we had two first-class chairmen of the Countryside Commission who approved and co-operated in all the policies I wished to develop. They were Sir John Cripps, son of Stafford Cripps, who was already in the job when I came into office, and Lord 'Michael' Winstanley, a former Liberal MP whom I appointed to succeed John Cripps. They both had the benefit of the tireless and extreme devotion to the cause of Reg Hookway, their director. I had many a brush with him but he could be forgiven all things because of his compelling enthusiasm.

The crisis at Exmoor certainly concerned 'the beauty of the land-scape'. It was drawn to my attention by Guy Somerset, formerly a Birmingham industrialist who had retired to live on Exmoor and who I had appointed to be the deputy chairman of the South-West Council for Sport and Recreation. Guy kept telephoning my office to tell us that a landowner was ploughing up bracken and heather that had been there unspoilt for hundreds of years. Officials from the regional office of my department and from the Ministry of Agriculture went off to see and they reported back that nothing untoward was happening. More calls from Guy Somerset. It was then revealed that the ploughing up was being done on the 'wrong side' of the hill. This turned out to be the fault of the Ministry, who had given a wrong map reference. Finally, we tracked down the offenders to a place called Stowey Allotments. Although I had powers to delay the ploughing up for 48 hours I could not postpone it indefinitely unless compensation terms were negotiated. Worse still, I discovered that ploughing to make land available for food production actually attracted a grant from the Ministry of Agriculture! I took the view that we had a crisis on our hands, our national heritage was being destroyed. The National Farmers' Union and the county landowners proved very helpful. They agreed to co-operate in an enquiry I wanted to set up and to ask their members not to do any more ploughing while the issue was being investigated.

The man to whom I turned to conduct the enquiry was my old friend Lord Porchester, Henry to us all, who had done such splendid work as a foundation member of my original Sports Council. Lord Porchester was now the Queen's racing manager but he agreed to take on the task on condition that he did it as a one-man enquiry. He was not going to be weighed down by any committee. I had sufficient faith in him to agree, but now I had to go to a Cabinet Committee chaired by the Lord President of the Council – Michael Foot – to seek their agreement. There was no difficulty about the purpose of the enquiry, but when we got to the name of Lord Porchester Michael Foot looked at me with a degree of apprehension and said, 'Are you sure about this, he's a bit of a Conservative, isn't he?', to which I could only reply, 'I've been around Whitehall long enough to know that if you want socialism brought about in this place you have to find a good Conservative to carry it out!' My proposal was endorsed. Lord Porchester did a splendid job of work, soon winning over the sceptics, who were certainly not all on the political left. He set up his headquarters on Exmoor at the Porchester Arms, named after his family. I had not realised that he had connections in those parts. In fact, this proved to be an advantage. The findings and recommendations of his report were published in 1978. They were an excellent analysis of the geographical and economic history of Exmoor and of the legitimate but conflicting interests involved between conservation and natural beauty on the one hand and improved agricultural production on the other.

Porchester went for a voluntary solution. He did not believe that it was feasible to solve these problems by any extension of compulsory purchase powers. However, he was adamant that the natural beauty of the moorlands had to be protected. He set out the following objectives: 'to secure for all time the conservation and management of the heathlands and other defined areas of moor and heath of exceptional value within the Exmoor National Park, and to promote the conservation and management of other appropriate areas of moor and heath within the park'.

To achieve these objectives he wanted two maps to be prepared. Map 1 would identify and define all the areas which were predominantly moor or heathland. Map 2 would define those particular tracts of land whose appearance the authority would want to see conserved, so far as is possible, for all time. He went on to say that in his view the heathlands in this proposal extended from Dunkery in the east to Chapman Barrows in the west. The report then praised the gentlemen's agreement approach for protecting these public interests backed up by an adequate system of notification so that Ministries, the Somerset County Council, the NFU and county landowners, as well as all the conservation and recreational interests, would have adequate notice of any intention to plough up or to change the character of the moorlands. 'There should', said Porchester, 'be a strong presumption against reclamation of any moorland shown on Map 2.'

The principal means of achieving all this was to be the Moorland Conservation Order which would in effect be a management agreement. Apart from the control of ploughing and planting it could also deal with ways in which pastures could be improved, fertilisers and chemicals controlled, and fences erected – quite a fascinating concept. Under these proposals the Ministry of Agriculture and its agricultural advisory service (ADAS) would refuse grants to farmers where this was necessary but propose a Moorland Conservation Order as the basis of compensation which would reflect the depreciation in the value of the land. The National Park Authority was recommended to pay management grants as part of conservation grants so that farmers would be encouraged to maintain public access to all these areas of superb beauty and keep them in good order for the nation.

Henry Porchester had fulfilled all my expectations, and I had no difficulty in persuading my colleagues to endorse his recommendations. I am delighted to be told ten years on that it is all working extremely well. But it seems that a new problem has now emerged: there is far too much grazing on the uplands which is seriously damaging the quality of the vegetation. Farmers are paid a sum of money for each animal they graze, an incentive to over-use if ever there was one. I understand that in some cases this amounts to 50 per cent of their income. I intend to return to this subject when I have time, for priorities have to be re-established.

My involvement in the battle to protect and preserve the Ribble estuary in Lancashire was another success story. It involved the Nature Conservancy Council, whose ever-vigilant and resourceful director, Bob Boot, came to seek my assistance in 1978 when the estuary was threatened by development. We had to act with great speed. Bob told me that the Ribble was the second most important bird sanctuary in Europe, home of the pink-footed goose. It was owned by the Scarisbrick Estate who had put it up for sale. A Dutch company wanted to acquire and develop it to grade 1 agricultural standards. There were 5,500 acres of salt marshes and mudflats. Bob Boot and his chairman, Professor Fred Holliday, explained to me how vital it was to preserve this site for the passage and wintering of wildfowl. The marshes also supported a large breeding bird community which would otherwise disappear. I was able to convince my colleagues that we should act with all speed. The owners had accepted an offer of £1.4 million and our attempts to reach a compromise met with no success. I was ready to support a compulsory purchase order if necessary, especially as more than 220 MPs signed a motion calling for the future of the site to be safeguarded.

The West Lancashire District Council then took an excellent initiative under the 1977 Town and Country Planning Act, the effect of which was to prevent development before prior planning permission had been obtained. I visited the site in July 1978 and announced that we would provide funds for the NCC to purchase the whole of the site. This statement was very well received in the House. On my visit to the site two fellow MPs turned up to meet me, Robert Kilroy-Silk, Labour, and Sir Ian Percival, Conservative, who both had constituency interests there. Kilroy may have been there but he was unprepared. He had come without his gumboots so he could not join Ian Percival and myself when we waded out into the mud. No gumboots, no pictures. I have never seen the self-assured Kilroy looking so downcast! Having agreed to fund the purchase it was left to the district valuer to determine the price the NCC could pay and in early January 1979 I was able to announce that the Ribble estuary site had been purchased for the nation at a cost of £1.72 million. Never has public money been better spent and I know that it provides great satisfaction for thousands of people. The NCC has done a splendid job here, and the Ribble has become a model for the integration and conservation of wildfowl. The birds have responded very well. They are staying longer and in greater numbers. In 1979 the numbers of widgeon totalled 4,500 and in 1988 30,000 were counted. Every year I receive a Christmas card from an old friend, George Sharrat, who served on the executive of the National Union of Railwaymen. He moved back to the Ribble and has a cottage over-looking the estuary. George shares his joy with me by taking a photograph of the migrating birds in full flight and makes it the centrepiece of his card. What a delight it is for a former Minister to have an annual reminder that his efforts are still appreciated!

Lead in petrol was a saga that continued throughout my second period of ministerial office when pressure from colleagues in the House persisted. I never had any doubts about the extreme dangers of absorbing lead into the body from any source. In March 1976 I set this out clearly in a speech in the House: 'It is the totality of lead to which we have to have regard. Lead can be consumed in a variety of ways. It can be consumed not only from breathing but from eating and drinking. Food and drink possibly play, in some parts of the country, a greater part in this consumption than the air that we breathe'. I also talked about the danger of lead in toys, pencils, paint, coatings and cosmetics. Apart from the petrol situation I initiated action to replace lead water pipes wherever they were found, which was mainly in the old industrial towns. My Scottish colleagues were also very active about the problem, especially in Glasgow. Aston University did a great deal of research measuring the amount of lead deposits at the kerbside in many busy streets, in school playgrounds and near to 'spaghetti junction', the famous M6 interchange at Birmingham. This work was championed in the House by Julius Silverman, my Birmingham colleague, and it was carried out in association with Birmingham University and the city's environmental health department. We found their work to be more relevant to our problems than the example of Professor Nieldeman from the US, who obtained a good press here. We were also under constant pressure from Bryce Smith, a professor at Reading University, but from our position we were more impressed by the work of a German researcher which seemed to us to be more relevant to the British situation. I was told that there were two problems associated with lowering the lead content of petrol. The first was that to take lead out of petrol would make car engines less efficient. Cars would consume more petrol on their journeys and this would add seriously to the balance of payments problem, an argument strongly advanced by the Department of Trade and Industry and supported by the Treasury. The second argument was that the British motor industry had not produced an engine to run on lead-free or lead-reduced petrol and would need several years' notice in order to do so. This was an argument strongly advanced by the Energy department. My environmental arguments were recognised, even sympathised with, but at best I could get agreement only to proceeding step by step at a snail's pace, reducing the lead content in petrol by minute amounts, what we came to call in my department the 'bacon slicer approach'. This was disappointing for me but an illustration of how an individual Minister has to accept responsibility for the collective decision of his colleagues. My own belief, oft expressed in my department, was that no one had yet demonstrated that any quantity of lead in the human body could be justified in terms of human health.

We had some forceful discussions in cabinet committee and I had to rationalise my concern by reference to the fact that, as inadequate as our programme was turning out to be, we were in fact making some progress! To achieve even this I had to adopt aggressive postures about the terrible dangers to health caused by lead consumption which my colleagues could not deny. The strategy agreed upon was to hold the position of discharges into the atmosphere at the 1971 level and that as the number of cars increased on our roads there would be progressive reductions in the amount of lead in the petrol. The EEC programme was set to be 0.4 grammes of lead per litre on 1 January 1976. In the debate in the House I announced a three-stage reduction for the UK, coming down to 0.5 grammes immediately; 0.45 grammes in 1978 and 0.4 grammes by 1981. We would be five years late in our programme but the cost of even this policy would be £70 million on our balance of payments account. To go straight to the EEC level would cost a further £100 million. However, I was able to report progress on the rest of the dangers, especially on food items and cooking utensils.

The breakthrough for me came when I attended an EEC Environmental Ministers' meeting where Gerhard Baum, the German Minister, who was also the German Minister for Sport, was present. We cooperated with each other to the full. News had reached me that West Germany had met the full onslaught of the oil companies but they had gone all-out for environmental protection and public safety. At one of our ministerial meetings I raised these matters with Baum. He told me that the case of the oil companies was flawed. The efficiency argument did not stand up to close examination, it was insignificant in his experience, and notice should be given to the motor industries to produce engines that could run lead free. He readily agreed to make full facilities available to my officials and I immediately despatched a team under Steve McQuillan, who headed the section in the department responsible for these matters, to work in co-operation with our German colleagues and to report to me on the results of their experience. They came back convinced that the efficiency and economic arguments advanced against removing lead had been greatly overstated. Furthermore, the oil industry was now saying to us that it did not really matter to them, their refineries would produce whatever quality of petrol we required. We had great resistance from industry. There was no sign that our car manufacturers were thinking of producing engines that could run lead free. Armed with our strengthened beliefs and the German experience, plus the positive EEC position, we were able to set a new target. We would come down from 0.4 grammes per litre to 0.15, a very big reduction. This was really a staging post on the way to going lead free, but it was as far as we could possibly go at that time because we had no mass car engines that would allow us to go all the way. It represented significant progress achieved in a difficult economic climate, but with hindsight I think it would have been a better tactic to have announced a date to go lead free at that time and so forced the industry to design their lead-free engines a few years earlier than has proved to be the case.

Yet another aspect of the dangers from lead emerged when Bob Boot reported to me his great concern about the way the swan population was dying from lead poisoning, thought to result from the swallowing of lead shot left on the banks of rivers by anglers or picked up by the swans from the beds of the rivers. This confirmed the observations my wife and I had made on our trips to the theatre at Stratford where we used to delight in watching the swans. In 1979 I authorised Boot to establish a working group to examine the problem and to try to get a solution acceptable to my good friends in the angling community as well as to the conservationists. Peter Tombleson, general secretary of the National Anglers Council, played a very constructive role on the working party. They found that some 250 tons of lead were being discharged into the environment in the form of lead shot – two pieces of shot per foot of river and canal. In an 18-month period 288 swans had been found dead, 40 per cent as the result of lead poisoning, the Avon, the Trent and Thames being the most dangerous rivers. To deal with these disasters a code of practice was recommended to anglers; zones were created where fishing was not allowed until the swan population had recovered and lead shot was to be phased out over a five-year period, with acceptable alternatives to be made available to the anglers. It was a very successful initiative.

My involvement over the whole range of environmental issues was a source of considerable satisfaction for me. I am delighted that these 'green issues' are moving ever more to the forefront of public concern and are indeed potent in our political life. They will not go away, more public money will have to be provided to promote them and all the agencies, especially the Nature Conservancy, the Countryside Commission, the Sports Council, and a whole range of voluntary bodies will have to take on Government, local government, landowners and any others with vested interests who stand in the way of the protection of our national heritage, which we must bequeath to succeeding generations.

Royal parks, dog licences, gypsy settlements, canals, the protection of birds, all had their place in my timetable, as did the ever-present situation in South African sport. This was now aggravated by the Rhodesian UDI and the attempt to smuggle Rhodesian teams such as the Ridgebacks cricket team into the country. I even received a letter of criticism from Joe Lister, the secretary of the Yorkshire County Cricket Club, couched in the strongest terms and protesting against my action to ban the team. I replied in similar vein telling him that I was surprised to find such an illustrious county with such patriotic connections believing that the Government could for one moment give any recognition to citizens from a country held by the highest courts in the land 'to be in revolt against the Crown'! That ended that correspondence.

EBB TIDE

The tide turned for Labour in 1978. The Government was bogged down by two issues and won neither of them. First came Scottish devolution, where the running was made by the Scottish Nationalists. They held a dominant position with our minority Government. We needed their votes and eventually paid the price of having to rely upon them. The second issue was over wages policy and when that collapsed, leading to the awful winter of discontent in 1978–79, we were really done for. The fact that Prime Minister Jim Callaghan and his Cabinet were right, and courageous, cut no ice with the British people, certainly not with the unions. It was a remarkable irony that just as the nation had at first approved of Ted Heath's stand four years earlier but turned against him when the full effects of the miners' strike were felt, so now lightning struck twice. There was great support for incomes policy but when the Government stuck to its guns and both employers and unions deserted us, whipped up by Mrs Thatcher's opposition in the House, the country had no stomach for the fight. The dam was breached by the Ford Motor Company and irresponsible unions with left wing leadership poured through it.

During most of this Parliament we had managed a working relationship with the Liberals with great success, so sustaining our tiny majority, and Michael Foot deserved much credit for this. David Steel, the Liberal leader, had no more wish than we did to see a Conservative government in office and as long as he could he worked closely with us. Ministers regularly consulted Liberal spokesmen to ensure that difficulties were foreseen and potential problems avoided. I had a very happy relationship with Stephen Ross, the Liberal Member for the Isle of Wight, who had responsibility for environment and sports policy. We usually agreed in both areas of policy. When the Liberals withdrew their support in November 1978 it was the beginning of the end. We ought to have had an autumn election – and we might well have won it – but Jim Callaghan would not take the risk. He was supported in this judgment by Michael Foot and by the Chief Whip, Michael Cocks, and almost all the Whips' Office.

The Cabinet was split over the election. The six wise men of the TUC – Alf Allen, David Basnett, Geoffrey Drain, Terry Duffy, Moss Evans and Len Murray – were united in their belief that an early election was desirable and that we could win it. They were all invited to dinner by Jim and Audrey Callaghan and they thought they were being consulted. Actually, the Prime Minister was trying to tell them in coded language that he had decided to soldier on, believing that a few more months to consolidate his improving position would be to our advantage. It turned out to be a disastrous decision but none of us knew it at the time. As a life-long trade unionist myself, believing that politics and economics, and therefore trade unionism, go hand in hand, I could never for one moment believe that the trade unions would behave with such crass stupidity as to desert their best interests and bring about such a reactionary Government as that of Margaret Thatcher. But they did.

The 'winter of discontent' saw us off. It came about because Jim Callaghan wanted to get pay settlements down from the level of around 10 per cent, where they had been throughout the year. He settled on 5 per cent as the norm for 1978–79. The TUC would have none of it, with left wing leadership raising the banner of 'free collective bargaining'. The phrase 'free collective bargaining' is a nonsense. There is no such thing, and the unions knew it, but it became the stick to beat us with.

Conflict became inevitable, although none of us believed it would be conducted with such violence. Five of the six wise men strove honourably to keep the movement united and reasonable and tried to create new working policies, but Moss Evans of the T&GWU and Alan Fisher of NUPE were rampant. Their union executives were in full cry and seemingly nothing would stop them. In a brilliant speech at the Party Conference Michael Foot spelled out the truth: 'If we were to see inflation going upwards – 10 per cent, 15 per cent, 20 per cent – it would certainly not assist the low-paid workers. If you have a Tory government, what sort of wages policy do you think you are going to have? You can have a wages policy imposed by mass unemployment, far worse unemployment than anything we have experienced. That is the Keith Joseph–Thatcher policy!'

Ten years on, with millions unemployed, cuts in the social services, the health service, pensions, education, housing – all the services upon which poorer trade unionists and their families depend – it is terrible to contemplate that Michael Foot's wisdom was rejected by an overwhelming majority. Thank goodness that my own union, APEX, stood firm. Roy Grantham and I fought our battle within the union and carried our conference with us. We were able to deliver our own vote and, for what it is worth, absolve ourselves from the disasters that were bound to follow when the movement chose to destroy the central economic strategy of Jim Callaghan's Government.

Fortified by the irresponsible decisions of the TUC and the Party Conference, Moss Evans, on behalf of his union, lodged claims of up to 30 per cent for the motor workers of Ford's and British Leyland. Not to be outdone, the local authority manuals asked for 40 per cent. The Government's 5 per cent norm, which meant 7 per cent overall in earnings, had no chance. The strike at Ford's was short-lived. Terence Beckett, their managing director, probably on instructions from the US, bought a settlement at 17 per cent. When later on Sir Terence assumed the post of director of the CBI and had the gall to lecture the nation about the need for moderation in wage settlements, all in support of Mrs Thatcher's utopia, I almost died of apoplexy. No Tory spokesman, neither Margaret Thatcher nor anyone else raised a voice of protest. Quite the reverse – they voted in the House to oppose any sanctions being taken against firms who breached the 5 per cent pay policy. When Mrs Thatcher came to office her pay policy totally expressed itself in the restraint of wage settlements for public servants, leaving the discipline of the marketplace, weakened trade unionism and large scale unemployment to set the agenda for the private sector. In a crucial vote the Tories were joined by the Liberals and the Scottish Nationalists and they defeated us by 285 votes to 283. Next day Jim Callaghan asked for a vote of confidence in the Government. The Scottish Nationalists changed sides; they had no wish for an early election. The Government enjoyed a temporary reprieve – we won this time by ten votes – but bigger trouble lay ahead.

This came in the form of transport strikes by lorry drivers, local government strikes, strikes in hospitals and, worst of all, strikes by grave-diggers. Alan Fisher of NUPE would not intervene to get his grave-diggers back to work and David Basnett of the GMBW could not succeed either with his graveyard members in Liverpool, although he tried. They preferred to bury the Labour Government! Never has public opinion been so bitterly expressed against the unions. I was myself, as Minister of State dealing with local government issues, involved in all these disasters. It must be recorded that David Basnett, Geoffrey Drain and Len Murray did their best to find some accommodation with the local authority unions, as did Terry Duffy and Frank Chapple on the industrial front, but all to no avail. Finally, the Scottish Nationalists tabled another vote of confidence. I doubt if they had any expectation of winning it. They were turning the thumbscrews in Scotland but the Tories embraced their motion and, joined by the

Liberals and others, the Government was defeated by 311 votes to 310. A General Election was inescapable. It was held on 3 May 1979.

We lost and departed for the wilderness. In fact, we did better than we could have expected at the polls. We actually polled better than in 1974. I was satisfied with my own result brought about by another fine campaign organised this time by my agent, Reece Thrupp, who had assembled a first-class team. Although I was away a great deal, speaking all over the country, I came back at least every other night to keep an eye on the vigorous campaign. Reece and his team canvassed every house, as we always do in Small Heath. The declared result was: D. Howell (Labour) 17,735; D. J. Savage (Conservative) 6,268; D. Minnis (Liberal) 4,470; M. Caffey (National Front) 490; C. C. Adamson (Social Unity) 349; Majority 11,467.

This represented a swing of 5.4 per cent, almost the national average. Adamson, the Trotskyist candidate, was the son of Sir Campbell Adamson, the director-general of the CBI! Margaret Thatcher moved into Downing Street with a majority of 71 over Labour. The Scottish Nationalists who defeated us to bring about the election went down from 11 seats to 2 and their Liberal allies from 14 to 11. There was some poetic justice in this, but not enough to account for Labour's loss of 38 seats.

It was a sickening blow. In two spells of office amounting to 11 years in all I had thoroughly enjoyed the challenge and believed I had made some solid achievements. At such moments, the only thing to do is to recover from the exhaustion of the campaign and the rigours of the election. Sleep is the great balm. Two days into my slumbers, the telephone rang at my bedside. 'Buckingham Palace here, the Queen desires to take leave of her departing Ministers.' I have never had the sack so eloquently expressed. When I got out of the train at Euston the realisation dawned upon me that there would be no Eric Adams waiting to pick me up. There was nothing for it but to take a taxi. When I gave my destination the driver asked me, 'Outside or inside?' He had never driven his taxi inside the Palace but I told him that as I had not arrived there in one either, it would be a new experience for both of us. During a very gracious chat with the Queen and in response to her enquiry as to how different we were finding things I explained my transport problem. 'How interesting', said Her Majesty, 'and how do you propose to get away?' Her lady-in-waiting quickly advised me not to worry, there was a good taxi calling service at Buckingham Palace! It seemed a civilised conversation with which to take my leave of office.

13

THE OLYMPIC IDEAL

INTERNATIONAL SPORT AND POLITICS

There is a fascination about the Olympic Games which is timeless and universal. Love sport or hate it, the magnificent feats of men and women who extend the boundaries of human achievement are forced upon the consciousness of mankind. They cannot be ignored. These days the wonders of television and radio elicit our interest in advance and compel us to become participants, even from our own sitting-rooms. This compulsion knows no equal in the world. The Seoul Olympic Games of 1988 was beamed worldwide and watched by an audience of hundreds of millions. No political leader and no religious leader can assemble any comparable audience to match that appeal. That is why the influence and the integrity of the Olympic Games are so precious and why the integrity of the Olympic movement has to be a subject of continuous debate and its ethical standards jealously guarded against every assault.

These concepts find a practical expression in the Olympic village even more than on the running track, in the swimming-pool, the sports halls or the fields of sport where competition takes place. For it is in the Olympic village that the youth of the world assembles, to live together, play together and compete together for some five or six weeks during the period of the Games. They do so on terms of total equality, irrespective of all the barriers with which men divide the world. Here they are of no consequence. The Olympic Games takes no heed of the colours of government, ethnic origins, religious beliefs, political prejudices or differences of sex. No other activity in the world can assemble such a truly international gathering dedicated to the pursuit of peace and harmony through healthy competition. That is the massive contribution which sport makes towards international goodwill. That is why, since I first understood its purpose, I have been committed to support and sustain its ideals. This determination has led me into the fiercest battles, but it has also rewarded me with moments of great joy which have been unsurpassed in my own sporting life.

The British contribution to the Olympic movement has been immense. When Baron Pierre de Coubertin, the great idealistic Frenchman who launched the modern era of the Games in Athens in 1896, learned about the way in which Dr Arnold, the great headmaster of Rugby School had applied, for the first time, the development of sport as an essential part of education he was enormously impressed. He became even more enthusiastic when he discovered that in Much Wenlock, Shropshire, a Dr William Penny Brooks had founded his own Olympic Games as part of a community programme to create physical well-being through sporting activity. He then wrote to Dr Brooks in terms which made it clear that these English initiatives had inspired him to start the Games of the modern era. The people of Much Wenlock still hold their Games every year and the unique museum they have built to commemorate the life of Brooks is a fascinating place to visit for all who treasure the Olympic story.

Of course, national pride asserts itself and often ideals are degraded. In an odd sort of way that only serves to underline their importance; the perpetrators of these crimes are demonstrating that Olympic accolades are beyond price. This was evident in Berlin in 1936, the first Games that I remember. The story is well-known. Hitler stormed out when the great American black sprinter, Jesse Owens, won his gold medals. Hitler was seen by millions, many for the first time, for what he really was, a tyrant and a racist. It was sport which removed the mask. Owens evermore represented the true Olympic spirit. I remember discussing all this at home and with my schoolmates, and we all agreed that the character of the person was the real triumph. It was a lesson which has stayed with me all my life. On the fields of sport, the only qualities that matter are the sporting ability of the sportsman or sportswoman and their character as people. Since 1936 that is what the Olympic Games has meant to me.

We must not disregard true national pride in which we all share through the reflected glory of our successes; I do believe, however, that these have got out of hand in recent years, especially with the publication of medal tables of which I thoroughly disapprove. Our admiration should be first for the achievement itself, irrespective of the nationality of the winner; national pride should always be secondary to that. If it is otherwise we are not true internationalists. Immediately after the end of the war my thoughts were concentrated upon these considerations in a quite remarkable way which left a profound impression upon me. A distinguished sporting journalist, Mr Capel Kirby of *Empire News*, came to speak at the Birmingham Referees' Association. He was asked to tell us the most memorable sporting occasion he had witnessed in a long career. His audience was spellbound as he related the great personal sacrifice of Philip Noel-Baker at the Stockholm Olympic Games of 1912, who decided to run a tactical race to ensure that Britain's victory was ensured. Philip was clear favourite to win the gold medal in the 1500 metres, but on the eve of the race he told our second runner, Arnold Stock-Jackson, 'You are going to win the gold tomorrow. I want you to get ahead of me as far as you can, the rest of the field will all be watching me, waiting for me to make my move. By the time that they realise that I am not going to do so you will be too far ahead to be caught'. The plan worked to perfection. Stock-Jackson won the gold. As with all such stories there has to be a happy ending. Philip was later to win a silver medal in the Paris Games of 1920. When I heard this story I was just contemplating entry into political life. As I have already recounted, Philip Noel-Baker first entered my life at the West Birmingham by-election of 1937. Capel Kirby's story confirmed my belief that sport and national pride go hand in hand.

When Clem Attlee formed his Labour Government in 1945 there had to be a place for Philip. He was appointed a Minister of State in the Foreign Office. He was therefore well-placed to add an influential voice when the IOC approached the British Olympic Association with an invitation for Great Britain to host the first post-war Games in 1948, especially as his brief included matters of disarmament. Britain was ravaged by the war, short of food and bomb-scarred, and it was an enormous tribute to us that we were considered to be the one country which could be relied upon to promote the resurgence of the Olympic Games. Cabinet papers now released reveal that doubts were expressed about the wisdom of committing resources to such a project when we faced an acute housing shortage. Another question arose about the availability of petrol, a commodity in very short supply and strictly rationed. Ernest Bevin, the Foreign Secretary, was the decisive voice. 'My foreign policy depends upon speaking to the world, the Olympic Games will be of great assistance to me.' Such were the imaginative concepts of that great man, but who can doubt that the promptings of Philip Noel-Baker were also decisive? The Games came to London. Despite the forebodings and shortages they were acclaimed to be a great success. Wembley proved to be a fine venue for the ceremonies and the athletics. The competitors were housed at Goldsmiths College and all the sports were found venues which proved to be adaptable and suitable for their purpose. Fifty years on from de Coubertin Britain can certainly claim credit for re-establishing the Games of the post-war era.

COUNCIL OF EUROPE SPORTS MINISTERS

My first direct involvement with the International Olympic Committee or with the organisation of the Games came about through the Council of Europe. Walter Winterbottom had become much involved in the official working party of the Council brought together to further European sport. This was known as the Committee for the Development of Sport (CDS). Soon after I had returned to office in 1974 he came to tell me of this new work and of the progress being made. Officials were preparing the ground for new initiatives such as the development which subsequently became Sport for All. They were also concerned about the politicisation of sport and sports administration in the East. Walter immediately secured my interest and my involvement and I agreed to add my weight to the idea that Sports Ministers should meet together just as Foreign Ministers and colleagues from other specialist interests meet. The truth was that after the creation of the EEC the Council of Europe, which contained many more countries, found itself overtaken in terms of political weight but it now emerged as a major and wider-based organisation, certainly as far as sport was concerned. I found that my ministerial experience in sport was considerably greater than that of other colleagues and I was soon regarded as the senior Minister. I presided over some of the initial meetings and found myself chairing a gathering of 23 Ministers for Sport from almost every one of the non-Communist countries of Western Europe, including a representative from the Vatican City, which was a member of the Council.

Very soon I developed a close working alliance with Gerhart Baum, the West German Minister, and various French Ministers who seemed to change office much more often than did either Baum or myself. Eventually Jean-Pierre Soisson took over the French post and he proved to be another good ally. However, at one of our meetings held in Paris with Soisson presiding – by that time we had come round to the practice of inviting the host Minister to preside – we were interrupted when Soisson was called to the telephone and summoned to see the President, Giscard d'Estaing. He left the room, inviting me to occupy the chair, and when he returned later in order to host our reception he was no longer Minister for Sport. He had been promoted to take charge of the forthcoming election campaign. He explained how sad he was to leave sport as he was a mad devotee of Rugby Union and what he wanted more than anything else was an English piece of headgear, a checked cap, such as he had seen at Twickenham. It was my task to express appreciation for his hospitality and this formality took an odd turn when I tore up a newspaper to measure the size of the Minister's head since he did not know his cap size. Immediately after the reception I had to return to London for a crucial vote in Parliament, returning to Paris the following morning. I asked Eric Adams, my driver, to take me to Heathrow via Piccadilly where I called at Simpson's. I explained that I wanted a cap for the French Sports Minister and this was his cap size, producing my piece of newspaper duly marked. It was measured, I made my choice and set off back to Paris. At the closing dinner I produced the cap from under the table and solemnly placed it upon Soisson's head. Everyone was delighted.

By now the Ministers had all become good friends with happy

personal relationships. This was to stand us in very good stead sooner than we expected. UNESCO, the United Nations Educational, Scientific and Cultural Organisation, was already giving some concern to the Western powers, who were mainly financing it, because of its pronounced radical views thought by some countries to be anti-Western. The Americans had threatened withdrawal and on sporting and educational matters were represented by an official of the State Department, Mr Christian A. Chapman, supported by one or two people representing US sports organisations. Roland Martin was the French representative while the UK sent a delegation of officials from Education and from the Ministry of Overseas Development and John Williams from my own Ministry. Peter Lawson of the CCPR alerted me to future problems. These reared their head in Nairobi in 1976 at a conference which stretched out from October to November. Its stated purpose was to discuss physical education and I had therefore agreed that we should be principally represented by members of Her Majesty's Inspectorate of Education. The conference established a committee of some 30 countries to become a 'permanent international sports body' and it adopted a resolution which alarmed Peter Lawson, who telephoned to give me advance warning, following up with a letter and a copy of the draft resolution which had been initiated by the French and supported by many Afro-Asian countries. It authorised the director-general of UNESCO to arrange organisation and funding for Ministers responsible for 'physical education and sport in the education of youth'. That seemed fairly innocent but one of the points in the resolution which called upon the director to draft guidelines for international sporting events was changed to 'analysing the difficulties with the staging of international sports competitions'. Lawson reported his concern that the organisation was to be based on the principle of one vote for each country, many of whom had no international sporting presence. This meant that important decisions would be taken by non-participating nations.

The stage moved to Paris, where the Nairobi resolutions were to be considered. I stayed close to my telephone on day one of the conference and all my fears were realised when I received a report that Cuba had proposed that UNESCO should take over responsibility for the IOC and that this seemed to find favour with Mr M'Bow, the director-general. I was furious at this development and not best pleased that our delegates had not been able to register an immediate objection. It seemed to me to require drastic action. I called Gerhart Baum in Bonn and urged him to be present at UNESCO next day or to be represented. He agreed to come and we fixed an early meeting next morning. My own journey caused some difficulty. I was invited to stay with our ambassador, Sir Nicholas Henderson, and his wife and we fixed a late plane from Stansted. There was some trouble in obtaining permission to land at Paris. It was well past midnight and when we finally touched down we were directed to the furthest part of the airport. It seemed that our special plane was believed to be carrying Idi Amin!

Baum arrived at our breakfast meeting next morning and Soisson sent Roland Martin. Chapman and his advisers from the US State Department were with us and could not have been more supportive. We shortly agreed a common approach and I was to take the lead. Cuba and some other countries soon left me in no doubt that they thought that UNESCO should take over responsibility for the Olympic Games and that a new political and, as they argued, democratically answerable organisation should be created if necessary. I waded in at an early stage making it very clear that we believed that it was a cardinal principle that the IOC should remain independent of governments or politics. We felt so strongly about this that if necessary we would have to consider our membership of UNESCO. We were not going to finance this sort of nonsense nor give it any credence whatsoever. Baum also spoke in strong terms. The battle was over by lunch-time.

Michael Killanin is unique. He is an Irishman who still sits in the House of Lords; in his time he has been a distinguished writer for the *Guardian* newspaper and he has a liberal approach to life as well as a healthy scepticism about his aristocratic heritage. He is a man of great integrity and, as we were to see during the 1980 Moscow confrontation, a person of considerable moral courage. He certainly had an understanding of the emergence of the third world nations in sport and of the damage of doing nothing while sport was increasingly used as a political weapon. His agreement to come and meet us recognised our stand at UNESCO and the battles we were prepared to fight at international level in the interests of free sport. He brought with him Madame Monique Berlioux, herself a French international swimmer, who had a strong and independent mind which she always displayed within the IOC where she was an outstanding secretary-general. She suited Michael Killanin perfectly well for he cherished the traditional role of the English amateur administrator (if he will forgive the expression) who was content for his principal officer to take charge of the 'professionalism' of the administration as well as to be the negotiator on behalf of the IOC with the international governing bodies of sport and with all the member nations of the Olympic movement. It was a most successful partnership while Lord Killanin reigned, but it could not survive the advent of President Samaranch, who wished to change the character of the IOC presidency into one with an executive role.

Our discussions with Lord Killanin got off to a good start since we were able to report to him that, before he joined us, the full committee had agreed as a matter of policy on 'the need to safeguard the independence and integrity of the IOC and the international federations'. Most of the Ministers present wanted to see a great reduction in the use of flags and anthems in international sport. We were also concerned that the size and cost of staging the Olympic Games should continue to be studied and that subjects of mutual interest, such as commercialism and sponsorship, should be matters of future discussions between us. For a first meeting between the IOC president and 23 governments it was a successful gathering. We had discussed some of the most difficult issues of sport and politics and asserted important fundamental principles. Both Lord Killanin and Madame Berlioux expressed themselves well pleased. They were relieved that Western European governments no longer intended to follow a policy of continual inertia while the Warsaw Pact countries, and the regional assemblies of sporting politicians from Africa and elsewhere, met to take decisions which affected the control of world sport. We agreed to resume our discussions in London in 1978. We were fortunate to have two British representatives in post within the Council, George Walker in the sports section and Jack Hanning from the press directorate. They worked in full co-operation with John Noulton, my own private secretary, and Vic Shroot. With Winterbottom in the lead, supported by an enthusiastic British team, our contribution proved decisive.

Professor Nicholaos Nissotis, the Greek adviser, was soon to be invited to join the International Olympic Committee itself, which we welcomed. The considerations which led to people being invited to become members of the IOC were shrouded in mystery but the veil was lifted for me when Lord Killanin spoke to me one day and asked if I would like to be considered. He was well aware that the two British members, Lord Exeter and Lord Luke, were advancing in years and might be soon thinking of retirement. Michael Killanin was keen to reduce the influence of the British peerage within the IOC even though he was part of it himself. He had the same ambition about the inclusion of royalty. He had been giving thought to these matters and believed that he needed someone who could be charged with looking after the interests of the IOC in dealings with Ministers and governments who might have other ideas. I agreed to allow my name to go forward. Killanin's other choice was Charles Palmer, who occupied several important positions in international sport, was chairman of the British Judo Federation and a member of the Sports Council.

When the time came to replace Lord Exeter at Baden-Baden in 1981 Juan Antonio Samaranch had replaced Lord Killanin and Denis Follows had become the chairman of the British Olympic Association. He conducted his negotiations in a very personal manner. He produced a shortlist of five including both Palmer and myself. The other names were Arthur Gold from athletics, Mary Glen-Haig, a long-time member of the Sports Council, and Christopher Davidge, a rowing man. Follows decided to conduct a private poll, the result of which was never disclosed officially, but I understand that I obtained more votes than the other candidates together. However, there were two great difficulties. First of all Denis Follows would not submit one name to the IOC. He told me, 'You are all friends of mine, it would be invidious'. He believed in the old system which the IOC itself was moving away from, that members should be chosen not nominated! I told him that since he had taken a poll he was not called upon to submit any personal nomination, all that was needed was for him to forward the voting figures and to advise the IOC that these represented the preferences of British sport. He never did so. The second obstacle was the opposition within the IOC itself to the idea of having what was considered to be 'a powerful politician' joining their ranks. In the absence of any specific nomination from Follows President Samaranch consulted widely, including Buckingham Palace, but not with Michael Killanin, and in the event Mary Glen-Haig was appointed. Ten years later there is still no member of the IOC who has combined both sporting and political ministerial responsibility. On the other hand, it does have as members Marat Gramov (the USSR Minister for Sport), Franco Carrera (Minister of Tourism in Italy), Jean Claude Gauga (Minister of Tourism for Congo and chairman of the Supreme Council of African Sport), Lamme Kieta (the Mali ambassador to the EEC) and, until he was deposed, Mohammed Mzali, the Prime Minister of Tunis.

When Lord Luke retired, he was replaced by the Princess Royal, an appointment warmly welcomed throughout British sport but one which was achieved in another remarkable manner. Without warning most of his colleagues, Ian Luke interrupted an IOC debate to announce that he was retiring forthwith and with the support of his colleague, Mary Glen-Haig, he was nominating the Princess Royal, whom ex-King Constantine of Greece, an honorary member of the IOC, had found to be willing to stand for office. There was no consultation at all with the BOA, whose chairman, Charles Palmer, was known to have aspirations to the position. I broke the news to him myself in his room upstairs where he was ill in bed. He was dumbfounded. There was no need to adopt such a procedure: there is not a shadow of doubt that the Princess Royal would have been selected if the normal procedures had been adopted. In my opinion she would have been elected unanimously. This resulted in an embarrassment for President Samaranch at his press conference because he was asked by John Rodda of the *Guardian* why a replacement had not been chosen for the Russian member, Andrianov, who had died. Samaranch announced that in their case it was necessary to consult with their national body! A total contradiction of the British procedure. There is no doubt that the IOC were delighted to obtain the membership of the Princess Royal and I am quite sure that she will be a first-class success as an IOC member. Indeed, she has such a knowledge of sport and such a sense of independence that the IOC have probably got more than they bargained for, and that will be good for Olympic sport as well as for British sport.

MOSCOW 1980

The campaign to protect the integrity of the Olympic movement in the Moscow Olympic Games of 1980 was the most epic political battle in which I have ever been engaged. The principle involved was classic, the need for sport to assert its independence from government. Ranged against us were the most powerful political forces in the world, led by the President of the United States of America and the British Prime Minister. The circumstances in which the conflict took place could not have been more dramatic: the invasion of Afghanistan, a sovereign people, by the host nation of the next summer Olympics, the Soviet Union. All of us who rallied to the Olympic cause felt just as passionately as any of our opponents about this outrage. However, we could never agree that military aggression should be confronted by sporting boycotts or that the assembly of the world's finest young people entirely committed to the peaceful pursuit of sport should be destroyed by government policy. We believed the Olympic ideal to be sacred, and beyond the reach of any government. We realised the strength of the forces against us; most of the media opposed us, high emotions were aroused on every side. Yet we won, and it was a famous victory.

The Soviet invasion in late December 1979 took the world by surprise, although the internal situation in Afghanistan had been deteriorating for some time. The first news reached the world by means of a Tass (the Russian news agency) report on 28 December that President Amin, who had himself taken office as Afghanistan President only some three months earlier, had called upon the Soviet Union to provide assistance for his regime, including 'military assistance'. In fact, the Russian airlift of some 85,000 troops had already taken place on 25 and 26 December. With the troops the Russians also flew in a new Prime Minister, Babrak Karmal. The President who invited them in was reported to have been put to death within days of the invasion. By any standards the invasion was a massive show of strength, carried out by the Soviets in text-book fashion. As 90 per cent of the Afghanistan population is Muslim, it was also an enormous gamble. The reaction of the Western world was immediate. President Carter cut short his Christmas holiday and took counsel by telephone with several heads of state and governments including Margaret Thatcher. He also used the telephone hot-line between Washington and Moscow. He publicly described the Soviet actions as 'blatant military interference in the internal affairs of an independent sovereign state'. His difficulty was as previously with the Soviet invasions of Poland, Czechoslovakia and Hungary – how to confront it without going to war. On this occasion he decided that the war should be conducted by international sport, through the boycott or the replacement of the Moscow Olympic Games due in August 1980. Many Western political leaders rallied to his support. Sporting leaders looked on with incomprehension at the proposition that the military alliances of NATO and the Western world were impotent and that our freedoms must be defended by Olympic sport. We had always believed that the Olympic Games represented the assertion of all our freedoms. We could not believe that our governments now wished to sacrifice them.

The Winter Olympic Games of 1980 were about to be held in the United States at Lake Placid, where 37 nations were represented by 1,067 competitors. As required by the Olympic Charter, the US Government had undertaken to admit to their Games all nations participating and that included the Soviet Union. The undertaking was honoured. But the Americans totally failed to appreciate that both the Lake Placid Games and the Moscow Games had been awarded to those cities by vote of the IOC taken on 24 October 1974 and amounted to a binding contract. Before the world arrived in the States in February 1980, the United States began their offensive against the Moscow Olympics without realistic plans for dealing with the Afghanistan crisis on either the military or economic fronts. It is true they delayed the signing of the SALT II agreement on defence limitations and imposed a ban upon grain shipments to the USSR, which was later rescinded when the farmers rebelled. Lord Killanin told in his own memoirs how he received a visit from Mr Lloyd Cutler, the President's special counsel, on 2 February at his home in Dublin, where Cutler made demands on behalf of President Carter that the Moscow Games be either postponed or cancelled. No consultation, no appreciation of the independence of sport from politics, no understanding of the contractual obligations. Never throughout the controversy did the Americans understand that IOC members are elected as individuals, they do not represent their countries and cannot be instructed by anyone. When the United States Olympic Committee, which originally opposed the boycott call, allowed itself to be dictated to by its Government, it was acting against its obligations under the Charter and was fortunate to escape retribution.

Before every Games the IOC holds a session of its committee. Normally, this is opened by the head of state, but in an unprecedented snub to the IOC Carter sent Cyrus Vance, his Secretary of State, who made a blatantly offensive political speech. He insulted all the athletes by suggesting that they were not fit to carry 'the burden of responsibility' for taking their own decisions which 'properly belongs to the leaders of the Olympic movement'. He made it very clear that no US citizens would be in Moscow, a grotesque statement which he quickly retracted when it was pointed out that in that case all the elections to office held by the international federations in Moscow would result in the control of world sport passing into non-Western hands. Vance got so carried away with his polemics that he actually sat down without declaring the session open. That had never happened before. When the Games began a few days later President Carter again reneged upon his responsibilities. This time he sent Vice-President Walter Mondale to represent him. In the presence of some 30 nations, Mondale made another speech which disgusted those present, full of politics, with little sporting content. No one was now in any doubt whatsoever: the Olympic Games was the chosen weapon of war with which the Russian invasion was to be confronted. This was underlined by another ludicrous gesture of President Carter's following a victory by the United States ice hockey team over the Russians in the semi-final. He promptly invited them all down to the White House to celebrate, but exposed himself to ridicule by forgetting, until reminded, to invite Eric Heiden, who had won five gold medals at these Games, nor did he invite any of the other members of the US Olympic team. The US national euphoria was so great it was becoming a substitute for the military conflict the US could not undertake.

The Lake Placid Games over, the Americans turned the heat upon the rest of the world. They did so with the wholehearted support of Margaret Thatcher and some other Western leaders, notably Malcolm Fraser, the Prime Minister of Australia. We were soon left in no doubt that the British Government intended to pressurise sport in every conceivable way to join the boycott. As soon as Denis Follows, the chairman of the British Olympic Association, returned from Lake Placid he called upon me to outline the serious situation facing the BOA, which relied heavily for its funds upon industry and commerce. The moment the Prime Minister had called for a British boycott the chairman of the British appeal, who was also chairman of Barclays Bank, resigned and made it clear that no appeal to send our team to Moscow was going out over his name, a fact that was soon made public. Follows was very pessimistic. 'No funds – no Olympics' was his comment. He then asked me whether I could get the trade unions to provide the funds which were now to be denied them by industry. I was attracted by the challenge but not totally surprised. Follows had previously been the secretary of BALPA, the airline pilots' trade union, and represented them at the TUC. He knew my position as president of APEX. More importantly, he understood the essential generous impulse of genuine trade unionists and instinctively realised that they would respond to ensure that athletes who had spent four years in total dedication and training, depriving themselves of all the creature comforts which the rest of us enjoy, so that they could represent their country in sport at its highest pinnacle, must not be deprived of their right to do so by the threats of politicians. Fortunately, I had just taken on Patrick Cheney as my researcher and adviser. Pat Cheney has a good grounding in politics, trade unionism and sport. We agreed to undertake the task and to co-operate with the BOA's appeal secretary, George Nicholson, in launching our new appeal. I did this from the platform of the APEX annual conference and received total support from the TUC. Every union in the country was written to, articles supplied for their journals, and the appeal was commended by most of the principal union leaders, headed by Len Murray, the

TUC general secretary. The response was magnificent. The trade union movement helped to make it possible for Great Britain to honour its commitment to the Olympic Games. The financial position assured, we were able to turn our attention to the political assault being conducted with great ferocity against the British Olympic movement.

Denis Follows was subjected to intense personal criticism, even abuse. He was very much the gentleman, refusing to reply in kind, overwhelmed by the forces ranged against him and deeply distressed by the attacks made against him and the BOA. The Prime Minister, having assured President Carter of her full support, took to the battlefield with typical wholehearted determination. She has in full measure the quality I admire most in politics, perseverance. She never lets up. An opponent has to be attacked on all fronts and by all means. This is her strength; it is also her weakness, since she allows her judgment and her personal generosity, which she has in good measure, to be overwhelmed by the aggression which eventually emerges from her perseverance. Follows had to be sustained. Pat Cheney and I got together a small group to work out the strategy and the tactics of our opposition to the Government. We met regularly, usually once or twice a week in my flat. Among those who joined us were Dick Palmer, the BOA secretary, journalists Frank Taylor of the *Mirror*, Pat Besford of the *Telegraph*, Nelson Fairley of the Press Association and two colleagues from the BBC and Reuters News Agency, who did not want to be named. We decided to meet the opposition head on. The *Telegraph* was the truest blue of newspapers, and favoured the boycott, but in February they agreed to take an article from me responding to their own attack on British participation in the Games. When it appeared they very fairly gave it considerable prominence. Our counter-attack was launched. I was able to expand our case at some length, pointing out the political importance of sport. 'This has suddenly been discovered and some governments care not whether they destroy international sport in the process of confronting the outrageous Russian aggression in Afghanistan. Sportsmen should care. Sport is one of the opportunities for men to draw together and express pride in the excellence of their personal achievements and in their association with their fellow men and women. It is as absurd to suggest that participation in this summer's Olympics is an endorsement of Russian policy as it is to suggest that our presence at Lake Placid automatically endorses American policy'.

I went on to recall that the 23 Ministers for Sport of the Council of Europe, under my chairmanship, had recently addressed themselves to the problem of national Olympic committees who acted as agents of their governments. We had come together to oppose a move within UNESCO which was gathering considerable pace and which originated from France and some Afro-Asian countries, to enable UNESCO to assume responsibility for the Olympic Games. In doing so we had had the full support of the US Government. 'Such a hard won victory must not be surrendered lightly.' An example of the irrational behaviour of the US Government was at hand for me to cite. President Carter had allowed a US boxing team to proceed to Moscow for a boxing tournament at the very moment he was advising their Olympic committee to boycott the Moscow Olympic Games. When I questioned this with one of his envoys I was told that the US boxers had a contract to fulfill and it had been decided that this must be honoured. I replied 'That is exactly what Lord Killanin says about the Moscow Olympics'.

I was able to turn my fire upon the British Government and its position on trade with Russia, which my committee had already agreed to be the weakness of the Prime Minister's position. A reply to a parliamentary question admitted that Britain was providing lower interest rates for capital goods to Russia by means of export credits than were available to British industry. 'The Government has decided that our trade with Russia will continue as normal.' As I had judged, with many sports people this proved to be a decisive argument. I underlined its importance: 'Governments are telling sport that it should not be participating in Moscow at a time when they are financing the capital re-equipment of Russian industry through which such exercises as Afghanistan are more efficiently facilitated. Sport should not tolerate such double-talk'. Turning to the consequences for sport of any boycott, I predicted that if half the world did not go to Moscow in 1980 then the other half would not go to Los Angeles in 1984 and the world championships of 40 or more sports would not escape the consequences. Finally, I concluded my argument by revealing that when I was Minister for Sport I had once told my Russian counterpart that the reason why I supported the decision to award the Olympic Games to Moscow was that Moscow would never be the same again. The influence of 25,000 sportsmen and women expressing their freedom in that city would be one of the most significant events of our time. I believed that sportsmen would appreciate that truth and had a duty to sustain it against all opposition. My decision to set out both the philosophical and the sporting case for going to Moscow proved to be well justified. President Carter and Margaret Thatcher had to be taken on if we were to get British competitors to the starting line. The administrators of British sport, overwhelmingly conservative in outlook, began to stiffen their resistance and to show their independence. Their response to my call became much more articulate and more emphatic as the controversy unfolded. We decided that every statement of Government had to be contested in Parliament and in the media. I submitted articles to all the quality and most of the tabloid press which were published by newspapers totally opposed to our view. It did them great credit. We also bombarded newspapers with letters, dealing point by point with everything of importance as it emerged. Our campaign was total.

Increasingly, the nation was divided on the issue. Families differed, friends differed, sportsmen and women differed and so did journalists. My long-time friend Peter Wilson, principal sporting journalist of the *Daily Mirror* and champion of many radical causes in his column, came out forcibly against competing in the Games. The *Mirror* generously allowed me to reply. I returned to my theme that 'the Olympics is the highest expression of man's freedom and liberty and it is a disgraceful fact that it is sportsmen alone who are being asked to confront the military might of the Soviet Union'. I also amplified the issue of growing trade with the Russians declaring that 'trade is to be encouraged, new power stations to be built, new chemical plants erected, electronic factories designed, all for Russia and paid for out of export credit guarantees provided by Britain'. By this time – March – the Government had refused facilities for any civil servants to represent their country in Moscow. I could only describe that decision as 'humbug'. The press war we were conducting proved to be vital in our campaign; we had to bolster the morale of British sports administrators. Pat Cheney did an excellent job in keeping in touch with them, encouraging them to go public with their views and to put to their committees the issue of principle not usually much thought about by governing bodies of sport. Meanwhile, the Government moved from one petty action to another, each one of which we had to publicise as part of our campaign. Early on we had greeted with disbelief the decision to penalise civil servants and members of the armed forces who might be selected to compete. I described in the *Times* how this 'assault that is now being made daily upon our Olympic sportsmen and women is quite sickening', saying that 'there is a great deal of political thuggery going on which brings no credit to the Government. Some of this behaviour bears close resemblance to the very type of intimidation which all of us condemn when it is applied to minorities and dissidents in the East'. Geoff Capes, our shot-putter, who was a policeman firmly stated that he would quit the force if necessary and Sue Reece, a DHSS officer in Birmingham, had to call in her union, the Society of Civil and Public Servants, in order to support her intention to go to Moscow. 'Nothing is going to stand in my way', she declared. 'I want my union to call me out on strike so that I can claim strike pay!' Lorna Booth, our hurdler, told the story of her dedication, training six days a week, year after year, in preparation for her once-in-a-lifetime chance of an Olympic medal. The meanness of the Government's response provided us with great opportunities to counter-attack. We publicised and responded to every move. After the decision to frustrate the civil servants and armed forces by banning them from enjoying special leave facilities came the announcement by Douglas Hurd, the Foreign Office Minister, that the embassy official in Moscow assigned to be our special Olympic envoy was being withdrawn. Our modern pentathlon team depended upon its members drawn from the armed forces but they were forbidden to take part under any circumstances, effectively ruling that sport out of the Games. Meanest of all was the announcement that the collections of money which had been made by our servicemen out of their very small amounts of pocket money as donations to the Olympic appeal could not be handed over to the BOA. I thought that was an outrage and pointed out that this was not Government money, it belonged to the men and women of the forces who had made a voluntary donation. It amounted to theft to prevent them paying it over to the organisation to which it had been donated. The Government soon reversed that decision.

The parliamentary battle was fierce and long. It started in January 1980 and continued right on until our team left for Moscow in the summer. In February the Prime Minister published in *Hansard* the text of a letter she had sent to Sir Denis Follows. It stated that 'British athletes have the same rights and the same responsibilities towards freedom and its maintenance as every citizen of the United Kingdom ... for British athletes to take part in the Games in Moscow this summer would be for them to seem to condone an international crime'. It concluded by asking the BOA to accept the advice of the Government in this matter. Tam Dalyell was able to take up the contradiction inherent in this approach to sport with the Government's position on trade and industry. 'What is the justification', he asked Hector Munro, our hapless Minister for Sport, 'for allowing the Moscow branch of the Chase Manhattan Bank to continue its commercial operations, allowing the EEC to sell butter to the Russians and keeping an ambassador in Moscow while saying to the athletes "you cannot go"?' The Minister replied that Tam was totally misguided, to which Tam responded as he so often does, with one word – 'humbug'. I followed up by asserting that 'it is intolerable to expect Seb Coe and other distinguished athletes to confront the Russian military might when ICI has just announced the opening of a new office in Moscow and another Minister has made clear that export guarantees with Russia will continue. Is it not disgraceful to discriminate against sport in this way?' Hector Munro replied: 'We have taken many steps against the Soviet Union in trade and technology', but he did not tell the House what they were. The stage was set for a unique parliamentary occasion, a debate upon sport initiated by the Government. It took place on 17 March when the Lord Privy Seal, Sir Ian Gilmour, moved the motion 'That this House condemns the Soviet invasion of Afghanistan and believes that Great Britain should not take part in the Olympic Games in Moscow'.

Ian Gilmour's political case was that this was the first occasion since the war when the Soviet combat forces had been used outside the Warsaw Pact area. We needed to take measures to convince the Soviet Union that it had misjudged the firmness of Western response. He made much of the US grain ban and announced that we would not be renewing our especially generous credit terms contained in the Anglo-Soviet credit agreement. He went on to cite the cancellation of the visit of the Red Army Choir to this country and of the English Chamber

Orchestra to the USSR as good examples which sport should follow. He was in difficulties over the continuance of normal trading relationships: 'We are not advocating the severance of all contacts in political, sporting, cultural or scientific fields ... nor advocating the severance of non-strategic capital goods'. Terence Higgins, the Tory MP for Worthing and himself a distinguished international athlete, intervened to ask if export credits were not still available 'to enable the Russians to buy our exports at a lower rate of interest than that at which British industry can invest'? He concluded that some of these exports might well go to help the Russian war effort.

Gilmour said the Government appreciated the sacrifices and dedication of our athletes in order to arrive in Moscow in peak condition. He announced therefore that the first efforts would be 'to get the Games moved from Moscow'. At that moment the Minister for State, Douglas Hurd, was in Geneva 'with a group from like-minded countries examining the possibilities of enabling sportsmen to compete against each other in conditions similar to those of the Olympics but without the moral conflict attached to attending the Moscow Games'. He concluded by telling the House that in Russia 'all activity is political', and that 'if our athletic bodies wish to give such a victory to the Soviet Union, so be it'. It was strong stuff, soon to be backed up by further moves from Carter and Mrs Thatcher to provide funds for an alternative Olympic Games. This was a major mistake on two counts. No sensible governing body of sport is going to allow governments to organise international sporting competitions, and no such sporting events could be held without the sanction of the international governing bodies of sport – 26 of them – who actually organise the Olympic events, and they had already stated their firm intention to go ahead with the Games in Moscow. I looked up at the collection of British athletes sitting in the Gallery, all wearing their British team blazers. They were a fine collection of sportsmen and women, assembled by Pat Cheney and Dick Palmer. They were obviously greeting Ian Gilmour's offer of an alternative Olympics with sheer disbelief.

Peter Shore opened for us, describing Gilmour's speech as 'unhappy' and regretting the fact that the Prime Minister had not opened the debate, but he was soon challenging my own opinions. 'There has always been a strong opinion in this country that international sport and international politics should be kept apart. I suspect that is the dominating opinion of sportsmen themselves who are concerned with pitting their skills and strengths against those of competing sportsmen. They are hardly concerned with the political systems under which they and their competitors live, or with the external policies that their governments pursue. I understand that point of view but I do not share it.' This was terrible stuff for me to have to listen to. It was not true. Many sportsmen and sportswomen get closer to the evils of the world by competing abroad than do many stay-at-home politicians. They serve the cause of peace by their example. It was a sad moment for me.

He supported our argument about double standards, drawing attention to the 72 Conservative Members now opposing the Games who had supported the British Lions tour of South Africa and he moved on into a more general criticism of the Prime Minister for moving her ground from attacking Denis Follows and the BOA to attacking the athletes personally. Peter's views were dominated by his reference to the sounds of national anthems and the starter's pistol in Moscow being drowned by the noise of gunfire in the villages and plains of Afghanistan. He clearly thought we ought not to go to Moscow but he also believed that the Government had botched the job and accepted that the BOA would be going. It was a fascinating debate. Geoffrey Rippon made a powerful speech totally opposing any cultural or sporting links at this time; so did Sir Frederick Bennett (Torbay) and Jill Knight (Birmingham Edgbaston). Other Tories showed considerable unease. Nicholas Winterton (Macclesfield) said he would have had no difficulties voting for the Government had it proposed a total boycott of trade, commerce, cultural and political activities; Eldon Griffiths (Bury St Edmunds), a former Minister for Sport, thought that Gilmour's speech was far from convincing. He did disclose, as a 'member of the smallest trade union in the House – Ministers for Sport' – of which at that time there were only three – that although he and I were speaking in the debate 'the present Minister is not even being allowed to speak on his own subject', which was a deplorable situation to which I also drew attention. Terence Higgins and Sir Hugh Fraser (Stafford) both had reservations about using sport as a political weapon. From the Liberal benches Clement Freud (Isle of Ely) was totally supportive of our case, as were Eric Heffer (Walton) and Tam Dalyell (West Lothian) but other speeches were quite hostile. My own Parliamentary Private Secretary, Michael McGuire (Ince), quite properly used the free vote provided on our side of the House to vote for the Government motion though deprecating the lack of a free vote on the Conservative benches; so did Jim Wellbeloved (Erith and Crayford). David Ennals (Norwich North) vigorously supported the United Nations' condemnation of the Russian . invasion but just as vigorously supported the rights of our athletes. Many other speakers had turned the debate into a great House of Commons occasion.

I proposed to use my 30 minutes to tell the House what sport had to say, because that aspect had been lacking in our debate thus far. I had to meet head-on the argument that politics could not be divorced from sport, with which view I had always agreed, but which was now seen to be a new-found conviction for many Members. This is totally different from saying, as the Government was now doing, that sport should be used as a political weapon. I set out what I called, 'the calendar of misery and shame, even extending now to an offer by the Irish Republic to give us diplomatic representations if we wish to have them. The Director of Public Prosecution might well consider the theft or fraud of our defence Ministers, who were refusing to allow money collected by our armed forces and their wives to be handed over to the Olympic appeal, and the refusal of the army authorities to allow Jim Fox, the gold medallist in the pentathlon, to appear on television must be condemned, even if it was consistent with the Government's decision to relegate the Minister, Hector Munro, to the substitutes' bench and not to allow him to say one word in this debate.'

Turning to the Geneva talks, which were about promoting alternative Games, I informed the House that I had the full authority of 18 international governing bodies to state that under no circumstances would they authorise such an event, which meant in practice that no national teams could take part. I had also discovered that only two weeks before the US decathlon team had been competing in Leningrad, how had they got there? Finally, and inevitably, to the question of trade: 'Only last week Guest, Keen and Nettlefold signed a £50 million contract at the Leipzig Fair, defended by the responsible Minister on the grounds that "the Prime Minister has always made it clear that we are still prepared to trade on a mutually beneficial basis with the Soviet Union". Sportsmen regard that as double standards'. When the Minister, Cecil Parkinson, intervened to defend trade but not sporting links I countered by describing that as a Marxist view concerned only about materialism. There were other interests to defend as well as trade; sport and personal relationships were among them. I concluded by quoting Polonius: 'Give every man thine ear, but few thy voice'. Our amendment sought to assert that right for Olympic sportsmen and sportswomen. It had been a difficult – even dangerous – speech to make given the near-hysteria in certain quarters, but I was satisfied that the case for our athletes wishing to compete in Moscow had been sensibly deployed.

The final speech for the Government was entrusted to the Secretary of State for the Environment, Michael Heseltine. He said not one word about Hector Munro, his junior Minister responsible for sport, not being allowed to participate, nor did he reply to very much of my own speech although he started by contrasting my speech with that of Peter Shore. He was soon into the 'trade war', as I was now calling it, but he only made the confusion worse by telling us that although our Government would do its best to prevent any more subsidised ship-ments of wheat, barley and bulk butter to the USSR, the European Commission 'recently decided to consider again tenders for the sub-sidised sale of surplus butter, but we will continue to oppose any sales involving subsidy', which seemed to suggest that if the Russians paid full price for feeding their army that would be all right. The House became restive. Heseltine got into further trouble with his colleague Terence Higgins by saying that we could not unilaterally change the rates of interest for export as 'the only benefit I can see would be to our competitors overseas . . . to take export orders which otherwise would flow to British factories'. Higgins intervened, saying that if the Government were to say 'we are not prepared to go on subsidising exports which can be used to increase Russia's military might and adventurism, then our athletes might be persuaded'. No such assurance was forthcoming. Instead, Heseltine put the responsibility firmly upon the athletes alone. 'We are asking the athletes, in this unique contrast of the Olympic Games and Afghanistan, to play a role which only they can play in the circumstances. They alone are involved in a particular event, the significance of which makes it a weapon out of all accord with anything else that is on offer to the Western world'. That damaging admission swept away any lingering doubts among our supporters. The athletes alone were the chosen weapon with which to confront the Russian invasion. We lost the vote by 305 to 188, but as I had indicated in my own speech, we would have no hesitation in advising the BOA to ignore this expression of opinion obtained on a whipped vote and loading everything on to the athletes.

Our strategy committee had no hesitation in endorsing that view. The 'trade war' was now the dominating argument. We decided to step it up. Pat Cheney was asked to research all the relevant statistics. He unearthed a piece of dynamite. A House of Commons librarian was able to make an immediate check on the computer of the Department of Trade and told us that in the first quarter of the year, at the very time when the Government was exerting maximum pressure on our athletes, British exports to the USSR rose by 63 per cent. That information together with the GKN announcement and the projected ICI trade deal really settled the matter. There was a sea change in the atmosphere in favour of our Olympic athletes participating in the Games. The Government's tactics now became quite intolerable. One after another, governing bodies were summoned to see Ministers; the swimmers went to meet Lord Carrington, the Foreign Secretary, and others to see the Minister for Sport. We used all our resources to counter these tactics. When it was thought that the secretary of the Amateur Swimming Association was being enticed by senior Ministers I rang up their president, Alf Turner, and discussed the vital sporting issues at stake. The press had been briefed by the Government information machine to expect the ASA to announce their withdrawal when they next met. A large contingent of London press gathered outside their Loughborough headquarters and waited for the secretary to emerge. When he did so, it was to announce that the swimmers would be going to Moscow to compete in the Olympics. He then disappeared back through the door in record time without taking any questions.

Colin Moynihan played a valiant role. His sport, rowing, was in favour of the boycott. Colin rallied his boat race crew and led a counter-attack within the sport leading to a reversal of the decision. Seb Coe, who had expressed a doubt as to whether he ought to participate in the Games, changed his mind when these genuine misgivings were used in Parliament by the Prime Minister and held up as an example to other athletes. He did not want to be used as a lever to influence the decision of his colleagues. In April the indefatigable Tam Dalyell raised the subject again in an adjournment debate, resting much of his case upon a statement by Chris Brasher, a former gold medallist himself, reminding us all that in 1956, during the Suez crisis when Britain was the invader, the Olympic Games were successfully held in Melbourne. My own office at Westminster and my flat at Dolphin Square were manned as if they were battle headquarters but it was all worthwhile as well as exciting. Calls were coming in from all over the world. We had an hilarious call from Les Martin, the chairman of the Australian Olympic Committee, telling us how President Carter's international pressure was being applied. Les kept a pub in Melbourne. One day at about 3.00 am he was awakened by the arrival of a large black chauffeured car and told it had come to drive him all the way to Canberra to meet the Prime Minister, Malcolm Fraser. Les told them that they would have to wait until he was ready, shut the door and went back to bed. The car was still there hours later. When Fraser wrote to the Australian Olympic Committee they simply passed on his letter to the I O C.

The United States Olympic Committee, originally in favour of competing, changed its mind under intense pressure from President Carter. But within months of their doing so, the pressure of the US farmers caused Carter to resume shipments of grain to Russia. New Zealand left the decision to each sporting federation but the pressure was tremendous. Prince Philip was put in a great dilemma; he was president of the International Equestrian Federation and obviously he could not go to Moscow, but he did help with the drafting of a suitable text supporting the holding of the Games. Tommy Keller, the president of the combined International Federations of Sport announced this fact at a press conference. Ian Wooldridge of the *Daily Mail* followed this up and with the support of his sports editor, Tom Clarke, wrote up the story. It was mutilated in the newspaper's office and another story appeared saying that Buckingham Palace denied any involvement by Prince Philip. Since only Wooldridge had written the story and his story had got no further than the first edition, this really was quite remarkable. Lord Killanin says that Wooldridge and Clarke came very close to resigning. The West German Government behaved in a quite disgraceful manner. Their National Olympic Committee were due to meet in Dusseldorf and they were given a reception the night before by the Head of State, President Kustens. When they arrived for their meeting next day they found their privacy invaded. The press were present and the whole of their proceedings were televised live – intimidation by television at the behest of government!

The arrival in London of Lloyd Cutler, ambassador extraordinaire to President Carter, was an event to be greeted with wonder. Here was the man who had travelled the world conveying the message 'they shall not go'. Not the troops, not the ships, not the planes but just the Olympians. He had argued governments into acquiescence, affronted sportsmen, intellectually seduced some and browbeaten others who defied his message, and now he was left with the British. We had to be brought into line. The invitation to meet him was impressively delivered to me personally by the US ambassador. The meeting was to take place in his own private office. It turned out that before coming to Grosvenor Square Cutler had met a small group, including Roger Bannister, at the ambassador's residence. As soon as he arrived the ambassador withdrew and left us to our private conversation. Within minutes it was obvious that Cutler knew little about sport and less about international sport. He started with a round-up of those countries he confidently predicted would not be going to Moscow. The Games would be a disaster, the President recognised that this would be a cruel blow to athletes who had trained for four years and the United States would provide finance to promote alternative events. I replied by asserting the unique importance of the Olympic movement. It was irreplaceable, nothing would compensate athletes for removing their rights to be true Olympians. It was as though he believed the Olympic Games was a commodity to be bought and sold on the money markets of the world. I explained my own belief that the Olympic Games uniquely expressed a sense of internationalism which transcended the national interests of the host nation, which is why it has to provide undertakings that every member nation in good standing with the IOC must be admitted, irrespective of the relationships between those countries and the country staging the Games. In Moscow such a situation had arisen over the position of Israel, which I for one had written to Lord Killanin about, and he had taken it up strongly with the Government of the USSR when it appeared that there might be some discrimination. In the event Lord Killanin received the assurances he had requested and they were honoured. Mr Cutler did not seem able to comprehend this situation and he had no reply to my argument that the United States itself had benefited from this position at Lake Placid. The IOC would not have tolerated any demonstration by any competing nation against the foreign policy of the US during the course of those Olympics.

Lloyd Cutler took up a new line of approach. 'I want to discover your breaking point', he told me. 'Would you call off the Games if the Russians invaded Austria or Yugoslavia? What do you think is acceptable?' I replied that no Russian invasion was acceptable to me but these were hypothetical questions in the context of the 1980 Olympiad. As far as Afghanistan was concerned, I could never agree that sportsmen alone should be expected to confront the Soviets in such a situation. The conversation was clearly getting nowhere. Cutler rose to take his leave, telling me that he had not met those arguments before. As he reached the door he told me that he was returning to his President, did I have any message for him? The only thought I could express was that 'this country is governed by Magna Carta not Jimmy Carter'.

As we approached the summer the Government was playing the numbers game. Douglas Hurd announced that 38 governments had now indicated disapproval of their athletes competing at Moscow. This was a reply to a question from Eldon Griffiths. I responded next day by asking Hector Munro, the Sports Minister, why he had not consulted the Sports Council about the arrangements and financing of the events which the Government were encouraging as an alternative to the Olympic Games and why he had not consulted the Central Council of Physical Recreation? The Minister replied: 'The Sports Council is aware that arrangements for compensating events are still very tentative', and in a follow-up question I asked, 'When does he expect to answer questions about the administration and statutory basis of the provision of funds for these alternative events?'. The Minister replied that the Government's contribution towards the financing of these events, should they take place, would not be met from the Sports Council's current grant-in-aid. Additional funds would be made available. The Sports Council chairman, Dickie Jeeps, had agreed that the Council would act as 'a vehicle for channelling these additional funds to the relevant bodies'. As we predicted, all this turned out to be an exercise in self-delusion by the Government, who stubbornly refused to believe that not a single international governing body of sport was going to sanction any such alternative games. When the United States and the EEC reversed their decision banning the shipment of grain to the USSR I asked the Prime Minister if she would reconsider her policy regarding the Olympic boycott or her subsequent advice to British athletes. She curtly told me, 'No. Nothing has happened to cause us to alter the advice we have given to the British athletes'. As late as July, one month before the Games, the Minister for Sport was confirming that he had met the governing bodies still intending to participate in the Games and he was hopeful that at least some of them or their competitors would think again. In a rather bitter exchange Mr Garel-Jones (Watford) complained that his socialist local authority had decided to give a donation of £500 to the Olympic appeal. No doubt this was in response to another initiative in which I had played a part at the request of the BOA. We desperately needed more funds for the BOA appeal if we were going to get our team to Moscow so we wrote to all local authorities who might support us, overwhelmingly Labour. Doncaster gave a wonderful lead and in all this appeal raised over £64,000. The gift of £1,000 from Hackney was actually challenged in the Courts, but Hackney's action was upheld and councils who had athletes chosen for Moscow rallied to help. Munro told Garel-Jones that he thought it astonishing that 'socialist-controlled councils are prepared to give large sums of money to the Olympic appeal'.

Tam Dalyell, as usual, was short and to the point. 'Like it or not, the athletes are going to Moscow, do Ministers wish them well?' The Minister said he was not going to dodge that one . . . he warmly applauded 'the efforts of superb quality last night by Coe and Ovett', a reference to a pre-Olympic athletics meeting, but added, 'I do not wish any of our athletes to be in Moscow this month'. He knew then that the Government had largely lost the battle. Great Britain had 307 official representatives in Moscow: 229 were competitors and 78 team officials. The sports which chose not to compete were: equestrianism, yachting, hockey (field) and shooting. The hockey side did not qualify for their event. We won five gold, seven silver and nine bronze medals. Our gold medals were won by Alan Wells (100 metres), Steve Ovett (800 metres), Seb Coe (1500 metres), Daley Thompson (decathlon) and Duncan Goodhew (men's 100 metres breaststroke). They all won on merit, and in my judgment the track and field men would certainly have done so against any competition. Duncan Goodhew, who had spent years training and competing in the States, might well have won against a full turn-out. In any event an athlete can only beat those who turn up to compete. No one can ask for more. Their names are rightly recorded in the history books. Those who stayed away or were prevented from taking part are never remembered – 'they fly forgotten as a dream dies at the opening day'. In all, 81 nations competed, more than half the number eligible. Lord Killanin could measure his disappointment over the boycott against the fact that he and his colleagues had saved the Olympic movement from extinction and made it certain that in spite of any deplorable retaliation four years hence in Los Angeles, those Games would also take place. The fact that both Moscow and Los Angeles proved to be fine examples of the fellowship of sport in action was a matter of the greatest satisfaction for me. It had all been so worthwhile.

Immediately before the Games took place I received several visits from the Soviet ambassador and other officials inviting me to be a guest of his Government. I was very appreciative but I declined after giving the matter careful thought. I would have loved to have been there but I too had been subjected to much hostility. I did not want anyone to say that I had played my part in the fight to get the British team to Moscow in order to enjoy the luxury of a free trip for myself. Vanity, no doubt, but that was my view. These refusals brought a telephone call in the middle of the night from the Kremlin itself repeating the invitation. I was touched but I would not change my decision. However, when the Soviet embassy approached Pat Cheney yet again with another personal invitation for me, Pat suggested that I would be best pleased if they offered free transport to and from Moscow for the British team and this they did. It was an enormous help. When Lord Killanin left for Moscow he wrote me a personal letter, which I treasure, telling me: 'I cannot leave the country without expressing my warm appreciation for all that you have done to support the Olympic movement'. It was reward enough for me, and typical of Michael Killanin's warm generosity, but I was overwhelmed when I received a cable from Monique Berlioux telling me that the IOC Congress had awarded me the Olympic Order silver medal, their highest award. It is an honour that I value next only to my membership of the Privy Council.

14

THE BIRMINGHAM OLYMPIC BID

THE CONCEPT

It was Sir Denis Follows who first talked to me about the possibility of getting the Olympic Games back to Britain, to London, in fact. Follows had become chairman of the British Olympic Association after the death of Lord Rupert Neville. Neville's long period of office had been well ordered and friendly, but certainly not adventurous. I doubt if he would have taken on the Government over the right to compete in Moscow in 1980, although he would have wished to do so. His position as secretary to Prince Philip would have inhibited the level of public commitment Follows showed. Denis Follows wanted to strike out in new directions and the attraction of hosting the Games was a natural expression of this ambition. When we discussed these dreams both he and I believed that London was the only runner. Wembley would be revamped to provide for the ceremonies and the athletics, Crystal Palace National Sports Centre had a swimming pool which would require vast investment to double and improve the spectator accommodation and improve warm-up facilities, but it was feasible. The cycling velodrome could be built there or in a London park and the Olympic Village could be developed in north London and sold off after the Games. It was an imaginative dream. I agreed to discuss it with Prime Minister Jim Callaghan early in 1979, and Jim agreed that I could include a commitment to support a British bid with financial assistance in the sports programme which I was to draw up for Labour's 1979 election manifesto. The Tory victory disposed of the commitment to provide any funds, if not the proposal itself.

When Sir Denis Follows died he was succeeded by vice-chairman Charles Palmer, who automatically assumed the chairmanship. Palmer took up Follows' ambition to enter a British bid, encouraged by the considerable commercial success of the 1984 Los Angeles Games. By 1985 the BOA had gone public with an invitation to any city to make its interest known. London was an obvious candidate, and the Lord Mayor put together a competent team of advisers drawn from both the city and from sport, laced with sporting journalists such as John Rodda of the *Guardian*, who had considerable knowledge of the Olympic movement. Manchester was also an early aspirant. The two cities made all the early running and attracted a great deal of publicity, Manchester using Pat Besford, the *Daily Telegraph*'s veteran swimming correspondent, the doyenne of sports journalists. Manchester's successful publicity aroused great interest in Birmingham. It was soon patently obvious to most of the leading members of the Birmingham City Council that Manchester could not be allowed to make an Olympic bid without challenge from Birmingham. Birmingham asked the BOA to extend the deadline for the submission of bids and when this was granted set about putting together a creditable proposal.

Councillor Ken Barton, the deputy leader of the Birmingham City Council and a former chairman of Leisure Services committee, and his successor, Councillor Bryan Bird, provided the initiative from the Labour benches and they were joined by a former Conservative chairman, Councillor Clare Fancote. These three members carried their colleagues with them but the inspiration for creating what was described as a 'Midlands-based Olympics' came from Jimmy Munn, the council's director of Recreation, a man respected throughout the country for his imaginative and pioneering role in sport and recreation. When Birmingham sought to make that appointment they had asked for my advice and that of the current Minister for Sport, Neil Macfarlane. We both recommended Jimmy. The original proposal was to base the Midlands Olympics on the facilities already available. In March 1985 Jimmy Munn was in touch with all the chief executives concerned and prepared the way for Ken Barton to invite the leaders of the relevant councils to discuss the proposals at a meeting in Birmingham. It certainly was an interesting package. Birmingham had in 1983 commissioned a feasibility study on the development of a new international stadium at the NEC which could stage the athletics as well as the opening and closing ceremonies; Coventry's international swimming pool could be brought up to Olympic standard; rowing and canoeing could take place at Holme Pierrepont in Nottinghamshire; the cycle track at Leicester was due for modernisation; all the indoor events could be held at Birmingham's NEC; shooting at Wolverhampton and the Olympic villages would be provided by various university campuses. The meeting was sufficiently encouraged to arrange a further examination of all these possibilities in the presence of Dick Palmer, the general secretary of the BOA, at Holme Pierrepont in mid-April.

At this time I was myself rather sceptical about such a bid and I expressed my doubts in public. Los Angeles had been very successful financially, largely due to an enormous television contribution and to some spectacular sponsorships, but the distances to be travelled and the traffic congestion had been a source of much criticism. In any case,

I was well aware of the fact that the Olympic Charter required the Games to be promoted and largely staged in one city, and my view was that it was unlikely that we should again see selected by the IOC any bid that spread out across a wide geographical area. The exceptions to this rule were for the rowing and yachting events. When Dick Palmer attended the Holme Pierrepont meeting he gave precisely the same advice to Jimmy Munn and his fellow officers. The BOA would be unlikely to support the bid as now proposed but they would welcome a more coherent Birmingham submission. The Birmingham councillors agreed and Munn was charged with the urgent task of creating the mark two proposals. His April report relied upon two major factors. First, Birmingham is at the centre of the nation's infrastructure, motorways and railways all meet there and the airport is near. Secondly, in Los Angeles the television contract had been worth $230 million, while in Seoul in 1988 it would increase to some $700 million. A Birmingham bid was feasible. The city agreed and allocated a sum of £110,000 to put it together. The firm of Ove Arup was appointed consultants. Ernest Irwin, their Midlands director, and John Harvey and his colleagues provided inspired leadership, calling in Emlyn Jones, the former director of the Sports Council, to provide specialist advice. Hill Samuel advised on funding and Saatchi and Saatchi handled marketing, promotion and sponsorship. Ove Arup, Jimmy Munn and their colleagues did a superb job in an amazingly short time. They jettisoned half-baked ideas and botched-up proposals and went all-out for a coherent package of first-class facilities that would excite the imagination of the BOA and could be sold to the world with confidence.

The centrepiece of this strategy was to be a new 80,000-seater Olympic stadium on the National Exhibition Centre site at Solihull, immediately next door to the exhibition halls, which would house the basketball, boxing, fencing, handball, judo, table tennis, volleyball, weight-lifting and wrestling. After the Games, the stadium would be roofed over and become a further hall for the NEC – the largest indoor hall in Europe and the UK's first superbowl. Next to the Olympic stadium would be the Olympic village, built to house 14,000 athletes and officials on a 105-acre site. The great beauty of this plan was that the land for both the Olympic stadium and the village already belonged to Birmingham City Council. So for 80 per cent of the Olympic events the athletes could walk from their village to the main stadium for athletics or to the NEC complex for nine other sports. It was indeed 'Olympic City', as we came to call it, and at its doors was the whole motorway system of Great Britain, the Birmingham International station and the Birmingham International Airport. Teams could fly in, clear their accreditation and security and be installed in their own mini village well within the hour. A unique feature of the village was the proposal for many smaller villages, separate villages for the very large teams, all linked together by the social, medical and community buildings. We planned to provide hundreds of bicycles for the athletes to pick up and drop down at their own convenience as well as electrically driven transport; walking would be easy too. Each of the NEC halls would house some 12 to 15,000 spectators who would be deposited at the gates by plane, train or car – 200,000 people could be watching the Olympic competitions in Olympic City, and there was no doubting the ability of the NEC to cater for them, since this is the scale of the numbers it already entertains for the Motor Show, the largest of all British exhibitions.

It was a brilliant and breathtaking concept. Almost all the other sports would be within the immediate vicinity of our Olympic City. At Stoneleigh, only half an hour away at the British Equestrian head-quarters and Stoneleigh Abbey, home of Lord Leigh, were first-class facilities which could house the equestrian, archery and modern pentathlon competitions. Originally, it was also planned to hold the shooting events here, but when we learned that Wolverhampton was the preferred site of the British Shooting Federation for their national shooting centre that proposal was incorporated into the plan – the site could be reached from the main village in some 40 minutes. At Perry Park, where Birmingham's present Alexander Stadium is located, not more than ten miles away from the main stadium, we would stage the hockey tournament. Gymnastics would be one of the major competitions and it was allocated to the Arena Hall at the NEC. Inevitably, rowing and canoeing would be staged at Holme Pierrepont, 40 miles away but with motorway from door to door. The Edgbaston Priory Club is already established as Birmingham's premier tennis club and stages international competitions, so there was no difficulty in upgrading the facilities. Football could be played at Villa Park and at the four other major grounds in the West Midlands. Inevitably, yachting had to be allocated to a coastal town and the Royal Yachting Association chose Weymouth, which not only has some of the finest sailing water in Europe but is a natural amphitheatre: spectators would have an unprecedented view of Olympic events from the clifftops. Weymouth also has a first-class holiday camp, ideal for a yachting village. Jimmy Munn and his Ove Arup team were left to find stadia for cycling and swimming. Britain as well as Birmingham needed a national facility for both of these sports, and Birmingham would provide them. The Leisure Services committee had already developed a strategy for swimming provision which rationalised existing pools and included a facility designed to international specifications. An Olympic swimming complex would cost £20 million. The cycling velodrome would cost £6 million, but this had long been a priority for the Sports Council as there is no such velodrome in the whole country. Staging the Olympic Games in Birmingham was no longer just a dream, it could be a reality.

When Jimmy Munn brought these plans to me all my doubts disappeared, I was overwhelmed. The Olympic movement had never before seen such a compact and practical complex capable of being realised. A Birmingham Olympic Games would be a successful Games, of that I was now convinced. Jimmy Munn had called not only to show me the results of the feasibility study and to get my opinion, he was also anxious to involve me in the campaign to secure the British nomination. It was going to be a fierce competition with enormous media coverage and Jimmy had advised his chairman and colleagues that I was the person who should be invited to lead the bid, advice that was acted upon by Ken Barton. I met the committee and agreed to take on the presidency of the Birmingham Olympic committee having first explained that they should consider the matter very carefully, for I could be a difficult person when faced with an overriding objective and, furthermore, I firmly believed that in campaigns such as this there had to be one clear and unmistakable figurehead. I had one more proviso: The city must be united politically in its determination to proceed with the project. Of course there would be some dissidents on both sides, but I had suffered in a previous attempt to secure the Commonwealth Games when a change of control in the city council meant that a bid that was going well was suddenly abandoned. There must be no risk of that with an Olympic bid. With these considerations explained, understood and accepted we set about our campaign with confidence.

We had barely eight weeks to get our plans on to paper, to cost them and to lodge our submission with the BOA. It was a period of great creativity accompanied by skilful marketing and astute politics. When I arrived I identified four subject headings which I believed to be crucial. These were the financial viability of the proposal; the security operation, which must be watertight; the athletes' village, which had to capture the imagination; and the selling of the whole project to the 32 voting members of the British Olympic Association. Ove Arup had a first-class economic adviser, Mark Bostock, who was fully supported by his colleagues from Hill Samuel. They were enthusiastic: the Birmingham bid would succeed because no other competing bid had such a low capital cost. We already had the eight halls of the NEC, a capital value of about £300 million. Our £20 million swimming centre would fall naturally to the recreation and community department of the city, which had intended to build it anyway as part of their development programme. The bungalows in our village were demountable, and could be sold off after the Games. Bostock and his team fed it all into the computers again and again. We already knew that we had Government support for our bid only if we could demonstrate a profit. The economists were satisfied that we could go to the BOA and forecast a profit. We put the figure at £200 million minimum. We would do more, we could propose how we would distribute it.

I had my own ideas about this which were agreed by the Birmingham organising committee. One third of the money would provide sports facilities in Birmingham and the other authorities supporting us, Solihull, Nottinghamshire, Weymouth and Wolverhampton. One third would be allocated to the BOA as a trust fund for the development of British Olympic talent, and one third would be used at the discretion of the IOC, probably through their solidarity programme, for the development of Olympic sport in third world countries. We would avoid the unseemly situation witnessed over the profits made at Los Angeles when the IOC failed to secure anything for use outside the USA. We approached the West Midlands Police Force to get their advice about a security plan. Geoffrey Dear, their Chief Constable, was tremendously supportive and practical in his response. He allocated to us, almost exclusively, Chief Superintendent Graham Trevis, head of the Special Branch. They realised the size of their task: 88 IOC members and 12,000 competitors from more than 150 countries, were to be brought together to live in one village for a period of six weeks or more and to compete together with the whole world looking on. They never hesitated to give me every support and encouragement and they produced a plan which won the admiration of the BOA and the world.

The athletes' village had to be special. Earlier thinking about building a new great estate and selling off the houses afterwards was soon jettisoned as being impractical. None of the builders approached by Ove Arup wanted to be involved. They all told us that the market simply would not take many thousands of houses for sale at the same time. Jimmy Munn and Ernest Irwin had an inspiration. We would build a temporary village of factory-manufactured bungalows which could afterwards be disposed of around the country to a variety of different interests, principally the leisure industry. Terrapin of Banbury agreed to co-operate and produced a bungalow which they erected at the NEC. It was a winner with everyone.

THE BOA DECISION

The campaign to win votes was fascinating. It was obvious to me, Emlyn Jones and to Patrick Cheney in my own office that the key was to get the 32 members of the BOA to Birmingham to show them the site, give them a presentation and generate their enthusiasm well before we got to the Café Royal in London on 12 July 1985, the day of decision. In addition to the BOA members, we had to win over the national officers of the various sports who would be participating in the Games. The plan succeeded beyond all our imagination. Almost all the BOA members came to Birmingham over a period of four weeks. We had no doubt they were impressed. We had to deliver our submission to the BOA two weeks before the day of reckoning and it had to be good. It was superb. The city council's principal promotions officer, Peter Mearns, and his colleague Ron Argyle, principal graphics officer (who was another tremendous find, indefatigable and irrepressible), produced literature of outstanding design. They were also able to include the model of the stadium from the earlier feasibility study that had been undertaken by Ove Arup. It was breathtaking. Together with the high standard of display material it was to make a great impact on our world travels.

When we arrived at the Café Royal we could not have been more confident. We believed we had 22 votes for our bid, but the national press was writing us off. *The Times* and the *Telegraph* were for Manchester and the *Guardian* for London. Under a banner headline 'Why the BOA should vote for Manchester in 1996', David Miller of *The Times* told his readers that IOC members would not be anxious to go to either Birmingham or Manchester. Manchester would have a main stadium with a sliding roof which would be used by Manchester City FC. He advised the BOA to ignore 1992 and set their sights on 1996. John Rodda told *Guardian* readers that 'the only choice is London'. He concluded that 'the Olympic movement is in need of revitalisation which only the sporting heritage and history of Britain and London can provide'. That was a jaundiced view if ever I heard one. Our presentation team made an excellent showing. Councillors Ken Barton and Clare Fancote emphasised the political will of a united city council; Jimmy Munn outlined our proposals with typical flair and commitment; Paul Sabin, our city treasurer, covered the financial strategy, while Emlyn Jones set the bid within an IOC context. I summarised each contribution within a coherent philosophy of the role of sport in society, both in the national interest and for the general community benefit. It proved to be a winning formula. London polled two votes, Manchester five and Birmingham 25. Birmingham was now an international city. We had achieved our first great objective, but I knew more than most that we had not just one mountain ahead of us but a whole range. And we had only 16 months to climb it.

Our success took Birmingham by storm. Nothing in my experience can be compared to it. Morale everywhere was sky high. In the schools, the shops, the offices, the factories, among all our people, the response was amazing, and it was to last throughout our international campaign. So great was the enthusiasm that it caused me much anxiety. The weight of responsibility was considerable. This is a feeling known to every parliamentary candidate at election time, when one carries on one's shoulders the hopes and aspirations of all one's faithful supporters. This time it was much greater – the whole city was willing us on. We faced a year of constant endeavour, total commitment and confident assertion. The whole team responded to the challenge.

Within days we had enlarged our campaign team and were attracting sponsorship and financial support. This was to be our biggest headache. The city lent their surplus office accommodation but it was not sufficient. My brother-in-law, William Willson, chairman of the Birmingham Building Society, came forward with an offer of two floors above their central premises which proved to be a tremendous asset. CSS, a sports sponsorship agency with which I have a consultancy, was taken on independently by the appropriate committee of the council to lead the search for sponsors and finance. They negotiated with

British Telecom to fund the cost of a London office which was not as successful as I had hoped, although this was in no way the fault of Emlyn Jones and Don Antony, both of whom were assigned to work from there. CSS obtained a valuable sponsorship from Austin Rover, who put cars at our disposal. Some £10,000 came from British Airways to move our team around the world and to fly in visiting members of the IOC, and another £10,000 from Trusthouse Forte for hotel accommodation. We launched our Birmingham and West Midlands appeal to industry and commerce, headed by Sir Adrian Cadbury of the CBI and Frank Graves, president of the Chamber of Commerce. It produced £350,000, which I considered to be very satisfactory in view of the recession in British manufacturing industry. The highlight of Birmingham's commitment to our campaign was a magnificently organised dinner masterminded by Ken Purnell and graced by the presence of Princess Anne. More than 1,000 people gathered at the Metropole Hotel to raise £35,000. We were supported by an excellent turn-out of gold medallists who joined us at a two-tier top table, something I had never previously seen but it looked remarkably impressive.

The City of London was our greatest disappointment. We approached them through the chairman of Lloyds Bank, which is the city council bank and which has its origins in Birmingham. The appeal produced only £35,000, which was quite disgraceful – one more sign that the City cares little for life north of London. Our merchandising operation in Birmingham – T-shirts, pens, ties and all the rest – sold out as quickly as we could obtain them, thanks to the work of Tony O'Brien, seconded to us by Royal Insurance, and Tony Freer of Lloyds Bank, who was responsible for fund-raising. To co-ordinate all disciplines and to act as his deputy Jimmy Munn brought in Richard Caldicott, a senior area manager within his own department with outstanding experience of sport politics and the workings of the governing bodies of sport. Tony Rickard, who had experience with the Rotary International conference so successfully staged by Birmingham, joined the team as office manager, while Ian Mackenzie from the chief executive's department was allocated responsibility for all travel arrangements for IOC members and incoming visitors. Press and media interest was proving to be enormous, and I wanted my own man at headquarters. My experience of ministerial press arrangements was that it is useless to rely upon help from one central office with a multiplicity of differing responsibilities. We were extremely fortunate to get the *Birmingham Post and Mail* group to lend us the services of their chief sports writer and deputy editor, Leon Hickman. Our headquarters team was completed by Jim Sadler, previously the regional director of the West Midlands Sports Council, who took charge of special projects, assisted by Charles Taylor, the athletics coach, and others who volunteered their services. We assembled the whole team in the course of a couple of weeks. None of us had any experience of conducting such an international campaign but everyone performed magnificently.

Ken Barton chaired the Olympic committee of the city council to whom we were all responsible. We met regularly and soon produced a budget of £1.5 million, our projection of the cost of our 12-month campaign. Birmingham had committed itself to provide £750,000 of this sum. In the final three months of the campaign the councillors and Jimmy Munn secured wonderful contributions from our neighbouring local authorities – £150,000 from Coventry, £100,000 from Solihull, £150,000 from Wolverhampton, £150,000 from Sandwell. Solihull, in which authority area the NEC is located, as were the village and Olympic stadium, were invited to nominate a member to our committee and their representative, Councillor Richard Lewis, was a tower of strength. I used to say that if the Birmingham Olympic bid never achieved anything else it got Birmingham and Solihull talking to each other for the first time, and a real spirit of co-operation developed between the two authorities.

We were able to concentrate on the other two items of cardinal importance. First of these was to satisfy HM Government that a Birmingham Olympics would make the profits we forecast. Right from the start the Government had made it plain that no Government money would be provided. The Prime Minister had made up her mind, and I accepted the fact even though my council colleagues Barton and Bird refused to do so. Like them, I found it difficult to believe that a British government would provide no funds to attract the finest sports event in the world – Olympic, European or Commonwealth – but I knew the Prime Minister better than they did. If these were to be the rules of the game then we had to accept them, and since I believed that we certainly would make a profit I had no worry on that score. I doubt very much whether any other city in the country could do so. We had the halls and the infrastructure, the key essentials. Convincing the Government that our figures would stand up proved to be a considerable task. Early on we invited Arthur Young & Co. to advise us. One of their economists, Rick Parry, who had experience with the Los Angeles Games Office, worked with Mark Bostock and Paul Sabin, the city treasurer, and his assistant, David Lewis, to put our projections through the most rigorous examination. In fact they stood the test of four separate surveys – those of HM Treasury, the City Treasurer, Arthur Young and Ove Arup. It was only then that they were accepted. The Birmingham Olympic Games would cost £500 million to stage. Assuming pessimistic income forecasts from television coverage – something under £300 million (now reduced in the light of experience in Seoul) – we could predict a profit of up to £50 million. It was only when these projections were accepted that Margaret Thatcher authorised her Secretary of State for the Environment, Kenneth Baker, to sign the letter guaranteeing the Birmingham bid to the IOC and also guaranteed the entry into Britain of all representatives of the 160 nations likely to take part in the Games, an essential requirement. That letter was the necessary symbol of support that Birmingham had to have from the Government. It was a great disappointment to us that the Prime Minister did not sign it herself. Some elements of the media based many of their criticisms of Birmingham upon that fact. The Prime Minister *did* go as far as to host a reception in honour of our bid at Lancaster House, but that was disregarded by the critics. Other competing cities took with them to Lausanne, where the IOC decision was to be made, members of royal families and Prime Ministers. We had only a letter signed by a Minister who had never been heard of in the world of sport.

Birmingham did, however, enjoy the support of some Government funds which had been allocated to us by the Sports Council. John Smith, its chairman, was always encouraging as was John Wheatley, their director. The Sports Council made a contribution of £250,000 towards the bid and also offered a grant towards the swimming pool and velodrome due to be built if our bid was successful. John Smith even joined our organising committee. This was a matter of considerable satisfaction to me for we had long been personal friends. I believe the manner in which he presides over Liverpool FC to be one of the keys of its continuing success. Tom Caulcott, the city's chief executive, and Paul Sabin were very concerned about the possibility of some unforeseen disaster affecting the Olympics. Here we met with more success in our negotiations with the Department of the Environment. These were handled by David Lewis and Jimmy Munn. At that stage the support of Tom Caulcott, who knew the department well from his long service there in the finance section, was invaluable. It was put to the Government that they really must underwrite our bid in case of disaster. Their initial response was that Birmingham should insure against this and Lewis responded by saying that Birmingham would insure against everything that could be insured against; however, apart from earthquakes, there were such potential disasters as boycotts – as the Olympic movement had already experienced – and international tension, wars and political crises of one sort or another which could affect the finances of the Olympics and would be completely outside the control of Birmingham. The team argued that allowing for the capital items Birmingham would provide in its own programme, the city could stand a loss of some £100 million, but we needed to be assured that a loss above that figure would be underwritten. We were delighted and frankly surprised when the Government agreed to this. It was a significant decision for us both in terms of the morale of our campaign and as an indication of Government endorsement.

PLANNING THE CAMPAIGN

With security and financial viability taken care of I was able to concentrate on the international campaign. It was to be totally absorbing and completely exhausting. In 12 months we had to make contact with each of the 88 members of the IOC, tell our story and hope to gain their support. My feet hardly touched the ground. Patrick Cheney and I worked out most of the strategy while Jimmy and his senior management team of Richard Callicot and Ian Mackenzie co-ordinated the head office operation and provided the necessary mechanics. We divided the IOC membership into their regional groupings and raised a file on each individual member so that we knew of their interests and requirements.

Having analysed them from every conceivable point of view we began to plan our visits. It was a complicated job. We first considered the regional assemblies of the Olympic movement. We would take a full team, offer an invitation to a Birmingham lunch or dinner and lobby members as individuals. Our presentation material was first-class – the video we showed on our stand and our model of the Olympic complex were much admired. Our literature was also good. I was keen to stage our receptions in the British style, with seating plans and members of our team assigned to host specific guests. This contrasted with the general free-for-all jamboree offered by our competitors and seemed to be appreciated. It was seen as a typical piece of British organisation although I ran into trouble in Seoul when I placed the Russian Minister of Sport, Marat Gramov, on the top table as a mark of ministerial respect – no doubt I was carried away by my own ministerial experience. Apart from the top table all the IOC members were seated in strict order of seniority as required by Olympic protocol. This upset Robert Helmick, the new US member, who complained, 'I see you prefer the company of your Soviet friends to that of the Americans'. I replied that I had not been aware that the US had a Minister for Sport present and that he was on table 44 because that was his order of protocol. I am afraid that lost us his vote. We could not get him to visit us in Birmingham even though we sent him an open-ended ticket. That was a pity because getting the IOC members to come to the city was the central objective of our strategy. We knew that we could only get our arguments across and our concept fully appreciated if we walked the course with each individual member.

First priority in our campaigning had to be the major IOC events beginning with its annual session. Then followed the regional or continental assemblies. On each of these occasions there would be an exhibition in which Birmingham would need to take a stand to receive these delegates and to demonstrate the details of our bid. Our early enquiries, confirmed by the two British IOC members, Lord Luke and Mary Glen-Haig, suggested that each candidate city would be expected to host a reception not only for the IOC members but also to include the International Federations of Sport representatives, the press and other organisations who would be present in an official capacity. Calgary and Seoul, the cities hosting the next Winter and Summer Games, would be specially important. We discussed all this in the organising committee and came to the conclusion that if such exhibitions and receptions were expected then Birmingham must be seen at its best. We would host the IOC with style, but not extravagantly. Our exhibition stand would be designed to show the central theme of our 'Birmingham' philosophy and its practical realisation. None of the other bidding cities, either for the Summer or Winter Games, had stands which so clearly demonstrated their detailed proposals. Indeed, we were told over and over again by many people that our model was the only one they thought to be relevant to the bidding process rather than offering a general display of the attractions of the city itself. Peter Mearns, Ron Argyle and their teams, together with the professional companies involved, did a first-class job. There was one other matter we had to consider: the delicate question of gifts. We took advice and discovered that it was the invariable practice to present gifts to members of the IOC on these occasions as well as when they visited the city. We decided that we would follow this custom, but that we would do so modestly, expressing our friendship and respect. We planned the diary of our campaign on these principles and around the major dates of IOC sessions.

We identified these as Lisbon in October 1985, where the IOC executive board was to meet; Seoul in South Korea, where two visits would be necessary, one in April 1986 when the IOC executive would again be in session and a second in September for the Asian Games, to which up to 20 IOC members could be expected. We also planned to be in Bahrain in December 1985 for the Asian assembly of the Olympic movement and in the same month to travel on to Ethiopia for the African assembly. All our other international visits and all our invitations to IOC members to come to Birmingham would be organised around this main programme. We immediately ran into difficulties at our first appearance in Lisbon. Our splendid model had to be driven across the Pyrenees into Spain and then on to Portugal. Customs delayed and delayed, and dark broodings about the Spaniards not wishing to give any help to rivals of Barcelona were hard to banish from the mind. Sir Geoffrey Howe, the Foreign Secretary, had already sent out a message to all our overseas embassies around the world that every practical assistance was to be provided for Birmingham's bid. It proved to be of enormous value to us throughout the entire year and a half of our campaign. The ambassador in Lisbon could not have been more helpful. The model was released from customs and, accompanied by an armed guard, arrived in Lisbon in the nick of time. Ron Argyle and his team worked all night to erect it and get the electronics working, and as it stood on our stand it looked so good it was the centrepiece of the whole show, not just of the Birmingham stand. The embassy were equally helpful in making the arrangements for the Birmingham lunch which the IOC members all enjoyed immensely.

The Lisbon experience convinced me that my own time was going to be totally absorbed by the campaign and I discussed the matter with my constituency party and my agent, Mike Sharpe. They were very supportive. We agreed that I would give priority to my constituency case work and my surgeries unless I was abroad and leave much of the routine political work to colleagues. My immediate constituency neighbours, Roy Hattersley and Terry Davis, another Labour front-bencher, were outstandingly helpful, but all my Birmingham colleagues agreed to help out wherever possible. Terry handled all my emergency or urgent immigration cases when I was overseas. Every one of my fellow Members agreed that I was promoting the interests of Birmingham and that essentially that was a priority for all of us. I never felt a moment's concern about any of these matters for the next 18 months as I travelled the world presenting Birmingham's case.

We began with a visit to Lausanne at the end of July to pay a courtesy call upon President Samaranch and Raymond Gafner, his chief of staff. Raymond was unfailingly courteous and helpful to us throughout our campaign. When we first met he told me that he had been to Sutton Coldfield for the World Scout Jamboree and it rained torrentially the whole time. I was able to assure him that I was now in charge of the weather and he need have no worries on that account! In September we were in Barcelona as I had to deliver a lecture on international sport. We thought it would be a good idea to take the Birmingham case into enemy territory. We did so to good effect, becoming good friends with our rivals. My feet hardly touched the ground in October. The European Olympic assembly was held in Budapest, and as our large scale model could not be transported there we took a small exhibition. Nonetheless that visit was one of the most useful. It introduced Birmingham to all the Europeans as a serious contender alongside Amsterdam, Barcelona, Belgrade and Paris. Pat Cheney and I proceeded directly to Vienna to meet Phillip von Schoeller, a very fine horseman who was thrilled by the possibility of the Olympic Equestrian events being held at Stoneleigh. From Vienna it was on to Lisbon and then straight to Amsterdam because the GAIFS (the general assembly of the international federations of all the sports, summer and winter) met there for its annual conference. We arrived to find ourselves in the centre of a hostile demonstration against the proposal to hold the Olympic Games in Amsterdam. Hundreds of protesters gathered outside our hotel and throughout the weekend they periodically burst in through the police cordon and shouted slogans until they were evicted. When the Mayor of Amsterdam entertained us to a trip on the beautiful canals the demonstrators stood on the bridges and bombarded us with flour bombs. One scored a direct hit on Frank Taylor, the president of the world's sporting press organisation and a Birmingham supporter. We were very sad for our Dutch colleagues who were genuine sports people trying to do a job for their country.

After Lisbon came Seoul, where all the IOC members were in session and where many of the international federations of sport were in attendance. So were all the bidding cities. We were invited to exhibit in the grounds of the hotel headquarters. It was a major undertaking to host a reception for all these people, plus the world's media, but it had to be done. We were interested in what sort of stands our competitors would mount. Seoul was to give us the first real indications of the plans each city would be submitting to the IOC. We were delighted with the comparisons. Birmingham's stand here, as elsewhere, actually represented the proposals upon which our submission would be based. Belgrade had an exhibit where visitors were called upon to release various balls, which rolled down with a message written on them making a point in favour of their city. Paris had a stylish model with statuettes and a ready invitation to enter into their sanctum where generous hospitality was provided. Brisbane provided an ambitious tableau at the entrance to their main reception – guests were welcomed by their Mayor, Sally Anne Atkinson, after negotiating a water feature with stepping stones. Unfortunately, the water took its own route. We were certainly amused, but very wet. Barcelona had a competent if not exciting stand, but made up for this at the final exhibition in Lausanne, where the floor of their exhibit was made of marble. This created an enormous impression. All the talk was about what would happen to the floor after the IOC session, but when Barcelona won the vote the floor served its purpose as hundreds joined in the champagne party, and it came through the ordeal with flying colours! Amsterdam provided a small exhibition at the front of their stand which led to a bar at the rear.

During the Seoul exhibitions the Dutch approached me with their view that all this money ought not to be spent in this way. Would we join them in submitting to the IOC a proposal that there should be no more exhibitions or receptions until we got to Lausanne for the final session? I readily agreed to this plan, but only if they secured the support of the other bidding cities. I was already acutely aware of the fact that the process of competition was getting out of hand both in terms of scale and finance. However, I had to point out to my Dutch friends that Birmingham was faced with the gigantic task of achieving in one year what other cities had achieved in three or four years. Amsterdam failed to get assurances from the other cities, especially Paris, so sadly the proposal got nowhere. This experience was to be a decisive factor in my later submission to President Samaranch as to how all this campaigning should be regulated for the future. A most pleasing relationship developed between the bidding cities arising from these exhibitions. There was a delightful camaraderie, with all the technical people helping each other to erect the stands and provide equipment and those of us leading the delegation sharing a warm friendship. We really became a club within a club – and a very exclusive one at that!

Hours spent in aircraft are the most demanding that I know. They are physically exhausting and mentally stressful. It is inevitable that you eat too many meals and drink too much wine and coffee. After much time spent in this way I would disembark in search of one, or occasionally two, members of the IOC who then had to be entertained cheerfully and convincingly. I have no doubt that this gruelling schedule brought on the circulation problems that still beset me.

In November Jimmy Munn and his team were organising the video which we had to send around the world to IOC members and to the sports federations as well as to scores of television stations wherever we could get a show. It really did serve its purpose in advertising Birmingham. It was a very successful production commissioned from United Television Artists. For the Expo '85 exhibition in Montreal we sponsored a narrow boat from 'Brummagem Boats', decorated with our logo and carrying our message to hundreds of thousands of people. We sent a delegation to Oslo for the world fixture congress of the International Amateur Athletic Federation and I used an invitation to speak in Cork at their city's anniversary celebrations to talk about the social purpose of sport, which enabled me to outline Birmingham's philosophy to a distinguished audience.

The Bahrain gathering of Asian Olympians was exciting too. I was refused admission to the country in the middle of the night because I had a stamp in my passport which showed that I had once entered Israel. I knew all about the convention practised by the Foreign Office and urged upon me by our diplomatic staff that in such circumstances one ought to have a second passport. I do not approve of such a practice and, as I explained, 'Israel is a member of the United Nations and it is most certainly a member in good standing with the IOC'. I was soon escorted to my hotel, much to the surprise of our embassy staff, and when His Excellency the Amir of Bahrain gave a banquet in honour of the occasion I was placed in a seat of honour as one of the Queen's Privy Councillors. Relationships between our two countries were obviously of the best. Sheikh Fahad of Kuwait presided at the assembly and graced our Birmingham lunch as did Prince Faisal of Saudi Arabia, both of whom were members of the IOC. I was able to use two incidents that occurred during the lunch in my speech. We had been determined to provide a formal English lunch since we knew this would be appreciated by our two royal guests so we arranged for strawberries to be flown in specially from London. I had to apologise for their absence from the table although they were on the menu – the baggage handlers had forgotten to unload them at the airport. 'At this very moment', I told my audience, 'your strawberries are being sold in the streets of Singapore to which country the plane was bound.' But my best story, as ever, concerned 'my reputation in our country as a miracle man'. I explained that this was due to my feat in bringing rain to our drought-ridden country. Our guests looked suitably puzzled until I informed them that I understood that Bahrain had not seen rain for two years, at which point I invited them to look out of the windows to see 'yet another miracle', the rain was pouring down. The hilarity and the cheering ensured the success of the lunch.

A week later we were in Ethiopia. Their country was in the middle of the disastrous famine, receiving help from all over the world. I was surprised that the African assembly went on but it did so we had to be there. We did not achieve much except to renew our friendship with Reggie Alexander, the veteran IOC member from Kenya. Reggie is one of the old school, number 12 in the order of protocol at that time. Most of his family still live in England so he comes here often. As an accountant he takes great interest in the financial affairs of the IOC and he has very strong reservations about the modern marketing of the Olympic movement which he voices with sturdy independence and, in consequence, not to universal approval. He also fervently holds the view that sport should be used as a bridge-builder with South Africa, not one I believe to be realistic. He had been commandant of the Kenyan Olympic team which was totally multi-racial, and he could not understand why this was not possible these days. My most remarkable experience on this visit was the supper given by Cortina, the candidate city of Italy for the Winter Games. They invited us all to dinner at 7.00 pm. Three hours later the talking was still going on in the assembly. They took my advice to start the meal without any African Olympic representatives and to persuade Reggie Alexander, who was the only person among us entitled to enter the conference hall, to go down and seek their approval for this arrangement. Thankfully it was granted so that we could all start our meal. The African delegates joined us just before midnight!

Our mid-winter tour of the eastern socialist countries was of very considerable importance. They could command or influence at least a dozen votes. We arrived in Moscow in late January 1986. For the first time in many years there was a thaw at a time of the year when many degrees of frost were expected. My hosts knew of my reputation as a miracle man with the weather and promptly gave me the credit! When we met the principal members of the Soviet Olympic committee we had a very full and frank discussion of considerable detail. Constantin Andrianov, their senior IOC member, and Yuri Titov, the international president of gymnastics, did most of the questioning. They were very taken by the concept put forward by Bryan Bird and Reg Hudson, our two councillors who represented both political parties, and by myself, of the development of sport and recreation in Birmingham as an arm of social policy. Bryan and Reg described the use of our schools for community-based recreation and the city's policy of attracting international sporting events. The bid to stage the Olympic Games was the apex of a policy designed to embrace sport at every level. Our Soviet friends told us that they found this an attractive philosophy.

Perhaps the most fascinating part of our discussions, which lasted a whole day, covered the increasing move towards commercialism and professionalism in the Olympic movement. They knew about my report on Sports Sponsorship (published in 1983) and were clearly concerned at the direction in which the Olympic movement was heading. I believe that they found Birmingham's community sports programme, based on community sport and embracing the Games themselves, an attractive proposition. For my part I gave my own view that the commercial merchandising of sport was justified only if its purpose was to extend the boundaries of sports development and participation, and provided that the amateur principle in the Olympic Games was always fully protected. I found the Russians fully shared my concern about recent developments and about the activities of players' agents who have no place in Olympic sport. Always the realists, they then explored our likely voting strength and we had our first discussion about tactical voting in Lausanne. The Bulgarian capital, Sofiya, was contending for the Winter Games and Budapest was running against us for the Summer Games. Andrianov made it clear that they could not commit their socialist colleagues to vote as a bloc any more than we could commit our own friends, but possible arrangements were obviously in their minds after their first round of voting in support of Belgrade. We left Moscow well satisfied with our reception and while the rest of the delegation returned to Birmingham Pat Cheney and I travelled on to Poland and Czechoslovakia.

There was no thaw in Warsaw. I have never been so cold. The temperature was many degrees below freezing and the conditions underfoot were dreadful, but again we were warmly received by the Polish Olympic secretary and Wlodzimierz Reczek, their IOC member. The discussions were interesting and we gained the impression that details of our talks in Moscow had travelled ahead of us. Two days later we were in Prague, but we found that their member, Vladimir Cernusak, was in his home town of Bratislava. Arrangements then had to be made for us to meet there. Cernusak is a distinguished professor, an academic as well as being director of the PE and Sports Facility Research Institute. The Birmingham philosophy was obviously of great interest to him and we had a very useful meeting indeed. I don't know what advance information or impression he had been given about me but when he took us to lunch he told me quietly but earnestly, as was his style, that he was so glad I had made the effort to go and see him – 'it makes a difference to talk to someone face to face'. We parted good friends and I was hopeful of his influence being used in the later stages of the voting.

In February we accepted an important invitation to view Sofiya's facilities and discuss their bid for the Winter Games. Hosting us for this visit was Ivan Slavkov, who in 1987 himself became a member of the IOC. He is a very flamboyant person who speaks excellent English, and we spent a great deal of time discussing the possibility of supporting each other's candidature during the voting process. In my judgment Sofiya made a fine bid. It was very similar to Birmingham's in concept, with all the facilities and the village being contained closely together near the city itself. If the IOC was looking to get away from the sprawl of Los Angeles and from continual traffic jams then we both agreed that Birmingham and Sofiya met the requirements. My visit to the home of the Bulgarian IOC member, 94-year-old General Vladmir Stoytchev, was astonishing. He lived on the top floor of a block of flats several storeys high and without a lift. This certainly did not impede his frequent trips abroad on Olympic business. His room was the most extraordinary that I have ever visited. Every conceivable war and sporting memento filled every nook and cranny. Pride of place was given to his war photographs which hung on the walls. He had been photographed with Churchill and Stalin and also with all his fellow Allied generals in the various victory parades. We never did get him round to discussing the merits of Birmingham or any other city, but Slavkov assured me that the Bulgarian Olympic committee would make it very clear to him who they wished him to vote for. I have never heard a more optimistic forecast. I could not imagine him taking any notice of anyone!

By contrast we had extremely agreeable and realistic talks with Mrs Nabedba Lekarska, a splendid Olympian lady who undoubtedly should have been the first woman member of the IOC, and would have been had anyone been able to persuade the General to retire, but no one could, not even the Bulgarian Government or Olympic committee. We also met the deputy Prime Minister and Minister for Sport and our talks with them were also very positive. One of the most lasting of all the impressions I brought away from Sofiya was of their cathedral. The singing and chanting were spell-binding. We attended their Greek Orthodox service and I could hardly drag myself away. I shall never forget the voice of one of the priests who sang from the pulpit. He had a bass voice which could have ensured world fame in any opera company – better even than Paul Robeson's.

I made two visits to Brazil, one in March for the world motor racing Grand Prix before moving on to Peru, and the other taking in the Caribbean and Central American Games held in Puerto Rico in late June and early July. The trips to Brazil were designed to enable me to meet IOC members who might be present but particularly to obtain wide media coverage in Latin America. We certainly got that on our first visit. CSS, our sponsorship advisers, had obtained the support of the British racing drivers in advance of our arrival. They all wore Birmingham emblems and carried our small logo on their cars. I was told that this would have cost us a small fortune to buy so we were very grateful. The media conference arranged by CSS was also a success. Jackie Stewart made a warm speech commending our bid to an audience which included Major Sylvio de Magalhaes Padilha, one of the two Brazilian members of the IOC, who responded generously. I found myself giving a succession of interviews to the world press, radio and television. I realised in Rio de Janeiro that whatever else we were going to achieve our aim of selling Birmingham world-wide as an international city for sport, conferences and investment had been reached. This view was strongly shared by my Conservative colleague Reginald Eyre, the senior Tory MP for the city, who was accompanying me on this trip as evidence of our all-party approach. However, throughout Latin America, it was impossible to escape the effects of the Falklands War upon the voting prospects for Britain and Birmingham.

Next on our programme was Peru, where we wished to lobby IOC member Ivan Dibos. The day before we were due to fly out from Rio we received a cable from the British ambassador in Peru informing us that there was a state of civil unrest, a curfew was enforced at 11.00 pm every night and our plane was due later than that. What was worse, a member of his own staff arriving on the same flight the week before had been shot at between the airport and his home. Reggie and I decided to keep to our schedule and make the trip. Pat Cheney and Richard Caldicott made up the delegation and we landed the next night at about 11.15 pm. No one was taking any risks to meet us, so armed with a piece of paper allowing us to be out during the curfew we managed to persuade a taxi driver to drive us to our hotel. Ivan Dibos and his wife were extremely hospitable and amazed that we had travelled halfway round the world to solicit one vote. They told us of the pressure building up among their Latin American colleagues to support Barcelona and, indeed, the assumption was that they would all do so. The Dibos family were most appreciative of Birmingham's claims but obviously their loyalties were stretched. We concluded that Birmingham would be the second choice if by any chance Barcelona was beaten. The embassy staff were also very helpful, and delighted that we had disregarded their advice. When they drove us back to the airport they told us that it was becoming a normal feature of their society for people such as Dibos – especially those who owned a Rolls Royce car – to be kidnapped. Dibos had already told us that one of his immediate neighbours, an executive with Coca-Cola, had been kidnapped and held for ransom. Ivan saw us off and his last words were that he had just agreed to his wife's demand that he should sell his Rolls Royce!

The assembly of Olympic summer sports (ASOIF) met in Rome in early March, presided over by Primo Nebiolo. We used the occasion to sit in and listen to our competitor cities. We were heartened by the comparisons, especially after hearing the Paris presentation, which we had assessed as the strongest rival to Barcelona on the first count. In short their case was based on the statement: 'We offer you Paris, the most beautiful city in the world'. Nothing much more was said and certainly little about sport or the Olympics. Nebiolo was in charge of this conference and at one stage it seemed that he intended to answer questions directed to the bidding cities. I hurriedly consulted my competitors and informed him that if we were not to answer these questions ourselves we would leave. Nebiolo had to give way to our challenge, allowing me to dominate the press conference for the next 15 minutes.

In April we were due to visit Seoul again where the IOC executive was to be in session. I was very conscious that in spite of our African trip we had not really concentrated upon the IOC's Arab members. I discussed this with Pat Cheney and we decided that our visit to Seoul should be via Egypt, whose member, Ahmed Touney, was known to be a strong character. We knew he would be influential with his fellow north African colleagues. He had built his own Olympic museum inside the national stadium and when we visited it he proudly showed us that it already contained the advance literature and other material sent to him by Birmingham. It was the only time in my life I have visited a museum dedicated to the person showing me around! However, by then all hopes of securing any Arab votes had already disappeared. We arrived in Cairo one day after our Prime Minister had authorised the United States Air Force to take off from British airfields to bomb Libya and Colonel Gadaffi. So much for the Arab vote. There was really nothing for us to do except to go and visit the Pyramids and look at the Sphinx, whose inscrutable smile said it all. Even though many of the Egyptians were understanding there was no way that we were going to get any Arab votes. The Turkish member was Turgut Atakol, who lived in Istanbul. I met him and his wife, a most charming couple, in their flat but it was clear that he was ill. His greatest concern was to host the IOC session in Istanbul. We were delighted that he lived to see that conference successfully accomplished. On that occasion Birmingham won the decision to host the 1991 session, and Mr Atakol told me that he was never more honoured than when a Rolls Royce pulled up outside his door flying a Union Jack and out stepped the British ambassador to deliver the official Birmingham bid. Well done the Foreign Office.

We sent other delegations to various sporting events or asked friends who would be there to represent us on at least a dozen occasions. These included the World Gymnastics Championships in Montreal, the meeting of summer Olympic sports, the World Swimming Championships in Madrid, the European AAA meeting in Stuttgart, the World Volleyball Championships in Prague, Badminton in Jakarta, the World Cycling Championships, again in Rome, and so it went on – wherever major international sport was being played or discussed we were there. I went myself to Budapest for their first-ever motor racing Grand Prix to try to talk to Pal Schmidt, the Hungarian IOC member, as it had been difficult to talk to him alone before. He made all the arrangements for our trip but in the event he failed to show up. On the day we arrived the Hungarian Minister for Sport was replaced and it was rumoured that Pal Schmidt was in difficulty.

Meanwhile, during and between all these expeditions we had to organise visits for the incoming IOC members, a task requiring tact and considerable attention to detail. Ian Mackenzie applied himself to it with great enthusiasm. By the time we completed that programme in late September we had received 44 members – exactly half, just as targeted – and had talked to almost all the others, making individual presentations. There were just one or two exceptions, the former Prime Minister of Tunisia, Mohamed Mzali, being one of them. He had been deposed, imprisoned and had escaped, making his way to the safety of the IOC in Lausanne, but in any case he was clearly not going to be voting. Mr Shagdarjan Magvan of Mongolia was impossible to track down either in the USSR or anywhere else. We told our Russian friends that we did not believe he existed. They were much amused. For all the incoming visits we followed a similar procedure which worked very well. It became a routine, but we never treated it as one. The two motorcycle policemen allocated exclusively to us by Chief Constable Geoffrey Dear would escort our guests, accompanied by Ian Mackenzie, from their port of entry. We entertained them for two or three days in Birmingham, where they could tour the NEC site, visit Stoneleigh and Holme Pierrepont, take a helicopter trip to Weymouth, the proposed site of our sailing events, and be modestly entertained by members of our organising committee. With one exception they all told us how much they approved of our proposals to 'give the Games back to the athletes', after we had explained to them that by this slogan we were emphasising the importance and convenience of the athletes as our first priority. They would live together in excellent accommodation and they would be able to walk to more than 60 per cent of the venues. All of them expressed total support for our security provisions, and acclaimed Graham Trevis's presentation of a Birmingham Olympic City closely contained and secured by three separate, safe perimeter systems. The close proximity of national facilities for rowing, canoeing, shooting and equestrian events was another obvious plus and no one could visit Stoneleigh and Nottingham without being impressed by their superb layout. We managed to have a lot of good social contact, too, which resulted in firm friendships.

Most of the members wanted to visit Stratford and were amazed that it was only 20 miles from Birmingham. Flor Isava-Fonseca, the first woman member of the IOC who hails from Venezuela was thrilled by Coventry Cathedral and went there again just to sit and meditate. James Worrall QC was the first member to stay, with his wife, at Highbury, the newly-refurbished official residence of the city of Birmingham. It was the home of Joseph Chamberlain and is a most attractive house. Jim must be the tallest member of the IOC so we had to make sure to get for him a bed of suitable size. It turned out that his family came from Bury in Lancashire and he wanted to find the family 'seat' and to visit Gigg Lane, home of Bury Football Club. It was all arranged. Reggie Alexander did not believe in visiting the bidding cities but told us that he believed his mother was buried in Birmingham. If we found the grave he would certainly come and visit us. Ian Mackenzie

discovered it in Harborne Parish churchyard. It was a most moving
moment when we arrived to pay our homage and discovered that not
only were Reggie's mother's ashes there but also those of his sister,
with whom he had lost touch. Jan Staubo of Norway had served in the
war with the RAF. He gave us much wise counsel and encouragement.
Sir Lance Cross from New Zealand wanted to visit the BBC Midlands
headquarters at Pebble Mill, where he had spent part of his training as
a broadcast journalist. Ivan Dibos, our Peruvian friend, chose to visit
us during the Birmingham Grand Prix, revealing a passion for motor
racing. He was overjoyed to find one of his Peruvian friends participating in the event.

We had a delightful visit from General Henry Adefope and his wife
from Nigeria. This was unfortunately turned into a press rampage
months later when certain councillors were questioning every penny of
our expenditure, having exercised their right to scrutinise our accounts.
Henry Adefope, like most of our guests, made his own travel arrangements and was recompensed by payment through our office. Mrs
Adefope required some medication for an eye problem and we immediately arranged for proper medication to be provided for her, as I
trust any civilised host would have done. To my great distress these
arrangements were scandalously blown up to provide headlines. I have
no doubt that a similar fate would have awaited me had the same people
had half a chance. One councillor even demanded a full statement of
the expenses I had claimed during my leadership of Birmingham's
campaign. He must have been extremely disappointed when the treasurer wrote back to him explaining that he could not provide this
information since Denis Howell had not claimed any expenses other
than for his telephone calls!

Apart from President Samaranch, we also received visits from the
two vice-presidents, Ashwini Kumar from India and Alexandru
Siperco from Romania. When Mr Siperco arrived he promptly questioned all our proposals. The village would be too small and not up
to good planning standards, the bungalows for the competitors were
inadequate. The fact that the village had been designed by the planning
officers of Birmingham and Solihull did not satisfy him; nor did the
fact that our own Birmingham international athletes declared they had
never stayed in better accommodation. He believed that aircraft arriving
and taking off from Birmingham Airport would disturb the village. He
also appeared to question our security arrangements. I had to go to the
House of Commons leaving Graham Trevis, our security adviser, to
take him to dinner and to get the planners to join them at short notice.
I have never seen Graham so indignant, but we heard no more criticisms
of this sort. It was an extraordinary visit but the only one of its kind.
In sharp contrast was the visit of Pasqual Maragal, the Mayor of
Barcelona, who told me that he was worried about the impact that
Birmingham was having in the contest which was why he had come to
see for himself. Having been shown all our plans and all our existing

facilities he said, 'Birmingham is indeed an Olympic City, but not for 1992'.

President Samaranch flew in one Sunday evening directly from the men's final at Wimbledon. I had not realised that he did not like helicopter flights but he was intrigued by what he saw from the air. 'The whole of England seems to be playing cricket', he told me. He toured the site of the NEC and visited Stoneleigh, and in spite of what was written afterwards by some of our detractors, he expressed himself in complimentary terms at his press conference. He was also keen to make a pilgrimage to a house in Ampton Road, Edgbaston, where the first game of lawn tennis had been played.

LAUSANNE

The Edinburgh Commonwealth Games of 1986 were always going to be of vital importance to us. The whole of the Commonwealth were expected to compete and we hoped that all their IOC members would be there. We decided to invite them all to come as Birmingham's guests if they were not already attending in a Commonwealth capacity, and we took one of the hospitality boxes offered us by the organisers which was excellent for our purpose. We backed this up by adopting an idea put forward by Richard Caldicott and his event team to offer a special coaching and acclimatisation programme for all the developing nations of the Commonwealth. Eleven countries accepted this invitation and Jim Sadler and Charles Taylor did a superb job in organising their programme for 39 athletes.

Alas, disaster struck even as they arrived. Margaret Thatcher had defiantly stood out in a minority of one at the Commonwealth Prime Ministers' Conference in the Bahamas on the issue of sanctions against South Africa. The majority of Prime Ministers reacted to this in a most hostile manner and it was obvious that African, Asian and Caribbean participation in the Edinburgh Games was in total jeopardy. Each day, as the athletes trained in Birmingham, more and more officials and competitors were ordered home by their governments. The independence of sport from government was clearly seen to be non-existent for most of these teams. Many of the competitors faced with the instruction to return home broke down in tears. It was a crushing blow for Birmingham. The Edinburgh Games were a most successful event for those who competed but out of 47 Commonwealth countries only 26 took part and they were overwhelmingly white countries. At one of the receptions my friend Lord Porritt – Arthur Porritt, an honorary member of the IOC and former chairman of the Commonwealth Games Federation – said: 'It is a great shame for Birmingham that it has all come apart here in Edinburgh'. I thought we might recover from this setback since Birmingham is genuinely multi-racial. I had written to every one of the IOC members explaining this and telling them that Birmingham had a declared policy not to have any commercial contact with any firm that directly or indirectly traded in or with South Africa. 'It won't make any difference', Lord Porritt told me. Nor did it – in the event he was proved right. But eight or nine IOC members did attend the Games, and those who had not yet been to Birmingham did so during their visits.

In the weeks before Lausanne Jan Antonio Samaranch acted to quell the growing disquiet, of which we had told him, about the cost and practice of all this campaigning. Nothing like it had been seen before in the history of the Olympic movement. It is to be hoped that nothing like it will ever be seen again. The problem was that there were absolutely no rules governing the extent of the campaign. No limit was set to the number of receptions which could be offered by each of the competing cities, nor on the money which could be spent upon them, nor upon visits by IOC members, nor on the gifts presented to them. I had no doubts that President Samaranch shared our concern. I was pleased when he wrote to the presidents of each of the cities bidding for both the Summer and Winter Games asking for their observations and recommendations upon these developments. Our replies would remain sealed and would not be opened until after the declaration of the votes in Lausanne in October. I had no hesitation in setting out my own views in full:

1. *Finality of Bid Proposals*:   It is not in the interests of good order within the Olympic movement, nor fair competition between bidding cities, for inducements to be offered which go beyond previously accepted IOC practice. Nor is it acceptable for amendments and new proposals to be made after submissions have been presented to the IOC on the date notified by them. When offers are made by any city which affect policy decisions by the IOC – as has occurred during the current campaign – then other cities are at a considerable disadvantage if they have no knowledge of the IOC position in respect of such proposals:

Detailed comments: i) Offers of free transportation for horses, and free accommodation in another country where acceptable rules of quarantine apply, made because of general concern about equestrian quarantine regulations in the country of the bidding city not only relate to the main question but provide a financial inducement beyond those offered by the other cities in their bids lodged with the IOC. This should be discouraged.

ii) Offers of free travel and free or partially free accommodation for competitors and officials are obviously attractive to the national Olympic committees but raise questions of a different kind for the IOC. It is important to make a regulation that no city should include any proposal in its bid which affects existing IOC policy without the consent of the IOC and, where that is given, other bidding cities should be provided with the opportunity to adopt such a proposal if they wish to do so.

Both the above illustrations have financial consequences for the profitability of any Games. The cost of free travel or accommodation must come out of the final surplus of the Games as the costs involved are included in the cost of the Games. This reduces the surplus available within the Olympic Movement and is therefore a policy matter.

2. *Campaign Budgets*:   Very few countries where competitive national elections are held allow totally unrestricted expenditure in the conduct of such elections. The campaign for the 1992 Games shows the good sense of such a practice. It cannot be in the interests of the Olympic Movement for those NOCs located in regions of poverty to be confronted with costly and extravagant campaigns. In any case these are in total contradiction to the purpose of the Olympic Solidarity Commission. The IOC needs to issue regulations to govern this situation.

3. *Expenditure Limits*:   If it is possible to set limits to the expenditure which any city can spend upon its campaign this would have considerable advantages and would seem to be fair to all cities. Two difficulties to be considered about such a proposal will be the geographical location of the competing cities and strength of their currencies. But if it is possible to devise such a scheme then it would be the easiest and most sensible way to control the campaigns. An alternative approach would be to regulate campaign activity under specific headings.

4. *Visits of IOC Members*:   It is important to provide opportunities for members of the IOC to make their own assessments of the facilities, organisational skills and related questions such as transport, security and health cover. The following questions arise and need consideration.

i) Should the number and extent of such visits be regulated or remain unrestricted as at present?

ii) Would it be reasonable to issue the air tickets through the office of the IOC even when they are provided by an airline as part of its sponsorship of the city's bid?

iii) Should there be a cost limitation upon any entertainment, hospitality or gifts and souvenirs provided in the course of such a visit?

Birmingham's experience leads us to believe that many IOC members would welcome such a regulation.

5. *Media and Entertainment*:   Any international campaign must have regard to the role of the media and the need for world-wide publicity. However, the total cost of such an exercise and the value of gifts provided either directly or indirectly should be controlled.

6. *Receptions and Delegations*:   The number and cost of receptions offered to IOC members whenever they are in session or where their various commissions meet needs to be considered. The

justification for such activity on behalf of candidate cities is that it provides the opportunity to make contact with IOC members who cannot visit their city. However, such receptions have now become a normal part of the organisation of such gatherings. They are very costly and must cause some concern, especially when repeated several times each year. Furthermore, it is very demanding upon IOC members to expect them to attend several receptions in the course of one conference or congress. It would seem to be reasonable to restrict the number of occasions when any city can provide such receptions in the course of any one year.

7. *Regional Games and Conferences*: Since it is now a regular practice to hold conferences of national Olympic committees on a regional basis, often in association with the staging of continental Games, then it is obvious that such gatherings do impress the national Olympic committees and the international federations with the strength of their bids. It would seem reasonable to restrict such promotional activity by any city to one event for each such gathering during the four-year cycle terminating at the congress where the IOC reaches its decision.

8. *IOC Congress*: The congress of the IOC, which decides the choice of host cities for future Games is the climax of the campaign of each candidate city. Inevitably, it must attract maximum international publicity. Excesses of expenditure are likely to be magnified when reported world-wide. Already, in 1986, advance experience suggests that the movement would benefit from some control upon this situation. Totally unrestricted activity and expenditure could well bring the Olympic cause itself into disrepute. Many countries find it necessary to establish financial limits in respect of the costs of national election campaigns. Also, many such election campaigns are not allowed to proceed after a given date shortly before the final day of decision. Since the campaign to stage the 1992 Games has covered a period of two or three years in most cases it is difficult to understand how extravagant last-minute expenditure can be justified. Furthermore, it is grotesque to expect members of the IOC to be subjected to mass invitations during the course of a final week's deliberations when they have a very heavy schedule of meetings.

There appears to be a strong case for proscribing all such activity at the congress taking the decisions upon the location of future Games. A possible exception might be the staging of exhibitions under the auspices of the IOC as occurred in Lausanne this year.

9. *Accountability*: The disclosure of campaign accounts is an essential feature of the control of expenditure required by many governments in order to ensure the proper conduct of elections. Without such a provision it is not possible to monitor campaigns and to protect against undesirable developments. The IOC might well consider the need to seek the submission of an annual statement

of account from each bidding city during the course of their campaign.

10. *Relationships with IOC Members*: Certain information, as yet uncirculated, which has reached us, suggests that offers have been made 'of employment or other opportunities' to the families of members. If this is correct it is very unwise, of course. Probably the new commission should consider some statement defining the proper relationships between bidding cities and members of the IOC.

As requested I sent a letter to this effect to President Samaranch before Lausanne. As a result of our experiences in Lausanne during the IOC session I decided to send to the president my further thoughts upon this subject, as follows:

1. *Pressure upon IOC Members*: These have been intolerable. It is quite destructive of the dignity of the Olympic movement to be simultaneously approached by representatives of several cities. Such pressurised canvassing has to be eliminated. Clearly, this undesirable situation arises from the presence of the exhibitions where the stands have been used as the focal point of such operations. The decision of the IOC to ensure that in future the Summer and Winter Games cities are not to be chosen at the same congress will reduce the scale of this problem, which is to be welcomed, but it will not eradicate it.

In my judgment it is important to consider whether these exhibitions should be allowed at all in the final weeks before voting.

2. *Campaigning*: The campaigning conducted around the congress building and the reports of high pressure campaigns within the IOC itself are highly damaging to the Olympic movement. It is very important to appreciate that the bidding cities are spending large sums of public money upon their exhibitions and final presentations. If it is thought that decisions are foregone and the presentations are only of marginal importance, this will act against the long term interests of the IOC.

One possibility could be to adopt the same procedure in force in some countries which prevents any electoral promotion or campaigning within a given number of days (say seven) of the voting. Another possibility which might be examined is to replace the present system by a selection process in which the IOC invites applicant cities to make submissions for evaluation and subsequently allocates the Games to their chosen city.

3. *IOC Commission*: My own view is that the newly elected IOC commission should have considerable authority to oversee the whole electoral process if the present system is continued. I believe that this should include consideration of all interests. It may be helpful for the protection of members if any interests are openly declared, as in the case of most western Parliaments. As I know from personal

experience this is a very helpful and protective practice.

Neither of these letters were acknowledged other than formally but when all the submissions had been considered by a special IOC commission chaired by Marc Hodler the following new regulations were adopted for the future:

1. No candidate city receptions or exhibitions are to be held during the year 1987.

2. A joint reception may be organised by the cities bidding to host the XVIIth Olympic Winter Games during the 93rd IOC session in Calgary, 1988. However, no exhibitions may be staged on this occasion. A further joint reception may be arranged at the 94th IOC session in Seoul, 1988 (the session during which election of the host city will take place). Cities may also stage an exhibition during the 94th IOC session.

3. Candidate cities bidding to host the Games of the XXVIth Olympiad may hold a joint reception at the 95th IOC session in San Juan, 1989. However, no exhibitions may be staged on this occasion. A further joint reception may be arranged at the 96th IOC session in Tokyo, 1990 (the session during which election of the host city will take place). Cities may also stage an exhibition during the course of the 96th IOC session.

In addition to providing these new instructions the IOC stated that it was still reviewing the issue of limitation of candidate city expenses.

Before these decisions were taken came the Lausanne session. We had to take a big team – there was much to be done on every possible front. To help with the general hospitality and reception work on our stand we had Bobby Charlton, whose fame was a great help. As soon as he walked into a hotel room with us spontaneous applause broke out and waiters left their tasks to greet him. The Ex Cathedra Choir, which is one of Birmingham's finest, came over to sing at the dinner we gave on the lake on one of the lake cruisers, 'La Suisse', which we hired for the occasion. Guests were greeted at the quayside by the West Midlands Police Pipe Band which also played in the foyer of the Palais de Beaulieu where the session was held. Our presentation team included Ron Pickering, who did a superb job, especially when we ran into serious technical trouble in the projection room due to the refusal of the Swiss technicians to allow any of our British production team into the room. Alan Hart, now head of the BBC's international department, who was a source of great strength, was furious that our technical people had let this crisis be forced upon them. Ron heard it all on his headphones and he quietly said to me out of the corner of his mouth, 'There is chaos among the technicians, they want me to keep talking', and without any member of the IOC being aware of the situation he proceeded to conduct a question and answer session with Seb Coe and Judy Simpson.

It was the best part of our presentation. Both Seb and Judy, who had expected to speak for only a couple of minutes or so, and did not know what was happening, responded magnificently. Senior IOC member Lord Luke then declared his belief in Birmingham. The team was completed by Charles Palmer, the BOA chairman, who delivered the endorsement with firm conviction. We fielded a few questions and left the hall to the generous applause of the assembly and the congratulations of our friends.

The French Prime Minister, Jacques Chirac, who was also the Mayor of Paris, scored a great hit when he presented his city's case. We were told afterwards that his very personal style and oratory swept many members off their feet although it did not appear to be totally relevant to the gigantic task of staging the Olympic Games in Paris. Chirac certainly captured some of the undecided votes although I doubt whether there were too many of them to be won. The immediate effect of Chirac's fervour was to generate enormous activity overnight among the Barcelona supporters within the IOC. This brought many complaints about the pressures forced upon the members. However, I think that such distinguished people ought to be capable of dealing with these. The significant decision taken immediately in the wake of Chirac's performance was to concentrate support for the Winter Games on the French city of Albertville. There can be no doubt that every effort was made by the Barcelona strategists to ensure a victory for Albertville in the belief that if they won that nomination then the prospect of a second French victory for Paris for the Summer Games would be undermined. It was a strategy which succeeded.

LOSING THE VOTE

When we arrived in Lausanne, I called my closest advisers together to make a realistic assessment of our prospects. We went over the 88 names of the members again and again and discussed what they had told us during the campaign, adding other intelligence we had gathered. We reached the conclusion that we had 24 firm promises to vote for Birmingham. I advised my colleagues that long political experience in such matters had taught me to reduce this number by at least a third, which left us 16. I then calculated the minimum number of votes required to bring into play the second preference votes of Belgrade supporters if Sofiya received significant support for the Winter Games. We decided that in this case we would need 12 votes. During the following 24 hours I had a meeting at the highest level with two of our Bulgarian friends who confirmed this arrangement. We also hoped to receive some Commonwealth votes if Brisbane was eliminated and one or two from Amsterdam, which we were sure by now would be the first city to be eliminated. If this transpired we had an exciting prospect before us. Within hours we were to learn differently. Friends who had been warm in their appreciation of Birmingham walked past our exhibition looking the other way, embarrassed to be seen on our stand now that their debts of loyalty had been called in by their friends. Some of them told us afterwards that they had no choice but 'it will be different next time, we shall not have the same torn loyalties to face'. Even worse for us, the South African question struck in a big way.

After we arrived in Lausanne Commonwealth leaders at the very highest level made their views known to their IOC members. The Bermuda Conference, where Britain had been isolated, meant that a vote for Britain or Birmingham was out of the question this time, it would be misunderstood. To my own certain knowledge this cost us at least four votes. Also, we were soon able to confirm that the Arab vote was a hopeless prospect after the Libyan bombings. It seemed that our committed promises were dissolving like snowflakes in the Sahara desert, and so it proved when President Samaranch declared Barcelona to be the victor and we examined the voting figures. The result of the first vote was: Amsterdam 5; Birmingham 8; Brisbane 11; Belgrade 13; Paris 19; Barcelona 29.

Amsterdam dropped out as expected. It was clear that our estimated requirement of 12 votes had been spot on. Those four votes could have made all the difference. In the second round we again received eight votes. Actually, we picked up one vote from Amsterdam and lost one from a supporter who thought he should now move elsewhere. Brisbane's tally was reduced to nine, only one more than us, so at this stage two of our promised votes would have kept us in the contest. Four votes would have seen us in third place as Belgrade had lost votes too, and now had only 11 votes. Paris picked up one and Barcelona eight. The Spanish bandwagon was rolling. The saddest part was that less than a handful of votes prevented our understanding with Bulgaria from falling into place. Indeed, in the third and final vote the Belgrade vote fell away and was more than halved to five while Brisbane gained one, finishing with ten. Paris improved to 23 but Barcelona gained another ten to reach a total of 47, more than the required 50 per cent, and so became worthy winners. There was one last irony: in the vote for the Winter Games Sofiya polled 25 votes, which suggested that commitments had been delivered, but the overnight surge to Albertville brought that city victory with a total of 51.

When in 1988 there was a further round of voting to determine the host city for the Winter Games of 1994 Sofiya's vote fell dramatically to 17, which appeared to confirm our understanding of the vote in Lausanne; in effect, then, those of our supporters who had promised to vote for Sofiya indeed did so.

BIRMINGHAM LOSES OUT

While many people throughout Britain thought that Birmingham's campaign had been an outstanding success – I personally received very many congratulations and two exceptional honours, being chosen as the Midlander of the Year 1986 and awarded the Fellowship of the Institute of Public Relations, which is my own professional body – it was never clear to me that our endeavours received similar acclaim among some of the British Olympic contingent. We received no expression of appreciation from the BOA though Lord Luke certainly did write to me in generous terms. I began to wonder about the bid for 1996. Nothing was heard. The sensible thing was to build a new bid for 1996 based upon all our endeavours and to do so without delay. However, a year or more went by before the BOA even thought about the subject. I mentioned the matter to Charles Palmer and Dick Palmer on more than one occasion. We were losing good campaigning time while reports kept coming in that Athens had launched a full-scale campaign, almost assuming that they had already been selected. This was a repeat of the Barcelona strategy. Toronto were also well into their campaign and all the IOC members due in Calgary for the Winter Olympics of 1988 were invited to call there en route.

Eventually the BOA stirred from its slumbers and announced that it would again invite submissions from bidding cities intending to enter the competition for 1996. They fixed the date of submission as the end of December 1987. Birmingham reviewed the position and decided to run again. We re-activated our committee and proceeded to produce literature and models of our amended plans. Out of the blue we received a letter from Charles Palmer telling us that Manchester had requested an extension of the deadline by a period of some two months. He wanted to know if other interested cities had objections. We certainly had. We were ready for the off; we knew well that every month of delay would be an obstacle to any serious campaign. Glasgow had also emerged as a possible candidate city and they supported Manchester's request. Palmer and his executive compromised and a new date was decided upon, 19 May 1988, which was after the Calgary Games. No more was heard of any Glasgow bid. It was Birmingham or Manchester.

My concern about all this procrastination heightened during my visit to Calgary. It was clear to me that Charles Palmer was certainly not going to support Birmingham. We did not believe that he had done so at the previous selection but we had no complaint about that. My judgment was that Palmer had expected to play a greater role in the presentation of our previous bid but there were two reasons why this could not be. In the first place it was Birmingham that had to be financially responsible. Secondly, Charles Palmer is an extremely controversial figure in the politics of international sport. His previously expressed views about sport and South Africa would be a hindrance with many sports and national Olympic committees. The socialist countries were also very wary of him as they made clear to me. These personal antagonisms had already led to criticism of his position as general secretary of the GAIFS (the General Assembly of International Federations of Sport) from which he was later ousted. He also lost his important position as president of the International Judo Federation, his own sport. All this was very regrettable. Charles Palmer is a very talented man, he speaks several languages, he is intelligent and good company. But the reaction he evoked from eminent people whose votes one sought could not be ignored. Horses for courses was my determining policy. There were some parts of the world, especially in the west and the southern hemisphere, where it was advantageous to have Charles in the vanguard. There were other regions where this was decidedly not the case, especially the Eastern Bloc, Africa and Asia. I do not think that he fully understood this situation and it often showed. In dealings with the members of the BOA I soon realised that many of Charles Palmer's fellow officers were hostile to his style of chairmanship.

In Calgary this opposition grew to a crescendo. It was impossible to talk about the merits of Birmingham's bid and the improvements we had made to it: all talk was about who could be nominated against Palmer, how his secretary Dick Palmer would not stay on as secretary if Charles remained as chairman, and on the chairman's side, how he could get someone to stand against the treasurer, Robert Watson, who was certainly out for a change. All in all it was a very disagreeable Games, not helped by the stretching of wings of some of the newer officers of our winter sports organisations. I was not surprised when Charles Palmer was taken ill, and his health was not improved when Princess Anne was elected to be the new British member of the IOC without any consultation whatsoever with him. In fact I broke the news to Charles myself as he lay ill in bed. He was dumbfounded. He was certainly not opposed to the nomination of Princess Anne but to the fact that the BOA had not been consulted in any way. The two British IOC members had by-passed the organisation officially. He even suggested that he ought to call an emergency meeting but he accepted my advice not to contest the situation and I believe that he subsequently had a very agreeable discussion with Her Royal Highness. I returned home earlier than I had intended as I could see no useful purpose in staying on in Calgary. I soon received reports that Manchester's Bob Scott had arrived, was being extremely urbane and spending a great deal of time in the company of Charles Palmer and some of the younger and newer administrators. What is certain is that the majority if not all of the winter sports representatives decided that they would support Manchester for the summer Olympics of 1996, even though their own sports would not be competing there! They proved to be a formidable block vote.

When we returned from Calgary we invited all the BOA members to visit us in Birmingham in order to show them around the new site we planned for the village. There was general approval. Other developments were also praised; particularly the location of the national swimming centre to cater for diving and water polo as well as for both competition and recreational swimming, to be built on a prime site in the new Heartlands project, a partnership enterprise created between the city and five major private developers. Of those delegates who came, at least half representing the summer sports, assured us of their continued support and I believe that we received it. Meanwhile, Manchester was also inviting BOA members to visit the Manchester Ship Canal and to hear their dreams for the future, based upon investment by three separate urban development corporations. As Birmingham had not been offered any financial help in its previous bid I wrote to the three Ministers responsible and asked if there had been a change of policy. They each replied very firmly that no change of policy had been introduced. Kenneth Clarke, one of the Ministers, reminded me that as he was a Birmingham citizen he was unlikely to give any such preference at the expense of our city. I wrote to *The Times* to point this out since its chief sports reporter, David Miller, had made much of the financial support Manchester was supposedly receiving. It was becoming increasingly obvious that Miller in *The Times* and Rodda in the *Guardian* were now very firmly backing the Manchester cause. They both belittled the National Exhibition Centre as a stage for international or Olympic sport. Later on Miller was to refer to this magnificent project, which makes a £12 million annual profit for the ratepayers, as 'converted warehouses'. I replied that these 'warehouses' had created an excellent impression when they hosted the Royal International Horse Show and the European Ice Skating Championships. I also pointed out that Miller had been a member of the organising committee of the Birmingham bid for 1992. With some justification I deplored that he had made no such criticisms at any of our meetings. My letter was never published. Months later Tom Clarke, the sports editor of *The Times*, wrote me a typically generous and understanding letter of regret about the situation which had arisen between us, and I responded in like terms.

Later on in Seoul, immediately before the 1988 Olympic Games, Great Britain put in a bid to host the World Gymnastic Championships at the NEC in Birmingham. The international president, Mr Yuri Titov of the Soviet Union, came to the British reception and responded to the welcome of Frank Edmonds, the British president, in the warmest terms, saying that he knew Birmingham and the Birmingham people and that in his view our Olympic bid was clearly the best on offer. It was a judgment that gave us much comfort even though, by then, we had been replaced by Manchester.

One of Manchester's deciding initiatives was inviting the BOA members to a reception at the London home of the Duke of Westminster. I was told that there was talk of 'the great houses of the north ringing with laughter' during their campaign. What did emerge was the concentrated attention paid to new delegates or substitutes who would be present at the BOA session for the first time. Our swimming friends told us of the individual pressures, in their case an invitation to be involved in the design of the Manchester swimming complex. Ron Eames of canoeing assured me at a sports ball five days before the critical BOA session that although he could not attend himself, canoeing, which Birmingham had proposed to hold in Nottingham-shire, would certainly vote for Birmingham. Understandably, Nottinghamshire County Council were distressed about the eventual decision in view of the considerable financial support their ratepayers provide for both sports. At the same ball my wife and I sat next to Mary Glen-Haig for several hours. She said not a word about the decisive meeting to be held in four days' time, nor did she wish us good fortune. As she had travelled the world as a member of our delegation supporting Birmingham's bid it was all very sad. Probably the most poignant incident was the visit to the House of Commons of Robert Watson, the BOA treasurer, who had not been able to come up and see us in Birmingham. He left assuring me, 'Don't worry, we are all behind you'. In fact, at the meeting where the voting took place he is reported to have asked Mary Glen-Haig and Lord Luke to advise the BOA which of the two bids would find most favour with the IOC. Mary refused to answer the question as a serving member of the IOC but Lord Luke does not appear to have been so reticent. I am told that he thought that Manchester was the answer. The afternoon had begun with lunch at the Café Royal. All my life I have been able to feel atmosphere; when I walk into a school, a factory, a hospital, it tells me what I want to know. So it was at the BOA lunch. One of our staunchest supporters, Eileen Gray of cycling, made a similar remark when she took her seat at the executive table, so did Wally Holland of weight-lifting, another Birmingham friend. Their forebodings proved to be only too accurate. The die was already cast, as it had been three years earlier. The fact was that more people assured us of their vote than voted for Birmingham.

We had given a good deal of thought to the presentation and we had sent every member a copy of our video several days before the meeting. It was an excellent video but it should have been a central feature of our presentation. We relied upon the two-year campaign, the fact that half the IOC members had visited us, that friendships had been established upon which we could build and, most important of all, that since our campaign we had won the IOC vote to hold their 1991 session in Birmingham. Our friends in the IOC had demonstrated their belief in our city; they would find it incomprehensible if having done so the BOA deserted us now. But they did. Manchester 20 votes, Birmingham 11. What is still incomprehensible to me is the fact that the BOA hardly considered the effect of Birmingham's campaign, of the great victory of obtaining the IOC conference for Birmingham, of Birmingham's commitment to host and to fund the Games. They seemed to have no idea of what we had done on their behalf and no sense of international strategy whatsoever. After the vote the only thing was to wish Manchester well, which I did as warmly as I could.

We returned home counting the cost. We had spent £2.25 million on our previous campaign; we had an investment of some £180 million at the NEC which was proving to be an outstanding success; we had a new swimming complex in the city programme. To add to the existing facilities at Stoneleigh, Holme Pierrepont and the Birmingham Alexander Stadium, we were building the new International Convention Centre – 11 conference halls – and the National Indoor Sports Arena with its six-lane athletic track capable of holding 15,000 people for a major conference or sports event. It seems inconceivable to me that such a gigantic investment programme can be reproduced in any other city. We can only trust that we are wrong if Britain's Olympic aspirations for 1996 are to be realised. We also knew that the Olympic Games in Birmingham could produce a profit on every possible pessimistic assumption. We had been required to convince the Government that this was so and we did. We also know that Birmingham's was a city bid, as required by the Olympic Charter, and as strongly urged upon us by Dick Palmer, the BOA secretary. Soon we were to listen to talk of Manchester's bid being a national bid. That may be sensible but the rules were not those we had expected to play to.

At the following AGM of the BOA Charles Palmer was voted out of office and replaced by Sir Arthur Gold, Eileen Gray succeeding Arthur as the vice-chairperson. Both Gold and Gray have been long-standing friends of Birmingham. A wry smile or two was in order. The gods were perverse in their timing and some of Charles Palmer's new friends, who had made common cause with him in Canada, seemed to have deserted him. Thankfully, a large part of Birmingham's Olympic ambitions are about to be realised. The Olympic family will be in Birmingham in 1991 and they will be extremely welcome in our.city. We intend to ensure that the organisation of their session and the welcome we will provide remove any doubts and confirm all the confidence of our friends. Birmingham is indeed an Olympic city to which they will all be delighted to return one day for even greater things.

Another remarkable chapter of events led to the IOC's decision to hold their 1991 session in Birmingham. I had convened a debriefing session of London-based members of our team at the House of Commons. During the discussion it emerged that the BOA had submitted Birmingham's invitation for 1991 to the IOC and that the matter would be decided in two weeks' time in Istanbul. No arrangements had been made by either the BOA or Birmingham to be represented in Turkey. I was horrified, especially when I learned that we would be competing against Paris, Monte Carlo, Moscow, Budapest, Nairobi and other attractive cities. Bryan Bird and I moved into action immediately and convinced Dick Knowles, the city council leader, that an invitation by means of a letter only would be massacred. As there were no councillors available to travel to Istanbul I agreed to go myself, accompanied by Ian Mackenzie. The publicity department managed to produce a fine brochure in something under a week and despatched a model of the new International Convention Centre where we proposed to hold the IOC conference.

Pat Cheney, my chief of staff, who was in Israel at the time agreed to proceed immediately to Istanbul to assist. Charles Palmer, the BOA chairman, was also in Israel at the same event, but did not find it possible to come to Istanbul to support us. In Turkey we found Dick Palmer, the BOA secretary, already in attendance upon the IOC, but he returned home as we arrived, leaving the Birmingham invitation without any BOA presence. Lord Luke and Mary Glen-Haig, the two British members of the IOC, were present of course, and offered their support. We installed ourselves on the top floor of the IOC hotel, set up our model, distributed our literature and modestly entertained our IOC friends. My confidence soared when Mr Joao Havelange visited us and told me, 'You have my word, I shall support Birmingham'. We won by one vote, aided by the fact that Mr Magvan from Outer Mongolia, who had supported Moscow throughout the voting, had left the room, and in spite of Lord Luke not finding it possible to remain and vote for us in the final session of the meeting! I was told that in the final vote Magvan still voted for Moscow, who had by then been eliminated, thus spoiling his voting paper and leaving us with the narrowest of margins over Budapest. So the IOC will be coming to Birmingham after all. Theirs will be the first conference to be held in the new International Convention Centre after it is opened by HM the Queen. It would be impossible to find a more important conference in sport to inaugurate the centre. The IOC decision reflected the very real appreciation of Birmingham's earlier endeavours and the impression we had created in our Olympic campaigns, as many IOC members told me. It was a pity that the BOA did not take the same generous view.

We are disappointed to have lost the confidence of the BOA for the time being but we can measure the great gains for Birmingham which our Olympic bid secured for us: an undoubted reputation around the world which is helpful to our businessmen and attracted new investment; 20 new hotels were being built or planned in the West Midlands and hotel occupancy reached an all-time high. The city is on the move. It would be quite wrong to suggest that all this results from the Olympic bid. The bid has proved to be an essential part of a developing strategy which began with the NEC, continued with the Motor Race Grand Prix, and was reinforced by the International Convention Centre and the National Indoor Sports Arena. The Olympic bid provided us with the highest possible international profile at exactly the right time. I believe too that it generated a new pride in our city. It was worth every penny spent upon it and every minute of devoted effort. That is satisfaction enough for me.

15

'LET US FACE THE FUTURE'

LIFE OUT OF OFFICE

The common misapprehension about Ministers leaving office is that it is the non-availability of the car and chauffeur that causes all the anguish. It cannot be denied that this is a great inconvenience, but so is the sudden absence of secretaries and press officers. The withdrawal symptoms are considerable and I certainly felt them after two spells of Government in four Parliaments, 11 years in all. But far outweighing these factors is the loss of power. No longer does the Minister take decisions which carry authority, which determine the course of events, and which may well become the law of the land. When one sees one's successors changing things for the sake of change, in order to demonstrate to the world that 'we are the masters now' or, worse, to assure the Prime Minister that the shop really is under new management, it is then that despair sets in. During my time as Minister of State for the Environment and as Minister for Sport I liked to think that I knew where I was going, and that I had some idea how to get there, but I believed that I had a duty to carry as many people with me as I could. This was a blindingly obvious requirement for sport. That is why, when I was in office, hardly a week went by but that I took the Opposition spokesman into my confidence as far as was practical to get as much common agreement as possible. This has never been reciprocated in the ten years since I left office.

Margaret Thatcher is extraordinary in her approach to political power. The famous question 'Is he one of us?' tells it all. There seems no room for bi-partisan policy in the House nor, on the surface, for genuine difference within her Government. I do not think, however, that this represents her true feelings. At moments of crisis she does yearn for consensus – the Falklands was an obvious example. And she does from time to time yield to other views in Cabinet. The trouble is that she does not want anyone to appreciate her desire for consensus unless it appears to have been achieved by concessions from others. It is a psychological phenomenon. It is a great pity because it is an attitude which is bound to create hostilities from the leaders of all the Opposition parties she has to deal with from time to time, and it has driven many former colleagues, relieved of office, into taking up public positions which are against her interests. We all know that she has in abundance the great qualities of courage and perseverance, which I regard as the most important of all the qualities in political life. She also has a personal loyalty to her colleagues, particularly when they are in difficulties, and a considerable sympathy with MPs who have met with distress, as my wife and I well know. By and large these are characteristics which are kept well out of public view for fear they might erode the image of great toughness which she needs constantly to reinforce. I believe this is a totally unnecessary attitude for her to adopt. I think that in the end it will be a considerable handicap to her. The caricature has triumphed over the person.

It is necessary to understand these characteristics in order to make any sense out of the comings and goings of all the Ministers for Sport during the reign of Mrs Thatcher. My own position, I believe, has been unique and has generated some reputation, so I think it was wrong for the Prime Minister to want a policy of doing everything differently. That I believe has been the undoing of Ministers. The British people are conservative with a small 'c', particularly sporting people. They do not want change for its own sake. They want the certainty of knowing what the policy is and where their next grant is coming from. It is a lesson which my party is learning afresh a little late in the day, but learning it we are. My own belief, as arrogant or as vain as it may be, is that the four Ministers for Sport who have held office during Mrs Thatcher's premiership have all been given as their first priority the need to establish themselves in the public mind as equal or superior to anything that I might have achieved. This is a serious mistake because reputations cannot be manufactured, especially in sport, unless they follow from hard achievements. As a public relations consultant myself I know that there can be no message unless it is one of substance. Mrs Thatcher's approach to sport rules out the possibility of any all-party consensus if it originates from the Opposition. Her Ministers have never initiated any discussions with me on any of the issues where an agreed approach would have been in the best interests of sport. This 'go it alone' policy is carried to remarkable lengths. During my years as Minister we held many Government receptions at Number Ten starting with Harold Wilson's party for the returning and successful British Olympic team in 1964 and embracing football, cricket, rugby, paraplegic sport and a host of sportsmen and women deserving such an acknowledgement. Always we ensured that the Opposition spokesman was invited and, invariably, his other colleagues known to have an interest in the sport in question. When Edward Heath was Prime Minister he followed the same pattern. I have never once been invited to any such reception at Number Ten during the Thatcher years despite the fact that I believe my personal relationship with Margaret Thatcher to be good, and with Denis Thatcher, who has a special interest in sport, to be very good. Life under the Thatcher administration is designed to be different but it has impeded rather than helped its relationship with sport.

The Prime Minister's first choice of Minister for Sport was Hector Munro, who had a proper sporting pedigree having been a former president of the Scottish Rugby Union. Hector had good relationships with the governing bodies and the CCPR. He was able to announce in the House that he could endorse the agreement which I had reached with the Treasury not to tax the Spot the Ball competition and so guarantee income for the Football Trust. He is relaxed in his approach and easy to talk to, so it is regrettable that he did not survive the 1980 Moscow Olympic fiasco. I doubt very much if Hector approved of his Government's boycott policy and he was certainly not allowed to take part in the famous debate in the House. However, a more likely reason for his early dismissal was his close relationships with South African rugby administrators which continued throughout his period of office and must have caused considerable irritation at the Foreign Office. Next in line came Neil Macfarlane, who also had a sporting background as a good player of both golf and cricket. Neil also knew a good deal about sports politics and the CCPR. He had been number two to Hector Munro when the Conservatives were in Opposition. I was surprised, then, that he got into so much trouble with the CCPR, including expensive litigation. He followed this up with a too-direct involvement in the affairs of the Sports Council – especially for a Government committed to a Royal Charter which guaranteed its independence. This led to the forced retirement of both the director and the deputy director and allowed me to have a field day in Parliament. After Macfarlane came Dick Tracey, who as far as I could judge had little if any sporting background. Tracey had been a broadcasting journalist which suggests that his appointment was made with presentational skills in mind. I don't think Dick knew enough about sport to make any real impact or to promote any new thinking and he seemed to make heavy weather in the House when dealing with housing matters for which he also had responsibility. Dick associated himself wholeheartedly with Birmingham's Olympic bid and he came over to Lausanne with us to indicate Government support, but it was inevitable that his inconspicuous period of office was the opposite expected of him on his appointment.

These deficiencies were certainly corrected by the appointment of Minister number four, Colin Moynihan. Colin is all go. An outstanding rowing cox of Olympic fame, he will take a new initiative about anything at the drop of a hat. He certainly has no respect for the conservative traditions of sport. It is all change with Colin. First, it was the Sports Council, which he reduced in size. This means that there can be no sensible dialogue with the governing bodies of the various sports, which inevitably leaves matters in the hands of the full-time officials. He is fortunate that the new director of the Council, David Pickup, is taking great pains to build his relationships with sport and he is a man that sport can work with, but the new direction being taken by the Sports Minister seems likely to undermine the whole edifice. No sooner had he started down this path than he underlined his purpose by calling together some very distinguished sporting athletes without the presence of their governing bodies and allowing them to criticise their absent colleagues. This I think was a bad mistake, it was certainly the opposite policy to the one I followed when I wanted to influence sport: to bring sportsmen and women into my counsel and offer them incentives to carry out agreed policies. Moynihan went on to compound his error by publicly attacking the administrators, about whom he seems to have deep prejudices, suggesting that most of them were too old, and saying that we need 'gold medal administration by gold medal winners'. If sport had taken this literally almost the whole sporting administration of the country would have resigned overnight and British sport would have collapsed! The situation was saved by Prince Philip, the president of the CCPR. He took advantage of the Minister's presence at the next AGM to utter a stirring response pointing out that he himself was still an administrator, and that he also represented Britain at his own sport, the carriage and four. Having delivered that broadside HRH called for a show of hands from the several hundred people in the hall, asking how many of these administrators had taken part in international sport or still participated in the sport they administered. The response was overwhelming.

Another mistake which Minister Moynihan makes is to cultivate exclusive relationships with selected journalists, usually from *The Times* which now devotes more space to sport than any other quality newspaper. By far and away the major disappointment for sport as far as Colin Moynihan is concerned is the situation which has developed through his handling of the serious issue of Association Football and the football identity card question. He started every meeting with all who came to see him with the statement: 'the scheme is not negotiable'. In other words, he was under orders from the Prime Minister and that is how sport now perceives him.

A Minister leaving office has to consider his future role very carefully. In Opposition I started where I had left off in Government, dealing with both environment and sport. Neil Kinnock quite rightly wished to bring on new people, in particular from among some of the younger Members who had supported him in his contest for the leadership. Sensibly, he included many others who had supported Roy Hattersley but wished to give every support to the new leader. It seemed that I came into this category and I thought it made sense to be asked to continue with sport but to pass on my environment portfolio. I resuscitated my public relations consultancy, Denis Howell Consultants. CSS

Consultants, founded by Barrie Gill and Michael Tee, my first clients, often describe me as 'the conscience of the company'. As I have enjoyed nothing but the happiest of relationships with this most professional of sports agencies I am delighted by the compliment.

Soon I was approached by my colleague in Government, John Silkin, and invited to join the new board of Wembley Stadium for which he was mounting a bid, and I have remained on it ever since. The Silkin bid foundered at the last hurdle and control passed to Brian Wolfson, an outstanding executive chairman with another valued, though more controversial, character, Jarvis Astaire, as his deputy. Together they have worked to transform our national stadium and so far £23 million has been invested to turn Wembley into an all-seater stadium, refurbish the Wembley Arena and build new exhibition halls. Plans are afoot for another exhibition hall and for other developments necessary to support the stadium itself since it cannot possibly be sustained by its own earnings. This point is not properly understood by the public at large, nor even by all sports administrators. We often hear talk of national stadiums in Birmingham, Sheffield, Manchester and elsewhere. Quite apart from the capital cost of such a stadium, which must be able to seat 80,000 people, and the vast acreage involved – it would need to be large enough for massive car parking and public transport – there are the considerable ongoing revenue costs. At London's Wembley we estimate that it costs £50,000 to open the gates! When we proposed to build a stadium for the Birmingham Olympic bid it was designed so that a roof could be added afterwards and to convert it into the largest exhibition hall in Europe as part of the NEC. I have never seen any proposals from other contenders suggesting how this revenue cost would be met.

Later on I also took on a consultancy with Merlin, a development company who, together with their partners Laings and Sheerwater, secured the contract to build our national indoor arena and supporting facilities in Birmingham. I also agreed to become a director of Birmingham Cable, who won the franchise for the city. None of these causes are demanding in time but all of them are close to my heart.

THE HOWELL REPORT ON SPORTS SPONSORSHIP

When the CCPR announced that it wished to sponsor an independent report into all aspects of sports sponsorship I was in wholehearted agreement. It was not a day too soon – sports sponsorship had been growing at an amazing pace, it was totally unregulated, and many governing bodies of sport feared they would be over-run with commercialism. In a few cases there was a danger that certain sports would be taken over. Power was being exercised over sections of the media, especially television, for which there was no accountability. Many sponsoring companies had little knowledge about the guiding principles upon which sport rests and simply measured their sponsorship in terms of television exposure, which their financial directors then judged according to the cost of straight television advertising. The commercial television companies were unhappy about providing such advertising for sports broadcasts at a cheaper rate than that at which they sold their direct advertising space, although they understood the desire of their sports departments to have access to the best sporting occasions. An increasing cause of concern was the advent of international sports agencies who seemed to dominate sport and were negotiating contracts, both for performers and governing bodies, in order to get television exposure and to assume more and more power. Many sports bodies were valiantly trying to maintain their control and many had perfectly acceptable relationships with their sponsors, but almost all of them wanted the subject examined and guiding principles determined.

Peter Lawson, the general secretary of the CCPR, twice approached me to chair the enquiry which he and his colleagues were determined to set up. Twice I declined on the grounds that I had a professional relationship with CSS, which was one of the largest British companies in this field. My time as the Minister for Sport had brought me into the discussion on many occasions, so my views on many aspects of sponsorship were well-known. It might be thought that all this prejudiced my thinking before I had heard a word of evidence, but Lawson thought otherwise. I suspect that he was strongly influenced by his attempts to find someone else to do the job, a search which was turning out to be fruitless. He came back to me yet again and told me that this was an enquiry to be conducted on behalf of the CCPR of which I was a former chairman, whose members all knew both me and all of my interests. They all supported his approach to me. I relented subject to three conditions. First he was to seek the approval of Prince Philip, their president, as I did not wish it to be a source of any embarrassment if I made any controversial recommendations. Secondly I wanted, within reason, to choose my own committee, and finally I would be provided with sufficient resources for the research and secretarial work. Prince Philip thought that the reasons for my hesitation 'only show that he knows what he is talking about', and the other two conditions were readily agreed to. The two-year enquiry turned out to be totally demanding but quite enthralling. Putting the committee together was much easier than I had feared. Marea Hartman from athletics and from swimming Harold Hassall, who had also been a professional footballer in his time, came from two governing bodies much involved in sponsorship. From rugby union I was able to secure the services of John Young, an international player of distinction and an executive at the Stock Exchange. Peter Hunt, a marketing director of Coca-Cola, represented the interests of the sponsors. Two old and dependable friends of mine would represent a regional interest – Tony Boyce, a most experienced solicitor and chairman of Torquay United, who well understood the feelings of participants in a sport where most sponsorship was concentrated at the top, and John Perry, who was one of my nominees on the regional Sports Council who also served on the South-West Tourist Board.

Following my normal practice of ensuring that sport should have an all-party approach I invited Colin Moynihan to become a member. As well as being an Olympic medallist and a business executive with Tate and Lyle, he was a Tory MP. Alan Purnell, an accountant from Birmingham, was also a good county player at tennis and badminton and brought another level of experience. John Wheatley of the Sports Council had served at both national and regional levels, which was very useful. Completing the team was Pat Besford, doyenne of sports journalists, who I knew could be argumentative, which she proved in good measure, but a professional journalist to her fingertips. She was largely responsible for writing the report, a labour of love. The CCPR more than met its undertakings on the administrative side by providing two excellent organisers, Niobe Wells and Diana Sabin. Finally, I had the great good fortune to come into contact with Gordon Andrews, who lectures on accountancy at Birmingham University and who has a tremendous enthusiasm for sport. He was undertaking a great deal of football research in connection with publications of his own and agreed to work on the project. The amount of statistical information that Andrews provided for us was enormous and we published much of it. In the years since our report, to the best of my knowledge not a single one of Gordon's published statistics has ever been challenged!

We interviewed more than 120 people, many representing organisations, but some having significant individual experience. The list of those interviewed reads like a sporting who's who. At the end of it all I don't believe that we left anything undone which we ought to have done. Our report ran to 15 chapters and 73 recommendations. The CCPR tell me that they have sold 2,500 copies. This met the cost of the entire enquiry and its publication and made a modest profit! Even more significant was the amount of international interest generated by the report, judged both by overseas sales and by correspondence and comment made to me on my travels. The Howell Report made a considerable impression around the world. It is disappointing that some of our recommendations and conclusions have still to be acted upon, especially those which we directed to the attention of the Government, where Colin Moynihan now sits in the seat of power. The concern we expressed about ethical conduct and conflicts of interest has grown rather than diminished since we reported, and ought to be tackled by a Minister who understands the importance of sport in the life of the country and the commercial standards which should operate within it.

The committee had no hesitation in accepting that sport serves the public interest and that its sponsorship is fully justified. We stated as categorically as we could that 'at all times' governing bodies should accept full responsibility for everything that happens in their sport and that above all, governing bodies need to protect the integrity of their sport. To this end we charged the Sports Council with the responsibility for supervising the principles and practice of sports sponsorship. They have given some attention to this, even securing sponsorship for some sports. We also required that they should report annually and publicly upon their stewardship in these areas so as to ensure continuous public debate, which is essential.

We found from Gordon Andrews' work that sports sponsorship had risen from £2.5 million in 1970 to an estimated £20 million six years later, and on to £84.7 million (including back-up services) for 1982. Gordon Andrews devised an ingenious formula to estimate the growth of sponsorship and we reached the conclusion that a year later, allowing for inflation, the figure would have reached £100 million. Our researchers revealed that the 1982 figure of television coverage for our top 20 sports was 1,870 hours 59 minutes. After a detailed examination of public attitudes we concluded that 'the sponsorship of sport is fully accepted by the British public'.

Colin Moynihan was given the task of collecting the opinions of the athletes. Steve Ovett, in particular, was concerned about the management of trust funds established for the benefit of athletes. He was understandably aggrieved that their future resources, much of it from sponsorship income, was on seven-day deposit, which was not good enough. Our members charged with reviewing financial matters examined the progress of the Sports Aid Foundation and we recommended that a significant improvement in marketing and public relations was called for, although we certainly did not under-estimate their achievement of raising £1.5 million between 1976 and 1983. As far as the governing bodies were concerned we hoped that the CCPR would accept responsibility for bringing about a more efficient marketing policy, but we urged them to guard against an over-reliance upon sponsorship income, the dangers of which are obvious. Sponsors can move out of sport as quickly as they come in and we recommended that sponsors should provide at least three years' notice if they intended to pull out. Tony Boyce did an excellent job of work in considering all the tax implications of sponsorship, bringing to bear not only his considerable legal experience in commercial matters but also in securing the interest and advice of an eminent Queen's Counsel. As a result I believe we were able to offer sport very good advice on tax matters such as forming charitable trusts although I doubt that many sporting bodies have acted upon it. It is also to be regretted that the Government itself has not acted upon a House of Lords report recommending that new legislation be introduced to make sport for educational purposes a charitable activity. We were also concerned about the effect of VAT upon sport and gave advice as to how this might be mitigated. We recommended that sport ought to be zero rated. An important conclusion concerned the need of the Government to give every possible encouragement to the establishment of an international sporting head-quarters in this country. British influence in international sport is needed as never before, yet we provide little encouragement.

Our researchers analysed the relationships between sponsorships and the media and Pat Besford guided us towards the appropriate conclusions. We reminded our media friends that their first duty is to report the news factually and accurately, an injunction which ought probably to be made week in and week out. In our turn, Pat constantly reminded us, sport also has a responsibility towards the media. The extent to which sport and television are inter-dependent was illustrated by the results of our researches which showed that in 1982 sponsored sport occupied 1,004 hours 45 minutes of our screen time against a total sporting coverage of 1,449 hours 48 minutes. This was an increase of 10 per cent on the previous year. A matter of policy importance was the drift of the Independent Broadcasting Authority away from providing a competitive service to that of the BBC, which we believed they had a public duty to provide. There has been some improvement in the area of major sport since our report was published but overall there is still cause for concern. We welcomed the substantial opportunity for sponsorship coverage provided by television, radio and the press and we urged the governing bodies to sharpen their perceptions in this regard. We concluded our review of media matters by asking the Government to take care that cable television contained a minimum British content in their programme output.

There can be no doubt that Chapter 13 of our report, 'Ethical Considerations', caused us more heart-searching and anxious discussions than the rest of it put together. It certainly attracted the most coverage. I suppose this was inevitable. When we took ourselves off to John Perry's Livermead Cliff Hotel in Torquay for a long weekend of contemplation these ethical questions dominated our discussions and I was determined that we should face up to them. We did, though not without misgivings on the part of some colleagues. I decided to write this chapter of the report myself and then to ask Pat Besford to edit it, a necessary step not only on journalistic and editorial grounds, but also because the report carried the signature and authority of our members, who would all be accountable for our conclusions and recommendations. Pat and I had some very fierce arguments indeed, but at the end of the day we managed to reach agreement on even the most controversial issues. Many of these arose from the response of the international agencies to our enquiries about the scope of their activities. I understood the concern but it would have been irresponsible to duck out of such consideration on account of sensitivities or financial muscle. Government-appointed committees are protected by total privilege which can be relied upon if necessary. Such a committee as ours has a limited protection. We were investigating a matter of public interest, and anyone proceeding against us would need to show malice on our part. Aggressive noises were made before publication and threat of legal action was made against me personally as a result of publication and subsequent media coverage, but they did not discourage us and soon petered out.

Indeed, the increasing dominance of the international agencies was a big source of concern and we spent a lot of time examining their influence and relationships within various sports and their interlocking financial interests. We considered the position of Adidas, who had been very much in the news following their private enterprise activities with certain Welsh rugby union players. The Welsh Rugby Union took grave exception to this type of sponsorship of individual players who wore the Adidas boot but soon changed their tune and themselves entered into an agreement with Adidas which provided for sponsorship for the whole team. Horst Dassler, the Adidas chairman, agreed to come and discuss all these matters with me provided that only two persons from either side were in attendance. In fact he arrived direct from a meeting with the Welsh RFU accompanied by John Boulter, an old acquaintance of mine. I decided that John Wheatley, director of the Sports Council, was the most appropriate member of my committee to join us. We had a pleasant and far-reaching discussion, and Dassler could not have been more forthcoming. In answer to my question, 'What is a shoe manufacturer doing becoming involved in sports administration?', he told me: 'We exist to sell boots and shirts and wherever the action is we need to be there'. This policy apparently took Adidas to world fixture congress for sport, meetings of the International Olympic Committee and anywhere else they thought would be useful. We went on to discuss the company's involvements in the election of officers of international sports organisations about which we were worried and again Dassler was very frank. 'We have a department which collects and files all information from all official publications of national Olympic committees, international federations and so on. We have a better overall view of the total situation in sport than would be possible for any individual. It is natural that if people seek information on who holds which position in sport they should turn to us'. He went on to say that he would make this information available to anyone who sought it.

We were astonished when we explored the relationship between Adidas and FIFA to be told that Adidas had undertaken an extensive programme of education in Africa on behalf of FIFA, the most powerful governing body in world sport. This certainly seemed to be above board but we thought it ought to be kept under review by some responsible sports organisation and we recommended that the General Association of International Sports Federations and the International Assembly of National Organisations of Sport should do so. To the best of my knowledge this has not happened. After we had handed our report to the printers we heard that Adidas and a Japanese company, Densu, had created a new company called ISL which had obtained extensive rights of marketing for both the World Cup (football) and the Olympic Games. I telexed Adidas to enquire about these developments and received a reply from John Boulter telling me that he was becoming increasingly concerned about the nature of my enquiries. We concluded from all this that 'all the international federations have a duty to ensure the fullest public confidence in their contractual sponsorship agreements and should maintain registers of their commercial and business arrangements with outside organisations'. This seemed to me to be a sensible precaution, but I doubt whether it has ever been implemented. In the light of experience it is clear that the ISL involvement has been very beneficial for FIFA and the Olympic movement. Their marketing has succeeded in attracting large sums of money for the development programmes of these organisations and I doubt whether any other organisation at that time could have achieved a similar degree of success, or whether any other organisation could have taken on such a huge assignment. I still believe, however, that it would have been in everyone's interest to have invited competitive tenders for the work rather than to have set up a new company to award it the contract. Given the success of ISL that is now an academic question.

We had rather less of a response from Mark McCormack of the International Management Group (IMG). All our efforts to set up a meeting with him came to nothing. Gordon Andrews had meetings at his London office with Ian Todd, his senior vice-president, who came to meet us for a lengthy session which was adjourned and never reconvened. Mr McCormack told us he would be coming to stay at the Westbury Hotel and Diana Sabin spent a lot of time trying to contact him there without success. I hoped to meet him at Wimbledon where I was told he might be available, but he left before I arrived. Nowadays when he is asked about my report he totally dismisses it on the grounds that I have never met him. How true! Our area of concern with IMG was about possible conflicts of interest, highlighted by the fact that McCormack represents sponsors and sports bodies, creates events such as the World Matchplay Golf Championship, negotiates television rights and even commentates on the event. In answer to our enquiries Todd told us, 'Without McCormack there would be no World Matchplay Golf Championship'. This is true, but after receiving other comparable evidence we concluded: 'It seems to us most undesirable that an organisation should be able to represent a governing body, sponsors, a significant number of top players, negotiate television, cable and satellite contracts and sell merchandising rights. The situation is pregnant with conflict of interests and cannot carry public confidence'.

We therefore proposed that 'Her Majesty's Government should refer to the Office of Fair Trading, for full examination, the relationship between IMG and important sporting events in the UK to establish whether any monopoly situation exists'. This has never been done and the present Minister for Sport, who signed this report, has not so far shown any interest in doing so.

We also met head-on the ethical question involved in tobacco sponsorship of sport and after a lengthy period of cogitation decided that these issues of principle extended into the areas of alcohol and gambling as well as smoking. We fully accepted that excessive indulgence in all these activities is dangerous. The dilemma for us was that all these pursuits are perfectly lawful and revenue-producing on a vast scale. We examined the voluntary agreements reached between the Government and the tobacco companies which I had been involved in negotiating when I was Minister. We considered the tax income from these products, which in 1982–83 was £4,590 million from alcohol; £635 million from gambling and £4,207 million from tobacco. This caused us to consider the tax structure once more and to observe that in this country all taxes go into the Exchequer pool and are then used to finance all government activity – housing, hospitals, arts, sports and so on. There is no way that income from any source can be divided up to be spent according to the wishes of any section of society. We were well aware, too, that there were strong views on what products were dangerous for us to consume and ought not to be promoted by sponsorship. In Victoria, Australia, I had myself come across a Minister who wished to outlaw 'aerated' water soft drinks. He had no objection to sponsorship by gambling interests. Perfectly natural in Australia, I suppose. At the end of all these considerations we concluded that the only acceptable test had to be a test of legality. Is the activity lawful? Is the nation as a whole prepared to benefit financially from taxes upon the product? We decided that 'where a pursuit is lawful and when the Government itself derives substantial income from such pursuits then there can be no objection in principle to the sponsorship of sport from these sources'. The freedom of sports people to decide these matters for themselves ought to be safeguarded.

It had been a fascinating 18 months. One of our main recommendations, which was to establish an institute of sport sponsorship and to establish a register of agencies who observed acceptable codes of conduct, is only now becoming a reality. As with all major enquiries in this country nothing happens overnight as a result of their findings. Implementation is a long-term haul. Their importance is that they provide a yardstick against which issues can be judged in the future. They challenge established opinion and provide an authority for those who wish to take up the issues. They can never be ignored. I was happy to have attempted the task, and so were all my colleagues. Seven years on the Howell Report is still seen in a good light around the world which must mean that we have made a contribution to an important aspect of sporting activity.

THE DUTY TO OPPOSE

Nothing is more fundamental to the concept of a free democracy than the presence of an elected Opposition with a duty to oppose the Government of the day. We are indeed Her Majesty's 'loyal' Opposition. We must take our duties seriously. I have no doubt that on occasion Her Majesty feels like assuming these duties herself! It follows from the concepts of opposition and democratic elections that sooner or later the Opposition is going to become the Government. Therefore, we have two duties. The first is to be constructive in our opposition. The second is to prepare ourselves for government. It is not always easy to carry out both duties simultaneously. To begin with, most Governments resent the Opposition. This is natural but unwise. Governments have to get their business through and they are foolish if they fail to understand – as Mrs Thatcher's third administration has failed to understand – that the Opposition seeks to achieve something from opposition. An Opposition which is going to be defeated time after time, not by the force of argument but by a solid mass of regimented votes in the Government lobby, becomes increasingly resentful and disparaging of Government. This does no good for the reputations of Ministers, and when those Ministers find themselves in Opposition they will experience the short shrift which, in office, they gave to Members on the other side of the House. Likewise, Opposition Members who oppose every proposal of Government will have a torrid time if ever they reach office. These are the guiding principles by which I have always tried to operate during my 35 years' membership in the House. I have not always succeeded, but I trust at least that it is recognised that I have tried to be reasonable. Having said that I must also concede that there are times when great issues are at stake – Suez is the most obvious in my time – or when the fundamentals of liberty are involved, the basic human rights of our ethnic minorities being a recent example, when reasonableness is in itself a failure of Opposition. Even so, we still have a duty to express our anger in parliamentary terms.

In the last decade of my service in the House I led for the Opposition on a range of important Bills in which these lessons became apparent. The one experience which was common to all of them was the failure of Parliament to provide for the efficient performance of Opposition. We were under-staffed in terms of researchers, lawyers and secretaries. The House of Commons library does excellent work but it cannot possibly serve the needs of Opposition Members meeting several times a week on a whole range of committees, and it would be wrong to impose upon it any duty to initiate Opposition, or to suggest lines of research. The responsibility to oppose is that of HM Opposition so far as Parliament is concerned, and theirs alone. All too often we are thrown upon the mercies of interested parties who do their best to come to our aid and provide us with back-up services and advice, but we know only too well that they cannot be disinterested in their approach to us. Of all the parliamentary reforms that I believe to be essential for the proper function of Opposition, both for individual Members and for front-bench spokesmen, this back-up service would be top of my list, closely followed by the reform of parliamentary procedures and timetables so that Members work sensible hours and have reasonable time to do their thinking and relax with their families, another essential of good Government and efficient Opposition.

The Wildlife and Countryside Bill was an excellent example of good Opposition strategy. This reached the Commons in 1980, having first secured its passage through the Lords. After our election defeat in 1979 I had continued to be Party spokesman on sport and the number two spokesman on environmental affairs, working to Gerald Kaufman. For this Bill we also had the stimulating presence of our science spokesman, Tam Dalyell. Kaufman and Dalyell opened and closed the Second Reading debate in the Commons in April 1981 and I took over from Gerald for the 26 sittings of the standing committee, assisted by Ted Graham, another of our environmental spokesmen. This was a Bill about which we were determined to be reasonable and positive. It was much needed and universally welcomed. The Ministers we were opposing were Michael Heseltine, the Secretary of State, who did not serve on the committee; Tom King, the Minister for Local Government and Environmental Services; Hector Munro, the under secretary who also carried the sports portfolio, and Michael Roberts who was an under secretary at the Welsh Office. On our side we fielded a very experienced and committed team including Ken Marks (Gorton) who had served with me as Minister, Peter Hardy (Rother Valley) one of the most enthusiastic environmentalists in the House – Tam Dalyell described him as 'an amenity society in himself' – Donald Anderson, representing Welsh interests and our Whip, Allan MacKay (Penistone).

We did good work with great humour notwithstanding the serious issues at stake. We were soon able to identify the points of contention. Chief among these were the sites of special scientific interest and the growing practice of the Ministry of Agriculture to make grants to farmers for the purpose of increasing their efficiency. This has resulted in the massive destruction of hedgerows, the home of so much of our wildlife, creating more and more fields of larger size for the benefit of farming. Early on Hector Munro accepted the basic statistics of our case on areas of special scientific interest – the Nature Conservancy Council had reported that its 1980 survey had disclosed damage in 8,700 hectares of such sites and, worse, 2,400 hectares had been destroyed. Munro's view was that as these figures only represented 0.7 per cent and 0.33 per cent respectively they were 'a minute fraction of the total hectares covered by these sites'. Stephen Ross (Isle of Wight), the Liberal spokesman, was a very useful member of the Opposition team and he was soon demanding protection for the otter and condemning the vile practice of otter hunting in Scotland. Munro excused this on the extraordinary grounds that 'in recent years the otter hunt in Scotland has hardly killed an otter but it has made a significant contribution to wildlife by killing a large number of mink'. The protection of otters, he said, was not a question of otter hunting but of the conservation of the habitat and control of pollution from which the loss of otters derives. All that we could make of that was that the Government hoped to improve the habitat to preserve the otter so that the Scottish hunts would have more of them to kill off! Andrew Bennett (Stockport North), a sterling member of our committee, said the Bill was 'like dealing with the problems of the countryside and wildlife while sitting in an oak wood on a stormy autumn day and trying to catch the falling leaves'. Tam Dalyell quoted John Stuart Mill and accused Ministers of 'the deep slumber of a decided opinion'. That was in 1980–81; no doubt ten years on Tam is justified in believing that such a decided opinion has now become a nightmare! I strongly believed that the loss of our hedgerows could only be halted by making any attempt at removal subject to planning control. Ministers did not seem to have any alternative proposals. I also made it one of the features of our opposition to demand that marine nature reserves should be designated around our coasts. Eventually this was conceded by the Government and made a great contribution to the success of the Bill.

We spent a lot of time on the protection of countryside footpaths, a matter on which I had felt strongly when Minister for the Environment. I had agreed with Alan Leavett, my chief countryside adviser, to a system whereby a public path could only be closed if an alternative path was created. This allowed for the needs of farmers and landowners sometimes to close a pathway but protected the public rights of way by providing an alternative. In my own Bill, killed off by the 1979 election, I had proposed that grants should be available for this purpose but such a proposal was not included in the present Bill. An example of the irritations suffered by Oppositions occurred when we repeatedly drew attention to the fact that the Ministry of Agriculture offered grants to improve farming efficiency with total disregard to their environmental consequences. It was obvious that Ministers agreed with us but could do little about it. The cause of agriculture triumphed over that of environment.

When the Committee stage of the Bill opened I followed my custom both in Government and in Opposition. This is to set out my stall as early as I can. When in Opposition this means letting the Government know the areas of the Bill where I consider it is important for us to get concessions or improvements, to spell them out and to tell the Minister that if he wishes for co-operation from our side he would be well advised to let us know as soon as possible what he can concede in each of these areas. In addition to support, what came to be known as the Sandford Amendment, moved in the Lords by Lord Sandford and carried against the Government by two votes, demanded major changes in the 'scope, administration and implications of the system of grant-aid for farmers'. I listed the sites of special scientific interest, the question of marine nature reserves, public footpaths, the use of snares for trapping animals, shooting at night-time and on Sundays, and the almost hilarious – except for ramblers attacked by them – problem of controlling bulls in fields. On this occasion Tom King responded to my list immediately, he thought it was eminently reasonable.

I hope that he had been encouraged in this response by my former officials. They had become accustomed to my practice when in Government of beginning all consideration of future legislation with the questions, 'What do the Opposition want to get out of this Bill?' 'Is there anything we can give them to ensure their co-operation? Please go and find out, it may save hours of committee time and several all-night sessions'. And they did – so did a succession of fine private parliamentary secretaries (back-bench MPs who serve the Minister's interest in the House by acting as his watchdogs and helping him to be informed of the views of colleagues on matters within his area of responsibility). I had every cause to be grateful for the support of Joe Ashton, Michael Maguire and Jim Callaghan (little Jim as we called him, to distinguish him from big Jim, the Prime Minister). My approach to legislation was often greeted with incredulity but it never failed me and I found it much more pleasant to proceed on the basis of achieving the widest common agreement rather than the pursuit of hostility, which is difficult to maintain. When a Government is determined to listen to no one, to amend nothing, as in the Football Spectators Bill years on, it loses co-operation in the House and respect in the country.

The Wildlife Bill was actually three Bills in one, providing for the protection of birds; nature conservation, countryside and national parks; and public rights of way. This was far too much for one Bill. The Government had to rely upon a constructive approach from the Opposition. The alternative was the imposition of a guillotine which would make them look ridiculous when they attempted to curtail discussion upon such matters as flora and fauna, which they were seeking to protect, not to mention species of birds listed in the Bill. In all, there were 780 such items. The strong and vocal organisations dedicated to these causes – bodies such as the Royal Society for the Protection of Birds and the Nature Conservancy Council – would certainly take offence and embarrass the Government. In these circumstances the Government had no alternative but to hand the initiative over to the Opposition. When I first looked at the mammoth list of protected species I could hardly believe my eyes. It was a gift for any Opposition. Tam Dalyell and my colleagues soon realised that all we had to do was to put down an amendment for each of the items to be protected, seeking to exclude them from the Bill and requiring the Government to justify the inclusion of each one. It would have destroyed the Government's timetable. There would have to be 780 separate debates,

and since the chair would not accept a closure motion until an amendment had been debated for at least two hours, the potential for mischief
was obvious. We decided to demonstrate this truth to the Ministers
who were reluctant to provide answers on the issues which we regarded
as important. Tam Dalyell was enthusiastic to throw down the gauntlet.
He assured me that single-handed he could keep the committee sitting
all night – 'Go to bed and leave it to me,' he advised, 'come back at
breakfast time'.

When he arrived in the committee room for this mammoth session
we could hardly contain ourselves. Ministers and Tory backbenchers
looked on with amazement as he heaved in armfuls of learned volumes
and spread them out before him, a scientific exposition of all the lists
of species he was prepared to debate. I shall never forget his speeches
on the natterjack toad and the Dalyell anus worm, which he told us
owed its discovery to a distant relative of his family. It was wonderful
stuff. Soon we were receiving assurances about marine nature reserves,
bulls in fields, better co-operation from the Ministry of Agriculture
and the other matters that we had raised. Peter Hardy was equally
useful when Ministers were reluctant to meet us on yet another issue.
Peter had been talking for over an hour about the golden-eyed duck
when Tom King beckoned me outside. 'Get him to sit down,' he said,
'you can have your concession.' Peter duly obliged. At the end of the
day the legislation owed as much to the skills of the Opposition as to
those of Government.

The Water Bill which reached the Commons in November 1982 was
an entirely different kettle of fish. It was a Bill which abolished the
National Water Council and the Water Space Amenity Council and so
transformed the control and management of the water industry, and it
did so without any consultation or public discussion. No satisfactory
explanation was offered to either House as to why the National Water
Council was to go and how its functions were to be discharged. It really
meant that the national planning of water resources was to be brought
back into the Department of the Environment from which a previous
Conservative Government had removed it. It also meant that national
wage negotiations would come to an end and be replaced by negotiations
at each water authority, although the Minister could not tell us how
and when. Most serious of all was the termination of the Water Space
Amenity Council which was the only effective guarantee to the public
that the regional water authorities would carry out their obligations to
provide for public access to the vast areas of land owned by the authorities, and which positively encouraged recreation and sport on the
rivers and lakes in their ownership. This was particularly important
for anglers and canoeists. Throughout the Committee stage of the Bill
we got no satisfactory answers to any of these questions. A clue to the
purpose of the Bill was contained in a sub-paragraph in one of the
schedules which excluded the press from access to any meetings of the
water authorities. I summed up our fears by saying that there would

be 'no Ombudsman, no public accountability and no public reporting of any sort'.

The General Election of 1983 was never going to result in anything but a Tory victory but there were other causes for anxiety. Labour's defence policy was impossible to sell. As I toured the country I could only despair as good men and women faced the dilemma of being multilateral disarmers saddled with a unilateral policy. Labour voters just would not buy it. We had other formidable problems: the Falklands War had created a surge of understandable patriotism which enormously benefited Margaret Thatcher. Her single-minded determination to confront the Argentinian aggressors had support right across the parties but the Prime Minister was always going to get the credit for leading that almost inconceivable defence of the islands. Probably even more damaging to Labour was the defection of the 'gang of four' – Roy Jenkins, Shirley Williams, David Owen and Bill Rodgers – to form their new party, the Social Democratic Party. They took many of our voters with them, which was disastrous for the socialists and social democrats alike as their leaders must have known. They believed they could crush the Labour Party. What they failed to realise was that they could not destroy the Labour movement, which represents the totality of Labour, the trade union as well as the political movement plus the co-operative movement. What the SDP achieved in two elections was the safe return of Mrs Thatcher's Government. Those of us who refused to have any part of it have been vindicated.

In 1983 the Party faced one final difficulty, the age and personality of Michael Foot. He was cruelly attacked in the grossest personal terms in the press and by the Tories, not on the basis of the politics he was advancing but simply upon grounds of personality. It was sickening. I had not voted for Michael when he was elected to be our leader but I always found that his reputation as a distinguished man of letters of real warmth and liberal disposition was fully justified. His assumed weakness was his unfailing kindness and courtesy, a different trait in his character to that generally suggested by his time as the radical champion of the Left in the days of Bevanite Opposition. No doubt the change had taken place when he was in the Cabinet, where he had proved to be a first-class Minister in charge of employment affairs. The only bright spot for me throughout the entire election campaign was the daily performance of Bob Worcester, the head of the MORI poll organisation. The campaign committee met every morning and as a member of the Party's National Executive, which I was for one year, I attended. Worcester had the latest update on public opinion trends, the importance of all the issues and the effect of speeches and television performance. Our tragedy was that we were in a straitjacket of predetermined policy, unable to take any alternative action. The result was inevitable. In Small Heath my loyal supporters campaigned well and effectively, especially while I was away speaking around the country. My result, in a terrible year for Labour, was a satisfaction for all of us: I secured 63.3 per cent of the poll with a majority of 15,252, 42.1 per cent of the vote.

When Neil Kinnock became leader of the Party I moved to the home affairs team. The reasoning behind this invitation, initiated by Roy Hattersley, was that my expertise in immigration issues would be useful. Once more I found myself embroiled in legislation. We had the Cable and Broadcasting Bill and the Mary Whitehouse-inspired Video Recordings Bill, to both of which I gave general but critical support. The privately-promoted Shrewsbury and Atcham Borough Council Bill proposed the take-over of Gay Meadow, the ground of Shrewsbury Town Football Club, where I had spent many a Saturday afternoon officiating League games. I was having none of that and when appealed to by the club I recruited John Golding to help me defeat the Bill. It was a wise choice for John was well-used to making long speeches – our only chance of winning this fight was to keep the debate going for three hours to force the promoters to move the closure, for which purpose they needed 100 Members in the lobby. I calculated that Golding could speak for an hour and I put him in to bat early on, saving my own innings for the tail end. It was an hilarious performance. John dealt with subject after subject. He finished the first section of his speech on the importance of Shrewsbury Town FC, looked down at me and said 'help me out'. I got up to intervene and ask him if he had considered the fact that for generations a market had been held on this site. John proved to be very knowledgeable about markets, even more so when I asked him as a keen salmon angler himself if he thought that the building of a new bridge would impede the progress of the salmon! Next came the fact that the football ground car park was used as an overflow for the Shrewsbury Flower Show. 'What', said Golding, 'does Percy Thrower know about this? Has he been consulted?' and he was off for another ten minutes. All this was in order under the existing and nonsensical rules of the House and we were perfectly entitled to take advantage of them. It was up to the Members promoting the Bill to muster their 100 Members in support. At ten o'clock they could get only 84 Members into their lobby, the Bill was lost and the football ground reprieved.

The Data Protection Bill was a much more formidable proposition skilfully steered through a complicated Committee stage by David Waddington, the Home Office Minister. Our fundamental concern was that none of the manual files kept upon a citizen would be available to that person for inspection. The Bill provided that there should be a right of access only to information stored in computers. We spent hours pointing out the illogicality of this. The voluntary bodies active in the social services field also had other serious concerns, especially whether confidential information entered on hospital medical records should pass, via hospital reports, to doctors and others, on to social service agencies and the DHSS. I followed my normal practice of starting our proceedings by outlining to David Waddington the six or seven matters of importance on which I would like to achieve some amendment or reassurance. David Waddington took them away and I met him once or twice to discuss progress. He was trying to be helpful but I had a group of new Members who were itching for a fight. Robert Kilroy-Silk (Knowsley North) was making his front-bench debut on this Bill as my number two. At times I thought he was asserting an independent leadership – so did David Waddington, who was clearly exasperated. Matters came to a head over the demand from Kilroy for an all-night sitting. It was his virility symbol. I was confounded, on my return from other duties up country to attend a meeting convened by Kilroy-Silk for all the voluntary bodies, to be told by the representative of the British Medical Association that it was the duty of the Labour Party to sit all night in order to oppose this legislation! I responded by asking him since when the BMA had become affiliated to the Labour Party. I was even asked on a television programme by an interviewer who had clearly been primed to do so why I was failing in my duty to sit all night on this Bill? The truth was that I was making remarkably good progress in my negotiations with David Waddington but I could not say so until he was authorised to deliver them to the committee. There was nothing for it but to have an all-night sitting. When David made his announcements, conceding almost all the points I had urged upon him, the BMA and the other agencies generously wrote to congratulate me saying that they never thought that I could achieve so much. This was a Committee stage which taught me a great deal and I believe too that it was an education for my new back-bench colleagues. What it taught Kilroy-Silk I do not know, but soon afterwards he gave up the political ghost as far as Parliament was concerned and resigned, preferring the lusher pastures of television presentation where he will not be troubled with the necessity of all-night sittings.

I was delighted to be asked by Neil Kinnock to return to my old duties covering sport. There was, however, no sports legislation to concern me in this Parliament so life was more gentle. Brenda did not want me to stand again for Parliament but I did not want to give up the House when we had new leadership and another election in the offing. Neil Kinnock and Glenys were brilliant throughout the campaign. For one brief moment we all thought that we might win, but Margaret Thatcher was able to rally her forces and get home comfortably. In Small Heath we performed extremely well as usual. We had a firm and able chairman in Mac Baker and in Mike Sharpe a new and loyal agent. I polled 22,787 votes, 66.3 per cent of the poll, on a much reduced electorate and won by a majority of 15,521, 45.7 per cent of the poll. It was my 12th, and probably my final, parliamentary contest. Overall Labour won 30.8 per cent of the vote, an increase of 3.2 per cent. This was an improvement of 42 seats for the combined Opposition but it still left the Government with a very comfortable majority. There was nothing for it but to soldier on.

The Football Spectators Bill was a measure that inspired the true functions of Parliament. Admittedly, it purported to deal with matters of major concern about public order considerations surrounding football matches, but it was introduced against the advice of every organisation with any specialist knowledge, all of whom said it was impractical. It was clearly designed to create the impression that 'something was being done', whether or not it infringed the civil liberties of millions of people, and might well prove to create additional hazards at the turnstiles by causing longer delays as thousands of people seek to get into our football grounds just before kick-off time. The measure started in the Lords and proceeded to the Commons and on no issue of substance did the Government listen to the arguments advanced against its various clauses nor concede an inch. From day one of the Committee stage it was made clear that the committee would meet three mornings a week from 10.30 to 1.00 pm, in the afternoons from 4.30 pm to 7.00 pm and evenings from 9.00 pm until the Government Whips chose to end the agony, not before midnight and sometimes much later. It was a monstrous abuse of our Parliament procedures, designed simply to clock up the hours of the committee's sittings so as to justify a guillotine motion to speed the Bill on its way with even more indecent haste. The only possible response was to argue every point and treat the whole proceedings with contempt. After 120 hours in committee of Government arrogance and inflexibility Lord Justice Taylor rejected the identity card scheme out of hand as likely to create hazards to safety. Exactly our position, and a total vindication of our strategy.

THE ZOLA BUDD SCANDAL

The Zola Budd affair was the most disgraceful Government scandal that I have met in my time in the House. My own feelings were reported in *The Times* on 9 April 1984: 'I think it is an outrage that in the interests of a newspaper stunt procedures of one of the highest departments of state can be manipulated with adverse effects on hundreds of genuine applicants and, in this case, the Olympic hopes of girls who have given years of their lives to compete'.

This small, slight young lady – 5 feet 2 inches in height and only 6 stones in weight – was only 17 years old. She had just taken seven seconds off the 5,000 metres world record and she was the fastest under 19 years old in both the 1500 and 3,000 metres – a tremendous achievement at such an age. She was studying in Blomfontein at the Orange Free State University with no thought of giving that up, becoming British or leaving her South African homeland. But that is what happened when the *Daily Mail* decided that she should compete in the Los Angeles Olympic Games of 1984 and that she should represent Britain. It is not without interest that she was taking a course in history and politics, which convinced me that she was not as naïve about sport and politics as some people would have us think. It had long been impossible for any South African to take part in the Olympics – the IOC were in fact the first of all the international sporting bodies to exclude South Africa from participation. Her British grandfather had emigrated to South Africa and her father had not shown any interest in taking up British citizenship by descent as he was entitled. The suddenness of her departure for Britain showed all the strategic planning and the flair of David English, the editor of the *Daily Mail*, who staged the coup. Professor Charles Niewoudt, president of the South African Athletics Union, reported that 'not even close members of her family knew she was leaving', but he thought it quite normal; 'South Africa is losing athletes all the time because of political problems'.

Only a few days before she left with her parents and her coach she had denied any such intention. Within days of arriving here she had applied to the Home Office Immigration Office at Croydon for British citizenship. The date of that application was 26 March – ten days later, on 5 April, it was granted. Such speed was totally without precedent and it has not, to my knowledge, been repeated since. In my view it was clear evidence of collusion. I have dealt with hundreds of applications for citizenship involving my constituents of Asian origin and I knew only too well that the thorough examination to which they are subjected takes many months, if not years, to complete. However, there was more damning evidence. Zola Budd could not achieve British citizenship if her father was not British. David Waddington, the Home Office Member, told Doug Hoyle, the Labour Member for Warrington, that Miss Budd's father had produced evidence in support of his application at the British Consulate in Johannesburg on 23 March, just three days before Zola's own application.

During these events I was the Opposition spokesman on immigration matters. For one year I had left sport to join the Home Office Shadow team, so I had another reason to lead the campaign against this monstrous piece of maladministration. The Data Protection Bill was in committee and David Waddington was piloting it through. I was leading for Labour so I was in close touch with him throughout and he courteously discussed the case with me. His contention was that she had exceptional talent and should be allowed her chance to compete. I did not get the impression that he was overwhelmingly enthusiastic about advancing such a justification. He certainly had no reply to the inevitable questions about the effect of such unprecedented priority for an athlete over the tens of thousands who were genuinely waiting their turn in the queue. This preposterous plan clearly had the support of David English and probably that of Margaret Thatcher. My regular contact with Home Office officials, the result of my constituency duties, left me in no doubt that many of them shared my view. Soon I was receiving a flood of letters, many from South Africa, from people who also had right to British citizenship by descent, just like Budd, but who were still unable to obtain it. Home Office Ministers had no satisfactory answers.

The British athletics world was also in a state of shock. They had not been consulted either and the extraordinary steps taken by the *Daily Mail* to surround Budd with 'minders' who kept everyone at bay were resented by more than rival newspapers. However, if Budd was to qualify for the Olympic Games she had to appear in a competitive race within three weeks. The British Amateur Athletic Board secretary thought that it was an exciting prospect to have this 'raw talent with us'. First she had to find a club – the women's section of the Aldershot, Farnham and District Club obliged by 14 votes to nil. As the number of places available to British women competitors at the Games was strictly limited it was not surprising that some of them soon expressed concern that their four years of hard work on the training grounds might be jeopardised. Their feelings were eloquently expressed by Wendy Sly, our leading middle distance runner, who had been training in Florida. Wendy had finished in fifth place in the World Championships in Helsinki in both the 1500 and the 3,000 metres and she threatened to boycott the British trials if the IOC waived the qualifications of one year's residence and three years' probation for an athlete changing nationality. Two months after Zola Budd arrived, and with no one apart from the *Daily Mail* and a few athletics officials who needed to do so having met her, she was competing in the British Olympic trials.

Another remarkable feature of this astonishing controversy was the low profile maintained throughout by Leon Brittain, the Home Secretary. He hardly uttered a word. He certainly took no part in the House of Commons debate which, by remarkable coincidence, was due to take place on the subject of fees charged for processing British nationality. I was determined to use this opportunity to ventilate the whole scandal, in spite of constant interruption, mainly from the Member for Richmond and Barnes, Jeremy Hanley, the son of the comedian Jimmy Hanley. He kept interrupting to say that my speech had no relevance. I was, however, aided by the deputy Speaker, Mr Ernest Armstrong, who reminded the House that I was in order if I related my answer to the cost of the nationality fees. This was not difficult: the Government proposed to charge £55 for processing the applications of children in my constituency, many of them very poor indeed, while charging the same amount for Miss Budd, for whom the *Daily Mail* had established a trust fund said to be worth £200,000. And my constituents had waited years for their British citizenship while Zola Budd had achieved it in ten days flat, an Olympic record in itself! I referred to the vitriolic article attacking me in the *Daily Mail* which occupied the whole of the front page. I dealt with it as contemptuously as I could: 'When any Member of Parliament decides that it is his duty to raise the role of the *Daily Mail* he must naturally expect to be given the fullest treatment of vitriolic filth for which that newspaper is justifiably renowned. I therefore consider it a supreme accolade yesterday to be associated in one and the same article with both the late Senator McCarthy and Dr Goebbels. Such compliments and the source from which they come may be judged by the track record of Sir David English, himself a distinguished exponent of the arts that he condemns. Was it the same Sir David English who was involved in the Millhench affair and the forgery on House of Commons notepaper? Was it the same David English whose disgraceful allegations about Don Ryder and a British Leyland slush fund ended so abjectly? I could go on to mention the Ted Short affair, not to mention the "12 lies of Labour" issued just before the General Election, ten of which turned out on investigation to be attributable to the *Daily Mail* and not to the Labour Party'.

I felt a lot better after that, but it reminded me that I had the privilege of Parliament on my side while others who were seriously libelled had no such protection and could not risk the bankruptcy to which these ludicrously expensive libel actions often expose them. In his reply David Waddington, the Minister of State, described my speech as 'mean-minded'. He told us that Zola's grandfather was born in Britain; her father was South African born and exercised his right to come here and bring his wife and daughter with him. He went on to make a point of much greater importance than he understood, telling the house that 'Zola applied for registration under Section 3, which gives the State discretion to register a minor'. In other words, she did not achieve her British citizenship by descent as was commonly believed. Indeed, this argument was understood to have been used by Charles Palmer, chairman of the British Olympic Association, to convince Juan Antonio Samaranch, president of the IOC, to allow Budd to compete in the Los Angeles Olympics. She had achieved her citizenship on the basis of a political discretion exercised by a Minister, a very different matter in terms of eligibility for taking part in the Olympic Games. I do not believe that if this fact had been known to President Samaranch and the eligibility committee of the IOC she would have been allowed to compete.

Waddington went on to say that 'had she been left in the queue she would have been denied the opportunity of competing for a place'. Against the fact that the British embassy in South Africa had reported a massive number of protests and enquiries from the thousands of people waiting in the queue to exercise their own rights, such a defence seemed totally inadequate, as it did to the women athletes who had trained for years for their chance and were now to be displaced. The Minister concluded his speech by trying to turn the tables on me. He referred to a foreword in a book called *The Precious McKenzie Story* where I had written: 'It was my privilege some years ago to be of some small service to him when he was establishing himself as a British citizen. I have enjoyed the tremendous satisfaction of being present when he has represented our country in sport'. As Waddington refused to give way so that I could state the true facts about the McKenzie situation I could only raise a point of order to say: 'There is no truth in anything the Minister has said about the matter. Had he given way I should have put the record straight as I did in the Press Gallery today'. What had in fact happened was that friends of South African sport had given Waddington this quotation of mine in an effort to divert attention from my political attack. The record is that Precious McKenzie was a most successful weight-lifter who won many Olympic and world records. He had lived in Britain for many years and had had two applications for British nationality turned down by the Home Office. He made a third application and his own governing body, the British Weight-lifting Association, wrote to me to ask if I could intervene to discover why he had been rejected. I did so and was pleased to discover that the Home Office was by then on the point of approving his third application. His case could not have been further removed from that of Zola Budd. I suspect that Waddington's refusal to give way to me meant that he knew that too!

I turned my attention to Budd's South African coach, a Pieter Labuschagne, who was here as a visitor. I knew that visitors are not allowed to do paid work. If they wish to do so they must obtain a work permit. The Minister confirmed this to me in answer to a question: 'He was admitted to the UK on 1 April for a four-month visit during the leave he has been given from the school at which he teaches. He cannot take employment'. I also had two further lines of enquiry, one of which proved to be prophetic. This was the question of whether the Home Office had sought or received assurances about Budd's intention to settle permanently in the UK if granted British nationality. The answer given was that 'minors seeking British citizenship are asked to state their intended country of residence'. I knew from my own constituency experience that this is the invariable practice. After the Olympic Games it soon became apparent that any such assurance did not amount to much. It was reported that Budd had stated that she would not be in this country for more than a year or so. I followed this up by asking which governing bodies of British sport had been consulted before the granting of British citizenship and whether they had confirmed that she would be eligible to qualify for selection. The answer was a flat 'None, qualification is not a matter for the Government'. In my experience of immigration matters I know of no other case where the stated purpose of an application for British nationality has not been thoroughly pursued, examined and satisfied.

The political fight having been fought out and concluded attention switched to the sporting scene. Miss Budd was subjected to constant hostility from anti-apartheid groups who were outraged by the precedence that had been given to her. This was understandable but misdirected. She was now a British citizen and entitled to be considered on her merits by the Olympic selectors, who had themselves been placed in an invidious position. They too had not been told that she had been granted citizenship on the basis of a Minister's discretion;

they believed like everyone else that she had achieved her status by descent. However, in my view, they had no right whatsoever to ignore the rules of Olympic eligibility which required minimum periods of residence and citizenship before selection. These were cardinal errors made first by the BOA and then by the IOC. As I had said in the House, 'Zola Budd might well be an outstanding athlete of great promise. On sporting grounds I hope she achieves the personal success to which every international athlete aspires. But she is the person for whom I feel most sorry in this case. She has been exposed to tremendous pressures by the antics of the *Daily Mail* and the collusion of the Home Office which would be far too great for athletes with ten times her maturity. No young girl at 17 should be put in that position. Nor should she have been allowed to cause such concern to her fellow and future sports colleagues, or to become such a cause of resentment to other citizens'.

Three months later I was taking my seat in the Royal Box at Wimbledon when I was tapped on the shoulder by Sir David English, who was sitting behind me. He was kindly making his peace with me so I courteously responded, but I was a bit taken aback when he told me by way of total justification: 'She will win us a medal, you know'. I could only reply that that had yet to be proved but, in any case, as passionate a supporter of sport as I was, I could not believe that ability at sport was a justification for priority in the granting of British citizenship. Sport is essentially about fairness of competition, and the Budd affair belied every rule of life that I had been brought up to believe in.

As the summer wore on both the public and the athletes grew more restive. Wendy Sly chose not to enter the British Olympic trials in June and therefore not to compete against Budd. This was an extraordinary challenge to the selectors. They wisely selected her for the Olympics nonetheless. In the event the Olympics 3,000 metres in August 1984 turned out disastrously for Budd. In the fourth lap Mary Decker, the US runner and, ironically, Zola Budd's idol, ran into the back of Budd, stumbled and fell. The crowd booed and Decker heaped blame on Miss Budd. Any objective viewer however could find no fault on the part of the British runner, but the incident was yet another mighty burden for her to carry. Budd finished seventh in the race, well away from the medals for which the whole affair had been contrived, while Sly was second to Romania's Maricia Puica and Lynn William, the Canadian, was third. Immediately after the race Zola returned to South Africa for her brother's wedding but in January 1985 she was back in England for just two days. She returned again at the end of the month and stayed until 17 February, running twice at Cosford, once at Ipswich and once at Birkenhead, where an inexcusable demonstration forced her out of the race. In March her talent blossomed and she won the World Cross Country in Lisbon spending, according to Simon Barnes in *The Times*, 36 hours en route for Lisbon and 48 hours on the way back. In October she was here to take part in a disgracefully contrived television race created by the USA's ABC television and Britain's ITV. It was a race at Crystal Palace which in my opinion should never have been sanctioned by the British Board. It was almost like an old-time prize fight, the stakes were high and the race had little to do with international athletic competition as we know it. It was Decker versus Budd, who was reported to have been paid £90,000 in appearance money, Decker getting much less. The real outrage for me was that the woman who won the gold medal in Los Angeles, Maricia Puica, was never even invited. The Olympic ethos has no part in this sort of promotion! The American, by now known as Decker-Slaney, won the race and Zola Budd finished fourth. No doubt American prejudices were well satisfied.

Throughout all this trauma Zola Budd refused to say one word about apartheid and the South African situation from which she had escaped to become British. If only she had done so it might well have eased her situation. Tessa Sanderson, the Olympic javelin champion, was reported to have demanded that Miss Budd 'should condemn apartheid' and Andrea Lynch, our former 100 metres record holder, who had been honoured with the award of the MBE, said, 'she is still seen as South African'. Judy Oakes, our champion in the shot event, was even more to the point: 'Zola has to decide whether she is British or South African, it's as simple as that. If she wants to live in this country that's fine, we'll treat her like a British citizen, but if she continues to spend almost all her time in South Africa then we'll know we're being used. And we resent being used'. Daley Thompson, our great pentathlon Olympian, was the one British athlete who spoke out on her behalf. The Amateur Athletic Association still supported her cause but when the Commonwealth Games Federation faced a massive boycott of the Edinburgh Games – 25 nations withdrew – because of the isolated stand of the United Kingdom at the Commonwealth Prime Ministers' conference, they were forced into action.

They had to consider the unassailable facts. Under Article 34 of the Federation's constitution only those athletes born inside a country were eligible to represent it at the Games in 1986. Miss Budd had been born in South Africa after that country had left the Commonwealth but the question to be decided was whether or not she was properly domiciled in England. She had bought a house in England but she had hardly ever lived in it. The Federation ruled that she had failed to meet the necessary residential requirements, as she had not lived here for six out of the previous 12 months, and she was ruled out of the Games. In the Olympic year of 1988, and before the Seoul Games, the International Amateur Athletic Federation entered the arena. They asked if she had transgressed against their rules by participating in a meeting in South Africa which did not have their sanction and was therefore an ineligible meeting. Zola Budd denied the charge, although she admitted that she had been present at the meeting in question. The IAAF upheld the complaint but called upon the British Board to deal with the breach of rules, adding a recommendation that she should be suspended for at least 12 months as 'at the very best she has been in breach of the spirit of the IAAF rules'. The British Board responded by setting up its own enquiry into the international board! A month later Budd returned to South Africa and that effectively ended the matter.

In 1989 she married a South African member of the Dutch Reform Church, 28-year-old Mike Pieterse. It was reported to be a very happy occasion although her father was not invited to it. I sincerely hope that the marriage provides much happiness for them both; she is clearly far more at home in the country of her birth than ever she has been in England, where she seems to have spent no more than 17 months out of a four-year period. So ended the most disreputable episode of Government within my experience. Not one word of regret or apology! There was one comfort left – the like of this complicity will never be seen again.

FAMILY JOY

When my daughter Kate told us that she and Michael Molloy had decided to marry we were overjoyed. She is our only daughter and I was delighted that they agreed to hold the ceremony in the St Stephen's Crypt at the Palace of Westminster. As Kate, like our three sons, had been baptised in the Crypt, I think that her marriage there was a little bit of history. No one can recall such a record. Kate's two sons, Oliver and Jack, were also baptised in the crypt, and I am pretty certain that I am the only Member who has seen one of his family baptised and married there and his grandchildren baptised there too. Leaving all the bridal decisions to Kate and Brenda I threw myself into the organisational arrangements for 25 February 1984 – the anniversary of the day they met. Mick was reared in a good family atmosphere, as was Kate, and as were both Brenda and myself. We believe that to be the bedrock of any marriage. I know that Joe and Lily, Mick's parents, share the same belief. It was a wonderful occasion: the Crypt is my favourite place in the whole of the Palace of Westminster, much older than any other part of the Palace. It is superbly decorated, with a stunning cloistered ceiling and a real feeling of holiness about it.

Normally, St Stephen's Crypt is said to hold about 200 worshippers but we brought in extra chairs and used the wall seats, originally provided for the sick and the aged who were given special caring – hence the expression 'weakest to the wall' – and managed to get the numbers up to 248. The congregation included our Speaker, Bernard Weatherill, and his wife, Mr and Mrs Jim Callaghan and numerous friends from the Lords and Commons, from sport and Birmingham politics as well as from both families. Canon Ronald Jennings, an old family friend, performed the marriage service assisted by Canon Trevor

Beeson, the Speaker's chaplain. When news of the wedding got out the Canoldir Choir, of which I am president, offered to come and sing. The Canoldir is Birmingham's Welsh choir, nearly 100 strong, and I could not possibly refuse. There was only one place where they could be accommodated – standing at the back of the Crypt. Their singing of two prayers, The Reverend Eli Jenkins' Prayer from Dylan Thomas' *Under Milk Wood* and the Lord's Prayer, had many in tears. The words and music seemed to haunt the roof of the cloisters. I felt we should take full advantage of their generosity so after the reception they gave a concert in the Members' dining-room to conclude our celebrations. When I was making the arrangements for this concert I learned that the Palace of Westminster owned no piano and that no choir had sung previously in the dining-room. It was another first which gave us all enormous pleasure. Roy Hattersley did the honours at the reception, with Canon Ralph Stevens providing full support. It was a day never to be forgotten, sheer delight, and a marriage from which we continue to draw great pleasure.

We treasure too the marriage of our eldest son Andrew and Ceri. They did not want anything like such a marriage feast, preferring to be wed quietly but very pleasantly in Birmingham. Ceri's parents – Ron and Elizabeth Ogden – are stalwarts of the Labour Party and the trade union movement, as are both Andy and Ceri, which is another source of contentment. So too are Mick, our second son, and Liz his partner, so we are blessed with a devoted and dedicated family who share our beliefs to the full. As they all live within a mile or so of our house the concept of a close, caring family is well maintained. Our family gatherings are never dull as we join together to set the world to rights.

FAMILY GRIEF

22 May 1986 was the most devastating day in our lives. David, our youngest son, then aged 21, died in the Frenchay Hospital, Bristol, despite the valiant efforts of surgeons and the great skills of the anaesthetist and nurses in the intensive care unit. Two days earlier I had arrived at the headquarters of the Iron and Steel Trades Union for a discussion about trade union and Labour Party matters to be met by Sandy Feather, who asked me to telephone home at once as David had had a car accident and suffered serious head injuries. Brenda was already on her way to the hospital, being driven by our eldest son, Andrew, and in great desperation I rushed to Paddington for the first available train. It was a nightmare journey and when I arrived at the hospital I could see at once that David's student friends from the Bristol Polytechnic shared our despair. They were present in a small group outside the casualty entrance just waiting for news. David's friend Michala was with Brenda and when I went to the room where David

was lying, being monitored and on a drip, I could see at once how serious it was. I was told later that he had received 12 pints of blood after the operation, which the senior surgeon explained to me had been to remove half of his liver. He explained the significance of this but seemed to be hopeful that a recovery was possible. Brenda and I thought the anaesthetist was less optimistic, although he assured us that he had known patients recover from such a situation. In the middle of the second night spent in the special rooms provided for relatives – a vital need in every such hospital as we came to appreciate – we were wakened by another of the doctors who told us that David's condition had deteriorated suddenly. He had called a neurosurgeon and rushed David off for a brain scan which had not been attempted before because the doctors were anxious not to move him. We had already been told by the orthopaedic surgeon that although David had fractured many bones in his legs and body he would not be in any pain from them as he was unconscious, and they could be dealt with later on. Early in the morning we went to see David again and learned the hopelessness of his condition. Brenda and I walked round the grounds of the hospital as dawn broke and prepared ourselves for the worst as the life support machine was switched off. Our prayers were for a quick and merciful release from his sufferings. The college chaplain, the Rev Sean Darley, was with us when the summons came that the end was very near. He had been in constant attendance throughout our ordeal, and he was able to commit David to the care and mercy of the good Lord.

We were desperately sad for Michala. She and David had developed a wonderful relationship together over the previous year and Brenda had only recently remarked that she had never seen David so pleased with life. We had no doubt that Michala had brought him great happiness. She often drove David back to his student accommodation but on the day of his fatal accident David had sat the second of his five papers for his final examination. Michala had to sit for a paper the next day so David left her working in the library and went off to find a lift. He was able to scramble into the hatchback compartment of an old car as all the other seats were taken. The car had only just been bought and was said to have been recently subject to a DOT test, but going down a steep hill the brakes failed, the driver swerved to stop the car, hitting a wall, and the back door flew open, catapulting David out. No one in the car was in any way to blame. David's tutors told us how well he had done in his studies and how much he had entered into the life of the student union and the college. He had been an active member of the Labour club and only a few months earlier he had proudly told me how he had gone into the union on the day of the local elections and got the students to turn out and knock on doors – 'it is no use bellyaching about grants and education if you do nothing about it' was his belief. To his great joy Labour won two very marginal seats in Bristol. David's other great commitment was against racism in any form and he took to the streets in the demonstrations of the anti-apartheid movement of which he was a member. He also played a full part in the sporting life of the college, especially in cricket, which was his passion, and football, for which he skippered the team. His tutor told us that he committed himself fully to life entirely on his own merits – until the accident the tutor had had no idea that he was my son. The college awarded him an upper second class degree posthumously and we collected it with great pride, as well as with gratitude for the contribution the Poly had made to his life.

The tragedy attracted enormous publicity and seemed to touch the hearts of so many people. Prince Philip wrote us a most warm and comforting letter as did Neil Kinnock who movingly told us that 'there are no words': so true. Both Margaret and Denis Thatcher wrote personal notes which we appreciated very much. So many friends in all walks of life wrote and we appreciated that. Although no one can adequately share such grief, it is a great comfort to know that others care. Most moving were the letters of parents who had also lost a son or a daughter, often in car accidents, sharing their experiences and commending to us various writings which had helped them. One piece by Canon Scott Holland, a former Canon of St Paul's Cathedral which starts, 'What is this death' was very helpful. Years later when called upon to comfort the bereaved of the Hillsborough disaster I shared my own experience with them and mentioned how comforting these words had been for us. I was so pleased to find that many of them had already been supplied with copies of this fine piece. Two comments were made to me repeatedly in all good faith which led me to ponder about the cause of disasters and the nature of God. One of these was 'You will get over it in time', to which I could only reply that neither Brenda nor I wished to 'get over it'. Nor have we. We have learned to live with our grief which is a different thing. We follow Scott Holland's advice and talk openly about David as if he is still with us, part of our life and our planning. His photographs surround us as do his cricket gear, his football and hockey clothes still litter his room, his pin-ups remain. We have a simple stone bearing his name on the rockery of a flower bed near where we sit in the garden. He is very much with us still. The other question asked so frequently is 'Why does God allow this to happen?' Canon Trevor Beeson, the Speaker's chaplain, now Dean of Winchester, who has also known a similar tragedy told me in his letter, 'We do not know the answer to that question in this world'. For my own part I cannot believe in a God who controls every moment of our destiny, it is a ludicrous proposition. I have often said in the House that I believe the greatest gift of God to man is that of individual free will. We make our own destiny whether it is to be found in individual tragedy or personal triumph. God provides us with a faith to live by not a life of total control. The sure knowledge that our God cares for every single person as being a person of infinite worth is my abiding faith, and it is a great comfort.

We held the funeral service for David at St Paul's Church, Birm-

ingham. The students of David's college paid him an enormous tribute
by obtaining the postponement of their examinations due on that day
and attending in full force. The whole service was very moving,
especially the 'young persons' address' given by Tessa Ward. She had
never given any address before and was not able to bring herself to an
end but although over-long it was very much 'David', and the students
all told me afterwards, 'she spoke for us'. Canon Ralph Stevens also
gave an address, telling how he had baptised David. He certainly spoke
with much feeling for he had lost his own son from leukaemia. Ralph
related an incident from a schools cricket match when David, fielding
on the boundary, had caught out the opposing captain who was making
a big score and then realised that his foot had been over the boundary
line. He signalled six and returned the batsman to the wicket. When
David told me this story he was delighted with the tribute paid to him
by the master in charge of the visiting team, who said that his action
had been in the best traditions of English cricket. At the service Tessa
and her husband played the guitar and movingly sang the hymn 'I
heard the voice of Jesus call, come unto me and rest'. One last tribute
delighted our family. Bristol College set up a memorial fund known as
the David Howell/Nelson Mandela Fund which each year brings over
an African student. The Students' Union meet the accommodation
costs and the college provides the tuition. There can be no more fitting
tribute to David's idealism and commitment.

FACING THE FUTURE

Very soon after the 1987 General Election Brenda and I took stock of
the future. Brenda was now on her own at home more often, which was
not a welcome situation, and my own health was not as robust as it had
been. I had exhausted myself on behalf of Birmingham's Olympic bid
and the sheer physical demands of ever-growing constituency surgeries
had to be kept in check. It is wise to concede the march of time. We
decided to consult our friends in the constituency about what was best
for the Party and to make the announcement that I would not be
standing again as soon as it was practical to do so. This was early in
the new year of 1989. As I have said often since then, I am not retiring
from life – I hope to retain all my old zest for life, and my love of
politics and sport, but to participate on my own terms, at my own pace.
I do not believe that any man should contract out of life and I have no
intention of doing so but I look forward enormously to being able to
do more things together with Brenda – to the delight of our family,
especially our two grandsons, Oliver and Jack – to more travel and to
the gentle life. It is tempting to accede to all the requests to look back
over the years and I don't doubt that it is not altogether possible to
avoid some of that. An autobiography is an indulgence in the past, and
quite enough of it, too! It is better, even as one approaches one's

declining years, to look forward and to use one's experiences as a stimulation for the future, so that one can offer good counsel, especially to one's friends. This new formed pleasure has to start some time so why not here and now? Let's take a forward look at sport and at politics, it seems as good a way as any of moving on from recollections of the past to prospects for the future.

I am much concerned about the future of sport. Not about the natural skills and abilities of British athletes, nor their character or willpower, but about government in all its many aspects. We are moving in the wrong direction to be able to deliver opportunities, provide facilities and develop all the talent. We shall have our successes, of course, especially where the individual personality triumphs over these adversities, but most of our young sportsmen and women need to be encouraged very early on to generate an absorbing love of sport, to develop an unquenchable enthusiasm and a mastery of essential technique. We should be providing these opportunities in abundance; instead we are creating obstacles and denying sport its proper role in society. In the modern world the impetus for all this must come from the Government, as it does now in so many countries, but in Britain the present Government has no philosophy as to the importance of sport and no strategy to provide for it. This is so in the field of all leisure resources. Our people enjoy the possibilities of more leisure time, better means of transport and access, but the leisure service industry is fragmented and the Government seems unwilling to bring the different agencies together and to provide for a comprehensive leisure policy. The Sports Council, the Countryside Commission, the Nature Conservancy Council, the water industry and the local authorities (including the education authorities) ought to be working together under ministerial leadership to provide unlimited possibilities from which people can choose their leisure time enjoyment. No such policy exists. I have always believed that the Arts Council and the tourist industry should be added to these to provide a new department of state, particularly since tourism is such an important economic industry with clout in Whitehall. I have long recommended such a policy to leaders of the Labour Party, including Neil Kinnock. It is becoming ever more important to bring this about, not only to provide for the enhancement and enjoyment of life, but also because failure to do so will increase boredom and frustrations, which can also cost society more than we need to find for the promotion of sensible and civilised leisure pursuits.

The greatest of all my fears for the future of sport lies in the fields of education and local authority provision. All over the country playing fields are being sold for development, and they will never be replaced. This is disastrous. When challenged the Minister for Sport takes refuge in the fact that fewer all-weather pitches are required than grass pitches. All-weather pitches are excellent for heavy everyday use but they are not a substitute for God's good grass upon which most team games should be played. In any case, only two teams can play at a time on one synthetic pitch.

The mania for the privatisation of local authority sports halls, swimming baths and recreational management is a disaster of monumental scale. All over the country young people who we need to encourage to play games and to participate in sport are being priced out of the necessary facilities while the police and the Home Office throw up their hands in horror at the effects of hooliganism and boredom! It is to be hoped that the ratepayers soon come to their senses by realising the effect of these policies on young people and also on their own pockets as they come to appreciate the financial sleight of hand which leaves them to pay the loan charges and maintenance costs while the private operators walk away with the operating profits.

Local education authorities have been told to sell off educational sports land. This is a betrayal of the future. If school rolls are falling the numbers of young people in our society are not disappearing, they are moving on to become young adults, or young married people; their recreational needs still exist, and the playing fields should be redeveloped for their use. In the area of community provision the cost of failing to provide is enormous as can be seen in every town and city in the country. As I never cease to proclaim, in this country the future of all sport is to be found in school sport. It is being systematically undermined. The continuous battle between Government and the teachers is having a devastating effect upon morale. It is not only low salaries – although salaries reflect the esteem in which society holds its public servants, and in my opinion no job is more important than the responsibility for the development of human character and personality – which is the lot of our teachers. It is also the place of sport and recreation in the educational curriculum. Under the new syllabus physical education is not regarded as a mainstream subject. It is not only the principal grass sports which suffer – swimming is badly affected. The first casualty of financial restraint forced upon education and local governments is the closure of swimming baths in the winter, and the withdrawal of transport essential for so many schools. The Swimming Teachers Association estimate that compared with 1980 only one third of our schoolchildren are taking swimming lessons. This is a national scandal.

Then there is the enforced requirement for teachers to 'clock in' and work 1,265 hours per year at their profession. Over 40 weeks and five days per week this breaks down to 6.3 hours a day. Many heads do not provide for sport, PE or the arts out of this allocation of time. The voluntary work undertaken by thousands of teachers in school sport after school time and on Saturdays does not count. Many teachers are responding angrily by working their required number of hours and no more. School sport is suffering, and although I am well aware that there are still wonderful examples of dedicated devotion being practised all over the country, the situation is not hopeful. As president of the

West Midlands Schools Athletic Association I recently attended their annual championships and found the organisers thoroughly depressed. Forty per cent of the pupils entered failed to take part because there were no teachers willing to turn out on a Saturday and Sunday. And the overwhelming numbers of our great national athletics champions will testify to the importance of school sport in their own development. It is all very sad. The effect will be long-term and that means the future of British sport is in jeopardy.

Another area of concern to me is the future of team sports. I am all for the enjoyment of individual pursuits, especially camping, caravaning, walking, mountaineering, canoeing and the like, but if these are provided for at the exclusion of team games then it will be a sad business for all of us. That danger exists. I know of no better way for youngsters to relate to each other in a happy situation than through playing games together. The need to win well and with generosity and to lose gracefully are among the most important attributes of life. Alas, they are becoming somewhat unfashionable in some professional circles. Recently I sat in on the appointments board of one of our most distinguished physical education training colleges. I decided that my question would be: 'What is the role of school sport in the life of British sport?' All but one of the applicants gave depressing answers. Recently the Inner London Education Authority (ILEA) took a lot of stick when they were reported to be opposed to team sports. My investigations proved that this was far from the case. The ILEA members were in favour of team sports, but they were being discouraged by education professionals who placed more emphasis upon individual activities. These activities in the schools were not the direct result of political control. My view is that the politicians have to assert more authority if we are to ensure the future of British sport.

Sport needs to campaign ceaselessly about these issues. The Sports Council should be in the lead but, as now conceived, it is a pale shadow of its original concept. It has become part of the managerial concept of government, streamlined by membership and with no sense of accountability to sport. The Royal Charter is supposed to guarantee its independence but, as I stressed earlier, the Minister's total control over the appointment of members and the allocation of funds means that it is an arm of the Government about whose decisions it is not possible to raise questions in Parliament. I am impressed with the appointment of David Pickup, the new director. John Smith, the retiring chairman, deserves credit for that imaginative appointment, but Pickup is an administrator not an idealist. He shows a willingness to work with the voluntary sector, including the CCPR, and we must hope that this relationship blossoms, but the structure created for him by the Government is fundamentally flawed. In a democratic society every institution should be accountable to a wider authority. Even the Cabinet is responsible to Parliament, but who is the Sports Council responsible to? The Royal Charter, if it means anything, means that it is not responsible to the Government, but we know that is not the position.

The CCPR is the only all-embracing forum for sport in this country, that is to say sport as represented through the governing bodies. I am well aware that many of them possess their faults, and we often bemoan their shortcomings, but in a free society there is no other way but to vest the control of sport in a democratically-elected governing body. The Minister only causes offence when he consults an assembly of distinguished sports performers, excludes any representatives of the governing bodies and calls for 'gold medal administration by gold medal athletes'. It is a meaningless concept. Instead he ought to be spending time with the governing bodies, understanding their problems, encouraging their greater efficiency and the expansion of their influence throughout the world, and providing cash incentives to achieve those policies. He would then earn their respect and would be listened to as he tries to encourage new blood into the administration of British sport. The CCPR, the British Olympic Association and the National Playing Fields Association are the chief agencies with whom the Minister for Sport should be working. They represent British sport and membership of the Sports Council should reflect that fact. Its accountability to British sport should be through their membership and to the public at large through representatives of local authorities and sport in education, and by individual appointments designed to acknowledge the needs of groups still at a disadvantage; women, the handicapped and ethnic minorities. A truncated Sports Council cannot possibly provide for this wider representation of interests. If we are to have a small executive Sports Council then there should be a much larger council drawn from all these interests to whom it is responsible and who can determine policy. On balance I prefer the much greater involvement of the CCPR, the BOA and the NPFA, which would have the important advantage of limiting the friction which so often afflicts British sport.

There is another important consideration. Sport needs a campaigning voice and that means a strong, knowledgeable and independent organisation. This has to be the CCPR. It is fully representative but it is not willing to involve its constituent bodies in a sustained campaign. Peter Lawson, the director, is forceful and resourceful. He is well supported by Ron Eames, his chairman, and by the executive committee and they battle on with important issues such as the sale of playing fields and the taxation of sport but although they are winning most of the arguments they are not securing the victories. Nor will they until the constituent bodies learn to get involved in politics. But sports people are notoriously afraid of this. It does not have to be party politics; indeed, the strength of the CCPR has to be built upon the fact that it brings together all the political interests and unites them in a common cause. The governing bodies must take the important issues into the regions. But the local authorities and the regional Sports Councils show little signs, except in exceptional cases, of responding to the needs of sport because sport does not force them to do so. A few non-party sporting campaigns at election times would work wonders but sport has to be responsible about this, more and better facilities need money; government, both national and local, has got to be told that facilities must be provided and sport must be willing to play its part in creating a climate of public opinion ready to accept the cost of doing so. It has long been a worry to me that the present generation of sporting administrators have not absorbed the traditions of their predecessors in respect of their need for a sturdy independence from government, or even from the Sports Councils and local authorities to whom they look for funding. We need a healthy relationship between sport and government and it can only be provided when the principles upon which it has to be built are understood by the governing bodies. This is a task to which the CCPR should turn its mind.

Commercialism is another growing concern. Time and again in the Howell Report on Sports Sponsorship we stated that the most important principle for sport was that at all times the governing body must govern. That principle is being eroded and sometimes flagrantly undermined. It is another responsibility for the governing bodies which cannot be shirked. Supporters' clubs and the Football Supporters' Association have worked together under my chairmanship to make an excellent contribution towards tackling the criminality known as football hooliganism. They have considerable collective wisdom which could be available to football. I hope football uses it and I hope, too, that individual clubs will bring their supporters' organisations into their confidence. It will pay them to do so. But when the Minister is faced with huge problems of spectator behaviour he does not consult or listen either to the football authorities or to the supporters. He talks at them, laying down his impossible ideas, refusing the supporters even a place on his newly-created football authority designed to meet their needs. How daft can you get?

The Football Trust has been an outstanding success and this must be built upon. The huge taxation on pools should be reduced – it is totally unfair when compared with taxation on other forms of gambling – and some of this money should be used to extend the work of the Trust in providing for better spectator comforts and sport in the community. But as important as football is it is not the only sport for which we have to provide. We also need new financial provision for the encouragement of cricket, athletics, swimming, tennis, rugby and the other sports not enjoying the support of the Football Trust. The Sports Council and the Central Council should create a similar trust for other sports. They might well be empowered to promote a national lottery. Only if we think in these terms can the future needs of British sport be met. It is only by providing for sport in the schools and in the community that we can create the foundation upon which it can prosper. After that we have to develop the talents which emerge right through the club structures and on to international level. This is a

policy which is quite capable of attainment but it will require a fundamental rethink by the Government, or by a new Government which
accepts these responsibilities and assists sport to meet them.

However, on the political front, a new optimism abounds in the
Labour Party and I share it in full. Neil Kinnock has done a superb
job in transforming the approach of the Party and relating it to the
realities of life. He has achieved this by the quality of his personal
leadership and by the partnership he has established with the newer
trade union leaders. His courage, an essential ingredient of high office,
has to be acknowledged, first, in taking on and destroying the Militant
influence in the Party and then in changing his own stance on defence
and on Europe to meet the public mood. For me personally, as I have
always been in the forefront of the multilateral disarmament camp of
our Party and serve as chairman of the Labour movement for Europe,
often maintaining these positions in the face of much hostility, it is a
great satisfaction now to see Labour set fair on these issues and to
acknowledge Neil Kinnock's great contribution. Labour now has the
most impressive front-bench line-up since the war, young and
immensely able. Their names are becoming known in every household –
Roy Hattersley, John Smith, Gordon Brown, Gerald Kaufman, John
Cunningham, Brian Gould, Robin Cook, Tony Blair and others, too,
specialists in their own fields. In due course they will make a formidable
Cabinet team and they will win as their policies come to be seen as
relevant and because they themselves command respect.

There is too a good sporting reason for expecting success. We are a
nation of cricket-lovers. The British people like to think from time to
time that it is only fair for the other side to have an innings and they
reach that conclusion when they sense that we need new people at the
wicket. That time is fast approaching. 'Enough is enough', is the
comment we hear more and more on the doorsteps. We all know what
it means. So I relish the prospect of offering my encouragement to the
team from the pavilion, a vantage point I trust that I have earned
during the 50 years of my adult life, most of it spent in the full glare
of public office. It will be a delight to offer my encouragement in the
company of my wife and family, for they too have been an essential
part of my story.

Postscript

The summer of 1989 provided me with a totally new experience and a new lease of life when I underwent major heart surgery at the National Heart Hospital in London. The problem had been developing for about three years. I started to feel pains in my calf muscles when I was walking and tension in my arms when under stress. I consulted my G P, Dr Paul Massey, who took my blood pressure three times and while I was dressing arranged for my despatch to the care of Dr Shyam Singh, consultant cardiologist at my cherished Dudley Road Hospital in Birmingham. He also called in Dr Kenneth Taylor, his diabetic colleague, who was later to gain prominence as the leader of the consultants' campaign to defend the N H S. After three days of tests they prescribed medication which we hoped would avert the problem, but with my lifestyle that proved to be impossible.

In the spring of 1989 I had a bad bout of angina during my holiday in Cornwall but I was reluctant to return to hospital while the Football Spectators Bill was in Committee day and night. By now the angina was causing discomfort in the throat during my speeches, usually after some ten or 15 minutes. Dr Singh wanted me back in hospital and clearly thought I was mad when I told him that as I was leading on the Football Bill I could only report to him after the final day in Committee. When I did so he performed an angeogram, which is a remarkable experience since the patient is able to watch the television set at his side relaying the pictures from inside his heart. I did not need to be told that an artery was blocked – I could see it for myself. What I did not know was that two other arteries were also blocked.

Birmingham has almost no facilities for heart surgery and when Dr Singh disclosed the results of his examination he told me that he needed a second opinion. He had arranged for this to be provided by Mr Graeme Bennett, consultant surgeon at the National Heart. Mr Bennett, an Australian from Brisbane, proved to be a keen sportsman. We had a mutual friend in Sally Anne Atkinson, Mayor of Brisbane, who had led the bid to secure the Olympic Games for that city when I was leading the Birmingham bid. It is indeed a small world! One look

at the videos and the X-rays was enough for Mr Bennett to tell me:
'You have two options: either I perform a triple by-pass operation or
you have a heart attack'. I could only say, 'That seems to be the end of
the conversation'.

Three weeks later the operation took place. The procedures at the
National Heart for securing the confidence of its patients are tremendous. My surgeon told me, 'We have a 98 per cent success rate'. This
was confirmed by the anaesthetist who breezed in and out – 'I have
looked at all the tests, a straightforward job, no worries'. Then followed
the intensive care sister – 'You will be with me for a day or two but
you will not see me again, as soon as I get the ventilator out of your
mouth and your breathing restored you will be off to the recovery
ward'; the physiotherapist – 'I shall be waiting for you to come round,
you will have a lot of phlegm on your chest, we have to get rid of it and
then get you out of bed and walking'. Then came the ward sister and
nurses – 'We shall get you to sleep and you will know no more until
you wake up. In the meantime here are ten throwaway razors. We want
you to shave every hair off your body, arms and legs'. Finally, the
junior surgeon explained that he would be taking a vein from one of
my legs, the entire length from thigh to ankle, and they would use three
parts of this to by-pass my blocked arteries. Everything worked out
exactly as predicted.

Brenda tells me of the wonderful team-work and attention that five
of us received in intensive care. Graeme Bennett came to talk to her,
explaining all the tubes and the instruments and reassuring her that all
was well, and tried to persuade her to go shopping in Oxford Street or
to visit the local galleries. She wanted to be there when I opened my
eyes so that she could tell the family. Graeme Bennett tried to convince
her that I would not be opening my eyes that day, and demonstrated
the fact by shaking my shoulder and pronouncing, 'There, you see,
he's not coming round today and if he does we shall put him out again!'

Back in the recovery ward I faintly heard the nurses: 'Come on,
Denis, the operation is a great success, wake up'. Tubes seemed to be
everywhere and an oxygen mask was aiding my breathing but I found
I had to do the Indian rope trick in order to sit up. The pain of
movement was considerable but I was instructed to pull on the rope
which was tied to the bottom of the bed. This brought me up to a
sitting position, achievement number one. In no time at all I was
standing at the bedside and then back in bed! Day two saw me taking
a bath. By days three and four I was walking up and down the ward.
On day five came the final test: walking up two flights of stairs. The
physio was satisfied that I could be returned to the outside world and
my consultant agreed.

The team-work, the quality of health care – medical, nursing and
auxiliary – was tremendous. Day and night, the ten of us recovering
from major heart surgery received constant attention and encouragement. And we encouraged each other. One day when I was not

feeling on top of the world I decided to stay in bed until Len, a lorry driver from Kettering, came over. 'Come on, Denis, this will do no good, get up and walk the ward with me.' We did not discuss much politics – most talk was about sport – but every one of my fellow patients gave me the message hard and clear: 'You tell them to keep their hands off the Health Service, tell them that the wages of those doctors and nurses are a disgrace'. Well, in part, this postscript is intended to honour that undertaking and to assert that two great hospitals, Dudley Road in Birmingham and the National Heart in London, represent the standards of health care which every citizen is entitled to expect, free and readily accessible in times of need.

Within days I was walking a mile or two a day, feeling fine and ready for a new lease of life. No one could be more appreciative that so many prayers have been answered, so many good wishes fulfilled, nor more determined to repay all this dedication.

APPENDIX 1

SPORTS COUNCIL 1965 – 1966

Membership (appointed January 1965)
Chairman Denis Howell MP *Deputy Chairman* Sir John Lang *International Chairman* (i) Lady Burton (ii) Robert M Gibb *Research and Statistics Chairman* Dr Roger Bannister *Sports Development and Coaching Chairman* A David Munrow *Facilities Planning Chairman* Lord Porchester. David M Bacon Menzies Cambell Sir Learie Constantine John Disley Dr Bernard Donoughue Michael Dower George Edwards Mrs Kathleen Holt Dr Stewart Mackintosh Clive Rowlands Dan Smith
Membership (subsequently appointed)
Desmond Brayley, Brian Close, Robert M Gibb, Mrs Mary A Glen-Haig, Peter Heatley, Cliff Jones, Clifford W Jones, Frank Leath, Laurie Liddell, Jack L Longland, Peter C McIntosh, Mrs Janet O S Sinclair, Arthur Tiley, M P, Leslie W Wood
Director Walter Winterbottom *Deputy Directors* Jack Barry, George McPartlin, Denis Molyneaux.

INTERNATIONAL

Grants to 47 organisations totalling £25,305
Grant applications invited for: (i) National amateur teams including Under-23, Youth and Schools; (ii) World, Commonwealth and other events of outstanding importance staged in England, Scotland or Wales; (iii) Delegates to overseas international conferences of importance or to working parties in the same category.
First International Grants for World and outstanding events staged in GB: Gliding, Wrestling, Horse Riding and Jumping, Scottish Sea Angling, Angling, Women's Rowing, Table Tennis, UK Conference on Sport.
Commonwealth Games in Jamaica, 1966: Contribution towards team costs – £5,000; Contribution towards officials – £5,000.

NB: The Steering Committtee wished to preserve the principle of voluntary appeal and requested only nominal support for the English team. Scotland and Wales were supported by their respective Councils.

RESEARCH AND STATISTICS

Initiated research projects into: (i) Sports Medicine involving physiology and psychology; (ii) Sociological Research – ownership and use of facilities, trends in popularity and demand; (iii) Documentation.

Grant of £2,500 towards the British Olympic Association enquiry into the effect in Mexico of competition at altitude.

Following the receipt of report from Dr L G C Pugh issued statement: (i) Relief to know no danger to health of participants; (ii) Hoped that never again would any such Games be staged in such special conditions of altitude or climate.

Grant of £3,000 to Royal College of Physicians for research into medical aspects of boxing.

Offered bursaries for research into physiology.

Established mobile research laboratory at Crystal Palace.

Responded to request from Council of Europe and asked governing bodies to investigate doping.

Dr Bannister and Dr O G Edholm to study physical fitness – 'Man and his physical working capacity'.

SPORTS DEVELOPMENT AND COACHING

Initiated study of financing of governing bodies.

Created new partnership with sport to provide: (i) Coaching facilities for beginners at local level; (ii) Increased international participation; (iii) Adequate and effective administration to be achieved over a five-year programme.

Supported essential voluntary autonomy of British sport but reminded it that it must be accountable for grants received.

Requested CCPR and Scottish Council of PR to organise annual course conferences for national coaches.

Initiated new federations or joint committees, e.g. Golf Development Council; Joint Shooting Committee for GB; National Anglers' Council and Met National Council for schools sport.

Capital grants to voluntary clubs established at 50 per cent. Grants made for 1965–66: England and Wales £627,051; Scotland £112,644.

Supported establishment of trusts for large sports centres and reviewed the finances and achievements of Harlow Trust.

Recommended Government grant of £75,000 towards Basingstoke Trust.

Recommended creation of National Recreation Centre for Wales in Cardiff at a cost of £425,000, supported by Sports Council for Wales and Cardiff City Council.

Examined major regional facilities at The Broads, Lee Valley, Polesworth and Aintree.

FACILITIES PLANNING

Established the nine Regional Sports Councils to bring together regional offices of H M Government, local authorities and sport and recreation.

Initiated regional conferences to review progress following circulars 49/64 from Ministry of Housing and Local Government and 11/64 from Department of Education and Science.

Analysed results and concluded: (i) Need to prevent duplication and overlap; (ii) Inadequacy of provision in indoor facilities and swimming pools; (iii) Need for national centres for international competition.

Produced list of facilities nationwide as at 1966: 500 indoor pools (three quarters needing replacement); 600 local authorities (excluding rural districts) have no indoor pool. Eleven of these catering for populations between 100,000 and 200,000 and 45 between 50,000 and 100,000; Recommended one international pool for each region; 176 sports halls approx. 80 feet × 50 feet; 63 sports halls approx. 120 feet × 60 feet, most of these provided by educational authorities, nine per cent by local authorities; Harlow multi-purpose sports centre commended, cost approx. £200,000; First priority for Regional Sports Councils to be an appraisal of major needs; Examined recreational use of all inland waterways – canals, reservoirs, wet sand and gravel pits; Recommended the C C P R produced 'Code of Conduct for Water Users'; Established Technical Advisory Service for sport to advise local authorities and voluntary bodies; Appointed working party to establish standards of Provision for Sport required to meet the leisure time needs of urban communities for sports grounds, swimming pools and sports halls; Requested all local authorities to consider how to co-ordinate sports and recreational facilities provided by different committees, i.e. Education, Parks, Baths.

APPENDIX 2

SPORTS COUNCIL 1966-70

National facilities, Grant provision: National Sailing Centre at Cowes
£100,000; Crystal Palace Tartan Track (GLC also paid 25 per cent)
£67,500; Meadowbank Stadium, Edinburgh (provided for Commonwealth Games) £750,000; National Sports Centre Wales £600,000;
National Equestrian Centre, Stoneleigh (British Horse Society)
£19,380; Stoke Mandeville Sports Centre for the paraplegic and disabled £30,000.

INTERNATIONAL

1968 Olympic Games at Grenoble (Winter) and Mexico (Summer);
BOA offered 50 per cent of travel costs and daily allowance for com-
petitors. BOA appeal raised £133,796, Government grant £8,635.
Considered national centres to provide for coaching and practice in ice
skating and skiing.
Bursaries offered for competitors aged between 15–18 and to provide
for residence, occupation, job training and sports coaching.
Four year programme of international preparation for all Olympic
sports leading to the Munich Games of 1972 arranged by Minister and
Sports Council.
International events supported by grants: 1967 European Cross
Country Championships, World Junior Modern Pentathlon Cham-
pionships, London Pre Olympic Hockey Tournament, 1968 World
Youth Fencing Championships, European World Junior Judo Cham-
pionships, International d'Alpinisme Congress, European Water Ski
Championships, 1969 International Squash Rackets Championships,
International Cross Country Championships, Congress of the Inter-
national Skating Union.

SPORTS DEVELOPMENT AND COACHING

Major development meetings with governing bodies of sport: 102 in England; 44 in Scotland; 28 in Wales. Produced four- or five-year programmes.

Full-time secretaries and administrative support provided for all sports.

Full-time national coaches doubled to 48.

Appointment of development officers recommended for each sport, grant aid as for national coaches.

Grant aid recommended for 92 bodies in England and Wales, 43 bodies in Scotland totalled: 1966–67 £828,487; 1967–68 £1,095,739; 1968–69 £1,432,685.

New governing bodies created and supported: MCC Cricket Council, Cycling Council of GB, Karate Control Commission.

Support urged by Sports Council for two major reports: Byer's Report into Athletics, Chester Report into Association Football.

Also for the creation of a full-time course in recreation management leading to a diploma.

Opposition declared to Selective Employment Tax on sport and recreation.

RESEARCH AND STATISTICS

Professor J B Cullingworth asked to chair a working party to advise upon studies required in the field of recreation and to advise on priorities.

Enquiries established into land use for sport, golf course provision and intensity of use of swimming pools.

Sport and Doping: governing bodies asked to review their procedures following Council of Europe resolution; a three-year project into the effect of anabolic steroids by St Thomas's Hospital grant aided.

Bursaries awarded for research projects into physiological research to 14 lecturers and also into the relationship between exercise and physical fitness.

Work commenced to encourage provision of NHS facilities for the treatment of sports injuries.

A national documentation centre was established at Belfast University.

Dr R H Stoughton, formerly a Professor of Horticulture, appointed to conduct research into sports turf use and maintenance. Assessment was conducted into all-weather surfaces and synthetic materials.

FACILITIES PLANNING

Support provided for the creation of 30 schemes of dual provision provided jointly for both educational and local authority use.

Following discussions between the Minister and Lord Pilkington, Mr R M Gibb of I C I and a member of the Sports Council considered the future of industrial sports provision in the borough of St Helens and endorsed its main recommendation that industrial provision should be used for the community at large.

Local authorities urged to acquire redundant Territorial Army drill halls or other service facilities no longer required by the armed forces.

Regional Sports Councils each form a water space committee into recreational potential of inland waters and coastlines.

120 water undertakers now opening reservoirs for sport and recreation including the newly constructed reservoirs at Derwent, Grafham Water, Chew Valley Lake, Errwod and Polesworth.

Schemes of zoning or timetabling recommended to resolve disputes between angling and boating.

Regional Councils asked to review gravel pits sports usage and to urge local authorities to use planning powers to provide for this.

Support was given for projects of major importance at the Lee Valley, Cotswold Water Park, Colwick Park and Holme Pierrepont.

338 Local Sports Advisory Councils now reported to be in operation.

National and Regional Sports Councils: **Scotland** *Chairman* Dr H Stewart Mackintosh (to 1968) Mr L E Liddell *Secretary* Mrs M K Brown (to 1968) Mr J K Hutchison. **Wales** *Chairman* Ald Philip Squire *Secretary* Mr H G Oakes. **Northern** *Chairman* Mr G S V Petter (to 1967) Earl of Lonsdale *Secretary* Mr A L Colbeck. **North West** *Chairman* Mr Paul Rose, M P (to 1969) Mr W F Roberts *Secretary* Group Capt J C Kilkenny (to 1968) Mr C A Ainsworth. **Yorkshire & Humberside** *Chairman* Mr Bernard Atha *Secretary* Mr F L Templeman. **East Midlands** *Chairman* Lord Winterbottom *Secretary* Mr R Logan. **West Midlands** *Chairman* Sir Frank Price (to 1969) Ald Edgar Hiley *Secretary* Mr J F Coghlan. **Eastern** *Chairman* Mr Brian Harrison, M P (to 1967) Lord Lindgren *Secretary* Mr G Richards. **Greater London and South East** *Chairman* Mr Jack Dunnett, M P (to 1968) Mrs Peggy Jay *Secretary* Air Vice Marshall R B Thomson (to 1968) Col B R D Garside. **Southern** *Chairman* Mr Edmund Gibbs *Secretary* Mr H Littlewood (to 1968) Air Vice Marshall R B Thomson.

Index